A GERMAN GENERATION

THOMAS A. KOHUT

A German Generation

AN EXPERIENTIAL HISTORY
OF THE TWENTIETH CENTURY

Yale UNIVERSITY PRESS

New Haven & London

Published with assistance from the Mary Cady Tew Memorial Fund.

Yale University Press books may be purchased in quantity for educational, business, or promotional use. For information, please e-mail sales.press@yale.edu
(U.S. office) or sales@yaleup.co.uk (U.K. office).

Designed by Mary Valencia.
Set in Sabon type by Newgen North America.
Printed in the United States of America.

Library of Congress Cataloging-in-Publication Data

Kohut, Thomas August.
    A German generation : an experiential history of the twentieth century /
Thomas A. Kohut.
      p. cm.
    Includes bibliographical references and index.
    ISBN 978-0-300-17003-0 (hardback)
    1. Germany—History—20th century. 2. Germany—Social conditions—
20th century. 3. Germans—Ethnic identity. 4. World War, 1914–1918—
Germany. 5. World War, 1939–1945—Germany. 6. National socialism.
7. Oral history—Germany. I. Title.
    DD232.K645 2012
    943.087—dc23
                                                              2011016844

A catalogue record for this book is available from the British Library.

This paper meets the requirements of ANSI/NISO Z39.48–1992 (Permanence
of Paper).

10 9 8 7 6 5 4 3 2 1

In memory of my father, Heinz Kohut, proud Austrian Pfadfinder and contemporary of those at the heart of this study

The historical events and decisions that really count play themselves out among all of us who are anonymous, in the heart of every accidental and private individual person. The most powerful dictators, ministers, and generals are completely powerless in the face of these simultaneous mass decisions, often made by people who are unaware that they have decided anything. And it is characteristic of these decisive events that they never appear as mass phenomena. . . . Instead these decisive events occur only as the result of the apparently private experiences of thousands and millions of individuals.

—SEBASTIAN HAFFNER, Geschichte eines Deutschen

CONTENTS

ACKNOWLEDGMENTS

Over the more than fifteen years that I have worked on this project, so many people generously provided advice and support that not all of them can be acknowledged here. I would like to begin, however, by thanking three historians whose support long predates my work on this project. Ronald Suny was one of my teachers when I was a student at Oberlin College. His courses prompted me to apply to graduate school in history. Ron's influence testifies to the power of a teacher to inspire a student, even when the teacher is standing at the front of a large lecture hall and the student is a wholly unremarkable undergraduate sitting quietly at the back of the room. Peter Gay and John Demos have been constant sources of inspiration and support throughout the course of my career, beginning in Peter's case when I was still a graduate student at the University of Minnesota. Their sophisticated, creative, and courageous scholarship has provided a model of psychologically sensitive history to emulate. What successes I have achieved as a historian over the years I owe as much to Peter and to John as to anyone. Indeed, when I sought a publisher for the manuscript of this book, I turned to John for advice. His willingness to read the manuscript and to contact the history editor at Yale University Press about it launched the process that has led to this book's publication. I would like to thank Peter Gay and John Demos most, however, for their faith in me as a historian.

I would like to thank Christopher Rogers, editorial director at Yale University Press, for his excellent advice to shorten the manuscript by about a third as well as for his more intangible intellectual and moral support. I would also like to acknowledge Christina Tucker, assistant editor at Yale, for her patience, gentle prodding, and intelligent suggestions, as well as Laura Davulis and the production editor, Ann-Marie Imbornoni, who has been a pleasure to work with. The thoughtful, knowledgeable, and insightful comments and suggestions of the two readers for Yale University Press about my manuscript resulted in a significantly improved book. Finally, I would like to express my gratitude to Robin DuBlanc. Not only did Robin do a masterful and meticulous job in copyediting the manuscript, she proved to be a wise, thoughtful, and understanding counselor and collaborator not only on the style but also on the substance of this book. She was wonderful to work with.

I would like to thank Dr. Susanne Rappe-Weber, director of the Archiv der deutschen Jugendbewegung, for providing the photograph by Julius Gross on the dust jacket and for granting me permission to reprint it.

I would like to thank the Köhler Stiftung. Its financial support in 1995–96 enabled me to participate in the research project "Die Freideutschen: Seniorenkreise aus jugendbewegter Wurzel—Ein Modell für sinnerfülltes Alter," sponsored by the University of Siegen in Germany and funded by the Federal Ministry for Family, Senior Citizens, Women, and Youth of the German government. Dr. Lotte Köhler and the late Dr. Hans Kilian, two intelligent, knowledgeable, and passionate supporters of psychosocial research, offered critiques of my work that helped sharpen my analysis of the interviews that were at the scholarly heart of the Siegen project. I would also like to thank the Academy of Science at the University of Siegen, where I was a member in 1995–96. The academy supported me financially and gave me an academic home while I was working on the University of Siegen project.

Additionally, I would like to acknowledge the president and board of trustees of Williams College for the sabbatical support I received over the three leaves I used to research and write this book. I would particularly like to thank Morton O. Schapiro who, as president of Williams, granted me a yearlong sabbatical while I was dean of the faculty, a leave that allowed me to make decisive progress on this book and to maintain my identity as a historian during the six years I was a college administrator. The support I received from the college testifies to the importance that Williams places on having a faculty of active and productive scholars.

I would like to express my gratitude to the three academics, then young, who conducted the interviews on which this book is based, Sabiene Autsch, Babett Lobinger, and Heiner Seidel. Babett and Heiner remained friends and colleagues long after the conclusion of the Siegen project on which we worked so well together. Heiner's recent, unexpected death casts a shadow over the publication of a book to which he contributed so significantly.

Helena Johnson, my former student at Williams, was my research assistant on this project. With her tenacity, intelligence, good historical judgment, and fluency in German, Helena contributed substantially to the historiographical essays that are an important part of this book.

A number of colleagues at Williams College, at Exeter College of Oxford University, and elsewhere in England, the United States, and in Germany offered valuable advice and/or support on this project: Richard Bessel, Elisabetta Brighi, Geoffrey Cocks, Robert Dalzell, John Downey, Stephen Fix, Lerke Gravenhorst, Regina Kunzel, John MacLeod, Judy Malone, Bojana Mladenovic, Ben Morgan, Simon Mortimore, Frank Oakley, Claudia Olk, Hanna Schissler, Roslyn Schloss, Olga Shevshenko, Paul Slack, Ileene Smith, William Wagner and James Wood. I would particularly like to acknowledge Georges Dreyfus for his help with the book's title and Pauline Nestor of Monash University in Australia for informing me that no press would accept for publication a manuscript that had 73,637 words of notes. Jeri Johnson's friendship and advice were of crucial personal and intellectual importance during the two years I was working on this book in Oxford.

I owe a special debt of gratitude to the historian Peter Fritzsche. Although he and I have never met, Peter graciously read and offered a valuable critique of a large section of the manuscript. Robert Jackall, a sociologist whose own work is based largely on oral interviews, read the entire manuscript and made a number of very helpful suggestions. The sociologist Kai Erikson, whose work is also based on interviews, read much of the manuscript. In particular, Kai's perceptive reading of the reaction of Germans (including those interviewed for this project) to the persecution and deportation of Jews during the Third Reich was both sociologically informed and analytically penetrating. In general, Kai has been a constant source of wisdom and counsel over the years I have worked on this book. Gerard Fromm, a psychologist and director of the Erikson Institute of the Austen Riggs Center in Stockbridge, Massachusetts, made a number of insightful contributions to this book. Similarly, Dorothee Wierling, a historian who is an experienced, sensitive, and analytically sophisticated reader of oral history interviews and who has herself written a model history of another German generation, provided crucial moral and intellectual support throughout this project.

I would like to thank Lydia Boetschi for her friendship and the use of her vacation home in a remote Swiss mountain valley where the most challenging chapters of this book were written.

There are three historians and friends to whom I owe a debt of gratitude that really cannot be expressed adequately: Ute Daniel, Alexandra Garbarini, and Jürgen Reulecke. All read the manuscript of this book at least once, all have offered innumerable suggestions that improved it significantly, and all have provided consistent intellectual and emotional support. This book would not have been written without them. Historical work is often lonely and isolating. Ute, Ali, and Jürgen have allowed me to overcome that isolation. I cannot imagine my life without them as colleagues and as friends.

Finally, I would like to thank my family. My two children, Sophie and Alexander, lived with this project during all of its fifteen years. I worked out virtually every vexing problem it raised, intellectual and otherwise, with my wife, Susan. She has been my partner in every sense of the word throughout the forty years we have been together.

INTRODUCTION

"We Have All, Always, Sought the Collective"

Some thirty years ago, when I began both my education at the Cincinnati Psychoanalytic Institute and my investigation of the psychological dimension of the past, I—like other "psychohistorians" of the time—analyzed the influence of the psyche on history. We studied the lives of historically significant figures ("great men" and, less often, "great women") in order to explain how their political attitudes and actions in adulthood could be understood as attempts to solve psychological problems encountered in childhood. We assumed that the historically significant attitudes and actions of such figures could be explained only through a psychological analysis of their early life. That is to say, I, like other psychohistorians, investigated the influence of the individual psyche on history.[1] I have since come to the conclusion, however, that the influence of history on the psyche is at least as significant as the influence of the psyche on history. Psychologically we are constituted in no small measure through our experience of the environment. That environment is constituted by history. Therefore, history constitutes our psyches.[2] Today I am more interested in the impact of history on the psyche than in the reverse and investigate how the experience of a historically determined environment shapes the self. Nevertheless, I remain committed to studying people—less "great men" or "great women" and more ordinary human beings—as makers of history. For, as the historian and journalist Sebastian Haffner noted in his memoirs, history is ultimately played out "in the heart of every accidental and private individual person" and made in response to "the apparently private experiences of thousands and millions of individuals," wholly unaware that their personal decisions have shaped its course.[3] I see it as my task, then, to study how the psyche and history mutually shape one another, or, put differently, how history flows through human beings.

At its most basic level, *A German Generation* is about how history flowed through sixty-two people. All were Germans, most born in the decade before World War I. All as adolescents had been profoundly influenced by their experience in the youth movement of the *Bunds* during the 1920s. Largely as a result of those adolescent experiences, all had joined the Free German Circle, an organization of former youth movement members, sometime after the end of World War II. All were approximately the same age, came from the same social milieu—the educated, generally professional, urban middle class—and most shared the same religion, Protestantism. As a result, they had similar historically determined experiences. Because those experiences were psychologically constitutive, they were also psychologically similar. In interviews they told similar life stories and told those stories in similar ways. This book presents their life stories and analyzes both how history shaped the psyches of these sixty-two people, as historical forces produced a series of losses for them beginning in the 1920s when they were adolescents, and how the psyches of these sixty-two people helped shape the course of history, as the solutions they developed to deal with those losses led them first to the youth movement in adolescence during the Weimar Republic, then to National Socialism in young adulthood during the Third Reich, and finally to the Free German Circle as mature adults in postwar Germany.

Founded in 1947 at the Altenberg monastery near Wetzlar, the Free German Circle sought to keep alive the spirit of the youth movement after the German defeat in the war. Initially a self-help organization for refugees, the Free German Circle rapidly institutionalized as West Germany emerged from the devastation of the war, with a national governing body, local chapters, a newsletter, annual "Fall Conversations," and annual national conventions devoted to a theme relating to the contemporary world. At its height, the Free German Circle had approximately 2,000 members. When the project on which this book is based began in 1988, there were still some 1,250 Free Germans, most in their seventies or early eighties. In June 2000 at the Altenberg monastery, the Free Germans held their last convention and dissolved the Circle, which had played a crucial role in the lives of its members—including the sixty-two people interviewed for this study—for more than fifty years.

Given their present circumstances and past lives, Jürgen Reulecke, perhaps the foremost historian of German youth generally and of the German youth movement in particular, developed a multidisciplinary research project on the Free Germans in the late 1980s. The project was sponsored by the Social Science Division of the University of Siegen in Germany and funded by the Federal Ministry for Family, Senior Citizens, Women, and Youth of the

German government. The project's title, "The Free Germans: Senior Citizen Circles with Roots in the Youth Movement—A Model for a Meaningful Old Age," helps explain the government's support, for it was hoped that the Free Germans—whose active and independent lives in old age seemed connected with the support of their generational peers—might serve as a model for an aging population. A more academic but by no means subordinate goal of the project was to produce a "collective biography" of the Free Germans, who, as Reulecke noted in the project's final report in 1996, comprised a generational unit of historically unprecedented definition and cohesion and whose lives spanned the course of the twentieth century.[4] These Germans had lived under four (and in some instances five) completely different political systems: Imperial Germany; the Weimar Republic; the Third Reich; the German Federal Republic; and, before eventually fleeing to West Germany, the German Democratic Republic. As children they experienced World War I on the home front, the German defeat, and the German revolution. As adolescents during the 1920s, they experienced the economic hardship and political unrest of the Weimar Republic, becoming, partially in response, members of the youth movement. As young adults during the Third Reich, they were for the most part active and enthusiastic National Socialists. They experienced the full force of World War II on the battlefront and on the home front and suffered in prisoner of war camps and in the ruins of postwar Germany. As mature adults, they participated in the reconstruction of West Germany and the so-called economic miracle of the 1950s and early 1960s. They were the parents of the rebels of the "1968 generation," which during the late 1960s and early 1970s helped transform the political, cultural, and sexual landscape of West Germany. And finally, in retirement and old age, they experienced the profound changes of the 1980s and early 1990s, including the increased emancipation of women, the emergence of a multiethnic, multiracial society, the advent of the so-called information age, the end of the cold war, and German reunification.[5]

My participation in this project began in the fall of 1995, but its origins date back to 1988–89, when Reulecke and his colleagues sent a lengthy questionnaire to members of the Free German Circle selected at random. Based on more than 150 responses, it was decided to conduct in-depth interviews with approximately sixty members of the group. These interviews were at the heart of the project and are at the heart of this book. Most were conducted between July 1994 and April 1995 by three German graduate assistants: two historians, Sabiene Autsch and Heinrich Seidel, and a psychologist, Babett Lobinger.[6] The three interviewers were born between 1960 and 1967 and were therefore closer in age to the grandchildren than to the children of the interviewees. This fact would prove significant, for the interviewees were able to speak more freely and above all more positively about the Third

Reich than they generally would have done with interviewers the age of their children, with whom many interviewees had experienced bitter conflict over their Nazi past. In the end, interviews were successfully conducted with sixty-two Free Germans. Most were interviewed individually, a very few in pairs. Most interviews were carried out by a single interviewer, although seven Free Germans were interviewed by two interviewers. Each interview was assigned a number and one or (in those seven instances) two letters, identifying the interviewers: A for Autsch, B for Lobinger (then named Baumgarten), and S for Seidel. The project was overseen by an advisory board of social scientists from various disciplines with expertise in the project's subject matter (the history of twentieth-century Germany generally and of the youth movement in particular, gerontology and gerontological psychology, social groups, and generational units) and primary method of collecting data (the oral history interview).[7]

Unlike oral history interviews structured around questions designed to get at their subjects' experience of specific issues or interviews focused exclusively on a specific period in their subjects' lives, the "biographical narrative" interviews employed in this project sought to elicit the life history of their subjects. Each interview had three parts. First, the interviewee was asked to relate the story of his or her life. These stories were told with little or no interruption by the interviewer(s) and consumed the bulk of interviews, which generally lasted several hours. Then, once the interviewee had finished, the interviewer(s) would ask questions elicited by the life story that had just been related. The third, generally briefest, part of the interview focused on the interviewee's current life situation. In addition to answering a series of more or less scripted questions about health, activities, and attitudes, the interviewee was asked to describe a typical day. Each tape-recorded interview was carefully transcribed using social science interview protocols.

Twenty-two men and forty women were interviewed. Half of those interviewed were born between 1900 and 1912; the other half were younger. The average birth year was 1912. The average age of those interviewed was eighty-two. The oldest interviewee was born in 1900, the youngest in 1926. The interviewees were well educated: 60 percent of the women and 71 percent of the men had an *Abitur* from a gymnasium, the secondary school that prepares adolescents for university study in Germany. Half of those interviewed had had some form of academic profession. Fifty-two of those interviewed identified themselves as Protestants; one interviewee as Catholic; one as Quaker; and eight as not religious or religiously affiliated. Twenty-eight interviewees were married; twenty-seven were widowed; and seven were single. Eleven married couples were interviewed.

As a historian of modern Germany with psychoanalytic training, I was brought into the project, with the financial support of the Köhler Foundation, to produce a psychoanalytically informed historical analysis of the interview transcripts. That analysis was to serve as my principal contribution to a "collective biography" of the Free Germans as what Reulecke called the *Jahrhundertgeneration*, the generation whose lives spanned the twentieth century.[8]

It was the sociologist Karl Mannheim who first focused the attention of social scientists on generation as a concept and as a social and historical phenomenon. On an epistemological level, Mannheim sought to use the concept to demonstrate how the two principal and competing traditions out of which sociology had emerged, the "positivistic" and the "romantic," could be productively reconciled.[9] Thus, according to Mannheim, a generation was determined by shared *objective* and *subjective* factors, each necessary but not sufficient to comprehend it.[10] As a result of biology (birth and life span) and geography, those belonging to a generation had a common, objectively observable "location in the social and historical process," a common exposure to the same social and historical circumstances. The shared experience of those circumstances led, in turn, to the development of specific shared modes of "behaviour, feeling, and thought," the shared subjective consciousness that ultimately characterized a generation for Mannheim.[11] Since the ways people organize and make sense of their impressions are established in early life, Mannheim saw the experiences of childhood and particularly adolescence as decisive in the creation of generations.[12] Those belonging to a generation could not simply share the same assumptions and worldview independently and in isolation, however. They needed to establish concrete bonds to one another, a "generational connection," growing out of the fact that all had been exposed to the same—generally destabilizing—social and historical forces in adolescence.[13] The generational connection in turn was the precondition for the establishment of what Mannheim called "generational units," as cohesive groups of young people belonging to the same generation responded to the same historical and social situation in radically different, often antagonistic, ways. Despite "the great similarity in the data making up the consciousness of its members," a generational unit need not necessarily possess generational consciousness or it "may consciously experience and emphasize" its "character as a generational unit," as in the case of Mannheim's paradigmatic generational unit, the German youth movement of his day.[14]

Thus Mannheim's interest in generation (like that of his contemporary, the art historian Wilhelm Pinder) was prompted by the dramatic emergence of generational consciousness on the part of young bourgeois Germans in the third decade of the twentieth century.[15] It was no accident that Mannheim's seminal 1928 article, "The Problem of Generations," appeared just

as the youth of the Bunds was openly and forcefully identifying itself as the
vanguard of a generation that would renew Germany following military defeat, political unrest, and economic hardship.[16] Mannheim's essay, then, both
explains the phenomenon of generation and testifies to its importance in Weimar Germany. Indeed, the enduring relevance of the concept to sociologists
and other scholars not only reflects the fact that it allows them to generalize
about the attitudes and actions of groups but indicates also that "generation"
as a way of defining and distinguishing the self was characteristic—perhaps
uniquely characteristic—of the twentieth century.[17]

Based largely on Mannheim's generational model, scholars have identified
four distinct twentieth-century "German generations," although they differ
slightly in how they define, characterize, and label them. The members of the
earliest, the "Wilhelmian youth generation" or the "front generation," were
generally born between the mid-1880s and 1900. The battlefields of World
War I defined this generation, which returned from the war decimated, demoralized, and disillusioned. Many of its members were filled with hatred for
the older generations, which they identified with the Weimar Republic and
blamed for Germany's defeat and "humiliation." This was the generation
that comprised the top leadership of the Third Reich.[18]

The second twentieth-century German generation, the "war-youth" or
the "Weimar-youth generation" born between 1900 and 1915, is the focus of
this book. Although the members of this generation were influenced by their
experience of war on the home front as children, their generation-defining
experience was of defeat in the war and of the disorder, division, and hardship during the Weimar Republic as adolescents. These events created a generation that sought to "redeem" Germany from its recent defeat and humiliation. In response to the conflict and disorder of the Weimar Republic, its
members yearned for discipline and order, to be realized in the creation of
a *Volksgemeinschaft*, a homogeneous and harmonious "community of the
people." In reaction to the anxiety and uncertainty of the 1920s, this generation was characterized by "coolness, hardness, and 'Sachlichkeit'" (an un-
translatable word conveying realism, privileging action over inhibiting sentiment or empathy).[19] Its members had "a love of absolutes" and a hatred of
the compromise and self-interest they saw as characteristic of parliamentary
democracy.[20] Their values were based on an idealized image of the soldier
at the front in World War I and of Germany's political and social unity at
the outbreak of the war. Already drawn to National Socialism during the
Weimar period, this generation put National Socialist ideas and policies into
practice during the Third Reich. After the harrowing experiences of World
War II, the members of this generation tended to abandon politics, throwing

themselves into the rebuilding of their lives and their country. Scholars such as Helmut Fogt and Ulrich Herbert see this as an expressly "political generation" that reinterpreted itself as "apolitical" only after 1945.[21]

The third twentieth-century German generation is the "Hitler Youth generation" or the "skeptical generation," those born between 1920 and the early 1930s. The older members of this generation fought in World War II; the younger served as so-called *Flakhelfer,* assisting with the civil air defense of Germany at the end of the war, or otherwise experienced the war as children on the home front. The consciousness of this generation was shaped by its socialization in the Hitler Youth followed by its experience of the war and the period of the Reich's collapse. After 1945 members of this generation felt a deep sense of betrayal and disillusionment. As the preceding generation had established National Socialism in Germany, the Hitler Youth generation established the two postwar Germanys. In the Federal Republic it most benefited from the "economic miracle" of the 1950s and early 1960s; in the German Democratic Republic it became known as "the reconstruction generation" and experienced upward mobility like no other generation in East Germany. In marked contrast to the passionate engagement of the preceding German generation, this generation in West Germany, largely as a result of the war, became, according to the sociologist Helmut Schelsky, "skeptical," mistrustful of ideology, idealism, and enthusiasm generally, adopting instead a sober, apolitical pragmatism.[22]

Finally, the fourth generation is called by some the "Kriegskinder," children of the war, and by most "the 1968 generation." These are the children, generally born between 1940 and 1950, of the generation of those interviewed for this study. Scholars who prefer the label "Kriegskinder" tend to understand this generation within a German context and see the decisive experiences that shaped its consciousness as occurring in early childhood: the experience of the war for its older members, the experiences of the immediate postwar period for its younger ones. The extraordinarily difficult conditions of life, the absence of the father during the war and then in POW camps, his demoralized return and the family tensions that accompanied it, the intense desire of the parents to make a new beginning and to distance themselves from the National Socialist past—all resulted in the parents of the members of this generation placing age-inappropriate and unrealistic expectations on them, expectations that led to feelings of inadequacy, resentment, and an unacknowledged but intense identification with the parents based on having to bear their parents' burdens.[23] These feelings laid the psychological groundwork for their rebellion in the late 1960s against their parents and the society their parents had helped create. Scholars who label this "the 1968 generation" tend to understand this generation within an international context and see the decisive experiences that shaped its consciousness as occurring in the late 1950s and early 1960s when its members were adolescents, experiences largely shared by their generational peers in other Western countries. The growing tension between established moral codes, customs, laws, and institutional cultures, on the one hand, and rapid economic, technical, and social change, on the other, produced a demand on the part of the self-consciously "young" to bring social norms, lifestyles, and political structures in line with these changes and brought the members of this generation into sharp political and cultural conflict with their parents and the political and social "establishment" with which their parents were identified.[24] What distinguished this generational conflict in West Germany from that in other Western countries was primarily the confrontation over the National Socialist past in the family and in society.[25] Deeply ideological, this generation contrasted sharply with its "skeptical" predecessor.[26]

Scholars, then, confirm that generational consciousness and identity were characteristic of twentieth-century Germany. The German generation presented and analyzed here is only one of several strikingly different twentieth-century German generations, each with its own unique identity and outlook, each responding to the history through which it lived in its own unique ways (indeed, there were different generations of Nazis and different generational responses to National Socialism). Finally, the formation of these four more or less coherent German generations and the differences between them confirm the authority of history over the psyche, as different historical experiences gave distinct shape to each German generation.

Although historians might like to think that their interpretations of the past are what command the interest of readers, most ultimately recognize that it is the past itself, our intrinsic interest in what has come before, that generally prompts people to read historical writing. The fact that readers are more interested in history than in historians does not make the historian irrelevant, of course, for it is the historian's task to render the past comprehensible to people in the present, in part by reducing its infinite richness and simplifying its infinite complexity. In effect, the historian boils the recorded past down into an extract. While containing traces of the past in all its richness and complexity, that extract serves as a comprehensible representation of what had come before. In the case of *A German Generation*, I can be said to have produced a secondary reduction and simplification of the past, for the sixty-two people, in speaking to the interviewers, had already distilled the richness and complexity of their lives into more or less coherent life stories. Indeed, those life stories were themselves based on previous distillations of experience, for the process of reduction and simplification is essential to the way human beings make sense of themselves and their environment. Thus the life stories I present here represent the interviewees' own representation of representations of what in the end is an unrecoverable original past.

In considering how to represent the representations of the interviewees, I was confronted with two problems. I was keenly aware that it was their interviews that would ultimately engage readers, but I did not find the interviews to be particularly engaging. Perhaps this is a common feature of oral histories, which present for the most part the testimony of ordinary people who have lived for the most part ordinary lives. A single life story contains its dramatic moments, but these are generally few and far between. It seemed to me that, although these sixty-two Germans had lived through an extraordinary century, their life stories were shallower and colder than one might have expected them to be. I was not alone in this assessment. I well remember my dismay, in part because it rang true, when Lotte Köhler, the head of the Köhler Foundation and a thoughtful and experienced psychoanalyst, dismissed what I considered to be the three most interesting and revealing interviews as being of little psychological (or historical) value. The uniformity of the interviews presented me with a second problem of representation. Lacking compelling individual identity, the interviews—and the interviewees—tended to blend together in my mind. Only a handful of interviews, and only a portion of those, stood out, and that was because they were atypical. Here too I was not alone in this assessment. One of the interviewers, Babett Lobinger, noted that the interviews exhibited "an astonishing homogeneity," attributable partially to the fact that the interviewees had presented themselves in them not as unique individuals but as members of a generational collective.[27]

With individual interviews that seemed intrinsically neither engaging nor distinctive, I was uncertain how best to represent them. Then, in a moment of inspiration and/or foolhardiness, I arrived at a solution. It came as I was thinking about the virtually indistinguishable descriptions by two different women in their interviews of the experience of living in an apartment expropriated from Jews during the Third Reich. It occurred to me that I might put these two descriptions together to create a thicker, richer account of their parallel experience than either description possessed individually. Indeed, it might prove possible to create "composite" interviews that would provide a thicker, richer account of the experience of the interviewees generally than any individual interview could do on its own. Furthermore, if I could create such "composite" interviews, I would demonstrate strikingly and forcefully the extraordinary homogeneity of this group of people, the fact that they told similar stories about similar lives, and that the hallmark of those stories and of those lives was the merger of the self with the collective.[28]

And that is what I managed to do. Altogether I created six composite interviews, two (one man and one woman) for each part of the book. The first part presents the interviewees' experiences in childhood and adolescence during World War I and the Weimar Republic. The second part presents the interviewees' experiences in young adulthood during the Third Reich, World War II, and the war's immediate aftermath. And the third part presents the interviewees' experiences as mature adults in postwar West Germany. I found it surprisingly easy to combine the individual interviews to create coherent life stories without having to change much beyond factual details like dates and places. Ultimately readers will have to decide for themselves how compelling, illuminating, and plausible they find the composite interviews. I hope that in reaching their judgment readers will compare the text of the composite interviews with the endnotes, which indicate precisely where one interview ends and another begins and every change I made to achieve narrative consistency or smooth transitions apart from very brief deletions. To be sure, readers will not be able to compare my translations with the original interview transcripts (at least until those transcripts become publicly available), but that inability is characteristic of any work of history written in a language other than the one used in the sources. Moreover, my translation of the interviews into English enabled me to iron out stylistic differences between the individual interviewees, and I eliminated the pauses, the coughs, and so on that are indicated in the interview transcripts. As Lutz Niethammer has noted, however, distortion in the presentation of oral history interviews is inevitable, not least through their transcription, which already smoothes out language and fails to communicate emphases and much nonverbal communication.[29] It is certainly the case that the composite characters I have created recall more experiences than a single life would normally contain. Perhaps the best characterization of the composite interviews is that they represent what Karl Mannheim's contemporary and fellow sociologist, Max Weber, called "ideal types," paradigms that simultaneously capture the recalled experiences of all the interviewees and of none of them.[30]

There are various reasons why it was relatively easy to create the composite interviews. In the first place, the interview situation encouraged the interviewees to relate similar life stories. All came to the interviews in their capacity as members of the Free German Circle and recalled their lives as former members of the youth movement. They knew that the interviewers were interested in their adolescent experiences in the youth movement and in the significance of those experiences for the way they had lived their lives.[31] On a deeper level, their life stories were so much alike because the interviewees belonged to what Mannheim characterized as "a generational unit." Born at the same time and living in the same place, they had been exposed to the same social and historical circumstances. The common experience of those circumstances led them to develop a shared generational consciousness and a shared sense of past, present, and anticipated future.[32] That shared consciousness and sense of themselves in the world helped to create a common way of remembering and relating their common past.[33] Moreover, as Lutz Niethammer and Dorothee Wierling have pointed out, the interviewees' life stories had been to a degree constructed collectively.[34] The interviewees had been sharing, creating, modifying, and affirming their life stories in conversation with one another for decades, many beginning already in adolescence. In a sense, as a result of those conversations, the interviewees can be said to be the original authors of the composite life stories presented here.[35] Indeed, as the sociologist Maurice Halbwachs famously argued, all memory is ultimately collective memory—shared, created, modified, and affirmed in a social and communicative process.[36] Specifically, Halbwachs believed that memory is collectively created and maintained in groups that are "confined in space and time" and that the identity of such groups is created and maintained by their collective memories.[37] The Free German Circle would seem to be just such a group, and the six composite interviews would seem to instantiate its "collective memory." Finally, and this reason is implicit in everything advanced thus far, the interviewees made the creation of the composite interviews possible by the way they lived their lives and by the way they defined themselves. Beginning in adolescence, these Germans consistently sought to belong to—to merge with—the group. Throughout their lives they privileged collective over individual identity. As one woman told her interviewer: "Actually we have all, always, sought the collective."[38] Although those interviewed would doubtless find much of what follows in this book objectionable, I doubt that most would be put off by the composite interviews and by the loss of their individual identity in them. The composite interviews are wholly consistent with what they sought to achieve over the course of their lives.[39]

The transcripts of the sixty-two recorded interviews comprise a substantial amount of textual material.[40] In reducing the material to manageable proportions, I tended to excerpt memories of historically significant events, memories of events and experiences of personal significance to the interviewees, and memories that I simply found vivid and compelling. Most fundamentally, I excerpted accounts of events and experiences that seemed significant within the context of the interviews as a whole, nontrivial commonalities, passages that seemed part of a pattern of experience and response to experience across the interviews. In the process, I also excerpted the exceptional, such as passages describing being partially Jewish during the Third Reich, those expressing empathy for Jewish people—or overt anti-Semitism, for that matter. Based primarily on what I deemed characteristic of the interviews, on the patterns I had identified in them, I produced a psychological and historical analysis of the interviewees for the Siegen project on the Free German Circle. That analysis forms the basis of the analysis sections that follow each set of composite interviews in the three parts of this book.

Although the composite interviews present life stories and the analysis sections interpret them, the two are more closely related than might first appear. In creating the composite interviews, I clearly was influenced by the analyses, which predated them, and I sought to use the composite interviews to illustrate and support the interpretations of the interviewees presented in the analysis sections.[41] Indeed, not only do the composite interviews present my analysis of the interviewees in narrative form, but my analysis of the interviewees presents a composite of their experience. In both, the individual identity of the interviewees is lost or at least severely reduced. Thus, in the analysis sections, I have generally assembled my excerpted data—lined up if not melded together—in order to make a case. To be sure, brief interview quotations preserve perhaps a fragment of the individual identity and experience of the interviewees (theoretically enabling the reader to discern any differences between them). Nonetheless, the quoted passages are not manifestly different from one another since the purpose of the analysis sections, as in most scholarship where evidence is presented in support of argument, is not to highlight individual difference but to demonstrate congruence. The analysis sections of this book represent more or less traditional historical writing, offering interpretations of the interviewees and presenting evidence from the interviews to illustrate and support those interpretations. The composite interviews also present evidence that illustrates and supports the interpretations in the analysis sections but do so in a way that preserves the collective narrative power of the sources, tapping into the attraction that history exerts on us when it takes the form of stories about the people of the past.

If I have a concern about the composite interviews it is that they may divert the attention of readers away from the historical material onto its mode of presentation. Nevertheless, I do hope that readers will come to believe—will *want* to believe—that, say, "Magdalene Beck" is a real woman and then will experience a fleeting sense of disorientation every time their eyes catch an endnote and they recall that "she" is actually thirty-one different women. And I do seek to remind readers that the histories we read are the distillations—indeed, to a degree, the creations—of historians. For as the philosopher and publicist Theodor Lessing wrote during World War I: "In no way does history uncover hidden meaning, causal connection, historical development per se. Instead, history is always history writing, that is, the creation of meaning, the imposition of causal connection, the invention of historical development. History does not discover the meaning of the world; it gives the world meaning."[42] It also needs to be emphasized, however, that historians do not simply impose themselves on the past; the past also imposes itself on historians, giving rise, shape, and substance to the history they write. The double meaning of the word *history* reflects the fact that there is no clear distinction between the past and its representation. History is the product of a dialectical process involving present and past, historian and historical material.[43] Or, put another way, history writing is a collaboration between the historian and the people of the past, in this case between me and the interviewees, who were themselves historians of their own lives.[44]

The very fact that interviewees, as autobiographers, apparently stand between the historian and the original past has prompted some to question the value of oral history. Specifically, these skeptics ascribe the unreliability of oral history to the unreliability of memory and contend that life history interviews are "artifacts" that reveal more about the present than about the past. This skepticism about the truth-value of oral history, however, is based upon the application of a positivist standard to oral history interviews that other historical sources would be unable to meet and naively presumes the existence of a recoverable, stable, original past that in fact never existed.[45] In defending oral history against its critics, Ute Daniel points out that "precisely the same problem characterizes every other category of source that is available to historians for analysis. Whether transcripts of parliamentary sessions or the texts of laws, whether wage statistics or photographs, historical sources are selective and reflect a point of view. Sources can never be taken as reflections of the reality of the past. What sources transmit is always an interpretation of reality, an interpretation that requires integration and assessment that is both interpretative and critical. Historians who conduct and analyze life history interviews are well aware of this fact, something one cannot always say about historians who base their work on the apparently 'hard facts' of history."[46] Indeed, there is an extensive, self-reflective, and epistemologically sophisticated literature on the problems and potential of oral history.[47] Its practitioners appreciate that contemporary experiences and concerns shape memories of the past—in what is recalled, what is revised, and what is left out—and they recognize that there is no such thing as an accurate, objective memory of the past as it actually happened.[48] But it is also true that the past shapes contemporary experiences and concerns, and life history interviews are not simply retrospective reconstructions.[49] Oral history interviews always reflect past and present, and it is clearly very difficult, perhaps impossible, to disentangle them.[50] Nevertheless, the influence of contemporary concerns generally seems secondary in the autobiographies narrated by interviewees, and in practice the past appears to predominate.[51] We are, after all, historical beings, less the creators of our past and more its creation, products of a history that exercises more authority over us than we may care to acknowledge.

Being able to disaggregate the admixtures of the present from the past in oral history interviews would seem to be an issue for historians whose interviewees function as "witnesses," typically to historically significant events. For such historians, the accounts in oral histories need to be corroborated by other, more traditional historical sources. The interviewees in this book, however, do not serve as witnesses to history, as potentially objective observers of something outside and beyond themselves. The interviewees in all their subjectivity are the subject of this book. And what is presented and analyzed here are their memories, historically valid memories to the extent that the interviewees sought to present their life experiences as best they can recall them. Therefore, no systematic effort has been made to determine which memories accurately reflect some supposed past reality and which reflect retrospective reconstruction. Where there are obvious discrepancies between the recollections of the interviewees and what is known about the past as reconstructed by historians using other historical sources, these are presented not to expose the falsity of those memories but to understand their meaning—indeed, to uncover their "truth" for the interviewees.[52]

Although this book focuses on the subjective experience of sixty-two people, the question of the representativeness of those subjective experiences arises inevitably. In fact, the question is posed by the book's title, *A German Generation: An Experiential History of the Twentieth Century*, which implicitly claims that the experience of these sixty-two people over that period was characteristic of Germans belonging to their generation. Like most works of history, then, this book is a case study. A particular historical phenomenon is studied systematically and in depth not only for its own sake but also with a view to making generalizations that transcend it. To be sure, the sixty-two Germans at the heart of this study cannot be equated with an entire generation. They are historically unique, not least because of their extraordinary homogeneity. Nevertheless, despite their uniqueness, they also manifest historically significant characteristics of the generation to which they belong, at times perhaps to a pronounced degree. An in-depth study of the lives of these sixty-two people, then, enables us to identify and to understand aspects of their experience and response to experience that they shared with generational peers. Although not drawn to scale, the following diagram depicts the relationship of the experiences of the sixty-two interviewees to the wider circles of experience in which theirs were inscribed:

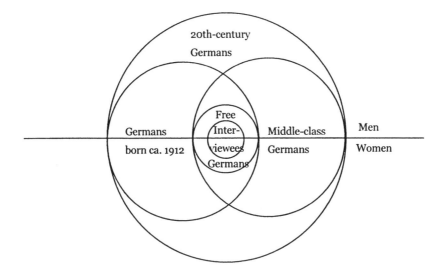

It seems ethically problematic to insist that the lives of the sixty-two interviewees represent more than themselves to be historically significant.[53] It
seems wholly legitimate, however, to place those lives in historical context, to
relate the experiences of the interviewees to the experiences of Germans belonging to their generation and social class and beyond. It also seems wholly
legitimate to place the findings presented in this study in historiographical
context, to relate my interpretations of the sixty-two interviewees to the interpretations of other scholars who have studied the experience of Germans
in the twentieth century. That work of historical and historiographical con-
textualization is done principally through the essays following each analysis
section. Bringing the history of twentieth-century Germany as presented and
interpreted by other scholars to bear on the lives of the sixty-two interviewees should enrich our understanding of those lives.[54] Bringing the lives of
the sixty-two interviewees as presented and interpreted here to bear on the
history of twentieth-century Germany should enrich our understanding of
that history.[55] The essays assess the sixty-two interviewees' "representativeness" by setting their lives in generational context, thus enabling readers to
determine which aspects of those lives were characteristic of their generation
and which not, and to transcend the experience of the interviewees to read
the history of a generation over the course of the twentieth century. Or, put
another way, the essays should enable readers to gain an appreciation of the
relationship of these sixty-two people to other twentieth-century Germans
of their generation as studied by other scholars. Although readers will reach
their own conclusions, it would seem that the presentation and interpretation

of the interviewees here are generally compatible or congruent with those studies that focus on "subjective" experience and take an empathic approach to that experience and are somewhat less compatible and occasionally incongruent with those studies that focus on an "objective" historical reality that can be disaggregated from subjective experience and take an empirical approach to that reality.[56] This book, then, contains three different types of historical writing. Taken together, however, the interviews, analyses, and essays seek to present readers with an experiential history of twentieth-century Germany: a representation, a distillation, of the experience of sixty-two Germans over the course of the twentieth century that in turn represents, distills, the experience of Germans belonging to their generation over the course of the twentieth century more generally.

Although some readers may be put off by the fact that I have subjected the interviewees to psychological interpretation or disapprove of the composite interviews, my principal concern about this book goes deeper. From the time I began to read the interviews until today, as I complete this book, I have been aware that I do not particularly like the interviewees. They are or were about the age of my parents. My mother was born in Milwaukee in 1912. My father was born in Vienna in 1913. Not only did my parents belong to the generation of the interviewees, they belonged to the same social class. Indeed, my father as an adolescent was a member of the youth movement during the 1920s in Austria. He was a Pfadfinder, or Boy Scout. When I attended the convention of the Free German Circle in Goslar in 1997, I was struck by the fact that those in attendance, including many of the interviewees, looked so very like my parents would have looked had they still been alive. And yet these sixty-two Germans stood on one side of the Holocaust and my parents stood on the other. Although neither of my parents identified themselves as Jewish, both, according to Nazi racial criteria, would probably have been victims of the Final Solution had they been living in territory controlled by Germany during World War II. Although from a German American family, my mother appears racially to have been a quarter Jewish, on her mother's side. And my father was racially wholly Jewish. Indeed, my father escaped the Holocaust only by fleeing Austria in 1939, and four of his five uncles and aunts, as well as cousins, perished in the genocide. In addition to what the interviewees had been in the past—Germans of the generation of my parents who for the most part had enthusiastically supported National Socialism during the Third Reich—how they came across in their interviews put me off as well. I found their smugness and sense of superiority annoying. To be sure, sympathy and empathy are not synonymous. One can sympathize with someone for whom one experiences no empathy (one can feel sorry for people in whose place one could never imagine being), and one can empathize with someone for whom one experiences no sympathy (one can understand people in order to exploit or even destroy them).[57] Nonetheless, I worry that my lack of sympathy for the interviewees may have limited my empathy for them.

Perhaps my interpretation of the interviewees' self-satisfaction and relentless optimism as a defense against sadness at a lifetime of loss reflects a wish on my part that they too had suffered. To some extent all historians inhabit an imagined world when studying the past. One not only imagines the past in one's head, the past imposes itself on one's imagination. While researching and writing this book and over a number of years, I inhabited in my mind the world of the Third Reich, and the world of the Third Reich inhabited me. This was a difficult and upsetting experience. Throughout my research and writing on that period, particularly in studying the relationship of the interviewees to Jews and to the Holocaust, I was constantly aware of my own potential victimhood, of my own potential helplessness vis-à-vis the interviewees. Perhaps in creating the composite interviews and in analyzing the interviewees I sought to counteract those experiences of fantasized helplessness by exerting intellectual control, even mastery, over this group of Germans.

Throughout this book I present the interviewees and, by extension, many of their contemporaries as sympathetic to National Socialism and as, for the most part, committed Nazis during the Third Reich, and I consider the roots and the consequences of that sympathy and commitment. I do so not to condemn the interviewees and their contemporaries but in order to be able to empathize with an aspect of their experience that seems alien to most of us. Despite my abhorrence of National Socialism, I seek in this book to present and to understand its appeal to the interviewees and, ultimately, to other ordinary Germans during the 1930s and early 1940s.[58] Specifically, I seek to account for the attraction of what I regard to be Nazism's fundamental ideological tenet, the racial collective of the Volksgemeinschaft, or "community of the people"—reflecting in part the attraction that collective experiences exert on human beings more generally. My aim, then, is certainly not to engender sympathy for the interviewees or for Germans belonging to their generation but to reduce the intellectual and emotional distance separating us from them, in part by thinking our way inside their unique historical circumstances, in part by recognizing that on some level they were as we are and that we have within us the capacity to be as they were.

But I do not want to conclude this introduction leaving readers in the world of the Third Reich, with its exemplification of the potentially destructive human need to belong and, consequently, to exclude. Empathy does not only confront us with the dehumanizing potential of human beings. It also connects us emotionally and intellectually to others, allowing us to recognize ourselves in those who initially seem different, even alien. Empathy is at the heart of the historical method and at the heart of history's appeal, the pleasure we derive from learning about people in the past, very different from us and like us at the same time. My own interest in history can be traced back to fishing trips with my father in rural Wisconsin when I was very little. I do not recall us ever catching anything, but I vividly remember listening with rapt attention as my father told me stories of the Persian and Peloponnesian wars as we sat in a little rowboat in the hot sun on a lake near Dousman. This book is based upon stories and presents stories, the stories of people and their lives set against a historical backdrop nearly as dramatic as the one that framed the stories retold by Herodotus and Thucydides and retold again by my father to me.

I

Germany during World War I and the Weimar Republic

1

INTERVIEWS

Youth

HEINRICH RATH

The story of my life in this troubled century is somewhat muddled and not so easy to relate.[1] I was born in Berlin in 1910. I came from a home shaped by literature and music, and both my parents played musical instruments. I had two brothers. The one became a violinist, the other a doctor. They were twins. They are missing in the East.* Our family was close and harmonious, a closed circle, a bit focused in on itself, of bourgeois origin but very artistic. My father was incredibly well educated, and I always admired him. My mother was fourteen years younger than my father. He was regarded by us as the patriarch or head of the family. I should also mention that my father was a nature lover who acquainted us with nature from early on.[2] He took hikes with us.[3] It was a family tradition that every Sunday afternoon we would go on a walk of several hours,[4] and when I got tired, there would be singing.[5] My father loved to garden, and we children grew up gardening. So that is how I encountered hiking and gardening.[6] Already as a schoolboy I was inclined to a life close to nature.[7] My experience in the family is unforgettable and shaped at least half of who I am. The other half was shaped by the youth movement and the Bund.†,[8]

---

* Missing in action on the eastern front in World War II.

† "Bund," literally "Bond" in the sense of union. The interviewee refers here to the national organization to which his youth movement group belonged. The youth movement of the 1920s is generally referred to as the *bündische Jugendbewegung*, or the youth movement of the Bunds, for during the Weimar Republic individual youth movement groups were organized in a series of national Bunds, each having a somewhat different philosophy and orientation.

The good years, certainly, let's say until 1923.[9] Childhood. Good years. Free years.[10] On account of the war, my parents sent me to live with my mother's father in Brandis.*,[11] I lived there from 1916 to 1919,[12] when I was taken back to Berlin.[13] My grandfather was the only doctor in Brandis, because Brandis and surroundings only had three thousand inhabitants back then.[14] I felt at home there, and my grandparents' home was a family focal point. Grandfather had a large villa, and the relatives would gather there on any sort of birthday, of which there were quite a few, for my mother had six siblings and the family was very close. We cousins were close, too, like the pipes of an organ, you might say.[15] My grandfather [also] owned a lumber-yard, a vegetable garden, and fields and meadows that stretched all the way to the woods. Those fields had to be tilled, the hay mowed and harvested. Even at age six I helped with the farm work. In May or June, when the potatoes would sprout as little green plants, the weeds had to be cut down. Then we children were given the task of carrying the heavy turned pans, drink hold-ers, up the hills to the potato fields. That's where the women were, my aunts mostly. They were provided with coffee and potato salad and bread, and we had to haul those provisions up to them at various times of the day.[16] Every day after school in summer I went into the forest carrying a basket woven out of wheat stalks to gather grass, moss, and pine needles, which were used as straw for the goats. Every day we brought something home in those baskets. Along the edge of the forest there was a brook that flowed over pebbles, and you could grab crayfish or trout under the ledges, although we couldn't let ourselves get caught doing it, since food was very short during the war.[17] It was a time of hunger, and thank goodness we had our potato fields. Potatoes were my absolutely favorite food. When a pot of lovely boiled potatoes was placed in front of me at the table, I'd peel them with my fingers. Even today I'm enthusiastic when I see boiled potatoes, especially when they've burst open so beautifully.[18]

So there I grew up, for that time.[19] I was fortunate. My mother's young-est sister,[20] who lived with her husband at my grandparents,[21] was extremely close to me.[22] She had no children[23] and cared for me as if I were her own child.[24] So I was the child of the house from 1916 to 1919.[25] I was very much influenced and impressed by her. She died when I was in the lower grades of the gymnasium.[26] Her husband[27] was the senior teacher in the school and the choirmaster.[28] My uncle was a very musical person, and he more or less ran the theater club in the village, which every year around Christmas put on

---

* Coupled with the Allied blockade of Germany, the notorious "turnip winter" of 1916–17 produced widespread hunger and suffering. As a result, children were sent to live with relatives in the countryside where food was more plentiful. Brandis is a rural village in Nieder Lausitz about a hundred kilometers south of Berlin.

some performance like the *Dreimädelhaus* and similar operettas. Of course this was very exciting since we children replayed the whole thing on the stage afterward. It's hard to believe that a village in the Lausitz could have been so artistically inclined. My uncle filled all the roles, following the model of the Dresden opera. Once a horse also performed, the baker's horse. He let his apples drop during the performance, which was something we weren't able to reproduce! So that was the cultural life that centered around the choirmaster.[29]

As far as politics were concerned,[30] in keeping with the style of those days, I had a picture of our emperor and of Emperor Franz Joseph over my bed.* Franz Joseph died in 1916 or 1917, I think, but he hung on the wall until then.[31] And [I remember] 1914, when I was four years old, how I went along the Schloßstraße with my mother. Suddenly my mother said, "Wait a minute." She ran across the street and came back as pale as a corpse because she had just seen a poster announcing general mobilization for the war. I can still see it clearly before me.[32] Then in 1919, I must still have been at the school in Brandis,[33] I remember how our teacher came in deeply shaken and told us about the end of the war and about the heavy, heavy, heavy burden that had been laid upon Germany. The men teachers were all gone, completely gone. The woman teacher, she came in dressed all in black.[34] And I can still see myself standing in our living room [back in Berlin] looking out onto the street; and a man with a red armband came, holding a horn in his hand. He positioned himself at the corner and tooted his horn: *Tatata. Tatata.* Then my father said, "And now it's going to start." I didn't know *what* was going to start. It was the revolution, you know. "And now it's going to start." That was the Kapp Putsch or something similar from those times.† "And now it's going to start," and he turned his back on the street.[35] Those are all, so, impressions.[36]

Yes, and I can also remember when there was butter for the first time after the war and when my father brought home a piece of Swiss cheese and how my father often took me along to North Schleswig, which is the old district of Flensburg, north of the current German border. We would visit Pattburg,‡ a little village about ten kilometers from Flensburg. They dried beet cutlets there, and I was allowed to eat a couple of beet cutlets when I visited. They tasted rather sweet. I'd be repulsed by them today.[37] Those are

---

*Kaiser Wilhelm II (1859–1941), German emperor; Franz Joseph I (1830–1916), emperor of Austria and king of Hungary, the leader of Germany's principal ally in World War I.

†A short-lived right-wing coup d'etat that took place in March 1920 in Berlin. The putsch was brought to an end after a few days by a general strike. The collapse of the putsch led to an upsurge of left-wing revolutionary agitation and violence. In general, political violence plagued the Weimar Republic from late 1918 until 1923.

‡Pattburg is today Padborg in Denmark.

early memories. I remember that everyone was terribly frugal. I didn't have leather shoes but rather wooden shoes and wooden sandals.[38] In the morning, when we sat in the kitchen drinking coffee, we would hear our neighbor, a teacher at the elementary school, clumping down the stairs in her wooden shoes. You heard her coming from *far* away.[39]

Yes, and I remember the plebiscites.* I was nine years old then. It was an exciting business. Flensburg was *drowned* in German flags and in Danish flags. Schleswig north of the Eidern [River] was divided into three zones. The first zone voted on the 10th of February 1920 and had a Danish majority. The second zone was Flensburg and surroundings with a solid German majority. The third zone held out no hope to the Danes, and so they had renounced holding a plebiscite in the third zone [already when signing] the treaties of Paris. But I remember the plebiscites very well: our sorrow when North Schleswig was lost, even though my relatives had traveled there from far away in special trains to vote.[40] Anyone who had been born there was eligible to vote, not just those who lived there. On the 13th of March, there was a large procession in Flensburg. It took over one and a half hours for the marchers, in rows of six, to pass through the city. My father marched with me. That was really something *awesome* for a little fellow. And I also remember the plebiscite on March 14th. In the evening we waited for the results, but I was not allowed to stay up. My father went into the city around midnight, and I had to go to bed and fell asleep. The next morning around seven my parents came in, my father came in, and I jumped up and asked, "Father, did we remain German?" It was a great moment when he replied, "Yes, you can be at peace. We have remained German."[41]

Although my memories of Flensburg are vivid, we only spent a relatively short time there. After spending much of the war in the countryside, in Brandis, I was taken back by my parents to live in Berlin once the war was over.[42] For me, Berlin was, well . . . When you come from a remote village in the Lausitz, Berlin was a gigantic cauldron. When I first arrived I used to greet everybody on the street with "Good day!" as I had back home. But then someone turned around and said, "Do you *know* me, then?" Human contact didn't exist there. Already on my first or second day in Berlin, I was unable to find our apartment. There were six floors, and I had to scour every single story before I was able to stand in front of the right one. Or going through a railway underpass. There was so much to look at that I smacked my head on a mailbox. Everything was so astoundingly new to me.[43]

---

* Plebiscites mandated by the Treaty of Paris were held to determine the national identity of territories having mixed populations, in 1920 in Schleswig (Germans and Danes) and the districts of Marienwerder and Allenstein (Germans and Poles) and in 1922 in Upper Silesia (Germans and Czechs).

But when I think of historical events, then it's the period after the First World War that I remember, the mass demonstrations of the various party organizations. Even as a child I already picked up on the unrest in the city.[44] Everyone was armed following the revolution of 1918. In Berlin groups and factions of all sorts formed and fought with each other: Spartakus, Rote Frontkämpfer, Reichsbanner, Stahlhelm.* Everyone had the urge to putsch.[45] When there were Communist demonstrations, my mother would quickly pull me back [from the window], saying, "Get away from there. Don't look at that. It's blood they have on their banners, on their red banners." Well, that was the attitude.[46] You can imagine what sort of comments were made around the dinner table about the saddler's apprentice, Ebert.† And the murders on both sides and Rosa Luxemburg. And when I tried to grasp what was going on, albeit from a nationalist perspective, then I picked up slogans like: "Shoot down Walter Rathenau, that goddamned, dirty Jewish sow!"‡ It was on all the fences and was the [work of the right-wing] underground. When flags were hung out on Sundays, there was no question which flag hung from our window: Black-White-Red.§ So we ridiculed democracy, because we were used to something different from our parents, because our parents were used to something different—to discipline, not a free-for-all in the Reichstag.[47] God knows, where I grew up in Berlin was not republican and my school wasn't either. It was named the Treitschke School.** Not once when any official occasion took place did the Black-Red-Gold flag [of the Republic] ever fly from the roof of the school. On Volkstrauertag [Memorial Day], the entire school was led into a room where pictures of the fallen were displayed.[48]

So I experienced the years after 1918 with amazement because people were not prepared for the outcome of the war.[49] I studied hard, for money had become very short at home.[50] The period of inflation arrived,[51] cutting deeply into our family, for the money we'd managed to save lost its value[52]

---

* The Spartakus Bund organized an abortive attempt to overthrow the Republic in January 1919 and establish a socialist state. Following the collapse of the uprising and the murder of the two Spartacist leaders, Rosa Luxemburg and Karl Liebknecht, the Spartakus Bund continued to be a political force in Weimar Germany as the KPD, or Communist Party of Germany. The Rote Frontkämpferbund was the paramilitary force founded by the KPD in 1924. The Reichsbanner was a paramilitary force also founded in 1924 by the parties supporting the Weimar Republic, especially the SPD, which engaged in fighting its rivals on the left and the right. The Stahlhelm was a veterans' organization founded in 1918, which became the paramilitary arm of the conservative opposition to the Weimar Republic.

† Friedrich Ebert (1871–1925), Social Democratic leader and first president of the Weimar Republic. The son of a tailor, Ebert had, in his youth, learned the saddler's trade.

‡ Walther Rathenau (1867–1922), foreign minister of the Weimar Republic, who was assassinated by a right-wing death squad while in office.

§ The flag of the imperial monarchy.

** Heinrich von Treitschke (1834–96), nationalistic right-wing historian and publicist.

in the inflation.*,53 My father was a civil servant.† My mother was helped by my grandparents, her parents who lived in Brandis.54 My grandfather was in good shape financially because, as I said, he had a lumberyard.55 My grandparents supported my parents, supported my mother. And when there were arguments at home between my parents, it was always over money. My mother was convinced that my father hadn't given her enough or ought to give her more. I must say that those arguments remain a dreadful memory for me.56

Around that time I had the good fortune to join what was known then as the Deutschnationale Jugendbund,‡ where I was accepted as a person in a wonderful way. From then on I was a member of the youth movement, the youth movement of the Bunds.57 Surely one of the most important decisions of my life or pieces of good fortune in my life was that I joined the group.58 Indeed, in the group, I had experiences that decisively influenced my development. I say that now, but back then I didn't realize how important the group would become to me. Back then I only wanted to join the group, whose members I had noticed and admired at school. There was one particular boy who would come to school in a tunic and short pants. When I asked him why, he replied, "I'm a Wandervogel.§,59 Come along with me on Thursday to the Düsseldorferstraße. There's some hot dancing there." Me, all of eleven years old. It was certainly very interesting, very interesting indeed. When we walked in there, the group just broke up laughing, for the girls were absolute Wandervogel girls in their outfits and demeanor. Then came a scene I'll never forget. I was put in the center of a circle of girls, and they started to sing:

> I take the glasses from my eyes,
> to see what books make me realize,
> and there I read quite clearly,
> that it's you I love most dearly.
> But to you, to you I'll say,

always with their fingers pointed right at me,

> what I carry in my heart today,
> is that I can no longer live,
> unless to me your love you give.

---

* The hyperinflation reached its high point in 1923.

† As a civil servant, the interviewee's father was probably on an essentially fixed income, which would have lagged significantly behind the soaring inflation.

‡ The Deutschnationale Jugendbund was founded in the fall of 1918. In 1924 it became the Großdeutsche Jugendbund. In both manifestations the Bund tended to have a paramilitary, nationalistic, folkish orientation.

§ Wandervogel, literally, "Wandering Birds," was the name of the German youth movement before the war.

The male members of the group were demobilized young war veterans who sat with a wolfhound in a corner of what was a huge barracks. One had a big, heavy pistol, and they were all waiting for a mouse to come out of its hole. Well, that was my first experience with the youth movement. It was pretty devastating, of course, and I thought to myself, "Never, ever again." But then a youth of about seventeen or eighteen came in wearing a big belt with one of those buckles with a crown of victory on it, and a game of dodge-ball began, which gave me more hope.[60]

From then on I'd go on weekends[61] with a group from the Deutschna-tionale Jugendbund[62] to areas outside of Berlin. We didn't spend the night but came home again in the evening. I was especially impressed when they spread a tent flap on the ground at midday and every boy tossed the sand-wich he'd brought with him from home onto it. Then everyone took what he wanted. It was a custom in the group that was supposed to prevent poorer boys from only getting a slice of farmer's cheese while the others ate thick ham sandwiches. I thought this practice good in principle, but I felt sorry for my mother because she had put a lot of effort into making sandwiches I liked. The second experience [that impressed me] was more animalistic. At one point I felt a bodily need, but there was only a meadow, without a tree or shrub, and I didn't know what I was supposed to do. So I asked one of the boys, and he said, "Here, take a spade, go two or three hundred meters away, dig yourself a hole, squat over it, and then you make a loaf." That was the jargon of the group; they called this activity making a loaf. It's unforgettable to me. I liked the boys. It took a while before I felt warm inside [the group], but then I belonged to the group completely.[63]

The center of our activities were so-called nest evenings, a name that came from the old Wandervogel, along with the excursions.[64] Every month we'd go on a somewhat bigger hiking expedition and smaller excursions on the weekends, when we'd explore the areas around Berlin.[65] I remember when we went on excursions on Saturdays we always took the train out somewhere into the countryside. The stations were *filled* with groups of young people. There were mountains of rucksacks piled up waiting for the train. And in the trains there was singing and dancing and guitar playing.[66] Then, with our rucksacks on our backs, we'd make our way.[67] Once a week we met for a nest evening[68] in Steglitz* in a little wooden hut, which the mother of a Wandervogel who had fallen in the war had built and made available to youth groups.[69] At our nest evenings[70] we'd recount what we'd done,[71] discuss forthcoming excursions, consider how to recruit new members, and tell stories.[72] But most of all what we did in the group was sing.[73] We always opened the nest evenings with singing. First we sang several songs, and then

---

* Steglitz was the birthplace of the Wandervogel movement.

something was generally read aloud and discussed. And then we sang again.[74] So the evenings consisted of singing, reading aloud, and discussion. But we *always* began with singing, and we *always* ended with singing. When we went camping, after we arrived at our campsite in the afternoon or evening, we would spend half the night singing, simply singing one song after another. And through singing, somehow, something [was] shared, something in common was created—how should I put it, a unison of spirit came into being. Then often nothing would be read aloud. Instead we simply sang ourselves into unconsciousness around the campfire. And the next day we'd go swimming or take a hike, but singing, singing together, was always a very significant ritual.[75] Friendship bound us together,[76] and the unity of the group was very powerful. Each person helped the other, each counted on the other. And whoever didn't fit in with the group didn't last very long and soon would say fare thee well. Anyone could join, but he had to meld with the group. He had to harmonize with the spirit of the group. He couldn't be contentious. It's hard to explain psychologically. The group was like a living body, a living body comprised of many individual cells.[77] For my part, I gradually grew so much into the group that I couldn't imagine my life without the other boys.[78] The group was a part of my life.

My parents' home in no way disappeared, of course, but I noticed that there were other possible influences on me besides my parents.[79] In fact, my inclination [toward the youth movement] came from my parents, especially my father. Although he had a technical profession, he was primarily interested in the world of nature and from early on had taken me on hikes.[80] At least once a year we had an evening for the parents. On those occasions we put on some sort of play, sang a few songs, and also showed them some of the games we played, so that our parents would say, "Oh, it's all right. They don't do anything foolish. They do some sensible things as well."[81] In fact, when the older boys went on excursions[82] with girls of the same Bund[83] everything was done with the utmost propriety. For you must remember that the girls were all good middle-class daughters. Indeed, when girls went along on excursions, their parents were initially very concerned. But then the group leader would pay a courtesy call on the parents in order to secure their permission.[84] When we camped together,[85] things were arranged so that we would spend the night in a barn with the girls on one side and the boys on the other.[86] The point was comradeship, boys and girls being together as comrades.[87] It was important to establish not a sexual or erotic relationship but a *genuine* relationship to women, to girls, to a pure person, to a natural person.[88] For that reason, the game of love was taboo for us. And by keeping the game of love taboo, we were able to achieve something.[89] On joint excursions, it was natural, it was pure. Being together was as natural as between brothers and sisters. One complemented the other, one was able to see life from the perspective of the other.[90] Boys and girls could even sleep all mixed up with one another in a haystack[91] or together on the forest floor, sometimes sleeping under the same blanket.[92] When we went swimming in a lake, everyone simply undressed. The girls didn't put on bathing suits. They simply went swimming. It was the most natural thing in the world.[93] For me it all took place without accompanying erotic thoughts or feelings. Instead, there was a very powerful experience of belonging together connected to the smell of resin, spruce, and the pines, the communal cooking and how wonderful it was to have cooked and eaten a noodle soup together. And also singing— singing is again bound up with it all.[94]

My group often did things with girl groups from our Bund.[95] We went on excursions with them to beautiful, romantic places[96] on Saturdays and Sundays, into the woods, where we gathered at a forest meadow, next to a forest pond, to play music, sing, and dance folk dances.[97] The girls really impressed me. They made their own clothes, bright skirts, colorfully embroidered blouses, and sang beautifully in two- and more-part harmony. The girls knew how to sing the upper parts to these songs beautifully, and inside I felt a yearning for the clean, pure inner spirit of those girls. It deeply affected my whole attitude toward girls and later also [toward women].[98]

Of course between boys in the group the erotic element played a role. Yes, one noticed, one noticed. The group didn't tolerate it, because such relationships led to individualism, and then the group had an unspoken egoism [within it]. As group leader, you had to pay attention. For, naturally, the awakening of the possibility of liking another person exceptionally well could reach into the sexual realm. But that wasn't the point, that wasn't the meaning of the thing, that was mistaken. But it was possible to set guideposts to block people later. And therefore I always . . . I also went to the parents in such cases. And I'd tell them exactly what I thought. I put several boys outside of the group for a year. I told them, "Think it through. You can remain outside for the time being." Because we really didn't like it. We had the feeling that children could be corrupted. Of course we were eminently bourgeois in many of our views. We were the children of our time and of our parents. That's clear.[99]

We lived naturally—on an island.[100] We *never* drank alcohol on our excursions. No one smoked. There weren't rules against smoking—it just went without saying. It was part of our special relationship to nature, which also went without saying. We would never leave our campsite without cleaning up.[101] In general, this drinking and materialism,[102] this smoking and skirt-chasing, all those practices, which were so widespread, those weren't our style, and we[103] consciously set ourselves against them.[104] We found popular

music and that sort of thing trivial. We stood against those things.[105] I remember vividly in this context how, after we had gone off somewhere on our
bicycles, when we came home and saw kids our age standing in front of the
movie theaters and so forth, we had an incredible feeling of superiority. We
had the feeling that we knew *how one ought to live*, how one can live *more
beautifully* than by sitting at home or going to the movies and perhaps drinking beer or doing something of that sort. So we had the feeling that we had
the better part of the world, although I must say that this "better part of the
world" was not always appreciated at home. When I came home my mother
demanded that before I did anything else I had to get into the shower and
hang up my clothes on the veranda, because she always claimed that I stank
of smoke and heaven knows what else. And so I had to change and literally
fit myself back into the bourgeois order by putting everything connected with
the weekend aside. But that wasn't difficult for me.[106]

Or [I remember] how, after a national convention of the Bund, we went
with boys from Breslau on an excursion along [the] Saale [River]. We visited
a professor, a relative of one of the boys from Breslau, and drank coffee with
him, and admired the [university] students who were there in Jena.[107] We in
the youth movement stood in complete opposition to the fraternity students
who seemed to dominate the scene,[108] all gussied up in their [fraternity] uniforms. We wanted nothing to do with their frippery. Part of the self-image of
the youth movement was that our uniform was simple, simple for the style of
those days. In fact, our uniform was so simple that it aroused the contempt
of people like those students, who loved uniforms or fashionable finery. That
was not our style, and we consciously tried to distance ourselves from it. In
my neighborhood[109] there was a promenade. On one of the main streets,
every afternoon, the gymnasium students would stroll along dressed to the
nines. And to set ourselves apart from these people, with their school caps
and so forth, we would pass through the promenade in our uniforms, if possible wearing pants filthy from an excursion. And with our sleeves rolled up,
you know, while the others promenaded up and down in their pretty little
suits and caps.[110] In fact, we distinguished ourselves from those who weren't
in the youth movement of the Bunds by wearing shorts, despite the cold win-
ters. A certain hardness was connected with this practice, which our parents
weren't so keen on, for they worried that we'd end up with rheumatism or
at least a cold.[111] Although there were hardly any youth hostels then,[112] we
avoided every youth hostel.[113] Instead we spent the night with farmers and
slept in the hay.[114] We had the most powerful sense of superiority. There certainly was something elitist about our group.[115]

We believed that if we instituted an upstanding, modest, simple, alco-
hol- and tobacco-free lifestyle, in the spirit of the youth movement, following

the principles articulated on the Hohe Meißner in 1913,* Germany would
become strong again and the shame of Versailles would be lifted. Although
those were the ideals,[116] there was nothing doctrinaire about them. No reg-
ulations or statutes were imposed. Rather these ideals developed of themselves, out of a secure instinct, only half consciously.[117] Thus when a boy was
initiated into the group and our badge was bestowed upon him,[118] there was
no official pledge. Twice a year we celebrated the solstice, each time on the
Blauer Mountains near Berlin. We'd build a pyre of wood and set it alight. At
this fire the new boys would be given the badge. And when the boy was given
the badge and his hand was shaken, then he simply made some kind of promise to remain upstanding and honest and tell the truth.[119] Still, in our group
there was a hierarchy. There was the novice, who had been accepted into the
group. And when things got serious, he'd have to pass a little test to become
a wolf cub. First of all, he had to be able to sing a number of excursion songs,
if possible while accompanying himself on a musical instrument. If he knew
less than five or six songs, then he failed the test and was not allowed to become a wolf cub. Additionally, there was a test of courage:[120] going through
a cemetery at midnight, for example.[121] Then he'd have to have some knowledge of terrain. And when he'd go along on excursions, he'd have to be able
to do certain things, like cook and set up a tent. He'd also have to be up to
the hikes physically. Anyone who wasn't a good hiker was bound to fail at
some point.[122] Part [of what we were looking for in our recruits] was something artistic and a certain boldness and physical capacity. They also needed
to be a bit independent. If this independence was missing, then the boys were
conformists and not cocreators. We wanted cocreators.[123] The esquires were
the next, the middle, level.[124] From this you can get a sense of what our ideal
of youth was. Romantic notions were bound up in the progression from the
wolf cubs, the little ones who had just joined the pack, through the older esquires to finally the knights. Our models were knights or forest scouts. And
one must concede that we were a bit militaristic. I recently found a volume of
our songs, and I had to acknowledge reluctantly that out of the eighty songs,
sixty-five were soldiers' songs, ten were hunters' songs, and then there were
perhaps six others. Of course none of them were love songs.[125] The history
of the youth movement can be told through its songs. The old Wandervogel
sang songs from the *Zupfgeigenhansl*.† They were mostly folk songs, love

---

*On 11 October 1913, on the Hohe Meißner mountain, youth groups had come to-
gether to adopt the pledge that German youth would shape their lives "at their own initiative,
on their own responsibility, and with deep sincerity."

†The *Zupfgeigenhansl*, songs of the Wandervogel, was edited by Hans Breuer and first
published in 1909.

songs, peasant songs. Then came the period after World War I when soldiers' songs were sung—pikemen's songs, military songs. Finally, at the end of the 1950s, songs came from the regions of southeastern Europe and Asia— Cossack songs, gypsy songs, pirate songs.[126]

So that was our group, and[127] all over Berlin there were other groups. The whole comprised a community called a "Gau,"* and above the Gau was the Bund.[128] Gradually the Bund became an increasingly dominating presence for us in the group, a dominating unity. We grew into it; we felt connected with it. And the consciousness that we were a part of a great community extending across the entire area of the Reich was exhilarating and made us stronger.[129] We were the Deutschnationale Jugendbund, later the Großdeutsche Bund.[130] The Bund had about six or eight hundred male members and about the same number of females at that time.[131] I could say more about organizational issues, but they aren't important.[132] [The first] national convention [of the Bund] was in Schwerin in Mecklenburg.[133] Some male relatives who were military enthusiasts had really turned me out for this convention of the Bund. I was given a green hunter's doublet and haversack. I looked like a caricature of a soldier. I must have looked [ridiculous] in this uniform, which was adorned with puttees. I didn't have real soldier's pants but rather breeches, you know, like those worn by the English, those checkered ones. And so I went early one morning to the Lehrter train station [in Berlin] and had to march past the workers, who doubled up with laughter as I passed by with my bows and puttees and incongruous uniform—I also had a hunter's field cap on my head. And so I began my life in the Bund. We all sat in fourth-class railway carriages, with wooden benches and a large open space in the middle where the market women used to put their baskets. Outside, the train was festooned with nothing but Black-White-Red flags. I will never forget our entrance into Schwerin. The Socialist Workers' Youth had their own convention there at the same time, and the two trains went singing past each other, glaring at each other with hatred: the one singing, "Germany, high in honor"; the other, "Brothers, to the sun, to freedom." I will never forget the scene. And then I was the absolute littlest and the absolute last one in a column that marched through the sand, the absolute last one. The dust and the dirt that washed over me at the back . . . When a song was begun in the front of the column, then it took five minutes to make it back to the end. But it was *exhilarating*.[134] Groups came from all the Gaus in Germany, youth movement groups, with their instruments, boys, and girls in their dirndl dresses and self-embroidered blouses. We also had our instruments along and sang and played and danced.[135]

---

*A word stemming from Germanic times designating an administrative district or region.

The next morning we went out to the large festival meadow. There were two large blocks, one was of girls in Wandervogel garb and the other was of military Freikorps people* and a small band of Wandervogel, like the one who had played dodgeball with us. But the greatest thing for me was that we had peas and bacon to eat. Naturally, the girls had put all their bacon into my mess kit so that I was completely stuffed. My only worry was what to do with all the peas. So I went into the palace park to a bridge, where four or five swans were swimming. It was a large estate. And then along came the leader of the Bund, Admiral von Trotha, a real live admiral.† He came through the park and saw me feeding the swans. I, the prototype of the militarist, smartly saluted as he passed. I would have liked to have seen the scene myself—how I, with my field cap, my puttees (no, I'd already gotten rid of those), greeted the admiral. He was actually very gracious. The little one and the great admiral. Trotha had been [naval] chief of staff at [the battle of] Skagerrak [in 1916]. He was a real Christian, a royalist Christian, with all the attendant to-do—pretty appalling, actually—but a decent and good leader of the Bund, who, out of this curious Deutschnationale Jugendbund, shaped a youth Bund that belonged with the best of them, the Großdeutsche Jugendbund.

The next convention of the Bund was on the Ley [River] at Erpel in 1925. The previous one had been in 1923; they were held every two years. This all occurred during a period defined politically by national resistance, for we had the French on the Rhine. Schlageter‡ was nearly a saint to us.[136] So we traveled into the occupied Rhineland.§ A former soldier was in our group, and he sang to us:

> Listen well, German boy;
> Listen well, German girl;
> No day should pass you by;
> No day should you be at peace.

---

* Right-wing paramilitary units of demobilized soldiers who violently suppressed left-wing workers and socialists between 1919 and 1923.

† Adolf von Trotha (1868–1940), vice admiral. During World War I, he occupied increasingly important positions in the naval high command, becoming head of the naval cabinet shortly before the war's end. After his resignation from the navy, Trotha became head first of the Deutschnationale Jugendbund and then of its successor, the Großdeutsche Jugendbund.

‡ Albert Leo Schlageter (1894–1923). War veteran, Freikorps fighter, and early Nazi, Schlageter was executed by the French for acts of sabotage in the occupied Rhineland.

§ When Germany was unable to fulfill some of its obligations set by the Versailles Treaty, French soldiers occupied the Rhineland in 1923. The French occupation produced an upsurge of German patriotism and bitterness at the terms of the treaty and led to a policy of passive resistance to the French. After this policy contributed to the hyperinflation in Germany, it was abandoned by the Stresemann government.

And then the same again.

> The French are standing on the Rhine;
> Let that pierce your heart.

The mood was unambiguous. It was intolerable for a conquered people to have the French on the Rhine.[137] In those days a Langemarck ceremony was held every year.* The Bunds would march out to a bonfire, and a wreath would be thrown into the flames. It was all very solemn and uplifting.[138] Naturally, in the group we read what was popular in those days, books like the *Rembrandt-German*,† Flex,‡ of course,[139] and Jünger.§,[140] It was a time of transition. We had lost the war, and the Versailles Treaty hung around our necks. We held politics in contempt, party politics.[141]

When you look back, *of course* we were *nationalistic*—we were the Großdeutsche Jugendbund. And we were Christian, which simply meant that we didn't accept Jews. We never even considered it.[142] There was one episode, but that was more amusing. A couple of Jews had formed a youth movement group called the Comrades. I had three Jews in my class, and two of them belonged to the Comrades. One night we spied on them. At one point we stole their pennant. From our perspective, allowing your pennant to be stolen was dishonorable and intolerable. [Later] one of the two Jews in my class came to me and said, "Look here, we know you were in the area; you have our pennant." And I said to him, "Then you must come to us and prove that we have taken your pennant away from you. That's what you have to do." And he said, "The pennant doesn't matter as much to us as it does to you." As a matter of fact, I didn't have the pennant, but the pennant had been taken and was not given back. We never got into a scuffle with them, and that was the only incident.[143]

After our experiences we had learned that nationalism was necessary, especially after the Versailles Treaty had taken away parts of the old German empire. We were proud to be nationalistic, but we had no connection to a

---

* Battle of 10 November 1914 that took place outside of Ypres in Belgium. The heavy losses sustained by untrained German volunteers made the defeat into a redemptive myth during the Weimar Republic.

† *Rembrandt als Erzieher*, by Julius Langbehn, was first published in 1890 and enjoyed great popularity during the Weimar Republic. In the book, Langbehn insisted that race is the decisive factor in human life. He also hoped that youth would redeem the German Volk from materialism and mediocrity.

‡ Walter Flex (1887–1917), poet and writer. His book *Der Wanderer zwischen beiden Welten*, based on his experiences on the front in World War I, captured the spirit of the youth movement and the camaraderie of the trenches. He was killed in battle after the publication of his book in 1916.

§ Ernst Jünger (1895–1998), decorated war veteran who wrote books celebrating battle as the quintessential way to get in touch with life, most notably *In Stahlgewittern* (1920) and *Der Kampf als inneres Erlebnis* (1922).

political party.[144] [Instead,] we mobilized ourselves on behalf of Germandom and kept it alive[145] by taking foreign excursions in the youth movement. We went up to North Schleswig and spent the night with various farmers in Appenrade.* We would hold a "German evening" with them. Those were lovely occasions. The farmers brought us big sheets of pastry.[146] I still remember our final evening. We had a table in the shape of a horseshoe, covered with crepe paper, overflowing with fruit bowls and candleholders, and behind us, the flag. It really had style. That was a difference between the earlier [prewar] Wandervogel, who were slovenly and untidy, and us.[147] And I will never forget my big excursion in 1927 when we hiked illegally into Czechoslovakia.† We had no visa and couldn't afford one. We decided to slip over the border at night. We made it by the skin of our teeth, for customs officials came toward us, talking loudly in the dark. We threw ourselves flat on the ground, and they only passed a few steps away. Our hearts were pounding, and we were glad they didn't have a dog with them.[148] We traveled through Czechoslovakia, through Oderberg,‡ Iglau,§ Brünn,**,[149] and eventually to Prague on foot.[150] Then we continued on to Krumau†† and Linz, sometimes taking the train. Because we were the Großdeutsche Jugendbund, we visited Germans [in Czechoslovakia] and learned about the tension between the Czechs and the Germans. Entire villages were German, and we heard about the tension directly from the inhabitants in whose barns we spent the night. We also would sing with them. I'd have to say that nothing distinguished us from them, except that for the most part they went to church more intensively than we did. They wore fantastic traditional costumes, and I can still remember those of the Germans of Brünn. All the men wore a little hat and long black trousers, and the girls had long white dresses. We became pretty angry at the fact that they had to pay for their own schooling. They had to clean out a barn to pay for a teacher. While at the other end of the village, near the station, a whole new school was built to accommodate the Czechs.[151]

[Earlier] I took part in [another] big excursion. We started in Ratibor,‡‡ a hamlet in Upper Silesia, and then went to visit Germans living in Bessarabia.[152] At the start of the trip,[153] we stayed in a Polish youth movement camp in East

---

    * Ethnic Germans living in territory ceded to Denmark following the plebiscite of 1920, in what today is the Danish town of Abenrå.

    † The Treaty of Saint-Germain-en-Laye, which created Czechoslovakia at the end of World War I, ceded Bohemia and Moravia to Czechoslovakia, areas with large ethnic German populations. German efforts to incorporate these areas into the Reich would lead to the Munich Crisis of 1938.

    ‡ Today Opava in the Czech Republic.

    § Today Jihlavà in the Czech Repubic.

    ** Today Brno in the Czech Republic.

    †† Today Krumlov in the Czech Republic.

    ‡‡ Today Racibórz in Poland.

Upper Silesia, the camp of the Sokel, which means "falcon." We crossed the border [into Poland] and pitched our tent in the camp of the Sokel. There were ten, twelve of us, something like that, and we were organized in a fully military manner. We had real original officers as our camp leaders, and we naturally tried to top [the Polish boys] through our conduct. We got up early, ran to the stream, and bathed there, whereas the Poles arrived much later. We were very proud that we were the ones with more mettle. You know how boys want to prove themselves. We sang songs in the camp, German songs; they sang Polish songs. And then we departed. We weren't angry but merely triumphant that we were better than they. As a boy, one fancies that one is better than others.[154] Indeed, the youth movement had such a big impact on me because it enabled me to compare myself with others and win their respect.[155] In the youth movement, you often faced challenges, and meeting those challenges was good for my self-confidence.[156]

On excursions, group leaders were especially important.[157] They had to be capable people. When something wasn't working, when everything fell apart, they were the ones who, through their own initiative, had to make everything right again.[158] I remember, for example, when we were on our excursion in Czechoslovakia,[159] we went swimming in the Sazawa [River].[160] Because the banks were overgrown with reeds, we left our clothes on a little boat that was moored there, and jumped off the boat into the water. This displeased the peasant whose boat it was. He shouted something, which we didn't understand, and came bounding down, swinging an ax over his head. He took away our clothes, and threw his ax at us, giving one of my friends a pretty bad wound on his behind. When we made it back to dry land, we were without our clothes, without anything. Then it was up to our leader to deal with this difficult situation. We cowered there until he had fetched help in the form of a pastor and a gendarme, who went after the peasant. It was our leader who freed us from this unfortunate situation, which took some courage, for the crazed peasant wasn't exactly harmless.[161] Or, on the Havel,[162] it was our leader who showed us how we could swing ourselves up onto loading cranes, climb up the crane, and jump into the water.[163] He was simply an alpha wolf for us. These leaders weren't elected. Instead, they crystallized out naturally.[164] And they remained leaders only so long as they were accepted as leaders.[165] There were certain rules of the game, you might say. When we went on an excursion, we had to look after one another. When we set up camp, a fire had to be made, a meal cooked, a tent pitched. It went without saying that each person took responsibility for completing these little tasks. No one in the group said, "You go gather firewood, and you go set up the tent." Rather, there was an unwritten law that one did these things of one's own accord.[166] Awakening that sense was important to us.[167] And when the little ones, the ten-year-olds, had sore feet and couldn't carry their rucksacks anymore, then the group leader didn't need to say, "You go take his rucksack for him!" Someone had done that long before. It was simply an unwritten law of being together, which worked without issuing orders.[168] The group leader certainly had the last word, but he also knew that nothing could be done against the will of the group. He could only demand or say what the group approved of.[169] In the end, everything depended on the will of the group.[170] Still, we were certainly no democracy. There was no voting and debating. We didn't do those things or think much of them.[171] So it wasn't a democracy, but it wasn't an autocracy either.[172] The group leader had to grasp what the group thought. Occasionally we did discuss things, but we always came together in the end. Not by the command of the group leader but as a true cooperative. Leadership flowed from the top to the bottom and from the bottom to the top.[173]

I was a leader for a while.[174] I had gradually grown so much into the group that I took over its leadership when the previous leader suddenly left. Perhaps a girl was involved. Anyway, one day he was gone.[175] I realized then that to be a leader you have, in a sense, to execute the will of the collective, a realization that became even more obvious to me in the military, of course. I became an officer, and as a first lieutenant, a captain, or whatever, you can't simply give the order: "Go attack the Russian lines and wipe them out so that we can march through." No one would obey. It's an illusion to believe that people will allow themselves to be killed simply because they have been ordered to do so. Every order you give has to be capable of being carried out. And that's what we learned in the youth movement, that you can't give the order: "March up to the moon." It can't be done. And you can't give the order: "Go get yourself shot dead." That doesn't work either.[176] You must recognize that the command of the superior is not what constitutes soldiery. Instead, the personal bond with the circle of your comrades is far more important than anything else. It was on this basis that we developed our notions of leadership.[177] I believe we were prepared to lead in the youth movement, and to that extent I think the youth movement was a preparation for war, but to say that we were preparing for war in the way we think of it today is something one can maintain only in retrospect or only in the sense that we were preparing to defend [the Reich]. *That* one can maintain.[178]

It's true that we did[179] fight other youth groups. Back then, our relations with other youth movement groups consisted of spying each other out on a Saturday and then beating each other up. It was terrific fun. That's how the relationship with my friend Jaspers developed. He belonged to the Bund Deutscher Pfadfinder.* On the Kaiser's birthday or some other occasion they had transmitted a radio message from one elevated area in the Harz Moun-

---

* Literally, Pathfinder or Trailblazer, the German version of the Boy Scouts.

tains[180] to another. We attacked the group to which my friend belonged on the Brocken.[181] We destroyed their Morse signal lights, beat them up, and then sauntered off, extremely proud of ourselves. Naturally, the next time things worked out the other way around. We were at an age when one needs to demonstrate one's strength, and we tested that strength by fighting among ourselves.[182] We [also] played scouting games, where two enemy teams would rush into a forest to capture a guarded pennant. The pennant pole had to be seized and carried through the chain of guards. The leaders who had set up this scouting game would then evaluate it in military terms. A pennant would be captured and carried off, and the bands around the wrists [of the defeated group] would be torn off. One was conquered, and if one was conquered, one had to withdraw from the game.[183] Not only did we play scouting games in the countryside, but we also played a similar game in the city.[184] I think it was in the fall—we'd have big scouting games pitting the individual youth Bunds against each other. One Bund had a blue band, the other a yellow band. Then there'd be a brawl, one colored band versus the other. Our group, which was pretty far to the right (most of our fathers were German Nationalist, I'd say), would really go at it with the Red Falcons, who were definitely SPD or KPD.* Afterward we would get along well with them, singing together. It was a quite decent business.[185]

Still, I must say that the youth movement was a bit elitist. I didn't feel myself to be elitist, but we were practically all college-preparatory students in our Bund—not in the Red Falcons.[186] In general the groups were bourgeois groups and came from bourgeois families,[187] but it did bother us that we had almost no working-class members.[188] Therefore we were proud when two working-class boys joined our group, and we were especially considerate of them and sought to make their lives with us easier.[189] For excursions, we pooled our money so that we could take them along. Still, apprentices simply had less free time than we did. We tried to recruit those whom we could recruit, but it was difficult even to come in contact with working-class boys. In fact, I don't know how we were able to recruit the few we had. One could speak to people on the street—there was the son of a druggist in our group—but we never discussed social issues[190] and certainly not politics. Of course, boys of fifteen or fourteen prefer to talk about Indians than about those issues.[191] Still, although we didn't engage in highfalutin sociological debate in our group, we were aware of the social dimension in practice.[192] We were influenced by the experience of the soldiers in the lost war. We had

---

* The Red Falcons had a socialist or communist orientation and was comprised mainly of working-class children.

little use for class identity and realized that the traditional social boundaries were no longer in tune with the times.[193]

I had already come in contact with National Socialism in 1926 or 1927 when I was about sixteen years old. I remained in the Bund but became a Nazi of course.[194] In the youth movement, we were upset about social inequality but had no clear conceptions about what to do about it. One of the reasons I joined the NSDAP* in 1928 was that I believed the Nazis could put into practice what we in the youth movement had only hazily dreamed about. The NSDAP sought to dissolve class boundaries just as we had tried to do in the youth movement. We had gymnasium students and working-class children in our group and realized that there is no human difference between the two. It was important to us that people from different classes get along and recognize and respect one another.[195] So around 1926 I encountered Nazism and believed that we from the Bunds could make the Hitler Youth into something like the youth movement. Indeed, the prospect of achieving that in Berlin seemed good since the Berlin Nazis were influenced by the Strasser brothers.[†,196] I belonged to the Strasser wing of the Party. I was a "National Bolshevist," which would later turn out not such a good thing for me to be.[197] Back then, however, I [supported] this brand of "national socialism." The two main forces [in the Party], the Strasser line and the Goebbels line,[‡] were in conflict with one another and there was fighting within the SA [Sturm Abteilung].[198] I belonged to a Bund that refused to call itself "Hitler Youth," calling itself instead the "Bund Deutscher Arbeiterjugend" [Bund of German Workers' Youth], which took an absolutely socialist line. After all, it was a desolate time [during the Depression].[199] And at the end, we built our own home and organized a "people's school" where unemployed people in the district were given free instruction in German, mathematics, arithmetic, and whatever else.[200]

As far as my personal experiences are concerned, they weren't so easy, for I went into the gloomy working-class district of Moabit and handed out leaflets. One person stood on the lookout while the other ran up five flights of

---

* Nationalsozialistische Deutsche Arbeiterpartei, the National Socialist German Workers Party.

† Gregor Strasser (1892–1934) and Otto Strasser (1897–1974). The brothers both served in World War I and in the Freikorps and became members of the Nazi Party. Both promoted anticapitalist ideas and were leaders of the socialist opposition to Hitler within the Party. Otto resigned from the Party in April 1930 after a conflict with Hitler in which he accused the Führer of abandoning socialism. Two years later, Gregor was expelled from the Party by Hitler. Whereas Otto survived the Third Reich in exile, Gregor was murdered in July 1934 on the so-called Night of the Long Knives, as part of the purge of the SA, the paramilitary arm of the Nazi Party.

‡ Joseph Goebbels (1897–1945) was head of the Nazi Party in Berlin and later Reich minister of propaganda during the Third Reich.

stairs and then [having distributed the leaflets] ran back down again. Moabit is where "Hitler Youth Quex" was murdered.* But that came later.[201] I did this around 1931 in Berlin. We were friends with a young girl who lived in the grim Charlottenburg [neighborhood] next to the Röntgen Bridge. One evening I went to visit her. I was wearing a black overcoat, a civilian coat, in other words, and crossed the bridge between Berlin-Charlottenburg and Berlin-Moabit, a gloomy part of town. As I crossed the bridge, a gang of adolescents approached me from the front and from the rear. They wanted to throw me off the bridge into the Spree canal. If they had succeeded, I'd have had it, but I was lucky. When one of them came at me with a dagger from the side, I was able to grab hold of it. That was 1931. I didn't have a uniform on or anything else to indicate I was a Nazi. The fact that I wore bourgeois clothes was enough to do me in. Such things happened around the edges in Berlin back then, and I credit my contacts in the youth movement that I was able to survive those times. No matter what happened, we stood by each other. That cannot be valued highly enough.[202]

But then everything went wrong, and the local Gau leader of our little Bund was expelled for resisting its incorporation into the Hitler Youth.[203] That was 1932, and so I left too. I hadn't held an important office, but I'd been influential within the Bund. I was naturally regarded as [representing] the socialist counter-pole [to Goebbels and Hitler].[204] So Hitler was already a disappointment to me then, and later he became more of one. Hitler's strength was his unbounded love of power. He demanded absolute obedience from his followers. If anyone had critical thoughts, he'd throw them out or have them killed. Those included Gregor Strasser, of course. People who followed Hitler unquestioningly were given freedom to do the greatest mischief. The main thing was unconditional obedience. This leader understood nothing about leadership, about how one really inspires people. He could only command, and that has nothing to do with leadership. Hitler was certainly a clever fellow, but not the most clever. There were others who were cleverer. But, for the time being, let's leave Hitler in peace.[205]

MARGARETE SCHULTE

My earliest memory is the outbreak of the First World War. I remember as if it were today. I was down in the courtyard with my doll carriage, and all around was such excitement. The next day my mother went with me to the military barracks, and there were the soldiers marching off. They had

---

* A fifteen-year-old member of the Hitler Youth, Herbert Norkus, was killed by Communists while distributing leaflets in January 1932. Norkus's death was subsequently made the subject of a movie, *Hitlerjunge Quex*, which premiered in 1933.

bouquets of flowers in their helmets.[1] Since I was born four years before the war,[2] I don't recall much about the war itself, only[3] the outbreak of the war and my father's enthusiasm.[4] Although he was already a bit old, my father volunteered[5] and served as an officer at the front.[6] I remember that when he was called up he told me, "When I leave to join the soldiers, then I'll make my walking stick shorter." That's what I remember.[7]

My father was a wonderful man. I admired him tremendously.[8] And the most important thing was that my father told me fairy tales at night when I was in bed—my father, not my mother. My mother sang songs to me.[9] Indeed, for as long as I can remember, music has played a crucial role in my life, and that's because I came from a very musical family on my mother's side. Music surrounded me from earliest childhood, string quartets at my grandfather's. My mother was an outstanding pianist who practiced the piano several hours every day. (We lived in comfortable circumstances before the First World War and during the war as well.) I would sit under the piano playing with my stuffed animals, absorbing the music. And every evening before I went to bed my mother would sing to me. I have a vast knowledge of old children's songs and folk songs. Later, after 1945, during the time of hardship, those songs proved incredibly helpful to me and to my own children. I sang those children's songs then.[10]

I was born in Posen in 1909, as the second child of my parents.*[,11] I had an older sister.[12] I was a disappointment to my parents[13] in that I wasn't a boy,[14] but I was somewhat boyish in manner. I liked to climb trees. I was good at sports. And I did have a very, very lovely childhood. My father was a real artist type. He was a decorative painter since he was unable to support the family by painting pictures.[15] I was very attached to my father. He was quite fantastic.[16] Being together with him was so natural.[17] I had many opportunities to talk with him, and from the beginning he set me on a course that led me to study.[18] I read books that my father had selected. He foisted them onto us in such a way that we didn't even notice we were being led on a string. Sometimes I went to his bookshelf and simply read what I found there, from A to Z. Once I discovered a medical encyclopedia. Although I understood little or nothing, I read the book from beginning to end. When my father asked, "Which letter have you reached now?" I replied, "G." "What are you reading about now?" "Gonorrhea!" "And do you know what that is?" "No," I said. I had no idea. When I was about twelve, he foisted the classics on us.[19] He'd always ask me, "Well, girl, what do you want to be when you grow up?" From the beginning he pointed me in the direction of a profession, something my mother also supported.[20] My grandfather was a rich man, [however], and he said to my mother (he was my mother's father),

---

* Today Poznan in Poland. The city became Polish as a result of the Versailles Treaty.

"But my grandchildren don't need a profession. They will inherit enough so that they won't need a profession." My mother was progressive, however (she belonged to the generation that emancipated women a bit), and she supported us in our desire to continue our education, which both my sister and I did.[21] School was a revelation to me, and I was an enthusiastic pupil, eager to learn.[22] Of all the girls in my school, I was the only who got her Abitur in the end.[23] In fact, one teacher said to my parents, "If I had anything to say about it, your daughter wouldn't get an Abitur. She should get married."[24] It was his opinion that "educated women were a waste of resources, for they get married afterward and then nothing comes of all that education."[25] In those days it was usually the case that married women didn't have a profession.[26] But my father had always told me, "You just persevere. You must learn all you can." He was a real fanatic about learning.[27] I got my Abitur, thank God. Still,[28] when I'd graduated, people said, "What shall we do with this girl now?" And then I remembered what my father had said:[29] "She will become a doctor or a lawyer."[30]

So I had a happy childhood, and that clings to you for a very long time.[31] My parents were simply there. I couldn't imagine it any other way. Whatever I needed, they provided;[32] basically I had everything I could wish for.[33] As things were back then, my mother was a housewife.[34] I would describe her as the more determinative,[35] the more dominant person.[36] I got a great deal from her,[37] and my relationship with her was also natural.[38] Still, my mother was always dissatisfied. Once when I had a new dress I climbed up a tree and fell down and ripped the dress through. My mother scolded me of course: "One doesn't go climbing trees in a new dress." I said, "But I could have broken my leg!" She found that a feeble excuse and thought it characteristic of me that I always came up with feeble excuses.[39] Although I was never beaten, my mother was quite strict.[40] Everything had to be done properly. If one came to the table five minutes late, there would almost always be a punishment. Still,[41] apart from this rather too irascible, strict manner of my mother, I really can't complain about my upbringing.[42] Today we'd say she had her standards, something I didn't grasp then. She was very strict, but she had to be strict. Otherwise she wouldn't have managed with us.[43] So, I can only say I had a good childhood. I understand her better today.[44] My mother had been very spoiled as a young person, but later [after the death of my father] she really developed magnificently. She had to manage on her own, which she had never been taught to do.[45] I must say that my mother was an independent woman—although not like today, of course.[46] Things are different today.[47] So I certainly didn't have a bad childhood.[48] In fact, we had it good.

During vacations we were always able to visit my grandparents, which was the loveliest thing imaginable.[49] We spent nearly every holiday there,[50] and I have lovely memories of those vacations.[51] The whole family would travel[52] to my grandparents' estate.[53] From the time of my birth until 1920, my grandparents lived in Eigenheim in the district of Hohensalza. Hohensalza is Inowrazlaw today.*[,54] My grandfather was a doctor there and still had a coach with horses. We accompanied my grandfather when he made his house calls. We weren't allowed to go with him into the houses [of his patients], of course, but we could play in the gardens while he was treating them. My grandfather had a profound influence on us.[55] I still remember a walk I took with my grandfather one summer day in Eigenheim. He took me by the hand and walked over the fields with me. It was a Sunday. He explained everything to me, and I looked up at his 1.9-meter height—he was so tall that the Berliners would turn their heads when he walked down the street. Fortunately grandmother was short so that we all didn't grow up to be giants. Anyway, he walked through the fields with me, a little one, perhaps four or five years old, in the way that a grandfather interacts with his grandchildren. It was very lovely.[56] My grandparents had owned a relatively large farm of some 568 acres, which was considerable at that time.[57] My grandfather had sold the farm and built a beautiful house. One of my mother's brothers had a farm next door, which was wonderful for me. I would sleep at my grandmother's and spend the day at my uncle's farm. There were dogs at his farm and doves, which belonged to my cousin.[58] Behind the farmyard, there were goats, chickens, pigs, turkeys, and geese.[59] There were fruit trees, berry bushes, and vegetables,[60] and there were many cows and horses.[61] During the bad times [during the war], that was wonderful to have, of course.[62] When the haying was going on, I was allowed to ride up on the hay wagon, which is something one doesn't see anymore, hay wagons loaded up with hay, where one could really sit way up on top as it was being driven to the barn. That is a lovely memory.[63] So that was my connection with farm life, when my mother would take us out to the farmstead of my grandparents.[64] I think my love of nature developed out of that experience.[65]

Another childhood memory is of our Christmas celebrations there. First we'd celebrate Christmas at home [in Posen], and scarcely were we finished than a sleigh would be standing in front of our door, with two sturdy horses and heated bricks and fur foot muffs. We'd be packed in all snug, and the sleigh would start off. We traveled to my grandparents in Eigenheim, where we would celebrate Christmas a second time. Once again there were presents and a lovely Christmas tree and all that comes with Christmas. Grandmother was virtuous, capable, and housewifely. Grandfather gave lovely speeches. He was a pious man, chairman of the parish council, chairman of the school board, and he could speak beautifully. So we celebrated Christmas a second

---

* A part of Germany that became Polish as a result of the Versailles Treaty.

time at my grandparents, after the wonderful sleigh ride through the forest with the tinkling of the bells. My mother's brother lived next door, and we were able to celebrate Christmas one more time with them—a third Christmas, in other words. As children we always celebrated Christmas three times, and each time we got a little something. Nothing like what children are given today, of course, but it was a lovely experience.[66] So, all in all, I had a lovely childhood.[67] Otherwise, I don't know.[68]

Oh, yes![69] My parents had quite a nice house in Posen.[70] Our house stood at the edge of a wood. We very often played out there as well as in our neighborhood.[71] My great-uncle had built the house. The house was really massive, with walls like a castle. There were very deep windows, and I felt protected and secure in that house.[72] Since my father was a painter, our house was decorated in a wonderful way. Because he would give his customers tours through our house, it would be redecorated every year or every other year. We had something quite special in our room as children. Each corner of the ceiling had a different theme. Not only were there painted themes, but also little stones were inlaid in the ceiling, little stones were glued up there. They glittered, which was completely fantastic. We also took pleasure in the fact that every so often one of the stones would fall down. My sister and I would make bets about which stone would be the next to fall.[73]

Then, under difficult circumstances, we moved in 1918 to Berlin.[74] It was quite a significant change,[75] quite a leap from Posen[76] to Berlin.[77] At first I was unhappy. I'd left all my friends behind. I had to go to a new school.[78] In Berlin I attended the gymnasium.[79] Then my grandparents . . . Then it became Polish . . . But first came World War I. In 1914 my mother had a hard time of it. My father went off to war, and my mother had to take care of the business and the workshop and the household and the two children.[80] It was a lot to manage. I remember that she became very ill once. She had to use a railing, like disabled people have nowadays, and she'd walk around the house with a sort of canelike contraption. It made me feel bad. I was still little. My mother's sister came to take care of her. I remember that.[81] I loved her sister. She was one of the first women in Germany to study and was a friend of Helene Lange.[82] Later, when I was a university student,[83] we'd go to lectures by Helene Lange and Gertrud Bäumer.*,[84] My aunt went to America and died of cancer in 1930—she was very young, forty-two years old.[85] I was sadder when she died than when my mother did. My mother had the usual

---

*Helene Lange (1848–1930) and Gertrud Bäumer (1873–1954) were collaborators, teachers, and women's rights activists. Lange founded the German Association of Teachers in 1889 and led the German Women's Association after 1902. Bäumer was a member of the liberal German Democratic Party during the Weimar Republic and was a councilor in the Interior Ministry from 1922 to 1933.

education that all [girls] got, but I was disappointed that she hadn't gone further with her education.[86] Still, my mother would have loved to study and supported me for that reason.[87]

My father came home on leave a few times. When my mother was ill, I think he was there[88] and cared for her then.[89] He would talk about the war a bit, but I can't remember what he said. I remember only how, when the war was over, he came home, and all the children had scarlet fever and diphtheria. My older sister had diphtheria.[90] We both had scarlet fever. We recovered from it nicely, from the scarlet fever and diphtheria.[91] I do remember the revolution vividly. I had gone to get milk and came upon others waiting in line to get milk. Grown people were weeping. I couldn't make any sense of it. Why were people crying in the street? I asked at home, of course.[92] My mother, very dismayed, showed me a special edition of the newspaper. I could already read (and actually read an incredible amount). I read: "Abdication of the Kaiser and of the crown prince."* I remember asking my mother, "Why also the crown prince?" She explained that not just one [emperor] had resigned to be followed by his successor but that the monarchy itself had been abolished.[93] Then at the end of 1918 there was the great disorder in Berlin[94] and shooting at the railway station. I was all of nine years old. I remember distinctly that[95] I saw sailors with rifles on my way home from school.[96] That was the sailors' rebellion.[†,97] Once, in the middle of the day, my mother and I were in the Wendel Boulevard, which is a major thoroughfare, when suddenly we heard a piercing whistle and we all had to get off the street into a neighboring apartment building. Something to do with this rebellion was going on. I was terribly afraid, and my mother wasn't exactly calm either.[98]

We lived at a big intersection in Berlin, in a corner house on the Frankfurter Boulevard. The whole German revolution played itself out at this intersection.[‡,99] The police station near us was fortified with sandbags. In the evening we had to black out our windows and turn down the lamps so that

---

*Wilhelm II abdicated along with his son on 9 November 1918 and fled into exile in Holland the following day.

†What the interviewee describes as the sailors' rebellion began as a mutiny in the navy when the fleet was ordered to launch a suicide raid against the British navy on 28 October 1918, despite the fact that the war was obviously lost. Beginning in Kiel and Wilhelmshaven, the mutiny soon became a general naval mutiny and, with the involvement of local military garrisons, spread across the northern and western parts of Germany.

‡It seems likely that the interviewee witnessed the Spartakus uprising in Berlin. On 6 January 1919 the Communist Spartakus Bund proclaimed the overthrow of the government of Friedrich Ebert and the establishment of a socialist republic. Armed Communists occupied newspaper offices and various public buildings in Berlin. The government's response was swift, brutal, and effective. Regular army troops supplemented by the notorious Freikorps, attacked the Communist positions in Berlin. By 13 January, the city had been brought under government control. More than one hundred Spartacists had been killed, including the Spartacist leaders, Karl Liebknecht and Rosa Luxemburg.

no light shone out onto the street that could be used by snipers to see their targets.[100] I remember one night,[101] my mother had already gotten up and wasn't in her bed when I woke up. I was sleeping in a room at the front of the house, and I was awakened by loud shouting. I jumped out of bed and pulled the curtains aside and looked out. They were shouting something I didn't understand: "Keep the windows clear!" There were policemen on the other side of the street, and one of them took aim at me up there, and I jumped back to my bed. We couldn't leave our house. We couldn't look out of the window. We did peek out from around the edge of the curtains. We were in a corner apartment and could see out diagonally. The leftists, the Communists, came down the Osterstrasse from the police station. The police came down the Hellkamp [Boulevard] with their rifles at the ready. I looked out on the intersection and watched as one crept up with his rifle and as the police crept up and so forth. We watched spellbound.[102] I can still remember how my father stood at the window[103] and said, "Look, another one just bit the dust." He looked down as my mother wiped the dust off the piano, which stood right next to the window. She had just finished her dusting and had joined us at the table, where we all were sitting down to lunch, when suddenly the glass pane burst, burst all over the piano. Something had exploded and had taken off the tower on top of our house. We could see the open sky from the floor of the room. Debris from the tower had tumbled down onto the glass pane and knocked it in. My mother could easily have lost her life. She had been standing right next to the pane.[104] I'll never forget that.[105] After that we slept on the floor, because bombs, shots were flying. Once there was a loud rumbling, and my father said, "That's artillery fire."[106] He had served at the front for four years and knew those sounds.[107] I can still see the images clearly before my eyes.[108]

What else was there of significance? Yes, afterward the elections. When I was little there were so terribly many parties. I can't remember all their names anymore. In any event, when they marched along the main street, I wasn't permitted to go down to the corner. When the polling places were set up, I wasn't allowed to go there either, for quite a lot of political rioting took place then. Before the elections, people hung various flags out over their balconies.[109] Across from us, on the other side of the street, someone always hung out the German battle flag from the First World War, with the emblem in the middle. I found it wonderfully pretty.[110] Then I remember all those strikes and the difficulty we had in getting what we were due with the ration cards we had and the bathtub filled with water and the curfews. Of course there was the great general strike called by the government on account of the Kapp Putsch.[111] As I was coming home from the dentist's office, a boy came up to me with a trumpet and blew a signal of some sort. When I got home my mother quickly closed all the shutters: "There's been shooting in the

Hellkamp." My father wasn't at home, and my mother was quite worried. A neighbor came down and said that "shrapnel has been falling from out in front here to the corner." That was the Kapp Putsch, which was another attempted coup d'état or the effort to resist it. It was quickly brought to an end [with a general strike].[112] You know, the general strike didn't have much of an impact on me, however. It didn't last very long, and after the experience of the winter of 1918–19, we were simply used to not knowing when things would be available. I am sure we filled up the bathtub again. I can still see that [filled bathtub] before me in our Berlin apartment.[113] In some ways I was hardened, already beginning in childhood. Outside the bullets were flying, and we slept on the floor on mattresses, and shards of flying glass could have cost my mother her life, and we could look up and see the open sky. We were caught up in the revolution. I was never really so terrified that I might have started crying or anything, but I was somewhat hardened by those events.[114]

And then, also after the First World War, came the inflation years.* They were certainly not easy times.[115] In school it would always be announced: "Inflation at such and such a rate."[116] It really was a very hard time.[117] There were all those strikes during that period† and all the unrest and all the fighting.[118] I must say that the whole decade of the 1920s was characterized by our having to be very frugal. My father was a great music lover and liked to attend symphony concerts. A subscription would have been too expensive, however, so instead we'd attend the dress rehearsals, which were open to the public.[119] And we still managed to read a lot.[120] Buying books was scarcely possible, but there was a so-called museum society that was open to the public, and it had a library. My father read books there, and I'd read there too—sometimes secretly, because they weren't meant for young people.[121] I can remember reading *Oliver Twist* secretly. I was shocked by the social conditions described in it. There is a streetwalker in the book, and Oliver Twist is drawn into thievery. I remember a book by Sigrid Unset, *Kristin Lavransdatter*. In the first place, I was always interested in old Norse [tales], and then there was the freedom of . . . how should I describe it . . . I realized for the first time that a woman could express herself sexually, to put it bluntly. That impressed me.[122]

---

*The result of having used loans to finance the war, the costs associated with ending the war, and German reparations payments stipulated by the Versailles Treaty, the hyperinflation of 1923 (in which the value of one U.S. dollar went from 345,000 Marks in July 1923 to 4,600,000 Marks in August to 25,000,000,000 Marks in October) had a devastating economic and psychological impact on the German middle classes. Although inflation was brought under control with the introduction of the Rentenmark in November, the demoralization and disillusionment engendered by the inflation caused many Germans to turn against the Republic and toward the extremist parties on the left and, especially, on the right.

†There were frequent strikes in 1923, as workers sought to keep their wages in line with inflation.

But back to the hardships of the inflation period.[123] It was a very bad time, the inflation period, a time of poverty,[124] and things went very badly for my parents.[125] We were quite poor and lived modestly—very poor.[126] My father[127] became unemployed.[128] He tried to find something new to do, but he had no talent for it. He was well educated and something of a scholar. He tried to find another position, but he was not suited to it. He always seemed to have bad luck, and things went dreadfully badly for us. Even after [the introduction of] the *Rentenmark*, the stable currency, he couldn't find a satisfactory position. It was increasingly difficult to finance my older sister's education.[129] To tell the truth, my father fell into foolish company and began to gamble, apparently wagering large sums on cards. Although we children only knew vaguely what was going on, I gather he acquired very high debts. On numerous occasions my mother was in a position through her family to pay off his debts, thank God.[130] Basically I think the marriage of my parents was good.[131] My mother did love him so very, very much.[132] They'd known each other since childhood.[133] It was a good marriage.[134] Still, there was terrible fighting sometimes.[135] Finally, after the inflation, my father found a job as a tradesman, which naturally affected the whole family.[136] On account of my father's [new] profession, my mother was often alone and had to raise us by herself.[137] My mother was a woman who was forced by the personal tragedy of my father to raise her children by herself. The marriage became strained then. I realized that. She had to give up everything, all her social possibilities. She really couldn't entertain, give an afternoon coffee for other ladies and that sort of thing. Her brothers and sisters were in a better position socially, and they supported her. But other than that there was nothing. My father was an unlucky man. He made himself independent with the money that my mother had inherited from her father, and then that was gone. It was really a bitter blow of fate.[138] Then, finally, my father had to spend[139] six weeks taking a cure in Niederlindewiese.[140] He had a terrible heart problem. Every time mother visited him, she would come back and say, "Papa told me again, 'If I didn't have you!'"[141] The two pulled together. She was there only for him, and I was left alone a lot.[142]

I was in school when my father became ill. He had to give up his work. All he had was his little officer's pension. He fell into a sort of a hole[143] and was in his sickbed for a long time.[144] Then the father I loved so much died. All my father had to do was look at me, and I'd do anything for him. This father, he became so ill,[145] and after a lot of suffering, he died.[146] After three or four days with bad anginal pain, he had to go into the hospital. It was a septicemic angina. He developed scarlet fever. Five days later he died during a tracheotomy. His heart just failed him.[147] My father died when I was fifteen.[148] Well, you know, that was a very bad time, when my father died,[149] a very bad time, and I suffered for a long time afterward.[150] I kept a diary during that period, which unfortunately was lost during the war, with thoughts about life and death. It all oppressed me terribly.[151] You see, I missed him. You know, one misses one's father.[152] This experience with my father, it affected my whole life. It really shaped me.[153] It really was a decisive experience.[154]

So there my mother stood, with two children,[155] before the abyss.[156] She was beside herself when my father died. She simply wanted to get away, head over heels, away from our possessions, our money, everything we had. She simply wanted to get away.[157] So immediately after my father's death, my mother sold everything,[158] and a half a year later we moved[159] to Magdeburg.[160] The family was very large and much concerned with holding together[161] and decided that we should move near them.[162] We had an apartment there.[163] The move was a big change.[164] I had still felt like a child before the move. It was really a major turning point, moving a half a year after the death of my father.[165] As a result of the family's circumstances, my mother had to go to work.[166] The year before my older sister had finished with the gymnasium and had begun attending the university.[167] So after the death of my father, I was alone at home with my mother.[168] Initially I had to enroll in a *Volksschule,** because there wasn't [yet] room in the gymnasium. I was mortally unhappy there. Some children actually had lice.[169] We only had one teacher, who had to teach all the grades. Her name was Miss Lange. This Miss Lange was a very strict person, and I greatly feared and respected her. She had a cane with which she would beat specific children, those who were dumb or didn't come to class or were lazy. I honestly don't know why. I still think about it. This systematic beating with a cane really upset me, especially one poor fellow, Felix Czigorczniski. I've never forgotten his name because I felt so sorry for him. It's funny how you remember some names.[170] Then I went to the gymnasium and was in the senior forms.[171]

In Posen we had played a lot with the neighbor children.[172] We walked on stilts, jumped rope. We played on the street in front of our house. To the annoyance of passersby, we'd draw patterns in chalk on the sidewalk, on which we'd throw stones and hop, skip, and jump. In the fall we made what we called "leaf rooms." We'd dump piles of leaves, and they'd be the beds, the armchairs, and so forth. There were plenty of kids [to play with].[173] We played so many lovely games.[174] And in Berlin we also[175] played in the street. We played when we came home from school and had finished our homework.[176] We would play lullaby, hide-and-go-seek throughout the neighborhood. We'd play in the evening when the swallows were whirring through the air.[177] But all that was gone[178] when we moved, all that was gone. I had no real friends, boys or girls.[179] Even in school, I didn't have classmates with whom I had contact outside of school.[180] I lived on this border region, on the border of simple streets with a simple population, fundamentally poor, you

---

* The Volksschule was designed for pupils not bound for university study.

know. I wasn't allowed to play in the street,[181] so that I scarcely knew another child on the block. And in school, I had hardly any friends there. No one knows anymore how deep a [social] divide there was between people then. I felt I didn't belong anywhere.[182]

Because I was limited in my opportunities for contact outside home, the Wandervogel gave me the chance to get out into the countryside, to experience something, to go on excursions.[183] The inflation affected all German families terribly, and recovering from it took a long time. We had had to move to Magdeburg[184] and, because my father died young, we were limited financially there too. The youth movement excursions compensated for what I missed at home.[185] And there was something else that was special about the youth movement, something I didn't get at home: we were encouraged to meet challenges. My mother simply didn't have time to do that with me. Other things were more important.[186]

So we moved, and I found my way into the Wandervogel. I've always said that the Wandervogel brought me back down to earth, after those years when as a young girl I had lived between heaven and earth only as a result of death. When I joined the Wandervogel, then came the period of joy. I had suffered terribly through the death of my father. Those were very, very hard years. While other children grew up happily, I lived in a different world. I always say that the Wandervogel brought me back to this world.[187] And I wasn't the only one who had these experiences. In my group there were plenty of others to whom things had happened just as they had happened to me.[188] I can't imagine how I would have turned out without my youth movement, without my Wandervogel.[189] I grew up and all that in school, but I have the feeling that I only came to life in the Bund.[190]

You could say that my father was by nature a Wandervogel,[191] often taking hikes—my father always had time off after Saturdays at noon,[192] and he loved to go hiking on vacations.[193] My mother preferred to stay at home where she'd have her peace and quiet. And later, in relation to the Wandervogel, my mother wasn't exactly charmed by it. She thought it wasn't fine enough for me. You know, we ran around. We weren't improper, but we did wear the appropriate clothing—braids, of course, and a bracelet, and then often island clothing and so forth.[194] That was my ideal, to have those island clothes, which were fabulous for folk dancing.[195] Mother would sometimes say we looked like working-class children because we ran around looking like that. But she let me participate.[196] Even when I was alone with boys, even when I ran with them, I was allowed to do so without stockings in summer.[197] She had no problems[198] with the fact that in the Großdeutsche Jugendbund boys and girls would sleep together in farmers' barns—divided, with girls on one side and boys on the other. And other parents allowed it too.[199] I must concede that there were certain things that didn't suit my mother. The clothing in particular didn't seem proper, but she didn't put any obstacles in my way and allowed me to go on excursions.[200]

I joined in 1927 with a friend,[201] who was also the daughter of a widow. We had gotten to know one another in the sixth form of gymnasium. We joined the Großdeutsche Jugendbund.[202] From then on I always participated, which meant a lot since I was the only child at home.[203] For me and my friend it was also extremely important that we had the chance to grow up with boys in the youth movement. We had no brothers, no fathers. The male element was missing in our lives completely. There we experienced a complete sense of comradeship.[204] Every week we'd have a so-called nest evening, and every Sunday we'd take a hike. It was just wonderful.[205] On school holidays I was always off somewhere with my group, on excursions. Outside of Magdeburg,[206] we had an old hut on the Lüneberg Heath[207] where we could go during vacations.[208] Once we invited our teachers there.[209] We'd spend the night sleeping in the straw.[210] We had afternoon sings, and sang very well together.[211] Singing is something that has stayed with me my whole life long.[212] In the final analysis, I'd have to say that[213] it was on a musical basis that our community was built,[214] the sense of comradeship, the group bond.[215] In essence it was all about the group bond, the sense of belonging together.[216] You knew that here are people who belong to you and you belong to them, and that provided such a sense of security and tranquility. It was lovely.[217]

The excursion was the high point of the year for us. The few *Groschen* we'd brought back from the last excursion would be the beginning of the next forty *Marks*. By the time next year came around, we'd saved the entire sum. Of course, it was a different era as far as prices were concerned, and we were used to saving money from our parental homes.[218] I remember it was 1928, and we were fourteen, fifteen, sixteen girls with a leader. We had a route, which our parents knew, with all the post offices marked on it where we could be reached, because the parents sent care packages targeted to get to us. Without those packages we wouldn't have made it with our forty Marks. We sent our dirty laundry back home in the boxes. Every two days we had to write a postcard. That's how we stayed connected to our parents.[219] I remember in particular a very lovely experience, a summer solstice fire on the Vistula. We spent the whole night outdoors and built a fire, sang, and slept. I was astonished and touched that my mother allowed me to do that,[220] accepted what I did. You know, it was very different from present-day Germany with its generation gap. There was nothing like that then.[221] It was also quite different from the older [youth movement] generation, from around 1903. They were more in conflict with their parents.[222] I came from a very bourgeois family, but my mother accepted the fact that we went on hikes and so forth.[223] No objection was raised when I joined the group and went on excursions. The only thing that produced offense was my

dirty windbreaker. In those days we all—girls too—wore jackets made of
tent material, windbreakers with belts. These were never to be washed. They
were to be as filthy as possible. That my mother didn't find proper;[224] she
didn't find it at all lovely when I'd return from hikes on Sunday evenings with
my rucksack and filthy boots and completely exhausted because we'd sung or
talked the night away.[225] But the bourgeois existence didn't appeal to me,[226]
this boring, respectable, bourgeois propriety,[227] the idea that as a girl one was
supposed to stay at home and do handicrafts and have afternoon teas[228] and
get all dressed up and take Sunday afternoon walks with one's parents[229] and
so forth.[230] In our way we wanted to break out. We didn't want to smash in
windows or anything terrible like that, but we wanted to behave differently,
and returning to nature was certainly part of being different.[231] I was so glad
when I discovered the youth movement at age sixteen,[232] and from then on I
was in the group.[233] How shall I put it? Fundamentally I didn't belong quite
as much to my home. I don't know how to express it. I was freer. I traveled out. I was together with boys.[234] I would not spend a single weekend at
home.[235]

But every group, or our group anyway, had a decidedly elitist attitude,
which began with the [prewar] Wandervogel. It was unusual for a member
to come seeking to join us. Instead we sought members out, after having
observed them in school for a quarter of a year. Looking back, that was probably not the proper way, but that's how we did it. We "rushed" them. Of the
ten we'd rush, perhaps only one would make it, and not all parents were inclined to allow their children so much freedom.[236] I have a friend, whom I've
known for a long time since having been together with her at Klappholttal,*
and she always says to me, "You know, we're different from the others." She
means that even today we aren't so concerned with externals. I find today's
preoccupation with acquiring money dreadful. I always say to myself, "Of
course we need money to live, but money is not the substance of life." And
that attitude certainly grew out of the youth movement, because even back
then we rejected such things.[237] You know, it was a different lifestyle—the
simple life, the natural life, a rejection of externals. I've always found makeup
and cosmetics amusing. My daughters have always wanted to know why I've
never used them. It's out of a sense of honesty or truthfulness that I don't
paint myself up. Back then we emphasized the simple life, the clean life, and
distanced ourselves from the bourgeois, from the ostentatious.[238] We lived in

---

* A youth movement campsite on the island of Sylt in the North Sea founded under the
auspices of the Freideutsche Jugendbund, a relatively short-lived branch of the youth movement that tried to keep alive the spirit of the prewar Wandervogel. In 1922 the Freideutsche
Jugendbund became the Freideutsche Bund, which administered the camp at Klappholttal,
under the leadership of Knut Ahlborn (1888–1977).

accordance with the maxim of Walter Flex: "In the art of living, staying pure and growing up is the most difficult and the most lovely task."

When I joined the group, I was told as a newcomer, "We want to tell you one thing: flirting doesn't go on here." I didn't even know what flirting was.[239] I had no idea.[240] Still, we were often together with the boys. We had our "home evenings" separately, but were together with the boys at festivals and on excursions and whenever there was something special.[241] When we took excursions together,[242] we were strictly separated [at night]. Although some of us married each other later, there was no necking or anything like that. We found people necking on the street repulsive. I mean, there were possibly some friendships that developed and some liked one more than another, but we disapproved of lovey-dovey stuff, as we called it.[243] It was a clear-cut ideal of the youth movement that sex was completely disapproved of and played no role.[244] Instead our relationships were comradely, like brothers and sisters. It would never have occurred to us to start any kind of romance or anything sexy or that sort of thing. I think that if those things had occurred, then those involved would have had to go, for those sorts of things would have destroyed the group.[245] I entered into marriage untouched. I went to dances and had friendships. I also was kissed and hugged on occasion, but when more was wanted, I always put an end to it. It seemed somehow just too dumb. I also had a guiding principle—You will wait until you are married—and I did wait. And my husband, he waited too. We knew each other for a year. And I expect we were not the only ones. The youth of the Bunds was so abstemious that I expect there were many others like us, but we never talked about it.[246]

As you know, Klappholttal was the first place where there was nude bathing. I can remember quite clearly when we were there in 1927 or 1928. Policemen stood on the dunes with binoculars or they were down below on the main path that still runs along the sea today. Sometimes there were dreadful people who stood and leered at us, as we, such young things, went naked into the water. Sometimes they leered so long that we had to spend an eternity in the water. Or we withdrew into our castle. Once there was a young man who also lived in Klappholttal, and we had the feeling that he would tag along behind the naked girls a bit. We informed Knud [Ahlborn] immediately of course, and Ahlborn gave this young man a talking to, explaining that if it continued he'd have to depart. It did continue, and he had to leave.[247] When I was there I got to know a couple of other girls, well-developed girls, and we decided to go out to the beach where people were bathing in the nude. It was so lovely, something so lovely. That was the first time I swam naked.[248] The experience meant a great deal to me and changed me greatly.[249] But my mother did get upset when someone intimated to her, before I'd gone there the first time, that nude bathing took place. I can still see my mother telling me: "We'll have to talk about it." But wisely I didn't tell her anything, and she never referred to it again.[250]

How I actually joined the Wandervogel came about in the following way. As I said, I was in the gymnasium in Magdeburg,[251] and there was a teacher. God, we must have been fifteen, sixteen. I adored her. Her name was Hanna Pallmann.[252] She was my mentor. She was quite young then,[253] under thirty perhaps, and had finished her studies. She was a Wandervogel. And I wanted so terribly much . . . I think that gave me the final impetus. I can still remember quite vividly. How I changed my hairstyle and so forth. I visited her sometimes. And then I started hiking with a group of girls,[254] because I found their way of life so wonderful.[255]

So then came the years in the Bund, and those were years I lived intensely. In those days we bore the weight of the burden of the war for Germany. Strangely enough, it never bothered me that we sang soldiers' songs from the war. We only really became aware that we had done so after the Second World War. I remained loyal to the emperor and was raised conservative.[256] I remember how I learned: "The Kaiser is a dear man, he liveth in Berlin"—singing, you know, I always had to sing for people as a child—

> And if it weren't so far away, I'd run right there to him.
> And what I'd with the Kaiser do, I'd offer him my hand,
> and present him flowers that were the prettiest in the land.

Although it certainly never came to that,[257] it all fit in very well with the Bund. Admiral von Trotha was *the* personality for us. That conservative political orientation flowed seamlessly into the Bund. It was the same as what I had experienced in childhood.[258] I didn't think much about politics, but the Weimar Republic[259] was disparaged and had a bad reputation.[260] I was powerfully impressed by the unpleasant number of parties.[261] We weren't politically active, but my father was nationalistic[262] and voted German National of course.[263]

Although we rejoiced or thought it right when the Weimar Republic came to an end,[264] female suffrage was very important to us.[265] You know, when the war was over, it must have been in 1919, women were allowed to vote for the first time. I remember very clearly how my mother said, "Oh, heavens, what is this? How should we vote?" But at the same time she was somehow very proud, and I sensed it, that now women voted too.* Of course my mother voted as my father did[266] and avoided all political conversation. She had always been German National in her thinking, and she was encouraged in that orientation by the fact that she had to live alongside such disparate types of people in our apartment building [in Magdeburg]. A single

---

* Ninety percent of the eligible women voted in the election to the Constitutional Assembly in January 1919, the first election in which women had the right to vote. Although the percentage would never be so high again, women still voted in large numbers during the Weimar Republic, generally for conservative parties.

piano teacher lived on the fourth floor. Either Communists or Social Demo-crats lived across the hall from us. We also had a Jewish neighbor. She only said to me, "Herr Meier is gone, and no one in the house knows where he is." It's interesting. No one knew where he'd gone, and I certainly didn't know that it had been a Jew. That was [after 1933] . . . Whether my mother knew, I don't know. Herr Meier was simply gone. But that's how it is when you have to live in an apartment building because there is no money.[267]

[When we were] in Berlin-Wilmersdorf, a great many Jews lived there, and the newspapers and theaters and everything were in Jewish hands. There was a lot of negative talk about this at home.[268] My mother once said to me—I must have been about ten years old and I had been invited to the birth-day party of a Jewish classmate (they were wealthy people and I very much wanted to go)—and my mother said, "That's completely out of the question. You wouldn't go to a Negro's house either." That was the attitude at home. And yet[269] I can remember that when a Jewish salesman named Schottländer was murdered in Breslau during the Kapp Putsch my father disapproved of it absolutely.[270] And I also had Jewish friends in my class whom I liked very much. There was a contradiction.[271] In my class in Wilmersdorf, half the pupils were Jewish and half Christian, which made no difference to us. I can only remember one incident that happened later, in Magdeburg.[272] There was a girl who must somehow have become very Nazified through her parents. I left school in 1929, so it must have been 1927 or 1928. She was an excep-tionally pretty blond girl. She painted a swastika on the palm of her hand and held it out to a Jewish girl in our class and said, "Kiss me." That outraged many of us. But otherwise we got along fine with the Jews. They weren't any more forward than we were. That went without saying.[273]

The First World War more or less passed me by. And politics only emerged for me[274] in that as children we always heard about the injustice of the Versailles Treaty.[275] It was depressing for me to hear how terribly unjust this treaty was believed to be.[276] Yes, [I also remember] how the big Zep-pelin was flown to America as a reparation payment to France and how people stood in the street and wept.[277] The Zeppelin flew over and made an amazing impression as it slowly sailed along.[278] When we did arithmetic in school we calculated how many tons of coal per day and per hour were being taken out over the border to France. Thus it was made clear to us children through arithmetic what the Versailles Treaty really meant.[279] Oh, yes, and I can remember something quite interesting about being punished in school. The worst punishment was to have to memorize the [clauses of the] Versailles Treaty. There was a little octavo notebook, and one had to go to the prin-cipal's office to be tested on it. The purpose probably was for us to develop outrage at the Versailles Treaty, for it really was an inhuman assignment. We were expected to know not only the territories that had been ceded but how many pigs and milk cows. Then I had to speak about the colonies, all of which had been lost, and about what size German Southwest Africa had been in relation to . . . I don't know anymore, to whatever else had been lost. The first time this happened I was not very old, perhaps thirteen, and the principal sent me away because I didn't know all the information. The second time I was a little older and managed to pass. Well, the first time he did let me go, but that was quite a strange school punishment—not dumb at all, actually.[280]

I remember that we celebrated Constitution Day in school[281] on the eleventh of August.[282] We had to go into the stadium, and I remember that I didn't much like seeing the Black-Red-Gold flag [of the Republic] but preferred the black-white-red [flag of the Kaiserreich].[283] When Friedrich Ebert died,* our classroom teacher told us that it had been decreed that a memorial service would be held in the school auditorium. She said, "You all have those black gym sweatshirts. That will look uniform. Put those on."[284] I still remember a picture of Ebert in swimming trunks hanging over the toilet at home, a newspaper picture, a caricature, or something. You know he was a saddler's apprentice and that was for my parents not the right thing.[285] We always told jokes at home because he wasn't considered respectable. When Ebert died, his coffin was transported somewhere or other in an open railway car, probably to the funeral. The train tracks ran past near us at Lichterfelde. We and other children went to a bridge that the train went under and spat down on [the coffin]. That was the orientation at home.[286]

Still, I must emphasize that my mother only allowed me to join the Bund because it was unaffiliated with a party and absolutely apolitical.[287] We were never associated with any party,[288] and politics played absolutely no role for us. I can't recall ever having a single political discussion. We had our nest evenings, our hikes, and so forth, but I don't know that we ever had a political dispute.[289] We didn't feel ourselves to be political. We were nationalists.[290] We loved our country, were devoted to Germany, and wanted all good things for it.[291] Every year we had a meeting of the Bund, often in border regions.[292] Once we hiked along the border in the Bohemian Forest. We'd been taught in school that Germans stacked their wood neatly, whereas over [in Czechoslovakia] they were slovenly. There was much agitation of this kind. We didn't engage in that sort of thing on our hikes, but when we crossed the border from Plauen our superiority and industriousness and so forth was much emphasized.[293] Nonetheless, when we came to a mountain hut on the Czech side, the people there were touching and generous to us even though money was tight in those days, and I have the best memories of those few days we spent hiking on the Czech side.[294] Our Bund was founded after the war and was therefore somehow romantic, devoted to the historical, to folklore, to

---

* President Ebert died in office on 28 February 1925.

preserving what was Germanic in the past, learning how to spin and collecting old songs and old sayings. As a child I had an album in which my father had written a saying from Fichte:* "Act as if the fate of all things German depended on you and on your actions alone, as if the responsibility were yours alone." That was the attitude in my family, to have a sense of social responsibility,[295] and in fact, many in the youth movement wanted a social occupation and had a social orientation.[296]

But then it was 1930, and the group[297] dissolved itself. We had been a small group of girls, all very pretty, and all at once it was over.[298] It was hard on me.[299] The plan had been for me to apply for a university scholarship, but it wasn't clear I'd get one. There was no way my mother[300] could afford to pay for another education after paying for my older sister's.[301] So I had to earn money by tutoring after school.[302] I had begun my university studies in 1929 in Berlin.[303] Initially I wanted to be a veterinarian, but that was simply an unacceptable profession for someone of my social class. And for a woman in those days—I would have had to deliver cows and horses—for a woman at the end of the 1920s that was out of the question. So I dropped the idea and matriculated in history and theology in order to become a teacher of religion and German. Initially I tutored and lived at home in Magdeburg.[304] I could travel from there to Berlin,[305] where I'd stay overnight with friends when the lectures ran late. There were no trains after eight o'clock in the evening.[306]

Of course Berlin during those years was incredibly exciting. The battle raged back and forth, and the university was the crucible. You could only get in with an identity card. Police were constantly on guard, because outside groups would sneak in and stir up trouble. When there were big demonstrations in the Lustgarten next to the university, then there was almost always rioting. Either brown [Nazi] groups came into the university or red [Communist] groups or the Stahlhelm, and there'd be a wild tussle and one could only flee. Once Jewish students were supposed to have been thrown out of a window. After an uprising, the university was generally closed for a week. Since there weren't refrigerators in those days, when there were riots, we'd go down to the cafeteria and buy up the food that would spoil quickly (pudding with raspberry sauce) for very little money. We'd eat all we could and then go swimming in the Havel.

The university operation was quite limited, however, and it wasn't clear in 1932 if the semester would count [toward graduation].[307] This was the time[308] of Brüning and his emergency decrees.†,[309] Most were unemployed at

---

* Johann Gottlieb Fichte (1762–1814), philosopher and patriot.

† Heinrich Brüning (1885–1970) was chancellor during the Depression. From 28 March 1930 until 30 May 1932, he headed a series of cabinets that did not command a majority in the Reichstag. He was able to enact legislation only by using President von Hindenburg's power of emergency decree.

that time,[310] and there was great hardship.[311] The years '30, '31, '32 were really bad, you know.[312] The mother of a friend of mine was very active in the Jungdeutsche Orden, which was comprised of various patriotic Bunds more sympathetic to democracy.* As a result of the massive unemployment, they began constructing camps, mainly barracks. The mother of this friend asked me if I would be willing to spend a half a year in the Work Service in order basically to play the role of a housewife there. I thought it important to do that because the unemployment had made an extraordinary impression on me. So I spent four months in a camp [in Oeynhausen].† There were about twenty young people there, all male. Most of them had learned a trade but had been unable to find a job. They were supposed to build up the park in Oeynhausen. It was a public works project. It was heart wrenching. These boys had completed their apprenticeships and were about sixteen years old. They had no prospects at all and came mostly from broken homes. The worst was on Mondays. Some of them would cry about what they had experienced when they came back from work as I stood there stirring the big soup pot. On Sunday they had visited their parents, if there even were two parents at home. There they experienced their drunken fathers, and they told me about it. I was keenly aware that I came from a proper family, and what they related bowled me over. But I also recognized the necessity of getting to know and getting along with these very disappointed and troubled young people. So in the evenings we played games with them. I brought a big atlas from home, and we'd try to find places on the map. It was all quite simple, but nothing else occurred to us. There was no television and no radio. The gramophone had to be cranked up, of course, and we did have one of those. We tried to sing in the evenings and at other times. In a group, they wouldn't say much of anything. They mostly spoke when I was working in the kitchen, spoke with me in order to be comforted. So I got to know a completely new world there. At times I had to cry. It didn't last more than a fourth of a year. Yes, in 1933 it was disbanded. And then came the other Work Service.‡,[313]

---

* Founded in 1920 by first lieutenant and Freikorps leader Artur Mahraun (1890–1950), the Jungdeutsche Orden sought to rebuild Germany after the defeat in the war. Although it pursued anticapitalist goals and sought the establishment of a community of the people (*Volksgemeinschaft*) and an autocratic state (*Führerstaat*), the Jungdeutsche Orden rejected monarchy and supported the Weimar Republic.

† Along with a number of youth movement Bunds, the Jungdeutsche Orden established work camps to bring urban, often unemployed young people belonging to different social classes together in nature to lay the foundation for the creation of a national community of the people.

‡ The Nazi Reichsarbeitsdienst, initially voluntary, became a mandatory six-month labor service for all male youth in 1935 and for all female youth in 1939.

2

ANALYSIS

Finding the Collective in the
Youth Movement "Group"

To the extent they recall it, the overwhelming majority of those interviewed remember World War I not as a time of anxiety and hardship but as an idyllic period in their lives. Almost without exception, they describe positive experiences associated with nature, the out-of-doors, and a rural environment. Many of the interviewees associate childhood with the years they spent living with relatives in the countryside during the latter years of the war. They recall this as a magical time, and their memories evoke what they call *Geborgenheit*, a sense of security, and *Nestwärme*, the warmth of the nest.[1] Thus their wartime memories convey images that are rustic and nurturing.[2] They also associate this period with fairy tales and the artistic: theater and music, especially singing. Indeed, perhaps because of its association with a romanticized childhood, singing has given interviewees a sense of security throughout their lives.[3] The memories of the interviewees convey the feeling of belonging to and being embraced by an extended family.[4] The grandparents and, occasionally, the aunts and uncles are presented as idealized figures offering protection and security.[5] Generally members of the local gentry, wealthy farmers and professional people (doctors, teachers, or ministers), they are venerated not only by the interviewee but also by the local farmers and villagers.[6] The memories of this rural idyll often flow into or parallel memories of an idyllic early life with the nuclear family in urban areas.[7] These urban memories convey the same warmth, security, and artistic magic as their rural counterparts.[8] These are uniformly positive memories, conveying a sense of the parents as self-confident and loving, protective and supportive, initiating their children into a world containing challenges that are exciting yet masterable, a world neither prosaic nor boring but always fundamentally secure.

The war is only dimly recalled by the interviewees and is presented as having had little or no negative impact on them. The one recurring image of the war in the interviews—its outbreak—is generally festive, with troops departing for the front, flowers, and cheering crowds.[9] Given the birth date of most of the interviewees, relatively few had close relatives who fought in the war. During this period, middle-class, educated German men generally married and had children only after they had established themselves professionally. As a result, the fathers of the interviewees were, for the most part, too old for military service, and their brothers, for the most part, were too young.[10] Of the sixty-two interviewees, three appear to have lost fathers in the war, and two lost older brothers.[11]

Whereas the interviewees remember the war as a time of tranquility and security, they recall the Weimar Republic as a time of disorder. In contrast to the dimmer and even festive recollections of the war, their memories of defeat and the subsequent revolution in Germany are vivid and disturbing.[12] Frightening, incomprehensible street fighting, putsches on the left or on the right, bullets splatting into the living-room wall are often indelible "historical" memories of those interviewed.[13] From the German Revolution and the Kapp Putsch through the "party chaos" in the Reichstag to the street fighting of the early 1930s, their memories of the Weimar Republic are characterized by images of conflict and chaos.[14] And whereas the interviewees remember the war as a time of physical and emotional sustenance, they recall the Weimar Republic as a time of deprivation. Their memories of the immediate aftermath of the war are of malnutrition and disease, which in many instances led to the disability or even death of a family member.[15] Although the later Depression would affect the interviewees directly, they appear to have experienced the economic hardship of the first years of the Republic, culminating in the inflation of 1923, as more devastating because of its impact on their parents and family.

That the interviewees appear to have been distressed more by the economic crises affecting their parents than by those affecting them directly reflects the fact that their experience of wartime and most of the Weimar period was generally mediated and in significant ways magnified by their parents and other adults. Thus the importance one interviewee attaches to his "first historical memory," of the declaration of general mobilization in Germany in 1914, derived from his mother's frightened reaction to the event.[16] Just as the outbreak of the war was experienced through its impact on the parents, so too was its loss.[17] In general, the interviewees' negative attitudes toward the Weimar Republic appear to have been assimilated from parents or parental figures.[18] Although the interviewees present themselves as distressed

by the violence and disorder they witnessed, what appears to have most upset them was the unease and even fear of adults important to them.[19] Similarly, the anxiety, discouragement, and sense of failure with which parents
reacted to economic hardship rendered it disturbing to those interviewed.[20]
The parents—and through them the interviewees—had a clear sense of "history" as an external force one was helpless to control that affected the family
adversely.[21]

Specifically, the interviewees associate the Weimar period with a series of
historically engendered losses. The first of these was of an idyllic, rural childhood as many interviewees returned abruptly to the cities after the war to live
with their parents. They associate this loss with a sense of alienation in an
unfamiliar, impersonal urban landscape.[22] In some instances the rural idyll
was lost irretrievably, either because of the death of a grandparent or because
the grandparents or parents had lived in a part of the Reich detached from
Germany as a result of the Versailles Treaty.[23] An accompanying loss was
Germany's defeat, experienced primarily through the demoralized reaction
of parents and teachers.[24] This was followed by the loss of the family as a site
of stability and security, with the revolutionary violence in the streets literally
penetrating the homes of several interviewees.[25] A more widely experienced
loss was economic and psychosocial, as the inflation of 1923 seriously damaged family prosperity and social standing. The impact of the inflation ranged
from being unable to afford books and having to check them out of a public library (sharing such a symbol of cultural status with the general public
would have been a humiliation to educated, upper-middle-class Germans)[26]
to paternal unemployment, accompanied by the loss of the family fortune
and home and thus of the interviewees' dreams for the future.[27] For some
interviewees, economic hardship forced a family move (in some instances the
second such traumatic move within a few years), which brought with it the
loss of home and neighborhood as well as of friends and schoolmates.[28] And
yet the most psychologically significant loss of the postwar period appears
to have been the loss of the parents as admirable figures, as a result of *their*
loss of self-esteem and self-confidence. Upstanding members of the educated,
upper-middle classes, the parents apparently felt for the first time in their
lives like little people, helpless victims of forces and circumstances beyond
their control.[29] The fathers, in particular, are often presented as failures in the
interviews.[30] Given that in patriarchal German society fathers were expected
to be the more responsible, more powerful, and hence more admired of the
two parents, the loss of the father as an idealized figure would have been
particularly frightening and potentially traumatic. A number of interviewees
appear eager to preserve an idealized image of the father in the face of his
manifest inadequacies, while contrasting him to the mother, who is regarded

with more open contempt.[31] The instability of the era, then, manifested itself in a family that no longer felt secure, in parents who suddenly seemed
unreliable—a moody, dissatisfied mother or a gambling, sickly father.[32]

In fact, some of the memories of disorder during the Weimar Republic
may represent externalizations of experiences within the family. The chaotic
economic and social conditions of the 1920s appear to have created chaotic
conditions, tension and conflict, within the families of those interviewed. The
interviewees were deeply disturbed by those tensions and conflicts.[33] In fact,
the interviewees' aversion to conflict and the premium they placed upon "tolerance" throughout their lives can be attributed in part to the fact that the
conflict they experienced within the family in childhood seemed so threatening.[34] In an effort to separate their parents from the disappointment and
anger they felt at the lack of a stable family environment, the interviewees
may have projected their sense of family disorder and tension onto society at
large. Tensions within the family and their own bad feelings thus could be simultaneously denied and explained away. These disturbing experiences were
not inside but outside the family. They were not to be traced to the failures
and failings of the parents but to the weak and ineffectual leaders of the Weimar Republic or to impersonal, historical forces beyond human control.[35]

The loss of the parents as admirable figures was exacerbated by the fact
that the health of many appears to have deteriorated over the course of the
1920s as a result of anxiety and discouragement, economic hardship, and
the long-term effects of wartime malnutrition. By contrast, the interviewees
were coming into their own. Not only were they physically more robust,
they were better able to adapt to the unsettled conditions of Weimar, which
created unprecedented opportunities for them. The interviewees' successes
emphasized the failures of the parents and gave these adolescents the sense
of having surpassed them.[36] And yet, despite the parents' failure, demoralization, and deterioration, the interviewees did not hold their parents in open
contempt.[37] These adolescents still needed their parents and sought to preserve and protect them as admirable figures.[38] And, as we shall see, society at
large provided an explanation for the parents' shortcomings that worked to
absolve them of blame. But the psychological and physical frailty of the parents robbed these young people of any age-appropriate sense of adolescent
triumph, leaving them only with the guilty obligation to execute their parents' legacy.[39] For, as one contemporary of the interviewees noted in 1932,
"The love of young people for their parents is never so passionate nor so
filled with shame as when the disintegration [Zerfall] of the parents occurs
before their very eyes."[40]

This series of losses culminated for nearly 40 percent of those interviewed
in the death of a parent, usually the father, often following a period of physi-

cal deterioration and illness, generally during the mid-1920s, when the interviewees were in early adolescence.[41] Although those interviewed frequently let this information drop without revealing how they had felt at the time,[42] it seems likely that the loss of a parent was so distressing that the interviewees were unable to confront it emotionally, propelling them in the direction not of mourning but of denial and activity. For those who experienced it, this greatest loss, then, rendered their break with childhood traumatically premature and precipitous. It encouraged the interviewees to suppress feelings, to escape painful reality in idealized fantasy, to substitute activity for introspection, and to value emotional hardness over vulnerability—and this in a culture suffused with Prussian and Lutheran traditions of stoicism that discouraged the working through of painful feelings and encouraged the denial of loss, disappointment, anger, and conflict.[43]

The losses suffered by the family were inscribed in the losses suffered by the nation. Through the ongoing public outcry about the injustices of the Versailles Treaty, these adolescents, like Germans generally, were constantly reminded of Germany's territorial, colonial, and economic losses.[44] The sense of national loss was underscored especially effectively in the schools, which often sought to preserve national conservative, antirepublican values by harping on the injustices of the Versailles Treaty and Germany's losses and humiliations at the hands of the Western democracies and, indeed, of the leaders of the Republic itself.[45] The losses on the national and the personal level were thus interconnected and reinforcing. The lost childhood idyll was linked to the lost national idyll. Germany's former greatness was contrasted to its current humiliation, and the Kaiserreich was presented in a nostalgic light as strong, stable, and secure.[46] The notion that the parents were the helpless victims of circumstance found confirmation in the officially promoted version that the nation was the helpless victim of an unjust, externally dictated peace, perhaps even of "a stab in the back." In contrast to the often unacknowledged losses within the family, however, Germany's national losses were a public preoccupation. In fact, the focus on loss at the national level may have enabled the interviewees to confront losses too threatening to be faced within the family. At the same time, the parents were protected from the interviewees' disappointment and anger at their shortcomings and failures, for the parents' travails were simply a part of the ordeal of the martyred nation.

Those interviewed dealt with these disappointments, disillusionments, and losses by clinging to the memory of an idealized past and engaging in idealized collective activity in the present. Virtually all the interviewees contend they had an idyllic childhood. Even the handful of interviewees who describe unpleasant childhood experiences characterize their early life as "happy."[47] It is important to emphasize that these are *memories*, which do not necessarily

reflect the reality of their lives during World War I. To be sure, people generally idealize childhood. Still, in the case of those interviewed, the idealization
seems extreme. These are not simply happy but *idyllic* memories which, when
set in the context of war and wartime hardship, are even more striking. Like
Germans generally, who yearned to return to an idealized past in response
to the disruptions of the early 1920s,[48] the recollection of early life as idyllic
represented an attempt on the part of those interviewed to handle the losses
they experienced outside and especially inside the family as adolescents. The
interviewees, instead of confronting these losses directly, condensed them
into a pair of acknowledged losses, the loss of a romanticized childhood on
a personal level and of a romanticized Kaiserreich on a national political
level.[49] The conception of an idyllic childhood was a way to convince themselves that, although life was troubled and disappointing now, it had once
been happier and more secure, a way to preserve in memory the image of that
more sustaining, tranquil time, and, finally, a way to express the hope that
what had been lost could be restored.[50] Idealized collective activity in the German youth movement represented, in part, an attempt at that restoration.[51]

In contrast to the prewar Wandervogel, who were in conflict with the parental
generation and critical of their society, and to their own children, the rebels of
the so-called 1968 generation, the interviewees saw the youth movement as a
way to carry on parental traditions.[52] Their youth movement activities built
upon positive experiences when their parents, especially fathers, seemed self-
confident and secure.[53] Indeed, the interviewees' youth movement activities
were generally encouraged by their parents, and a good many were actually
initiated into the youth movement by members of the older generation.[54] The
fact that so many of those interviewed joined conservative and nationalistic
Bunds helps to explain their parents' approval. Thus, rather than rebelling
against the older generation, the youth movement of the 1920s can be understood as a way for the interviewees to stay connected to admirable aspects of
their parents and to live out dreams that their parents and other psychologically important adults had been unable to realize for themselves.[55] With its
emphasis on nature and music, on folklore and folk customs, and with its
rejection of the modern, the material, and the urban, the youth movement
can also be understood as a way those interviewed could live out the memory
of an idyllic, often rural, childhood, a time remembered as nurturing and
secure.[56] The youth movement seemed to recapture what had been lost in the
family during the 1920s, Nestwärme and Geborgenheit, the warmth of the
nest and feelings of security and belonging. Significantly, the weekly group
meetings in the youth movement were called "nest evenings" and "home
evenings." It is difficult to overemphasize the importance of "belonging" and
"fitting in" for those interviewed.[57] Responding to the disruptions within the

family and without, the youth movement gave these adolescents a sense of place and of purpose. In contrast to the disorder and conflict of the Weimar Republic, the youth movement group provided a harmonious communal haven. As a dynamic national movement, the youth movement restored a sense of agency and authority in the face of the passivity and helplessness experienced by the family.[58] Thus, the function performed by the youth movement for those interviewed was fundamentally conservative—and not only in a political sense. It looked not forward but back to an idealized past. It sought to preserve that past and restore what had been lost—in themselves, in the family, and in the nation.[59]

The fact that these adolescents sought to recover feelings associated with an idealized past helps account for the centrality of singing in the youth movement, the activity mentioned repeatedly in interview after interview as having been its single most important and attractive aspect.[60] The group-sing created a *Rausch*, a magical high or heady experience, the feeling that one belonged and was connected to others like oneself. The individual voice joined, was lost in, swelled the voice of the group.[61] And yet singing was impractical and ephemeral, and when it was over there was only silence and the warm afterglow of communal harmony and exhilaration. Although it accomplished nothing beyond the momentary experience, the singing symbolized and strengthened the feeling of belonging in and to the group. And, metaphorically, those whose voices did not fit in, did not swell the harmony, were excluded from the community. The group discussions about politics or philosophy also served primarily to create an exhilarating momentary experience. These discussions had no practical consequences but existed solely for their own sake. They allowed participants to feel sophisticated as members of an intellectual elite standing outside and above bourgeois society, but because these discussions did not lead to action, they were risk-free. They never confronted individuals with hard choices or antagonized anyone within or without the group. As a result, it was possible to read radical political thinkers and to accommodate different political philosophies without controversy.[62] Had these discussions the potential to lead to action, they would have threatened the harmony of the group and exposed it to the ominous outside world the youth movement was designed to escape. Precisely because the group was to be a haven, conflicts that could disrupt its cohesion and harmony were to be avoided at all cost.[63] Given that the youth movement sought to capture or recapture an affective state, interviewees found it difficult to articulate what characterized the youth movement of the Bunds, let alone define its leading ideals. In fact, it appears that the youth movement consciously rejected any articulated philosophy or program in favor of a vague "feeling of life" that was unthreatening, adaptable, encompassing—all things to all its members.[64]

Group singing and discussions, then, served to create experiences of belonging and power, of self-esteem and self-importance, without confronting the underlying losses that had produced the need for these experiences.
Similarly, the youth movement allowed these adolescents to express and to
avoid sexuality in a way that was simultaneously grandiose and unthreatening. On the one hand, the youth movement enabled these young people
to interact with members of the opposite sex in "natural," tolerant, yet socially acceptable ways.[65] Although most groups were single-sex, they came
together with the opposite sex on occasions such as joint excursions or at
youth movement conventions.[66] For a number of women interviewees, the
contact with boys in the youth movement was especially important since they
had little interaction with male figures either at home or at school.[67] In addition, there was greater freedom about exhibiting the body, and even homo-
eroticism was acknowledged and to some extent tolerated. Although girls
were expected to assume male models of behavior, there seems to have been
a blurring of traditional gender roles in the youth movement.[68] On the other
hand, what was not acceptable in the youth movement was sexual activity,
either heterosexual or homosexual. Sex and especially the body were elevated
to an aesthetic ideal, but sexual feelings were never acknowledged, and as
far as sexual activity was concerned, prudery reigned. Nude bathing was
encouraged, even celebrated, but woe betide the young person who showed
sexual interest in the bodies of the nude bathers.[69] Boys and girls went on
overnight excursions together, but they never touched one another.[70] Just as
their politics were apolitical, so too their sexuality was asexual.[71] Those who
were sexually active—whether homosexual or heterosexual—were generally
levered out of the group, conceived as threatening its harmony and cohesion,
as destroying its pristine magic, as transforming an ideal life into prosaic,
frightening reality.[72]

The reaction against sexual activity needs to be understood within the
context of the general asceticism of the youth movement.[73] Smoking and
drinking were frowned upon as well.[74] This asceticism can be interpreted,
perhaps, as a manifestation of the fear of letting oneself go, which in turn
might lead to the expression of feelings better left suppressed.[75] The need
to maintain rigid self-control may also have been a response to the sense
of those interviewed that they lived in a disordered world that had escaped
human control. As ascetics, they could at least impose order on and exert
control over themselves. And finally, the youth movement's attitude toward
sexuality and the opposite sex can be understood as an attempt to deal with
sexual development outside the family. Clearly, adolescents need peers to
help them with these developmental issues, and sexuality propels children
away from the family and dependency on the parents. Here, the working
through of sexual feelings seems often to have taken place in the absence of

significant interaction with admired and emotionally available adults. Consequently, mature, active, adult sexuality was rejected in favor of an adolescent sexuality that was aestheticized and asceticized, kept safely and securely in the realm of the ideal.

In seeking to become adults, these adolescents found in the youth movement group what was missing in the family and became, as members of the group, what they wished their parents to be. Taking on the very experience that had brought their parents low, these adolescents, like bourgeois young people generally, transformed hardship into a virtue.[76] Through their anti-materialism, they denied that the things their parents had lost or had failed to achieve were important in the first place. Indeed, the deprivations that had been forced upon their passive parents they took on actively.[77] What had rendered their parents weak and disappointing would make them strong and admirable.[78] In the wake of the defeat of the nation in the war and of the subsequent and related defeat of the father, brawling between various male youth movement groups became a way to reassert the lost masculine and military virtues and to prove oneself a man.[79] But the model of the man to be emulated was based not upon sustained interaction with actual, admirable, adult males but upon exaggerated adolescent fantasies of what a man was supposed to be. For both sexes, the youth movement excursion provided the primary opportunity to exhibit the toughness, resilience, and resourcefulness that the actual parents had for the most part failed to display. The "grand excursion" represented the high point of the year for most youth movement groups, and considerable time and energy were invested in planning these trips. In contrast to the chaotic conditions of Weimar, which had overwhelmed the parents, the excursion was an exercise in mastery, something to organize and carry through, an opportunity to embrace hardship and meet challenges with initiative and imagination.[80]

Nevertheless, on the excursions, as generally in the youth movement, there was always the risk of humiliation, the possibility that one would not measure up, that one was not tough or resilient or resourceful enough to meet the challenge.[81] The various initiation rites in the youth movement both spoke to and regulated that anxiety.[82] The self-idealization of the youth movement put pressure on its members to live up to the high standards they had set for themselves. The idealization of the self as a member of an idealized group responded to that pressure. The individual did not need to achieve greatness on his or her own; greatness was achieved with and through others. The group was always there to reflect back the greatness of the individual. And the group was always there to enhance the individual through the power of the collective.

Although the youth movement helped the interviewees to grow up and compensated for what had been lost in the family, an underlying sadness can occasionally be detected in the interviews, a sense of unacknowledged loss and loneliness that was covered over by intense activity, exaggerated independence, and militant optimism.[83] Despite the camaraderie of the youth movement, a dream remembered by a man from this period, the only dream he can remember from the whole of his life, conveys self-idealization and isolation: "But I can remember one single dream. I was already a member of the youth movement. I can still see it before my eyes. Strange. I was in a star-filled sky. Not a single person, there were only stars. The sky was gold, the stars were golden. And I was in the middle, not as a star. No. I have never forgotten that dream."[84] Indeed, the dependence of the interviewees on collective experiences throughout their lives can be understood as an attempt to counteract feelings of loss and loneliness.[85]

Not only did the youth movement compensate for what had been lost within the family, it also sought to repair the national losses in which these personal losses were embedded. Consequently, most of the youth movement Bunds of the 1920s were militantly nationalistic.[86] Various paramilitary games played by male youth movement groups served to enact and prepare for the war that would restore Germany's lost national territory and lost national honor.[87] Although less obviously militaristic and exaggeratedly masculine, the excursions to ethnic Germans living in territories lost to the Reich as a result of the Versailles Treaty were experienced as daring assertions of German identity.[88]

Nonetheless, the youth movement was not wholly conservative. The intense need for collective experiences, the yearning for cohesion and the aversion to conflict, when translated into the national social context, made traditional class divisions seem problematic. Instead of providing a sense of order and place, class lines had become divisive and confining to these educated, middle-class adolescents during the late 1920s and early 1930s.[89] As a result, there was an effort to recruit a certain number of working-class boys and girls and to integrate them into youth movement groups.[90] Although the youth movement sought to become more socially inclusive than the prewar Wandervogel had been, the bourgeois character of the youth movement of the Bunds was never seriously threatened by a handful of working-class members.[91] In the youth movement of the Weimar Republic, members of the educated middle class set the tone. As we shall see, one of the prime complaints of the interviewees about the Nazi youth movement was that the demolition of class barriers was carried too far and that the Hitler Jugend and the Bund Deutscher Mädel were no longer dominated by bourgeois children but had a decidedly proletarian or peasant character.[92] Indeed, what troubled some of those interviewed about the Nazi youth organizations was that, through their populist character, these organizations lost much of their bourgeois elitism.[93]

And, along with belonging, elitism was at the heart of the appeal of the youth movement as an "aristocracy of youth."[94] These young people had the sense that they had proved themselves superior to the vast majority of their fellow Germans in being able to transcend materialism and bourgeois comforts as well as the social snobbery of peers and parents.[95] Nevertheless, the youth movement remained deeply conservative and safely bourgeois.[96] As these adolescents carried on many of the social prejudices and political traditions of their class, their elitism took the form of a lifestyle. They lived a critique of bourgeois materialism and propriety, one that expressed the widespread neoromantic revolt of bourgeois youth against bourgeois society during the Weimar period.[97] Even in their rejection of the modern and the urban and in their celebration of the traditional and the natural, they remained within a well-established bourgeois tradition.[98]

Given their association of politics with disorder and their fear of discord in the group, it was important for the interviewees to maintain that the youth movement was apolitical.[99] Because overcoming the "shame" of the Versailles Treaty and breaking down traditional social barriers promised to promote harmony in Germany, neither seemed "political" to the interviewees and their youth movement peers.[100] Instead, they equated "politics" with the Weimar Republic, and along with other young people of their social class, rejected the latter along with the former.[101] Indeed, the "aristocratic aestheticism" of the youth movement, "which at heart held the masses in contempt," encouraged its members to reject parliamentary democracy as the tyranny of the mediocre, the vulgar, and the grasping and to reject politics in general as divisive, self-interested horse trading.[102] To the extent that they were rebels, the members of the youth movement rebelled against the decidedly political Weimar Republic, with its urban character, its pluralism, its interest groups, its social disorder and political strife, its men in dark suits and top hats. And it was a completely safe rebellion that never took a more dangerous form than a song, a discussion, or a hike up a hill. It was also a completely safe rebellion since it was not directed against parents and teachers but was generally in conformity with their national conservative politics,[103] their hostility toward the Weimar Republic,[104] and their anti-Semitism.[105] These adolescents actually had no need to rebel against the parental generation—for, had they chosen to, they could easily have seen themselves as having defeated their parents, but they did not want to see their parents in a defeated light.[106]

Despite its conservatism and nostalgia, the youth movement partook of the twentieth-century breakdown of sexual and social barriers, a breakdown facilitated by the chaos of Weimar, which forced sexes and classes together in unprecedented and often liberating ways. Although girls were often discouraged and dismissed in school, they were accepted as equals in the youth movement, even if they had to adopt certain male standards to achieve equality. In general, the Weimar Republic, including its disorder, had benefits for women[107] and, above all, for youth. The contrast between young and old in their ability to adapt to and even enjoy the conditions of Weimar Germany comes through in the interviews most poignantly in the words of the suicide note written by the much-older sister of one of the interviewees: she killed herself "to make way for the younger ones."[108] Despite lost educational opportunities during the 1920s, the hardships and the breakdown of established structures enabled women to take opportunities for work and for pleasure that had only been a dream for their mothers.[109]

The turbulence of the 1920s exacerbated class tensions, and it is fitting that the interviewees' memories of Weimar open and close with street fighting. Nonetheless, those clashes, like the experience of the interviewee in the bourgeois coat fighting for his life against Communist youth on a Berlin bridge in 1931, testify to the breakdown of the social barriers that had kept the classes apart and preserved social order.[110] Even in fighting each other, bourgeois and proletarian young people were interacting in unprecedentedly intimate ways. The chaotic conditions of Weimar reduced the physical and psychological distance between the classes, encouraging the interviewees to view social divisions not as inevitable but as permeable. Those conditions created opportunities for young people, enabling them to cast off not only traditional gender roles but traditional social roles as well. The economic hardships compelled the interviewees to be downwardly mobile in ways they could experience as liberating and exciting, like the middle-class boy who dropped out of school to become a locksmith's apprentice and factory worker; like the upper-middle-class boy who became a locomotive driver and then a migrant laborer in the United States; and like the upper-middle-class girl who became a maidservant in the United States.[111] Although these occupations would have been a social humiliation for their parents, the interviewees recall these experiences as providing them with an opportunity to escape stultifying social conventions, prove themselves, and live a life of adventure.[112] Making a virtue out of necessity, the interviewees, along with others belonging to their class and generation, "glorified the—actual or feared—social descent of bourgeois youth as a sign that class conflict was being overcome."[113]

The economic hardship awakened what one contemporary of the interviewees and member of the youth movement called a "consciousness of social community" in this generation of Germans, encouraging them to become socially aware and active.[114] Perhaps the loss of financial security and social status experienced by their own families made the lower classes seem less alien, enabling those interviewed to develop empathy for people lower on the social ladder.[115] The social engagement of the interviewees during the early 1930s marks a transition between the paternalistic charity of the parental and grandparental generations and the radical social-political activism of the generation of their children. Thus by working in a soup kitchen during the Depression, one young woman carried the tradition of her admired grandfather, the stately country doctor, forward into the urban social welfare setting of a work camp.[116] This transitional position is reflected in the fact that the social engagement of the interviewees on the one hand transcended class boundaries and on the other reaffirmed them. By mixing with the lower classes, the interviewees appear to have experienced a sense of liberation and of superiority. A new world opened up to the upper-middle-class work camp cook as she learned about the lives of proletarian young men, and yet their stories allowed her to feel, despite the deprivations she and her family had suffered, a sense of social elevation.[117] Still, the contact with the poor and unemployed during the 1920s and early 1930s laid the foundation for the social activism of the interviewees during the Third Reich and beyond.[118]

In conclusion, the youth movement responded to the disorder and disintegration that followed the German defeat in World War I. It offered emotional security at a time when the family and other institutions that normally would have supported these adolescents had been weakened by military defeat, political disorder, and economic hardship. The youth movement was a source of security that tapped into a fantasy of prewar and wartime rural stability, served as an alternative to the weakened family, and provided a set of communal ideals to restore and replace those that had been lost in the defeat and the events that came in its wake. But by the beginning of the 1930s, having been provided by the youth movement with a "nest" in adolescence, those interviewed were entering young adulthood. Most had graduated from the gymnasium and were ready to move beyond the campfire. The Third Reich became for them the youth movement's age-appropriate extension.[119]

3

ESSAYS

THE EXPERIENCE OF WAR, REVOLUTION, DISORDER, AND INFLATION

Like the interviewees, other middle-class Germans belonging to their generation experienced the war not as a terrible but as a wonderful, even exhilarating period in their lives. Certainly that was the view the journalist and historian Sebastian Haffner expressed in his posthumously published autobiography. Born in 1907, Haffner experienced the war as a schoolboy in Berlin. Rather than dangerous or frightening, the war seemed to him a "grand game," and looking back as an adult, he was convinced that "a whole generation of Germans experienced the war in childhood just as I did or experienced it very similarly."[1] Haffner's contemporaries confirm his impression. Thus for Klaus Mann, born in 1906, the war assumed "almost the character of entertainment."[2] And E. Günther Gründel, member of the youth movement of the Bunds and National Socialist, was convinced that the experience of the war on the home front had instilled an intense generational consciousness in Germans born after 1900, creating what he called "the war-youth generation."[3] Indeed, Haffner believed that the experience of war not by soldiers on the battlefront but by schoolboys on the home front provided "the fundamental vision of National Socialism." Although a committed opponent of Nazism who left Germany for England in 1938, Haffner regarded his to be "the true Nazi generation."[4] Historians have followed Gründel and Haffner in identifying a cohesive political generation of Germans based on the shared experience of the war "as youthful fantasy" on the home front and in seeing that generation, affected by defeat, disorder, and hardship during the Weimar Republic, ultimately becoming the leading Nazi generation.[5]

The youthful fantasy came to an abrupt end for those belonging to "the war-youth generation" with the revolution that accompanied the German defeat. Haffner experienced the revolutionary violence as a youngster in Berlin. The revolution "had exactly the opposite effect on me and on those my age as the war," he wrote in his memoirs. "Whereas the war had had a simple and clear existence, the revolution—with all its crises, strikes, shooting, putsches, and demonstrations—seemed contradictory and confusing. One never understood exactly what it was all about. One could not get enthusiastic. One could not even really understand."[6] Klaus Mann also found the revolutionary period disturbing. Keenly aware of the outside world, Mann, as a twelve- and thirteen-year-old, kept a diary in which he recorded his reactions to the disorder. "The ground has become shaky beneath my feet," he wrote following the collapse of the revolution in Bavaria; and "like an animal before an impending earthquake," he "sensed that the economic and moral order was going to the devil. . . . One is awaiting a catastrophe."[7]

The reactions to the political violence described by Haffner, Mann, and the interviewees reflect not only their experiences but also the age at which they had them. By the time of the revolution, this generation of Germans had become conscious of the outside world in a way that no longer allowed it simply to be incorporated into a child's universe (the war as a "grand game"). Now the outside world was apprehended as something that had the frightening potential to impinge upon and change that universe in powerful and seemingly arbitrary ways. The events of the revolutionary period and the stage of cognitive development reached by this generation, then, brought the idyllic world of childhood to an abrupt end. Certainly E. Günther Gründel experienced the defeat and disorder as a caesura. "The world of the fathers and of everything that until then had been valid" fell apart, and with "terrifying" suddenness. "Within a few days everything that had dominated the past four years and had stood at the center of our lives collapsed . . . everything we had experienced and were still meant to experience. Basically the entire world of the older generation was completely bankrupt."[8]

The bankruptcy of the older generation was realized, literally and figuratively, in the inflation of 1923, which dealt an economic and psychological blow to the middle aged and the middle class and turned them against the Weimar Republic.[9] Not only were their savings wiped out by the inflation, their value system appeared to collapse along with the currency. Hard work and thrift were replaced by "a get-rich-quick mentality" that, in the words of Richard Bessel, rewarded "the unscrupulous rather than the industrious"; traditional standards "dissolved in an anarchy in which sound moral values appeared to count for nothing."[10] As captured in Thomas Mann's story "Disorder and Early Sorrow," young people adapted better than their elders to the inflation, a time that rewarded impulsiveness and the ability to grasp quickly changing circumstances and that punished caution and the wisdom gained from experience.[11] Erna von Pustau, who experienced the inflation as a young adult in Hamburg, described the demoralizing impact it had on her parents' generation. Living in a world that seemed governed only by "chance and degree," older Germans "lost their self-assurance, their feeling that they themselves could be the masters of their own lives."[12]

In a patriarchal society, the collapse of what in retrospect seemed the stable, hierarchical social order of the Kaiserreich and of the monarchy, symbol of patriarchy, was experienced as a frightening blow to the authority of German men and to German masculinity.[13] Like Gründel, many of his contemporaries had concluded, in the words of Claudia Koonz, that "the world of the fathers had gone astray."[14] The weakening of patriarchal authority at the national and societal level seemed to reflect a weakening of patriarchal authority within the German family. Lacking "the firm hand of the father," young people appeared rudderless, even "out of control," according to Bessel.[15] Indeed, because of "unemployment, hunger, impoverishment, and the political unrest of the period," fathers "did not and could not fulfill their paternal functions in the family." Either absent or demoralized, these men "did not provide a particularly convincing picture of a father." As a result, according to the psychiatrist Hartmut Radebold, boys belonging to the war-youth generation frequently lacked a secure sense of masculine identity.[16] The apparent ascendance of women during and after the war compounded the loss of paternal status and authority in the family and in society.[17] The manifest weakness of the father deprived adolescent bourgeois males of paternal figures to admire *and* to rebel against. The literary scholar Karl Prümm noted that autobiographical novels written between 1928 and 1933 about adolescence during the early years of the Republic present fathers as oppressive and weak. "As a result, revolt and bitter struggle are unnecessary. The power of the fathers has been broken, and they have given up along with the bourgeois world."[18]

Given the sense that the family—and particularly the father—had been weakened by military defeat, political unrest, and economic crisis, bourgeois young people sought to find the strength and support normally provided by the family (and other traditional institutions like school and church) in their own generation. In 1932, in an essay entitled "Sons without Fathers and Teachers: The Condition of Bourgeois Youth," Peter Suhrkamp, a forty-year-old teacher and war veteran, argued that fathers and father figures were absent as sources of strength and stability for the younger generation either because they had fallen at the front or because they returned too immature to provide the paternal security that the younger generation craved. In the absence of admirable fathers and father figures, bourgeois youth had turned from family and school to its own generation: "Youth finds in the youth group the education that it seeks and the ideals that it needs, even in the form of shallow slogans. Above all, young people find in the youth group a sense of human order. . . . The influence of comrades in communities of young people is greater in every way than that of parents and teachers, even when these are much loved."[19] Whereas Suhrkamp sympathized with German youth, Otto Baumgarten condemned the youth movement in 1927 for seeking the "emancipation of the younger from the older generations." Rejecting the education provided "by teachers and older people," young people believed that "genuine education came only through comrades and peers and through their own experiences." Baumgarten attributed this unfortunate tendency toward independence and self-importance on the part of youth to the fact that, with their fathers at the front during the war, youngsters had been deprived of a proper home; boys had taken on paternal roles and become overinvolved with their mothers. Economic hardship generally, and inflation in particular had completed this unhealthy emancipation, according to Baumgarten, confirming young people in their contempt for the older generation, its values, and the bourgeois order as a whole.[20]

The youth movement of the Bunds was not the only bourgeois generational collective to flourish during the 1920s. The Männerbund provided an especially attractive and intense group experience for young men slightly older than the interviewees. Homoerotic and misogynistic, elitist and self-idealizing, this closed circle of young bourgeois males became, like the youth movement, a compensating alternative to the weakened family and especially to the weakened father during the Weimar Republic.[21] The investment of young Germans in the generational unit came at the expense of the family, which was subordinated first to the youth movement group and the Männerbund and then to the national "community of the people," the Volksgemeinschaft—a subordination that would be aggressively promoted by the National Socialists.[22]

Thus, the common childhood experience of war on the home front, the common adolescent experience of defeat, revolution, unrest, and inflation— and the attendant weakness of the family—helped to forge a powerful generational consciousness on the part of bourgeois Germans the age of the interviewees. In response to the insecurity and uncertainty produced by these events, they turned to the generational collective as a source of order, stability, and purpose and as a model for the regeneration of German society through the creation of a harmonious and powerful national collective.[23] In attempting to create a sense of community, first in the group and ultimately in the nation, the youth movement looked back to the national and social unity that had prevailed in Germany at the outbreak of the war in August 1914. Thus E. Günther Gründel claimed that the roots of the attraction to the Volksgemeinschaft for the members of his generation could be traced to their dim childhood consciousness of the first years of the war, which produced an "unusually early commitment of the child's soul to the whole, to the collective experience itself. At an age when other children have no conception of one's own people and one's neighbors, we had *lived* these great connections already. The *Volk*, the nation, the evil enemies were already the most active factors in our harmless childhood world."[24] Perhaps, as Gründel suggested, these vague childhood experiences at the outbreak of the war laid the foundation for the yearning of members of this generation after 1918 for the collective at the personal and the national level, or perhaps this ideal of community was transmitted to them by parents and postwar society at large. Whatever its source, this yearning crystallized in response to the political disorder and social divisions of Weimar Germany, propelling most young bourgeois Germans in a conservative—some in a radical—right-wing political direction.[25] As Peter Stachura puts it, the youth movement represented an "answer to the fragmented society of Weimar" and "the national community (Volksgemeinschaft) in miniature, living proof of the indissoluble bonds which tied all Germans together."[26] The desire for the Volksgemeinschaft, then, looked back to the social and national unity of 1914 and to the lost emotional world of childhood and looked forward to national and social renewal, with the youth movement as the bridge connecting them.[27] Not only would the youth movement group serve as the model for the national collective, but the unity of the Volk over classes, parties, and religious confessions would be secured by the group's model of leadership, the fundamentally antidemocratic "leadership principle" or *Führerprinzip*, which also looked back to the idealized relationship between frontline officers and their troops during the war and anticipated Hitler as the embodiment of the popular will.[28]

The war-youth generation was not alone in yearning for the creation of a unified and powerful national community. Historians have noted the powerful attraction exerted by the idea of the Volksgemeinschaft on Germans across the political and generational spectrum during the Weimar Republic, as a way to recapture the "spirit of 1914" and overcome the bitter political and social divisions of the 1920s. And historians have also noted that the electoral successes of the National Socialists during the Weimar Republic can be attributed in part to their having responded to the desire, particularly of middle-class Germans, for a populist national community by making the Volksgemeinschaft a central tenet of their ideology. Indeed, Peter Fritzsche has argued that it was the Nazis' ability to appropriate and promote the popular notion of the Volksgemeinschaft that brought them to power in Germany and made "Germans into Nazis."[29]

GEMEINSCHAFT, GESELLSCHAFT, AND THE COLLECTIVE

Throughout this book, I have tended to translate the word "Gemeinschaft" as "collective" and not as "community," which would perhaps be the more

conventional choice. In German, the word has had specific ideological con-
notations ever since the sociologist Ferdinand Tönnies famously distinguished between "Gemeinschaft" and "Gesellschaft" in the late nineteenth
century.[30] In an implicit critique of contemporary bourgeois culture, Tönnies
saw Gesellschaft, or "society," as having something artificial about it. The
Gesellschaft was a rational association that the individual consciously and
intentionally joined in order to realize his or her self-interest. By contrast,
the Gemeinschaft was a natural and organic association—encompassing institutions like the family, the kinship group, the ethnic nation—to which the
individual belonged as a result of blood or tradition, regardless of consciousness or free will. For English speakers, "community" fails to convey the organic, romantic quality of Gemeinschaft. Although Gemeinschaft is the word
that the interviewees most often used in describing what the youth movement represented for them, it too is not an exactly accurate characterization,
conveying as it does more the ideal than the reality. For, unlike the organic
Gemeinschaft, whose prototype was the family, one *chose* to join the youth
movement. Still, the youth movement was not a Gesellschaft either, for it was
not designed to realize the rational self-interest of its members.[31] Indeed, at
the beginning of the 1920s, the sociologist Herman Schmalenbach sought to
add "Bund" as a third category of association to accompany Gemeinschaft
and Gesellschaft. Bund was meant to convey a distinct, autonomous possible
collective, one that people willingly joined but not in order to realize their
individual self-interest.[32] In any event, "collective" seems both to capture the
powerful feelings engendered by the Gemeinschaft of the youth movement
and to convey its intensely communal, anti-individualistic spirit.

SEXUALITY, IDENTITY, AND EQUALITY IN
THE YOUTH MOVEMENT

In 1911, the prominent Wandervogel and editor of the *Zupfgeigenhansl*,
Hans Breuer, expressed concern that androgyny would be fostered in the
youth movement should boys and girls interact extensively. Therefore, in an
article entitled "Das Teegespräch," he advocated that the sexes be segregated
in order to prevent the girls from becoming "feral" and the boys "soft."[33]
The sociologist Elisabeth Busse-Wilson suggested that Breuer's fears had been
realized when she wrote in 1920: "The 'unaggressive' male-type encounters
the 'neutralized' girl-type in the youth movement, which is transformed into
a 'playground for the sexless.'"[34] In 1925, Busse-Wilson expanded on this
theme with considerable ironic affection. Arguing that the youth movement
had contributed more than the women's movement to the emancipation of
young German women, she saw the asexuality of the youth movement as
essential to creating and preserving the "comradeship" that enabled "the

woman, for the first time, to experience true equality." In contrast to bourgeois morality, which regarded woman primarily from the perspective of pro-
creation as needing a man to fulfill her biological destiny, the youth movement had produced "one of the most unique relationships" between the sexes
"in the history of human society. Can you imagine? Boys and girls in that
first period of youth, where one experiences the greatest hunger for life, are
alone together. . . . In meadows and in moonlight, on June nights, in isolated
forests, singing their sentimental, passionate folksongs, songs which do not
even attempt to draw a veil over the nature of their yearning. And these men
and girls do not touch or even fall in love with one another. Instead, they
regard their sexual neutrality as normal and unexceptional." In their "conscious *rejection of eroticism*," these young people were able to experience
a sense of "moral superiority" that was enhanced by their "secret triumph
at having proved (despite the envious disbelief of the bourgeoisie) . . . that a
human relationship between the sexes is possible." They were further "richly
compensated" for their abstinence by "the security [*Geborgenheit*] of the collective" that asexual comradeship made possible. Busse-Wilson believed that
both sexes contributed to the asexuality of the youth movement. The "shy-
ness" of the men "about every loving touch and their distance from women"
derived from "the predominance of a homosexual orientation" growing out
of the ideology of the Männerbund. And the typical woman drawn to the
youth movement was a "worker bee," "a splendid and healthy, if sturdy
specimen." "It is no accident that the mass of girls not oriented toward love
would stream to the youth movement," Busse-Wilson concluded. "For this
type of neutered girl seeks to find just this type of unaggressive man, she is
practically his correlate."[35]

Like Busse-Wilson, Luise Riegger, writing in 1931 as the senior woman
member of the Bund of Wandervögel und Kronacher, saw the youth movement as promoting the emancipation of women, enabling girls to realize their
own potential and to achieve equality with boys in the group. And also like
Busse-Wilson, Riegger regarded the asexuality of the youth movement as
essential to that promotion. Indeed, she believed that on this asexual basis
"a comradeship of the sexes was established which no one had previously
thought possible." Riegger saw the "girls of the youth movement as having
provided an inestimable service by breaking down a wall of prejudice and in
contributing to winning a rich land of freedom for women." She concluded
hopefully: "Given how these girls and boys have grown into women and
men, it is to be hoped that a generation free of all repression of women, with
mutual respect for the individual value of the other, is emerging."[36]

Although Busse-Wilson and Riegger were convinced that the youth movement contributed to the emancipation of German girls and women, historians have been more skeptical about the nature and extent of that contribu-

tion. Ute Frevert, for example, acknowledges that "youthful interpretations" of traditional gender roles "were freer" during the Weimar Republic and that "the cult of youth in the 1920s" reduced the importance of differences between the sexes. Moreover, "the self-confidence of girls" was enhanced in the youth movement, which partially freed them "from parental influence and the strict familial observance of stereotyped sex roles."[37] Similarly, Dagmar Reese sees the "new girl of the youth movement" exhibiting qualities not traditionally associated with bourgeois women: physical activity and exercise; practicality and rationality; lack of pretension; and the ability to meet challenges. For Reese, the youth movement made "a definite, though ambivalent" contribution to the emancipation of women. "Above all, it operated with a notion of basic equality between the sexes—if only for a limited phase of their lives. But in aligning themselves with the broader category of youth, young women sacrificed all claims to a specific identity as women." Thus, for Reese, as for Frevert, the liberation that women experienced in the youth movement ultimately came because they were young and not because they were women.[38] Not only did the liberation of women during the Weimar Republic apply only to "*young* people," according to Frevert, it was highly circumscribed even for them: "Although sexual divisions had been eradicated in formal terms, specifically female domains emerged afresh, not least because of the dominant presence of men and their decision-making powers."[39] Rosemarie Schade is more unequivocal: "The youth movement contributed little to changing the subordinate position of women in the society of that time."[40] Like Reese and Frevert, Schade sees the youth movement as having empowered girls because of their age, not because of their sex.[41] As a result of their relatively small numbers and because they generally belonged to all-female groups, girls and women tended to play a subordinate role in the youth movement, which was dominated by men at the level of the Bund.[42] Schade concludes that "the entire female youth movement of the Bunds was decidedly antifeminist; its members did not share the feminist conviction that women were especially disadvantaged in German society and regarded the injustices suffered by the nation as far more important than any problems women might face." From "a liberal standpoint," the youth movement could not "advance the emancipation" of its female members because of its overall "fundamentally conservative orientation and the ideology of separate spheres for men and women, which was rooted in biological determinism and a component of conservatism."[43]

As we will see in considering the role of women in the Third Reich, however, the assumption that conservative or even fascist movements cannot promote the emancipation of women is at least open to question. And as we have seen, the women interviewed for this study were convinced that the youth movement promoted their emancipation as women, providing them with liberating experiences that would resonate throughout the rest of their lives.

THE YOUTH MOVEMENT AND NATIONAL SOCIALISM

There has been considerable debate among historians of the youth movement over its relationship to National Socialism. Matthias von Hellfeld and Felix Raabe play down the political links between the two.[44] Thus Raabe notes that the youth movement of the Bunds rejected National Socialism, not least for offending the bourgeois and elitist sensibilities of its members, and he concludes that, while the youth movement contributed to the failure of the Weimar Republic, it cannot be held responsible for the success of the Nazis.[45] By contrast, Michael Kater emphasizes the ideological links between the youth movement and National Socialism. In his view, historians like Hellfeld and Raabe overlook "the degree to which the worldview of the National Socialists was already anticipated before 1933 by essential aspects of the ideology of the youth movement of the Bunds. . . . The institutional fusion of the Hitler Youth and the middle-class youth movement that occurred between 1933 and 1939 was the logical consequence of a basic, shared ideological outlook, whose roots are to be traced back both to the politically conservative disposition of the Wilhelmian middle classes, which laid the groundwork for fascism in Germany, and to the orientation of the early National Socialists that was pseudo-revolutionary, antirational, and hostile toward civilization."[46] Peter Stachura expressly rejects Kater's claim that the youth movement was "pre-fascist." Instead he characterizes the youth movement as "ideologically neo-conservative rather than National Socialist or proto-Nazi." Stachura attributes the ready absorption of the members of the youth movement by various National Socialist organizations, including especially the Hitler Youth, less to ideological affinity and more to the opportunism that he believes generally marked the response of Germans to the advent of the Third Reich. Stachura, like Raabe, believes that the youth movement can legitimately be indicted for failing to support the Weimar Republic. Nonetheless, the "Bündische Youth, not being an ideological precursor of National Socialism, did not actively or passively promote Hitler's cause. Its responsibility, from an ideological point of view, was no more than that of many other right-wing organisations."[47] Jürgen Reulecke also takes issue with Kater, arguing that his approach of reading the ideology of the youth movement through the lens of National Socialism fails to appreciate the ideas of the youth movement in their own right and on their own terms. The ideology—or ideologies—of the youth movement pointed in a number of different directions, and during the Third Reich, among its former members were both enthusiastic Nazis and courageous resistors to National Socialism. Reulecke also notes that the National

Socialists themselves certainly did not regard the youth movement of the Bunds to be an extension of their movement but saw it instead as a potential rival, which they moved energetically to suppress. Reulecke sees the attempt to brand the youth movement a precursor to fascism as dehistoricizing the youth movement by taking it out of the social and cultural context of the 1920s. It was, in his words, "a child of its era." Just as one cannot claim that the coming to power of the Nazis was the inevitable result of German history, so one cannot claim that the youth movement, in a simplistic process of cause and effect, was a precursor to Nazism.[48] Although one can debate whether the youth movement of the Bunds was "pre-fascist," certainly most of those interviewed for this study and a great many of their youth movement peers would embrace National Socialism and flourish during the Third Reich.

II

Germany during the Third Reich and World War II

4

INTERVIEWS

Young Adulthood

FRANZ ORTHMANN

Basically I was raised apolitical and grew up apolitical, but when Adolf Hitler was named Reich chancellor I wasn't exactly astonished.* On the one hand, I didn't see coming what ultimately did come, which I suppose was a good thing. On the other hand, I certainly found the way the state was represented by the National Socialists impressive—in contrast to the top hats and suits, the dark clothes of the representatives of the Weimar Republic. They didn't impress me.[1] The Weimar Republic was saddled with the divisiveness of its political parties and of its politics, and of course we were well aware of the unemployment and the housing shortage. But now we had the sense that positive reconstruction work was being accomplished. There was a new, powerful sense of revitalization. Everywhere one was invited to pitch in.[2] The negatives that came increasingly to the fore, those were not seen at all,[3] and of course the Nazi Party held the reins of power. If you wanted to accomplish something in Germany, you could only do so within the system, not outside it.[4] Still, I must concede that I was absolutely susceptible, like many middle-class sons, I was absolutely susceptible to National Socialism. I joined the Party,[5] and as a result, things were considerably easier for me and I had wonderful opportunities. I was completely uncritical of those opportunities

---

*Hitler was named Reich chancellor on 30 January 1933, at the head of a coalition government of the National Socialists and conservative parties. Although the Nazis had presented their coming to power as inevitable and some of their political rivals had become fatalistic about eventual Nazi rule, the naming of Hitler as chancellor came as something of a shock to many Germans.

back then. It's something I reproach myself with today—and not only today. I've reproached myself about it for a long time.[6]

This initial period of National Socialism was a curiously open time. There were people from the SA, of all things, who contributed modern ideas*,[7] At first nothing much happened. We continued to publish our [youth movement] journal, *Trace*, but we were not able to escape the intoxication of the reconstruction or the new beginning. We didn't want to miss out on anything. We wanted to be a part of everything. And so we decided in April or May of 1933 to join the Party. The man Hitler fascinated us. Some things repelled us, but we didn't have the perspective or we closed our eyes to what was dangerous. Some things we didn't want to see, and we believed that everything would turn out all right. The publisher of our journal collaborated actively with the Hitler Youth, but our journal had to cease publication the moment the Hitler Youth claimed and enforced its exclusive right to represent German youth. In May 1933, I traveled one last time with my Bund, in a truck, to the Lüneberg Heath. There, at the Munster encampment, a huge convention took place of the Großdeutsche Bund, which had formed at the last minute out of the various large Bund associations under the leadership of Admiral von Trotha.[8] We had hoped to establish a counterweight to the Hitler Youth by bringing people together who represented the true youth movement way of life. The goal was completely illusory, but we didn't realize it back then. So both Freischar flags and swastika flags waved from our truck on the way to the Munster Camp.[†] I would say we were intoxicated, enthralled—less for National Socialism, perhaps, than for our Bund. There the Munster Camp was banned and broken up,[9] dissolved by Baldur von Schirach.[‡,10] The Bund was also prohibited.[§,11] The Bund had been an abso-

---

* Along with its well-deserved reputation for brutal street violence, the SA had a more radical, socialist orientation within the Party.

† Created in 1926, the German Freischar was more socially engaged, politically active, and moderate than most other youth movement Bunds, although it was still nationalistic and critical of the Weimar Republic. After the death of its founder in 1930, the Freischar moved steadily to the right.

‡ Baldur von Schirach (1907–74) was named Reich youth leader on 17 June 1933, a position he held until 1940 when he became the Nazi leader of Vienna, where he remained until the end of the war. Prosecuted at Nuremberg, Schirach was sentenced to twenty years' imprisonment for crimes against humanity. He was released in 1966.

§ In an effort to preserve the independent youth movement, many of the larger Bunds merged on 30 March 1933 to form the Großdeutsche Bund. After its leadership had pledged loyalty to Hitler, in May 1933 a convention of fifteen thousand members of the newly united youth movement Bund was held in the Munster Camp on the Lüneberg Heath. The camp, surrounded by police and storm troopers, was dissolved by Schirach. The action was directed from an airplane. Along with the camp, the Großdeutsche Bund and all other independent Bunds were disbanded. Several weeks later, the offices of the larger Bunds were raided and occupied by armed commandos of the Hitler Youth, their accounts closed and their money confiscated. In the following days, Hitler Youth violently suppressed the "homes" of youth movement groups.

lutely wonderful experience for me. Until the ban in 1933, I was thoroughly molded by the Bund.[12] But then in [January] 1933 the National Socialists came to power, and the end of the youth movement appeared over the horizon.[13] After that there were only informal contacts, close personal contacts of old friends, friendships that endured beyond the war . . . insofar as people didn't die in the war.[14]

Then I joined the Reich Work Service,[15] for after all, one has to belong somewhere.[16] Having just gotten my Abitur, I did one year of work service[17] in the Voluntary Work Service, as it was called then.*,[18] Later that year it became simply the Reich Work Service.[19] We worked in the vicinity of Küstrin in a forest and removed the resin from pine trees, which would be used somehow in industry. We also dug out a stream with the most primitive tools, handheld shovels that one dragged through the river. It was a six-hour workday.[20] We had a fine spirit of camaraderie[21] there too, since we were all volunteers. Most or almost all of us were unemployed, of course. I was the only one with an Abitur. As a result, I was allowed to do certain things, such as measure the exact number of cubic meters they had dug up. It was a lovely time, especially because sports were strongly emphasized—even more than the work, perhaps, at least from our point of view.[22] In school, I had boxed for an hour every week over the course of two years. My knowledge of boxing helped me in the Work Service in that I could protect my skin very nicely by challenging people to box, especially the ones who mocked those of us who had attended gymnasium as cowards. By boxing I could demonstrate that we weren't simply spoiled but could defend ourselves.[23] It was a lovely time for me. After having been in school, I could cut loose.[24] So that was the Work Service. It was really very nice,[25] and I have fond memories of the Work Service.[26]

Still, it was an experience ruined in retrospect by the war and the conditions after the war,[27] fleeting images, which in retrospect are overshadowed by the uncritical collaboration with National Socialism. I didn't harm anyone. But then again, most people didn't. I reproach myself most because as students and as a member of our youth movement group we should have been the most critical. How the children and sons of the apolitical, educated,

---

*The Voluntary Work Service grew out of work camps developed by various youth movement Bunds and became part of the Brüning government's efforts to ameliorate the effects of mass unemployment on youth caused by the Depression. Taken over by the National Socialists, the Work Service initially retained its voluntary character but was vastly expanded and its administration centralized. In addition to responding to unemployment, the National Socialist version of the Work Service was designed to symbolize and create the Volksgemeinschaft. In 1935 it became obligatory that young men serve six months in the Work Service. With the outbreak of the war in September 1939, it became obligatory for young women as well.

upper-middle classes, who belonged to the youth movement . . . [28] Still, I suppose we really had no experience in dealing with the manipulations of 1933
to 1935. We had only experienced the helplessness of the previous bourgeois
government, and we yearned for something completely different. We had the
feeling that we could create something different. What was created, however,
was quite different from what was being proclaimed at the time. For me the
first experience was the 30th of June 1934, when the Wehrmacht—that was
the biggest disappointment—allowed itself to be bought.[*,29] Indeed, I began
to distance myself after the 30th of June 1934.[30] I restricted my participation
in the Party. I was shocked by the events of the 30th of June 1934, when the
leadership of the SA was eliminated and all those personalities around whom
an opposition to Hitler might have crystallized. I will never forget the speech
that Hitler delivered about what in the future would constitute justice in our
state. I was totally repelled.[31] My father, as a judge, was deeply disturbed by
the Röhm Putsch. He simply could not reconcile his conscience as a judge
with the murder of Röhm, Schleicher, and the rest without trial. That was a
serious violation of the rule of law for my father. I would describe him as a
conservative nationalist, but with serious reservations about the Third Reich.
National Socialism seemed to him to be the rebellion of the street, and he
consciously kept his distance from Nazism. He used to joke, for example,
about the fact that the janitor in his courthouse had become the local [Nazi]
group leader. He was unbelievably impressed by the *Anschluß* with Austria in 1938, however. The old idea of a Greater Germany was realized for
him.[†] Not without inner reservations, he joined the Party in 1938 after the
Anschluß, remarking, "One must use different standards to judge this era.

---

* After the establishment of Nazi political control in Germany, Hitler declared that the
National Socialist "revolution" was over. Nonetheless, there remained on the left wing of the
Nazi Party, especially the SA, many who called for a "second revolution" in which a vaguely
understood "national socialism" would be put into practice and in which traditional state
institutions would be replaced, with the SA as the potential revolutionary successor to the
German army. Its penchant for street violence had become a liability now that the Nazis were
in power, and its vague social revolutionary agenda was incompatible with Hitler's plans for
European conquest, which required collaboration with industry and the army. As a result,
Hitler and the top Nazi leadership, in collusion with the army, moved against the SA on
30 June 1934, arresting and summarily executing most of its top leadership, including its
head, Hitler's old friend Ernst Röhm. In addition, Hitler used the opportunity to take revenge
on at least eighty-three of his enemies and opponents, including a number of prominent
conservative political figures, such as the former chancellor, General Kurt von Schleicher
(1882–1934). A law passed by the Reichstag on 3 July 1934 legalized the murders retrospectively as acts of "National Self-Defense." Two weeks later, Hitler justified the purge in a
radio speech to the nation. With the so-called Röhm Putsch, Hitler consolidated his power in
Germany and gained the allegiance of the leadership of the army.

† In March 1938 Austria was annexed to the German Reich, thereby fulfilling a dream of
German nationalists who since the nineteenth century had sought the creation of a "Greater
Germany" comprised of ethnic Germans living in Europe.

Perhaps I'm too bourgeois to understand." That was his point of view, more or less.[32]

After the Work Service, I volunteered for military service. I joined the army in 1935 when it was still voluntary. Then in 1936, as I was preparing to leave, the service became compulsory, so I had to stay on another year, until 1937.[*,33] I should add that my military service was a liberating experience for me, also socially.[34] I spent a year and a half doing general service,[35] and then came one of those strokes of fortune proving that my life has been determined by the youth movement. I had an old friend from the Bund. We met at Pschorr[†] on the Potsdamer Platz and had a glass of beer. He told me that he was in the Ministry of Propaganda with Dr. Goebbels, in the Literary Division. They were looking for people with publishing experience and wondered if I had any interest. Needless to say, that was a pretty tempting offer for a young father[36] (actually I wasn't a father yet but already married). He urged me to apply, which I did. For several weeks I didn't hear anything. Then one day I received a letter: "You are hereby summoned to report to the Reich Ministry for Popular Enlightenment and Propaganda[‡] on 1 July 1937 at such and such a time to Senior Executive Councilor Pumpelmann." I was obviously in seventh heaven. I will never forget how the friendly official calculated my income, which was many times what I had ever earned before. My future was secured.[37]

I was already married then. I got married in 1935. In 1936–37 I received a letter from the authorities with the following contents: "We inquire why your marriage, which was contracted in 1935, has remained childless until now?" I wrote back: "I hereby humbly inform you that in our marriage, our recent marriage, a son is expected next year, 1938. Heil Hitler!"[§] You know, one did hear about all sorts of things, about the Social Democrat who was thrown from a train, about another who was given a thrashing. You were denounced if you didn't fly the flag outside.[38] But when I think back today, I must concede that I never gave a thought to what it all meant, and there was much about the Propaganda Ministry that one shouldn't simply dismiss out of hand. I joined the Literary Division, where I found a bunch of old friends from the youth movement or those who would soon be my friends. I officially had a position there until the collapse of the Reich, although I was not there

---

[*] The law decreeing universal military service for one year was passed on 16 March 1935. After the fall of 1936, the term was increased to two years.

[†] A beer hall in Berlin run by the Pschorr brewery.

[‡] The Reich Ministry for Popular Enlightenment and Propaganda was responsible for promoting National Socialist ideology and for generally controlling information in the service of the regime.

[§] The Nazis, for ideological reasons and to reverse the decline in the birthrate, actively encouraged racially suitable couples to have children.

consistently since I was a soldier most of the time, but I was assigned there and ultimately became a government official. Perhaps I should say that for all those years I was a "dream dancer." I always tried only to see the good, always only to recognize the positive. When someone says today that one ought to have seen what was coming, then one can only reply: "You can only say that with hindsight. Back then everything was simply different." My job was to work in the loan and factory library branch, and I got to know many interesting authors, poets, and people. Then my son was born, and we lived a happy family life in Berlin.[39]

In Berlin we met the other members of the [youth movement] group again [and] talked about what we would do next and about who hadn't been drafted yet. I had been called up, since I had already served.[40] And with this group[41] I made one very significant bicycle excursion[42] to East Prussia.[43] We traveled through the Polish Corridor.* For us it was actually closed at that time. The cars were sealed, we were inspected, and traveled over. It was fun. A Polish sergeant came through with a machine pistol. We all had served as soldiers. I lay up in the suitcase rack. He didn't see me for all of his staring about. We traveled through.[44] That was in August 1939. Our excursion had been planned long in advance, of course, but before we took off there was concern about whether we should even go, since it was clear that war would soon break out. Nevertheless I and a couple of others pounded on the table and said, "We're going!" On the 13th of August we were back, and on September 3rd I was a soldier again. We got in under the wire. By the way, two years later, in 1941, I marched along the same path—from Marienburg to Tilsit. One night I peered about, reading the signposts: we were marching along the same road where I had ridden my bicycle! Our company was trudging along, and I gave my neighbor a nudge and said, "Two years ago I rode my bike here." "Wild horses wouldn't bring me to this desolate spot," he replied.[45]

Back in the youth movement,[46] we would read aloud descriptions from the First World War during our "home evenings." And it was this orientation that led me to become an officer.[47] I always regarded my service as a soldier, as an officer, from the perspective of the youth movement of the Bunds. It was a life lived outside orderly bourgeois society, with improvisation, especially when we were on the move. It was also an opportunity to lead other people in the service of a goal.[48] I began the Balkan campaign[49] as a lower-ranking officer and had "my group." I regarded those ten or twelve men as if they were a youth movement group and based my treatment of them on my expe-

---

* The Versailles Treaty created an independent Poland after 150 years of partition. To give the newly created Republic of Poland access to the sea, a strip of land between thirty and ninety kilometers wide was made a part of Poland. As a result, the German province of East Prussia was separated from the rest of the country by the "Polish Corridor."

rience in the youth movement. Whereas other officers of my rank slept in a tent by themselves, I had three tents put together so that all twelve of us could sleep in the same tent—with the officer smack dab in the middle. And I must say the boys really played along. I could ask anything of them.[50] So it wasn't orders and obedience, but rather it was conviction and cooperation, just as in the group.[51] We wouldn't have been able to endure the extreme conditions of wartime if we hadn't helped one another survive. Then orders don't matter. And when you are trying to winter at forty degrees below zero at night on the Arctic Ocean and when everything that moves is presumably Russian, then those are conditions where orders don't achieve a thing. That's when it was suddenly as in the group, where one makes things better by setting an example, through cooperation, conviction, collaboration. Without that, nothing works—if one doesn't have the feeling that there is someone at one's side, no matter his rank, and that one is responsible for the other person.[52] This human connection is what awakens the readiness to expose oneself to the dangers of war, not love of the fatherland and certainly not the order of the regimental commander. I had one company commander who had served in the First World War. He was concerned only with his own safety and made himself scarce whenever things got dangerous. As a result, I took responsibility for maintaining discipline. I had the feeling that the more restless the men became, the more important it was that I remain calm. The more restless they became, the more nervous, the calmer I became. And with my calmness and simple self-possession, I was able to calm the men. Not through commands or shouting, which was what the company commander had done. I said not one word. I tried only to radiate calmness. And that did it. Human qualities are far more important than the power of command. Nothing can be achieved with commands—rather only with leadership that sets an example by how one conducts oneself.[53]

The general mobilization came on 3 September [1939]. I went directly to Stuttgart, where I was inducted. I was assigned to the artillery, since previously, from 1935 to 1937, I had been in the horse-drawn artillery.[54] When the war broke out, I participated in the Polish campaign.* I marched from Czechoslovakia to Lehmberg† and back. There I had my first bitter experiences of attacking and the death of good friends. But in the end we believed—I believed that I was serving in a great cause and that we needed to put our lives on the line.[55] Following the Polish campaign,[56] I joined an officer's training program[57] in Berlin Starnsdorf in the Ludendorff Barracks.

---

* The German invasion of Poland on 1 September 1939 marked the beginning of World War II. Seventeen days later, Soviet troops invaded from the east. Polish resistance quickly collapsed, and Poland surrendered by the end of the month.

† Then a city in southern Poland, now Lviv in Ukraine.

There I experienced a hard period of training,[58] which never hurt anyone, and we reminded ourselves that we had volunteered for it.[59] We were twenty-five young soldiers who all wanted to become officers.[60] Soon after I was sent, as a young lieutenant, to the West Wall,* and then[61] I participated in the French campaign under the command of the later-notorious General Schörner.† After the French campaign (which was relatively brief for me, because I was a part of the so-called second wave across the Vosges Mountains into central France‡),[62] I was reclaimed by the Reich [Propaganda] Ministry where I spent the rest of 1940 and [the beginning of] 1941 at my desk. But I wanted to be released from my position at the ministry since it was unbearable to be sitting at a desk while people were out there dying.[63] So I returned to my unit[64] in Romania. From Romania, we marched through Bulgaria, participated in the Greek campaign, storming the Metaxas Line, and marched on foot to Athens.§ In a variety of ways this campaign was an extremely important test for me. The physical strain was incredible, and, as an artillery officer, I felt responsible for my team, for helping them through, for enabling them to handle the strain. It was a challenge in keeping with the spirit of my old ideals. From Greece, we saw action in Crete as an airborne unit with dreadful experiences. The experiences were dreadful, on the one hand, because so many fell there, among them good friends; on the other hand, because there I experienced for the first time how dreadfully people of the Wehrmacht

---

* The West Wall was the German line of defensive fortifications running along the German border with France from Lörrach, near the Swiss border, to the point where the Rhine flows into the Netherlands.

† A convinced National Socialist, Ferdinand Schörner (1892–1973) rose steadily through the ranks over the course of the war, serving in the invasion of France, in the Balkan campaign (against Yugoslavia and Greece), on the arctic front west of Murmansk, and in the Ukraine, ultimately becoming commander of Army Group South. In July 1944 he was put in command of Army Group North in the Baltic. In January 1945 he was made commander of Army Group Center, whose forces he kept relatively intact until the German surrender. He was made field marshal general on 5 April 1945. He became known, especially during the German retreat, for his brutality, ordering the execution of numerous soldiers for cowardice. After being released from Soviet prisoner of war camps, he was sentenced to four years' imprisonment in 1957 for ordering the summary execution of soldiers under his command.

‡ The German invasion of France began on 10 May 1940 with an assault through Belgium and Holland and through the Ardennes Forest. By mid-June Holland had surrendered, Belgium was overrun, and Paris was occupied. By the time of the German "second-wave" invasion across the Rhine into Alsace-Lorraine on 14 June, German forces were engaged primarily in mopping-up operations.

§ When Italian forces suffered setbacks in Greece after Italy's invasion of that country in October 1940 and when an anti-German, pro-Soviet coup took place in Yugoslavia, Germany began a campaign in the Balkans on 6 April 1941. By 17 April, the Yugoslav army had capitulated. At the same time, German forces invaded Greece and by late in the month had defeated a combined Greek-British force. On 24 April Athens was occupied by German troops.

mistreated the indigenous inhabitants, who during the occupation turned against the German invaders, which became an occasion for many German soldiers to exact bitter vengeance.[*],[65]

In June of 1941[66] those of us junior officers who were candidates for promotion[67] were sent to Marienburg,[68] were given seven days' leave, and then began the march into Russia.[†] I don't unfortunately have the photo of the tattered Polish children who came to our field kitchen and whom I had to urge two or three times to take some of my food. They came with tin cans and battered bowls and took the food away.[69] Later in the campaign I often went to houses to fetch water for washing and cooking. Once I gave a chicken to a Russian woman, who was very happy to receive it. Often the inhabitants offered us something at midday, a kind of pumpkin or melon or those grain dumplings or honey, and were happy when we ate it. One old woman said to the soldiers who were in her parlor, "Ast, ast, ast." We said, "But you have nothing to eat yourself." "Yes," she said (she spoke German too). "My grandson is also a soldier, and when you eat then he's eating too."[70] Before the war we had often held discussions at the house of our school director. Once we discussed the book by Moeller van den Bruck.[‡] There is the sentence in it: "A young *Volk* has a right to living space." "Yes, and where is that living space?" the author asked. "Of course, it's in the East. We are always drawn to the East, we Germans." "Yes, but the Poles and the Russians are there."[71] "Well, we've simply got to throw them out or kill them off." And, as I witnessed myself, that's what happened during the Russian campaign.[72] During the entire Russian campaign I was never able to overcome my feeling of sadness about the invasion.[73]

In 1940, when[74] a fellow soldier described atrocities, I had thought he was a pig. It was inconceivable to me. He never spoke of it again, but his last words were: "I saw it with my own eyes." Later on [in Crete] I experienced things myself,[75] but I will never forget one incident during the Russian campaign.[76] At the entrance to a village in the Ukraine a banner was stretched across the road with the message: "Welcome, Germans, Liberators from So-

---

[*] The invasion of Crete began on 20 May 1941 with a German airborne assault on the island, which was defended by British, Australian, New Zealand, and Greek soldiers. After ferocious fighting, with high casualties on both sides, Crete was in German hands. Local inhabitants supported British and Greek forces by taking guerilla action against the Germans. In response, the German commander, General Kurt Student (1890–1978), ordered brutal reprisals against the civilian population.

[†] The invasion of Russia, reflecting the Nazi ambition to acquire living space in the East, was launched on 22 June 1941.

[‡] Arthur Moeller van den Bruck (1876–1925) was a conservative writer, popular during the Weimar Republic, who argued that Germany's renewal lay not in the West or with Western ideals but, spiritually and physically, in the East.

viet Dictatorship."*,[77] When I was off duty that evening, I walked through
the village. We met a family with a little girl who spoke very good German
and could converse with us. All of a sudden people came running up the village street with mattresses and packed suitcases, shouting in Russian, "Russians! The Russians have come and in a village four kilometers away have slit
the throats of the people. Their tanks are following close behind!" Now, we
were there with our truck, a single vehicle parked in a hollow planted with
alders. The two of us went right back to our truck when we heard about
the tanks. The Russians didn't come. But after us, on that same night, the
SS Viking Division arrived.[†] They had antitank weapons with them. There
was firing all night long. At the village [the next morning] an officer said,
"Don't go through the village, there are too many dead lying about. The SS
Viking [Division] has shot them all." It was the village with the "Welcome,
Germans" banner.[78]

Much later, near the end of the war, when I was traveling back from the
front on leave,[79] I was taken along, as a hitchhiker, by a provisions truck
from the concentration camp Oranienburg.[‡] I got into a conversation with
the driver. I asked him what sort of people those were in the striped uniforms
working over there in the fields. "Yes," he said. "They are probably here
from one concentration camp or another in this area." After I'd given him a
couple of cigarettes,[80] he trusted me. He told me . . . He wasn't at all opposed
to what was . . . Rather, he actually seemed to approve . . . He was quite a
young guy, twenty-two years old. He'd just finished an apprenticeship and
got into the war. Labor service and then the war.[81] He volunteered that he
was a food supply driver for the concentration camp Oranienburg. Every
day, he said, about four hundred new inmates arrived at the camp, but the
amount of provisions always remained the same. I asked him how that could
be. It made no sense. He explained to me that people were gassed there in
gas chambers.[82] He went on to describe how those little towns with Jews in
Galicia, for example, had been dealt with—you know, how little children
were tossed up in the air and spitted on bayonets and such things. So I knew
then[83] about the extermination of the Jews and the system of extermination
camps.[84] I couldn't believe my ears. I must say, at that moment a world col-

---

* German forces enjoyed a series of stunning early successes against the Soviet Union.
By early October 1941 virtually the entire Ukraine was in German hands. The indigenous
population frequently greeted the Germans as liberators from Soviet oppression.

† The SS Viking Division was one of the most notorious and militarily effective German
units fighting on the eastern front. It was part of the Waffen-SS, the military wing of the SS
(Schutzstaffel). In addition to their military activities, these units were centrally involved in
the extermination of the Jews of Europe. They also executed prisoners of war and committed
atrocities against the civilian population in Eastern Europe.

‡ Oranienburg/Sachsenhausen was a concentration camp north of Berlin. More than one
hundred thousand people from twenty nations died there.

lapsed inside of me.[85] I'm grateful to fate that I didn't learn about the whole business with the concentration camps earlier. I can only say that the great mass of my comrades, that all of my soldiers, I've never heard of even a one who knew anything about it. When I hear Herr von Weizäcker say in his famous speech on May 8th that we all knew exactly, well, he doesn't know what he's talking about.* It's not true. My father-in-law, he certainly knew exactly, but he never said anything to me or to my wife, in order not to demoralize me. I think that was quite the proper thing for him to have done.[86] If I had known about it beforehand, then I would never have been able to fight wholeheartedly for the Führer or for our cause, in quotation marks. It was my conviction that National Socialism and the Führer wanted the best for Germany, and this idea was worth sacrificing one's life for if necessary. I would have been deprived of that justification. I mean, I would have kept on fighting. After all, I couldn't have objected and thrown everything overboard. I had responsibilities that I couldn't and shouldn't have given up.[87]

So I only learned about the mass exterminations late in[88] the war. It always upsets me when young people say, "Of course you knew everything." That's simply not true. We knew about some inhuman activities, but this almost industrial mass extermination I only learned about late in[89] the war. I was somewhat naive perhaps. Earlier[90] during the war I went on a trip to Heidelberg. I continued on in a sleeping car to Vienna. In my compartment was a big, fat man who was something of a loud mouth. As we traveled one morning through the rubble of Munich, he actually said, "They deserve it, those big-mouth Munichers." I thought to myself, "My God, what sort of man is this?" But I was cautious. When he left the compartment, I looked quickly at his luggage tag. He was the SA Obergruppenführer from Mannheim. Then I turned the conversation to the persecution of the Jews. I asked, "How have you solved the Jewish problem in Mannheim?" He replied, "Let me tell you. They all got the message within"—I don't remember anymore, six hours, twelve hours, could have been twenty-four hours—"they had to get out. They could only take what they could carry. I ordered two extra trains from the railway. They asked where I wanted the trains to go. I told them it was none of their business, and ordered the trains to leave." So I asked him, "Well, where did you send them?" He replied, which I don't believe today, "To southern France. They've all been set free there." I'd never believe that. Although one could suspect that terrible things were being done,[91] still, I only

---

* Richard von Weizäcker (1920–) was president of the Federal Republic of Germany from 1984 to 1994. On 8 May 1985 Weizäcker delivered a speech in the German parliament commemorating the fortieth anniversary of the Allied defeat of the Third Reich as the "liberation" of Germany. Weizäcker's most controversial and courageous claim concerned German knowledge about and responsibility for the Holocaust.

learned about the mass exterminations late in the war.[92] Can you understand
why it upsets me when it's said over and over: "You knew about it all"?[93] We
only fully appreciated the negative with the collapse in 1945.[94] Only with the
end of the war came the recognition that everything had been inverted and
all that had happened, which we hadn't fully known about, fully known how
bad . . . Perhaps we didn't pay enough attention.[95] Gradually an attraction
to the figure of Hitler had developed in me, which I can only understand in
that he had an undeniable radiance.[96] I was convinced back then that the
Führer, that Adolf Hitler, was the best thing to have happened to Germany
perhaps in its entire history.[97] I can only use the term "dream dancer" and
the effort to repress that which one thought worth repressing.[98] And also
one was at the front. There one has other worries, you know.[99] So that's that
chapter.[100]

In the fall of[101] 1941 I was transferred to[102] the Arctic Ocean, where I
served under the most extreme conditions.* We had to go from Altafjord
[in German-occupied Norway] to the front, over six hundred kilometers of
marching night and day, at a time when there was already snow up there.
Those were stresses and strains that could only be endured through an idealistic attitude, which I had then, still had then, which enabled me to endure
everything and to bring the troops, who had been made my responsibility,
where we had to go. I remained up on the Arctic Ocean until 1944. It was
positional warfare under the most extreme conditions.[103] I experienced the
Putsch up on the Arctic Ocean.[†,104] I would later become bitterly disappointed
in Hitler and the National Socialists,[105] but back then I wanted nothing to do
with the people of the 20th of July. I was of the opinion that it was unconscio-
nable for an officer to mutiny in the middle of a war.[106] During a war there is
only the question of whether we win the war or whether we lose. I thought,
first we have to win the war, and that will only happen if Hitler remains in
power. Thus I was utterly astonished by the Putsch against Hitler.[107] I was in
an intact military unit and had, for that reason, *absolutely no understanding*
for the assassination attempt.[108] I thought, "What are they *doing?!* We can't
suddenly switch horses in midstream."[109] We had the feeling that if we don't

---

* Following the Russo-Finnish war, which ended in March 1940, Finland became an ally
of the Third Reich, joined by shared hostility toward the Soviet Union. As a result, when the
Germans invaded the Soviet Union in June 1941, they were able to attack the Soviets from
positions in Norway, which had been conquered by Germany the previous spring, advancing
on the Soviet port of Murmansk and on Kandalaksha. Finnish troops advanced on Leningrad. By December, German and Finnish armies had bogged down and for the next several
years fought primarily to maintain their positions, under appalling conditions in winter.

† On 20 July 1944 members of the traditional military and conservative elites attempted
to overthrow the National Socialist regime, beginning with an assassination attempt on Adolf
Hitler. Hitler was only slightly wounded, and the attempt to seize power quickly collapsed.

defend ourselves up there, if we don't do our duty, then we are lost. Then we would have no chance of ever getting back home.[110] That was when one said yes to National Socialism of necessity, adding, "Afterward, when we've won the war, that's when things will work themselves out."[111] In our time up there we experienced the defeats on the eastern front above all else through news reports, and our faith in final victory was shaken more and more. Yet we held our positions till the end, more out a sense of duty than out of a sense of conviction. I did my military duty, as I believed right, as I then believed right, till the very end.[112] The collapse of the Reich was a devastating experience for me. I did not experience it as a liberation but as a defeat, even though I know that a victory for the Germans would have led to further catastrophes.[113] And for me, of course, the war represented above all else my service as a young officer.[114] The war posed the complete challenge.[115] On the Arctic Ocean I was in command of a unit with one thousand people. An entire sector, I was responsible for the defense of an entire sector. Those were challenges that really tested me. I was filled with a sense of inner pride and satisfaction that I was able to do the work entrusted to me, that I was able to do my duty.[116]

In the fall of '44, I[117] was able to get out of Finland. I was sent to the Courland bridgehead, where I experienced the heavy defensive battles at Mittau.* By this time I had become the divisional commander of an artillery unit. I was wounded, and on account of the wound and of the fact that I was an experienced officer, I was pulled out of the East and sent to Italy. In Italy I also commanded an artillery unit, assigned to defend the Futa Pass in the Apennines.† Then I was pulled out once again[118] and sent to Prienitz to my re-formed division, which had nearly been obliterated in the meantime.[119] I met many of my old comrades in Prienitz, those who had not remained behind in the East.[120] We were quickly thrown into the general retreat that had developed in Poland.‡ We were to delay the Russian advance.[121] There were a large number of Russians in one place where I was. I don't remember the name. It was a little village. They had fought on the German

---

* Mittau (today Jelgava in Latvia) was the scene of heavy fighting in the fall of 1944.

† The Futa Pass stands on the road between Florence to the south and Bologna to the north and was a key German defensive position on the Apennine front. On 10 September and again on 2 October 1944, British and American troops launched offensives, but German resistance proved so tenacious that it was only in April 1945 that the Allies were able to break through.

‡ The second half of 1944 witnessed the gradual military collapse of the Third Reich. By December, Romania and Bulgaria had been knocked out of the war and the Red Army had reached Yugoslavia, Hungary, and East Prussia. Polish territory east of Warsaw was also in Soviet hands.

side.* They were men and women. They were working with the local farmers. We stood opposite the Russian front. We heard that the front was getting
closer and closer, and so *we* were pulled back, to the north. The Russians
stayed there, where they all surely met their doom. It was a very "lovely"
thought for us, but we were able to save ourselves.[122]

Of course there are always decisions in one's life, decisions that I had
nothing to do with . . . If, as only an example, I think how I was sent out
of Russia back to Italy. We had to assemble in Kufstein at a barracks. We
counted off, one-two, one-two. The "ones" were sent to Italy. The "twos"
were sent to the Balkans. I was a "one" and went to Italy and am alive today. Those who were "twos" went to the Balkans. Most of them were killed
miserably by the partisans or later lost their lives working in the mines down
there. Hardly any of them returned alive. Such are the decisions made during
wartime, and there were many such decisions. They were of course fateful
decisions. Perhaps I had good luck; others, bad. I had no influence over what
happened.[123] I had come to terms with my life and accepted that what will
be will be.[124] Looking back, the worst part were all the comrades with whom
I was together from the beginning and who bought it there—all but three
or four. Of my schoolmates . . . In 1985 we had our fiftieth reunion and all
gathered together. Of a class of seventeen [boys] who got the Abitur, there
were only four left. That was my generation. Of the Bund, of the twelve [in
my group], there were only three left. You know it was really an antiselection
that took place as a result of the war.[125]

I was wounded on the *Autobahn*† on March 4th, 1945 in Königsberg.‡ I was fortunate. I was evacuated and shipped out through Pillau.§ I
was taken to a military hospital in the Teutoberger Forest[126] that had to be

---

* These Russians were apparently remnants of the so-called Vlasov Army, a force
made up of approximately fifty thousand former Soviet prisoners of war, forced laborers,
and volunteers under the command of the captured Russian officer Lieutenant General An-
drei Vlasov (1901–46), who fought alongside the Germans in order to liberate Russia from
Bolshevism.

† One of Hitler's dreams was to create a network of multilane highways connecting
the principal German cities. The construction of these roads, called Autobahns, was begun
in 1934, but by 1939 only three thousand kilometers had been completed. By that date, a
strip of Autobahn of about one hundred kilometers had been built running southwest from
Königsberg (today Kaliningrad in Russia) to Elbing (today Elblag in Poland).

‡ On 12 January 1945, the Soviets launched their "grand offensive" against the Third
Reich, conquering western Poland and pushing north into East Prussia. By the end of February, the Soviets had reached the Oder River, well inside the eastern border of Germany. At
the same time Soviet armies reached the Baltic, cutting off German forces in East Prussia. In
mid-April, the Red Army began a final offensive from its positions along the Oder and Neisse
rivers. On 25 April, American and Soviet forces met at Torgau on the Elbe River. Berlin fell
to the Soviets on 2 May 1945.

§ Today Baltiysk in Russia.

dispersed because the Americans were approaching. I got myself released to a reserve military hospital in Minden,[127] where my relatives had found refuge in the meantime.[128] I had only been there three days when we heard artillery fire from the west. So once again I took off, this time with my arm in a sling. I wanted to head for Potsdam, since I had the idea that I should go to where the remnants of one of my old units might be, for I didn't want to be slaughtered as a lonely soldier.[129] But it was too late.[130] For the first time in my life, I saw armed Americans belonging to some paratroop regiment.[131] The bridges over the Weser[132] were already in American hands.[133] So I decided to swim across the Weser. I had everything prepared. I had an inner tube.[134] After a stealthy creep, I made it to the area south of Nienburg.[135] I learned, however, that there were officers on the other bank. They were SS and were trying to get their tattoos removed. I learned that the SS was concentrated between the Weser and the Elbe and said to myself, "Better to be taken prisoner."[136]

I was taken prisoner in the military hospital in Minden.[137] But we weren't imprisoned. Instead, after the 9th of May, after the armistice, we were interred. The officers could keep their weapons, which meant I could continue to carry my pistols. I had to wear a white armband. In June the Americans began releasing the German prisoners of war.[138] When I was to be released, I think it was a major, an American, he asked me if I'd belonged to the SS or if I'd been assigned to the General Staff. Those were the only questions. I could readily answer them negatively. Then they checked to see if my blood type was scratched into my upper arm. That was the sign that one belonged to the SS, who all had their blood type engraved somewhere. I didn't have that.[139] I was released into the Russian zone where, along with all other officers, I was immediately seized by the Russians.*,[140] The entire transport of officers was freighted out in a goods train sealed with barbed wire. It was rumored we were going to Siberia, and our mood sank to the bottom.† But after three days our trip ended in what was obviously a German town, for the railway men who were working around the cars were speaking openly about Frankfurt an der Oder. So I landed in the Horn Camp at Frankfurt-Oder.‡ There we had to take all our clothes off and stand naked in the street in front of the

---

* It was not unusual for German officers who had been imprisoned by the Americans and who were released into the Soviet zone of occupation to be taken prisoner again by Soviet military authorities.

† Between 11 and 12 million Germans were prisoners of war. Of these, 8 million were in Western hands, generally American. Although most German prisoners of war returned home in 1948, this was not the case for the approximately 3 million Germans in Soviet POW camps. It was not until more than ten years after the end of the war that the last Germans in Soviet captivity returned to West Germany. Of the 3 million German prisoners of war in the USSR, only 2 million returned alive.

‡ The Horn Camp in Frankfurt an der Oder was the principal transit camp operated by the Soviets in Germany.

camp in order to be disinfected by a Russian woman doctor. She would pinch us here or there and then would call out: "Diphtheria 1," "Diphtheria 2," "Diphtheria 3." Thank God, I had diphtheria 3, which meant I was too emaciated to work in Siberia. There again we eked out a right miserable existence with inadequate provisions until our release.[141]

When I got out of Russian imprisonment, I didn't want to have to register [with the Soviet authorities] in Berlin.[142] Already during my imprisonment word had gone around that you should do anything to get into the Western occupation zones, that it was better to live in an earthen shack in the West with only a couple of potatoes to eat than to live under Russian control.[143] In any event, I wanted to get to my family [in the Western zone] as quickly as I could,[144] and so, with much luck and, yes, initiative, we took off.[145] Two of us in a three-week trek[146] through eastern Germany finally made it to the Elbe.[147] But already in 1945, the border was sealed off with Russian troops manning watch towers with orders to shoot. When I crept across the border, I was shot at.[148] Still, I made it over and about a week later[149] arrived at the[150] farmhouse near Minden[151] where my family had found refuge.[152] No one had seen me. I went to the farmhouse and only heard English being spoken. I thought to myself, "My God, what's going on here?" It turned out that my wife and mother-in-law and someone else were taking English lessons. She said, "The lesson is finished." So I was back home, and then the misery really began.[153]

MAGDALENE BECK

My name is Magdalene Beck.[1] I was born on 15 March 1914 in Hanau.*,[2] When I was six years old I was sent to a private school and stayed there four years. Then I transferred to a special girls' school, where I studied hoping to become a teacher.[3] In my last year of school we got a new school principal, a real 150 percent Nazi.[4] After he arrived, there were[5] two tracks to the Abitur: one in literature and natural science; the other we called the "pudding Abitur." On that track one was taught the barest minimum about the natural sciences and the rest was devoted to the household. We hadn't had that track until 1933.† It was typical of the Nazis that we suddenly had to take an examination in cooking, which was all part of "the German woman belongs at the hearth and bears soldiers for the Führer." A "Mother's Cross"

---

* A city in Hessen just east of Frankfurt am Main.

† The "pudding Abitur" can be traced back to the Weimar Republic. In the Third Reich, however, home economics was required of all girls before they could advance to the senior grades, and after the tenth grade girls could choose between two-year courses in languages or home economics.

was even awarded, a medal for having children!*,[6] In my last year of school,[7] in 1933 and 1934, there were continuous celebrations, and[8] every Monday morning the entire school had to assemble in the auditorium. Once another class went on strike and told everyone not to report to the auditorium. The school principal stood up and declared that this was "treason!" That was the word he used, "treason." "And the punishment for treason," he continued, "is death! In comparison to death, the punishment this class has received is mild." So instead of the traditional homily we heard such rubbish from him.[9] When he would give a speech, he would begin by saying, "My dear German virgins!" Naturally we'd all begin to sputter and stick our handkerchiefs in our mouths to keep from laughing. He noticed, of course, and said, "I repeat. My dear German virgins!" That really made an impression on me.[10] But those were my last impressions, since it was my last year of school.[11] I was eighteen[12] when the Third Reich began.[13] I can't think of a single teacher who ever sought to dampen my enthusiasm for National Socialism or ever said, "I don't care for Nazism." I think the teachers were perhaps somewhat afraid. There were teachers and pupils who made denunciations, although not at our school. There were children who denounced their own parents. So I'd like to believe that the teachers were afraid. It was easier for them to go along. Professor Baring, for example, he could have said to me, "Beware! Hitler is a rogue. Just wait and see where it will all end." But you know, I never would have believed him, which is probably another reason why he never said anything like that to me.[14]

During my last years of school,[15] beginning in 1930, I belonged to the youth movement of the Bunds, to what was then called the Jungnationale Bund. Later it became the Großdeutsche Bund. The overall leader was [Admiral von] Trotha.[16] Then 1933 came,[17] the year of the great historical event[18] when we were banned at the[19] last huge national convention of the Bunds at the Munster Camp.[20] I was a group leader at the camp.[21] There the entire Bund was dissolved,[22] outlawed by Baldur von Schirach,[23] who flew overhead in an airplane.[24] SA men were standing at the edge of the encampment.[25] What an atmosphere! It was boiling.[26] I remember the camp vividly.[27] In the middle was a flagpole surrounded by bundles of straw wrapped in cloth. The boys carried these bundles, singing some pretty grim songs. We asked, "What are you doing there?" "We're carrying a corpse to its grave, Balduria von Schirachia."[28] Our leaders weren't very keen on that for they feared it would produce conflict, but our boys went ahead and did it anyway.[29] Still, the whole event was endlessly sad[30] and the hardest thing any of us had ever

---

* The National Socialists introduced the Cross of Honor for German Mothers in 1938 for women bearing four or more racially pure and healthy children. Through September 1941, 4.7 million Mother's Crosses had been awarded.

experienced.[31] On Whit Sunday[32] there was a last parade past the admiral, the national leader of the Bunds,[33] and one by one the groups gradually,[34] sadly, returned home.[35]

So all at once it was over.[36] We were finished,[37] outlawed.[38] And our group was immediately[39] incorporated into the BDM.*[,40] By contrast, the boy groups were broken up. They were frightened of the boys, whereas they simply incorporated the girl groups into the BDM,[41] and we were offered leadership positions.[42] 1933 was an extraordinarily intense time. People were streaming into the organization. They didn't have enough leaders, and the situation was critical.[43] Our national leadership ordered us to reconcile with the Hitler Youth and participate. Our goal or mode of life had always been to contribute and cooperate[44]—I sought the group experience,[45] and when you live in a little city like Hanau,[46] you know the higher-ups in the Hitler Youth through school and other things. So we did our best. I did my best. As a result[47] I joined the BDM in 1933[48] and became a squad leader.[49] I did just what I had done before [in the youth movement].[50] We still did our group work.[51] We still had our "home evenings." We still sang our songs.[52] The Hitler Youth had simply appropriated all of our forms—only the greeting was different—and they acted as if everything had been their own invention.[53]

We weren't particularly interested in politics.[54] We only found politics irritating.[55] And that was our great error of omission and where our guilt begins. We didn't concern ourselves with political ideas and principles. Because we were young, because we were happy being together, we simply did what we had been doing before.[56] We attempted to adapt and tried to make the best of things in the BDM and to raise the standards a bit.[57] We didn't notice that in the meantime, underneath or over and above us, there was a completely different worldview. We simply didn't worry about that sphere. If only we had read *Mein Kampf*—and we all owned the book—if only we had read the book thoroughly.†[,58] We did sing a great deal,[59] and looking back, I'd have to say that National Socialist ideology[60] was conveyed most effectively in the songs we sang. They carried the message that you exist for the Volk, for your people, that you, individually, are nothing and that the Volk is ev-

---

* The Bund Deutscher Mädel, or Bund of German Girls, was founded in 1930 as an amalgam of different National Socialist organizations for girls. The BDM was designed to mold the "new German girl," who was to be physically fit, willing to sacrifice herself on behalf of the Volk, and who ultimately would bear and raise racially pure children for the Führer. In 1936, membership in the BDM became obligatory for racially suitable girls.

† Written (actually primarily dictated) in 1924 while Hitler was imprisoned in Landsberg after the abortive Beer Hall Putsch, the book sets forth Hitler's worldview, conceptions of a future National Socialist state and society, racial program, and plan to acquire living space in the East.

erything. Otherwise the ideology was transmitted through the work the girls did and through cultural activities. With the boys, there was much more military indoctrination. Reading them today, I can't believe the lyrics of the songs that we sang out so lustily back then. In the youth movement we at least sang old lancers' songs, [soldiers'] songs from a bygone era. Perhaps those songs weren't exactly appropriate for girls to sing. Still, the new songs, the ones by Baumann and Schirach, they were designed to prepare us for war.[61] I mean, Hans Baumann* was, when I think about it today, a catastrophe with his wonderful songs, songs that were wonderful to me. I'd have to struggle not to cry. They were sentimental. Hans Baumann himself later conceded, "I glorified war"—which meant that war was glorified for us as well.[62] But we were politically uneducated, we were naive and foolish.[63] Still, I never felt completely comfortable,[64] and so, after less than a year,[65] I left the BDM.[66]

By Easter 1934 I had my Abitur and made my way to the countryside[67] to join the Work Service[68] because I thought that *there* one could carry on the spirit of the youth movement[69] and because it was voluntary and moreover apolitical.[70] When I joined, it was still the Voluntary Work Service. So I became a work maid, earning twenty *Pfennigs* a day,[71] in Hessen, at Spangenberg, which lies south of Kassel. The camp wasn't in the town but outside, a half an hour away on foot.[72] The location of the camp was lovely, surrounded by forest and fields.[73] Still, it was a barracks' camp, and life was hard there.[74] So when I arrived at the Work Service camp, I had my problems.[75] A little troop of us, four or five "maids" or farmhands, would go out to the fields with the farmers.[76] Now that was hard, physical labor. I began thinning out beets. We worked in a row, so I had to be just as fast as the rest of them and worked incredibly hard to keep up. The rye harvest came later in the year. I'd climb up into the barn where the rye was unloaded. It was extremely heavy. I'd stand on the edge. I'd take the pitchfork with the rye and pass it to the back to the woman who would pack the rye and store it in rows. After an hour I thought I couldn't do it any longer. But I couldn't tell them that I had to give up. So I kept working. No one was more surprised than I when at four in the afternoon I still stood there. I was almost in a trance. I was unable to speak and about to collapse. But I didn't collapse. I stuck it out.[77] When one comes directly from school with an Abitur and has to work, really *work*, with Hessian farmers in the fields, well, then one is simply completely physically exhausted at the end of the day.[78] If we didn't do farm work, we had inside duty. Then we had cooking or laundry service. The camp had about forty girls and the leader, all of whom had to have their clothes cleaned.[79] I spent four weeks washing dishes and then four weeks washing clothes and then

---

* Hans Baumann (1914–88) was active in the youth movement in the 1920s. He was a committed Nazi and composer of songs for the Hitler Youth.

four weeks cooking.[80] I had never peeled potatoes in my life, and I was given a bucket full of them: "Now go peel those potatoes."[81] The loveliest part was in the morning when I was on kitchen duty. Everyone else had to get up at five o'clock in the morning, but we'd get up at four.[82] I really had to push myself.[83] But I did it, and I was as happy then as at any time in my life.[84]

There were a few advantages in having an Abitur. Once a week we had to give a report from the newspapers. Then it was always: "Women with Abitur to the front!"[85] So we had work or constant instruction. We were only free on Wednesday afternoons. It was very Prussian in the first camp.[86] There couldn't be any wrinkles in the wool blanket or the sheets on our beds, just as with soldiers. We were inspected, and the whole bed was torn apart if there was anything the least bit incorrect about the way it had been made. I had to learn how to do it—and in three minutes.[87] Eight of us stayed in a little room, with double bunk beds. We were all volunteers and came from all sorts of backgrounds. We were thrown together and became good comrades.[88] I can remember one, who had attended a convent school and was Catholic, would cry at night. I simply couldn't understand her. I'd always say, "But we have it so good here!" It didn't hurt anyone to work with the farmers.[89] After all, we came from a social class, from families that had effectively never had any contact with working-class children.[90] And in the youth movement of the Bunds we lived in a bell jar. We were always together with people just like ourselves, whose parents were alike. And now we were together with some-one like the girl from Silesia who had been abused by her father. As a result she had been sent by the authorities to the Work Service to get her away from her family. She came from the backwoods of Pomerania. It was apparently a very primitive family, which had nothing to do with the fact that she'd been abused. It was just that way. And she was with us and was always treated exceptionally nicely by the others.[91] For the first time in my life I experienced not printed words but real *people*, people of that sort. We'd always seen people like that from a distance. But now we established true rapport with them.[92] Especially coming fresh from the Abitur, it was so good to experience so dramatically that there are so many other things in this life and that in some of them you are the dumbest and most backward[93] and every salesgirl knows how to do them better than you.[94] And it was important for girls with an Abitur to come to a village and learn about the conditions there, to sleep next to a girl who had attended a Volksschule, and generally to learn about the whole situation of the other girl.[95] It was a transformative experience for many people.[96] Hitler introduced the Work Service[97] so that we would become one Volk. We were guided by such slogans, which we heard all the time.[98] I found it to be a magnificent experience from a human perspective. I wish everyone could have it.[99] If it were up to me, we'd have a work service again in the twinkling of an eye.[100]

[Since] I was deeply convinced of the importance of the Work Service,[101] I wanted to become a Work Service leader.[102] So I went to a leadership school south of Königsberg in the county of Preuß Eylau.*,[103] I was there during the winter, and it was brutally cold. We had to wash up in a former pigsty. There were bowls of water, and in the morning the water was either frozen or the early shift had heated the water in a tub. We had to run through the snow from the main house to the sty and back again. It didn't hurt us. I am still hardened by the experience.[104] For a half a year, as a leader in training on probation,[105] I was sent to Wutrinen in the county Allenstein,† in the southern part of East Prussia, where we lived in wooden barracks.[106] [Then] I became a camp leader in Reuß, in the county of Treuburg, which was then called Marggrabowa.‡ Back then the border was so close that at night the Poles would steal our bicycles out of our rooms, which we naturally had not locked. We'd see their tracks running through the meadows. I was camp leader there for a half a year.[107] I had thirty-six work maids. One of the work maids was a countess. Her father lived on an estate in Görlitz. It was 1936. By then the Voluntary Work Service had been renamed the Reich Work Service, but it was still voluntary [for women]. There I had work maids from Mazovia, who had never seen electric light and who had never traveled on a train, who were from villages in the backwoods, and I had cheeky girls from Berlin. But they all learned from one another.[108] It was a wonderful, lovely time.[109] And then[110] I was asked if I was prepared to go to Hinter Pommern.§ I went gladly.[111] We were continually being transferred, just like the soldiers.[112] We lived in a villa that had been expropriated and had our girls there.[113] We always used old manor houses.[114] In the spring of 1937[115] I was assigned to my last[116] camp, [at Burgkampen] in the county of Ebenrode.** Right smack dab in the middle of the East.[117]

In the winter of 1937 I was sent to Königsberg, to the district headquarters. We had to make preparations for the processions from East Prussia to the Reich Party Day celebrations.†† As camp leader, I had been present at the Reich Party Day in 1936,[118] in Nuremberg, of course. They certainly knew

---

* A town just south of Königsberg (Kaliningrad) in East Prussia, today Bagrationovsk in Russia.

† Allenstein is today the city of Olsztyn in Poland. Wutrinen was a village south of Allenstein.

‡ Then a town in East Prussia near the border with Poland, Treuburg today is Olecko in Poland.

§ The portion of Pomerania east of the Oder River. It became a part of Poland in 1945.

** Today Ebenrode is Nesterow in Russia.

†† The Reich Party Day was the annual convention of the Nazi Party held in September in Nuremberg from 1927 to 1939. The event was less the convention of a political party and more a spectacle designed to demonstrate the power and dynamism of the National Socialist movement.

how to organize celebrations that would sweep young people away. I stood there in a total daze. One simply can't underestimate the power of suggestion that flowed from those mass festivals, although I am someone who becomes enthusiastic very easily, who gets carried away. I got goose bumps.[119] Now, we had to organize ship and train transportation to the [1938] celebration. I enjoyed doing the work and did a good job, for my main talent is organizational.[120] It had the result that I left the Work Service.[121] Since I had been a Work Service leader,[122] I wanted to continue working with young people[123] and had planned for a long time to become a community welfare worker.[124] Things turned out as follows.[125] The authorities were desperately trying to find someone to work in family services in the Reich Youth Office.[126] So I went to Berlin, where I was made responsible for the district between the Silesian railway station and the Alexanderplatz.[127] It gave me incredible pleasure to organize that work.[128] I never once missed not having studied at university when I was doing this work.[129] I never received any support from anyone older than I, from higher-ups—I didn't even know the higher-ups.[130] I was truly independent and given complete responsibility.[131] It was wonderful work.[132] In Berlin[133] I really became acquainted with social work: the fourteen-year-olds who had left school and were unemployed, who found no apprenticeships, who simply had no idea what they were supposed to do. So we created what were called "reeducation camps" for the youth of the city. It was an action jointly coordinated by the Hitler Youth and the Labor Department, along with career counseling. The youth of the city was trained to do farm work. And that was a lovely and gratifying assignment for me. In the process we overlooked what National Socialism actually meant. We believed we were doing good.[134]

I was enthusiastic about National Socialism.[135] At the beginning of the Third Reich, of course, we rejoiced.[136] Many things made a positive impression on us.[137] There were so many good things,[138] and the successes were so visible. The unemployed were no longer on the streets.[139] These unemployed people would always hang out in front of the bars, drunk or not drunk. It was an awful burden for everyone when they were unemployed. And then Hitler came along and built the Autobahns and took so many people off the streets and gave them work.[140] Right from the beginning it was fascinating to see the unemployed vanish from the streets.[141] And I thought to myself, "He's the right man for the job, he helps the unemployed. You should join the Party." So I joined the Party.[142] And, because there were no more unemployed people, a certain calmness prevailed.[143] You could walk alone in completely deserted areas without anxiety. There were no criminals of that sort.[144] Throughout my time in Berlin[145] I would walk to work, past the zoo and then through the park. I'd return around midnight. I never had any trouble. I was never frightened. Never.[146] One was lulled by experiences like that.[147] I must confess that of all the times in my life, the carefree time was the 1930s.[148] You know, we talk about the "*Wirtschaftswunder*" today,* but the real economic miracle actually occurred before the Second World War after 1933.[149] And national pride and self-confidence grew, which had been very low since Versailles. One felt proud to be a German again.[150] Like when the Rhineland was liberated in 1936![†] You know, that was a real historical event, and we really celebrated.[151] There was this whole atmosphere, this sense[152] that things were happening,[153] that everything was about to take off.[154] Now, my father was downright "reactionary," as we said in those days. He was of the old school and not inclined to go along with the National Socialists, whereas we younger ones were taken with them.[155] I remember a conversation with my father and brother on the subject, probably near the end of the 1930s.[156] My father said, "Keep your distance. That's an evil man."[157] And the two of us, we replied, "Oh, Father!" we said. "You're old," that's what we said. "You've lived your life, but we have to have something to inspire us, something we can devote ourselves to."[158] It was a wonderful period in my life.[159] We were together and had the feeling to be out there, doing something different, experiencing something different.[160] At the beginning of the war it was still bearable, but then it became difficult. And the postwar period and the last years of the war, they were very bad, very hard.[161] But until the war it was a wonderful time.[162]

I experienced the outbreak of the war[163] in Münster at the district leadership.[164] We were directed to go to the railway station to provide assistance to the Wehrmacht trains passing through.[165] The trains traveling east were depressing, filled with soldiers and mounted with huge artillery pieces.[166] They were filled with soldiers who had been in training in camps in the north, on the heaths of Schleswig-Holstein. They came with bouquets of heather. It was September.[167] There was no jubilation, no songs.[168] We were supposed to hand them cups of tea. But they didn't want tea. They wanted newspapers. They wanted to know what was happening, how things were going. I remember that every time there was laughter and waving and then, when the trains had left the station, I had to cry bitterly and wondered which of them would return.[169] It was a bitter time.[170] Who knows how many of them died at the front?[171]

---

* The Wirtschaftswunder refers to the rapid expansion of the West German economy during the 1950s.

† According to the terms of the Versailles Treaty, the Rhineland was to be demilitarized. On 7 March 1936 German troops crossed the Rhine and established a series of military bases west of the river. Seen as an act that "broke the chains of Versailles," the remilitarization of the Rhineland was greeted with popular enthusiasm in Germany.

My fiancé was drafted on the first day of the war.[172] I had met my first husband at a party to which I'd been dragged against my will by my girlfriend.[173] She brought me and my husband together by telling him about me. He had been with her brother in a [youth movement] group, the Geusen.* She had told him about me. And my husband said, "Oh, I'd like to get to know her." So it happened.[174] After the first glance, everything was all over for me. Later he told me that it was the same for him. We didn't actually dance with each other all that much.[175] We had endless things to talk about.[176] It was 1938, a wonderful time.[177] We decided to get engaged during the Sudeten Crisis.[†,178] It was interesting psychologically—the whole world of that age was getting engaged then. I was twenty-four, and the world around us was pairing up. It was a sort of [mass] psychology. Perhaps everyone saw the war coming.[179]

I continued working in social services.[180] Otherwise we couldn't have afforded to get married.[181] We did finally get married after he'd passed his civil service exams. He had been sent directly to the West Wall and was given leave to take his exams in October 1939. Then things began to get delayed. Maybe he didn't want to get married so much, for he'd say, "I don't want to make my bride into a widow." It turns out he was prescient.[182] But then we got married in 1940,[183] in February 1940 on an ice-cold day, twenty-five degrees below zero,[184] on a day when Hitler delivered a speech in the Reichstag. We had to delay our church wedding, because nothing could happen during a speech by the Führer. Everything was delayed by two hours. We barely managed to get through our civil ceremony before the speech began. At the registry [where the civil ceremony was held] we received not the Bible but, bound in black like the Bible and in gold script, *Mein Kampf*, with the dedication: "To the young couple." That survived [the war]. Of all things, that survived.[185] So then we had our wedding,[186] and then we had a week.[187] We used every minute so we'd have as much of one another as we could. It was a sort of bright spot in the middle of 1940.[188] I remained in Berlin,[189] while my husband was sent to France,[190] not to the front but as part of the occupation.[191] When he would come home on leave, it was a bit strange. Later, when he was in the middle of Russia, it was stranger still.[192] He was sent to the Russian front, to the East.[193] He never saw action until the beginning of the Russian

---

* A right-wing youth movement Bund founded in 1919 with pronounced *völkisch* leanings.

† The Sudeten Crisis unfolded over the course of 1938, with the organization of Sudeten Germans living in Czechoslovakia and Hitler demanding the incorporation of the Sudetenland, an area in northern Bohemia bordering Germany with 3.2 million ethnic Germans, into the German Reich. By early September 1938, Europe appeared on the brink of war. War was averted when England, France, and Italy largely capitulated to German demands in signing the Munich Agreement on 29 September 1938. The agreement transferred the Sudetenland to Germany and made other territorial adjustments demanded by Poland and Hungary. Czechoslovakia thereby lost one-third of its population.

campaign,[194] first in Lithuania and then up there in Leningrad, Novgorod. Finally he was transferred to the south, to Kiev, and experienced the retreat there. He was wounded numerous times, a couple of times there.[195] Then East Prussia was brought into the action, and he was wounded again. He was wounded a total of five or six times. I can't remember anymore whether he was wounded five times and fell the sixth time, I can't remember anymore.[196] So at the very end he was sent to East Prussia to defend the eastern frontier. In December of 1944 he wrote me where he was: "We aren't actually permitted to write where we are, but you know this place very well." He was in my last camp, which I had helped to build myself.[197] He was at the neighboring manor house, and at that manor house was where he fell. I suspect that something of the sort occurs pretty infrequently in the annals of war. [Later] when I received the news that he had fallen in Burgkampen, it was confirmed. But when I learned where he was and that the Russians had broken through, I said to my mother, "He'll never get out of there. It's all flat and even." He was never buried, of course. The Russians rolled right through. It was on the 14th of January 1945. I only learned of his death in April.[198]

So, my husband was drafted, and then we got married, and then my first child was on the way.[199] I allowed myself to be given a leave of absence to "Uphold One's Duty to the Family."[200] My first child was born in 1941.[201] A year[202] later I was pregnant with my second child and had to manage the birth all by myself.[203] My daughter was born on the 25th of December 1942.[204] My husband returned frequently on leave, at times as a result of being wounded, so that on 17 August[205] 1944 my third child was born. I was even faster than my mother had been in producing three children.[206] My youngest daughter[207] was born in Altdamm.[208] My husband never saw his son,[209] for my husband died in 1945, in January.[210] The boy was already on the way when he died. I had the feeling that things were different than when the girls were born, so we were both sort of expecting a boy. At least my husband knew that when his life came to an end.[211]

So I had a lot to deal with during my husband's military service.[212] In 1942 I was reactivated[213] and transferred for nearly a year to Stuttgart, where I was put in charge of[214] a home up at Waldau for 140 women streetcar conductors, conductor maids, doing their second year of war service.[215] I asked, "I already have one child and another[216] is on the way; how can I possibly work?" They replied, "Oh, we'll give you a nanny." So I received a nanny and household helper.[217] Someone from the National Socialist Frauenschaft* came to my house, looked over my household, my daughter,[218]

---

* The NS Frauenschaft was the Nazi Party women's organization, whose purpose was to support women, primarily within the home and family.

and me, and sent a "service-year girl" to help with the household.* She was a girl who had just finished school, sixteen or fifteen years old, very nice, and a big help to me. In those days there were no washing machines, no vacuum cleaners, and so forth, and as a result, there was a lot to do. We got along well.[219] In general, the Third Reich was a very children-friendly state,[220] and I have often thought that one could easily institute a service-year girl program again. It was a lovely arrangement.[221]

So in 1942, my husband was on leave again, and again, on leave for being wounded,[222] and I was supposed to begin working in Stuttgart,[223] but I wasn't entitled to live in Stuttgart.[224] So there I sat with one child and another on the way[225] and didn't know where to go. Our district [Party] leader inquired of the Gau leadership, and the Gau leadership allocated an apartment to me in Haigerloch,[226] which had previously belonged to a Jew.[227] Haigerloch is one of many little towns that had a large Jewish community. They were all livestock dealers and lived good lives. Haigerloch is on the edge of the Swabian Alb, charming and beautiful, and descends steeply down into the Eiertal. We were given a large,[228] six-room apartment[229] that had been abandoned by Jews, directly on the slope,[230] with steps leading steeply down into the Jewish quarter. There wasn't a single Jew left, but for some reason being in this apartment sent shivers up my spine. We were told that they had been deported to work in the East. I didn't know what that meant, and I didn't inquire further. Had I known, I couldn't have continued to live there. I didn't want to know, just as so many others didn't. When I moved into the apartment, it was ice-cold. It was exposed to the east wind and had old windows. In any event, we lived up there, and a Slovenian family lived underneath us. The Slovenians had been resettled by Hitler because they could be Germanized, and he wanted to be able to push southward without harming them.[231]

Long after the war my daughter[232] asked me, "Mommy, how did you experience Kristallnacht?"† I tried terribly hard to recall: "Actually not at all." But the younger generation doesn't believe it.[233] I didn't really know any Jews. Those that had been in my school suddenly disappeared. They emigrated in time, thank God, and I didn't experience any loss in that regard.[234] In chemistry our teacher was Dr. Lederer, who of course had to go away later

---

* Following the passage of a law on 1 January 1939, all girls and women under the age of twenty-five were required to perform a year of public service as a precondition of employment.

† The infamous Night of Broken Glass, a pogrom against German Jews that occurred on 9 and 10 November 1938. SA men, other members of the Nazi Party, and ordinary Germans destroyed synagogues, seven thousand Jewish-owned businesses, and twenty-nine department stores. Jewish homes, schools, and community centers were demolished. During the course of the pogrom, at least ninety-one people were killed. Approximately twenty-six thousand Jews were sent to the concentration camps of Dachau and Buchenwald.

because he was a Jew.[235] And the girls' school [I attended] still had a Jewish pupil in 1933. She later had to disappear, of course.[236] She was gone all of a sudden. Yes, she was gone. Yes, one knows . . . One asked once, "Where are the Levis?" That was their name. "Where have they gone?" One was never able to find out. But it really didn't have much of an impact on me, you know.[237] I remember neighbors in Berlin,[238] they shared a balcony with us. It was a mixed marriage. The woman was a Jew, and they had a little daughter.[239] Then I heard that her husband had left her.[240] The man had divorced his wife on account of her race.[241] She was taken away, and the child was taken along, and they were never heard from again.[*,242]

For me, the Nazis . . . But that we had negatively . . . There were so many things I just didn't know about. One has to accept the fact. It's simply so.[243] I must honestly say that we had absolutely no experience of this other side of National Socialism.[244] Those things, the concentration camps, not to speak of the extermination of the Jews?[245] We knew little about those . . . About those gassings, we knew absolutely nothing.[246] I know it sounds unbelievable, but it's so. It's terrible, but it's so and resulted from naiveté, I realized later.[247] But we did know—I knew—that the Jews were discriminated against.[248] When I lived in Berlin,[249] there were a few stores boarded up with nails. I simply didn't think too much about it.[250] And in Berlin I experienced Jews with the Jewish Star.[251] I remember when the Jewish Star was introduced.[†] There was a residential area along the Grünewaldstrasse where a large number of Jews lived. I saw elderly people there with the Jewish Star. They slunk along the street—they looked so frightened, I'd have to say. I thought to myself, "That simply can't be."[252] And then I once saw in the Bachstrasse[253] that people were being transported away.[254] I once saw that Jews with stars . . . and actually numerous families, Jewish families, lived there.[255] But then I saw . . . I came, I can still remember exactly, I came from the side, and saw that Jews were literally being herded together. I saw it, and I looked away, and I thought about something else. I continued on my way and didn't get upset about it. How can something like that happen or that one registers what is actually happening? But I know I saw it. I can still see it exactly before my eyes. They wore the star and were literally being herded together on the

---

* Jewish people married to non-Jews were afforded a certain protection in the Third Reich. Although some Jews married to Aryans ultimately perished in the Holocaust and all experienced discrimination and persecution, they avoided deportation longer, and many, indeed most, appear to have survived. By divorcing his wife, this neighbor probably condemned her and their daughter to deportation and death.

† The Jewish Star was introduced on 20 August 1941. After 19 September 1941 all Jews over the age of six were required to wear the yellow six-pointed star on their left breast. This ordinance completed the process of the exclusion of Jews from German society and signaled the beginning of their deportation to extermination camps in the East.

street. And in retrospect I consider that to be our guilt, that we didn't concern ourselves about it. I thought about prettier things than about that. Already after taking three steps I was thinking about something else. I basically didn't acknowledge it to myself, although I still know it and can still see the picture exactly before me. Back then, I—I won't say I repressed it—I simply didn't consciously acknowledge it, not consciously.[256]

But specific knowledge, no, we didn't have that.[257] Later, of course, but earlier one simply had no idea. I can recall how I once traveled from Leipzig to Reichenbach, it only came to me later, really. A railway car stood there in Altenbaum, and there were people inside. I think they wore blue and white striped uniforms. It was a curious business, but I couldn't figure out what was happening. It probably had something to do with the concentration camps. But you know, I didn't give it much thought.[258] I had heard that there were concentration camps and that Jews had come to them. But I'd assumed that concentration camps were work camps, in the way I knew work camps, perhaps with slightly harsher restrictions, such as not being able to leave, that one had to remain for better or for worse, that one was basically imprisoned.[259] Furthermore, one heard unbelievably many rumors. My grandparents lived in a village relatively close to Flossenbürg,* relatively close but still far away. A soldier, also from the village, home on leave, once said to me [when I was visiting], "Do you know? Do you know?" In other words, a peculiar odor in the air. "Do you notice?" And I said, "No, I don't. I don't have a very good nose." He said, "In Flossenbürg Jews are being gassed." "What?" I replied. "Gassed?! What do you mean by that?" I said, "That's completely impossible. I can't . . . How could that happen? I can't . . ." I couldn't begin to imagine that such a thing was possible. He claimed he knew. He never told me how he knew. But I couldn't imagine that such a thing was possible, that there were gas chambers into which Jews were driven. That couldn't . . . I thought that so . . . That was beyond my ability to fathom. Today one can so easily say that, I know. But that was something monstrous, you know. One cannot imagine how tightly, how tightly the Nazis kept their . . . how tightly secret they kept it. Yes. That, that, that one didn't know. Also one didn't have . . . yes . . .[260] We had no idea. You know, that is sometimes . . . Only those in the higher echelons in part, perhaps they had more knowledge. But we? We had no knowledge about it.[261] These death [camps], these terrible cruelties, I only learned about those after the war. But that's not an excuse, and I expect you'll hear the same from many others.[262]

Everything changed completely after [the war]. I now know the historical facts and know the truth and know . . . But I have to say I honestly didn't

---

* A town in the Upper Pfalz in Bavaria. A concentration camp was established there in 1938. Approximately thirty thousand people died in the camp.

know what went on in the concentration camps. I knew they existed, for all of a sudden our pastor was gone. And it was said: "He has gone to a concentration camp." And after about a year, there he was again. We heard nothing from him—naturally, they were silent, they weren't allowed to speak about what they'd experienced.[263] Very many people [were afraid]: "For heaven's sake, don't say anything, don't express your opinions, don't expose yourself, otherwise something will happen to you."[264] You are asking someone to resist who knows exactly what will happen to him and to his family if he opposes such a dictatorial regime. He'll implicate his whole family. You try that! You try that![265] You would have been stood up against a wall![266] But no one understands! No one understands anymore.[267] I remember that we had a technician of some sort and he listened to a foreign radio station, stupidly along with the woman who owned his apartment, or she caught wind of it, I don't know. Anyway, she reported him. He was sent to an army penal company.[268] And in Stuttgart[269] an editor was arrested for making fun of the Nazis. He apparently knew a good deal about internal issues. It was said he was shot trying to escape.[270] And on the advertising columns I can still remember seeing a large poster announcing that a twelve-year-old boy had reported his parents for subversion. Both parents were executed. One could see such a thing on an advertising column, and it was horrible. Such things happened all the time. Can you imagine what sort of an impact such things had? And all of this occurred at a time when a human life had no value. All that built on itself and simply terrified people.[271] And there is something else. The first years were the years of reconstruction.[272] Things were getting better.[273] To everything else that went on, one said, "My God, it will all improve, these are only the first years."[274] We always believed that Hitler had freed us from unemployment and had done heaven only knows how many other good things for the people.[275] Economically things were easier during that period.[276] Then, after six years, the war came along, and the war dominated everything.[277] The war and all that it caused restricted our view.[278] For us, in living our lives, it simply meant: "We must survive the war." We never thought much about why the war came.[279] And then of course the war was over, and we experienced a terrible end of the war, you know.[280] Our worry about survival stood at the center of our consciousness. I only experienced the Nuremberg trials* on the edges, I only experienced the political on the edges: all these revelations, and the lost war, and the central worry about survival.[281] When one has nothing

---

* The most famous of the trials against the Nazi leadership. The trials took place between 20 November 1945 and 1 January 1946 before an international military tribunal. At Nuremberg, twenty-two politicians, officials, and leaders of Germany's armed forces were prosecuted by the Allies. Of these, twelve were sentenced to death (the most famous being Hermann Goering), three were acquitted, and seven were sentenced to prison for between ten years and life.

to eat oneself, then one doesn't say to oneself, "You deserved it all." Instead one tries to see where one is. One has to come to terms with one's own fears, the fears in the air raid bunkers, during the raids, when one . . . Then one doesn't think about others but about oneself.[282]

I still have anxiety dreams about the times I literally had to run for my life in Berlin. When I hear a sound like a siren or a cuckoo's call, then I wake up or I dream—dreams where I run and run and am held back for some reason.[283] The raids were horrible.[284] I was in a neighborhood in Berlin, not where I lived but where I worked. And we had to go far to reach the bunker at the railway station.[285] And of course the railway station was one of their targets. Whenever there was an air raid siren, we had to run.[286] We had to run with the spent antiaircraft shells already crashing to the ground.[287] Sometimes I didn't make it to the bunker, and I'd see the bombs falling in the sky.[288] Sometimes we were in the city park during the worst raids. One lay down flat on the ground under a tree.[289] It still haunts me a bit.[290] A couple of times in the night—but you forget about it afterward. It belongs to the past, and you try to repress it. But it still comes back up again, out of the unconscious.[291]

On Christmas Day, 1942, I had my second child and two months later returned to Berlin from Stuttgart—just as[292] the severity of the war reached Berlin, with massive air raids.[293] I hadn't been there four weeks before the first heavy raids began.[*,294] We had had continuous air alarms, of course. One went into the cellar with the children. And then came the Stalingrad catastrophe,[†] and one realized that the war was coming to an end and the bombing was ever heavier and came ever closer.[295] We knew that massive raids were going to be launched by the Americans and the English. They were only waiting for favorable weather conditions.[296] In the course of the year 1943—already in the spring of 1943—our lovely apartment suffered partial damage. Then in the summer of 1943, in August, again more damage, but without losing anything.[297] The parents of my husband, they lost everything in the bombing.[298] Then Berlin was evacuated, and I went to my parents, who were then living in Frankfurt, thinking, "Here nothing bad will happen,"[299] [since] heavy bombing hadn't started [there] yet.[300] And then all hell broke loose.[‡,301] The first raid lasted from twelve until six in the morning.[302] I had the children,[303] and we stood down there in the cellar, our only protection being what was over our heads.[304] One had seen, heard that whole houses had collapsed, and that people who were in the cellar were either instantly

---

* The first major Allied air raids against Berlin were launched in March 1943.
† The battle for Stalingrad resulted in a crushing and highly publicized German defeat with the surrender of the Sixth Army on 31 January and 2 February 1943.
‡ The first major raid against Frankfurt was launched on 4 and 5 October 1943, but the city was not the target of further significant Allied bombing until March 1944.

killed or never brought out again.[305] I heard of one instance[306] when coupled explosive and incendiary bombs crashed from the roof down into a cellar. And in the cellar, because the building contained a café and at the café there had been a wedding, in the cellar were seventy wedding guests. All of them perished in the cellar.[307] But we were in the cellar of a large house made out of stone near the edge of town.[308] At six when the all clear was sounded, we came out and could see the city burning. The seven church spires were burning torches, which didn't collapse but stood in flames.[309] And then[310] in March 1944[311] we were totally bombed out, totally burned down.*,[312] The whole house burned down.[313]

So we were bombed out,[314] and I went to Altdamm, outside of Stettin,[315] with my mother.[316] I moved to my sister-in-law,[317] who had asked me to live with her.[318] It was there, during an air raid on Stettin,[319] that I had the child.†,[320] Altdamm is about ten kilometers east of Stettin.‡,[321] When the low-flying planes came, then we caught it too.[322] But at night the [Allied] air force squadrons would bomb Stettin.[323] The entire sky was red, and there we sat.[324] When the parachute flares were shot off, it looked fantastic. What a wonderful fireworks display, if only it weren't all so sad.[325] Five months[326] after we were bombed out, our [third] daughter was born. It was really quite lovely, to come through the flames and through the bombs.[327] It was really a unique experience, when one emerges from the bunker and: "I'm still alive, and the sun is shining, and I can still breathe, and things still exist even if there is rubble all around, but the earth is still there, and the trees are still there." Normally one doesn't have this experience of physical life. I'd not have missed that experience for the world.[328] Apart from daily life, one's existence during the war was basically comprised always only of anxiety and yearning. That was one's essence. But one lived life to an unimaginable degree with an eerie intensity, an eerie intensity. In part it was due to the notion that today is perhaps one's last.[329]

It was while we were in Altdamm that[330] the period of the steady downfall began, always dressed up, always broken up, with vague hopes, such as especially the whole idea of the V2 and the V1.§,[331] And I began to hear from friends from the East, above all from East Prussia, about experiences

---

* A series of Allied raids on Frankfurt between 18 and 23 March 1944 killed about 1,500 people and left 175,000 homeless.

† On the night of 16 and 17 August 1944, the British launched a major raid against Stettin, killing more than a thousand people.

‡ Today Dąbie in Poland, Altdamm was a city of about sixteen thousand inhabitants in 1939. Stettin is today the city of Szczecin in Poland.

§ Abbreviation for the so-called Miracle Weapons, a flying bomb and a missile, which were supposed to turn the tide of the war. Of almost no military value, these weapons were essentially the last arrow in the quiver of the Propaganda Ministry in its efforts to sustain popular faith in German victory.

of flight.[332] The women had begun to be evacuated and[333] beginning in January [1945] we experienced uninterrupted refugee treks[334] from the East, people moving west. Individual soldiers who had lost their units also passed by in tattered uniforms. All that was moving from east to west can hardly be described.[335] The fighting became worse, always worse, and the Russians came ever closer,[336] and there we sat, in the deep snow, watching the treks pass by, and heard about the horrors of freezing to death and children dying and so forth.[*,337] We experienced everything more or less at a distance until early 1945, when the danger was really there,[338] for the Russians were approaching. Their first armored units had been seen along the Oder-Neisse River.[†,339] So there we sat in Altdamm,[340] and on came the Russians.[341] Then we received a notice instructing women with little children to prepare to be transported out.[342] And of course we had to get out.[343] So I said to my mother, "If you ask me, we should try to get to the Elbe."[344] My mother,[345] as nervous as she was, said, "Oh, God! We must flee too!" We had heard so much from East Prussia about how women were being raped there, and she wanted to get out.[346] So she made up her mind. And my father had said to me once, "I can't help you. Distance yourself from the Russians. That's my advice to you." You can probably imagine how it was. My mother was forty-nine years old in 1944, and my sister-in-law and I were twenty-five and thirty respectively.[347] We were all ripe enough for the Russians. My only enlightenment on the subject had come from my mother, who once said to me, "If you ever have a Russian child"—she never told me how this would happen—"we'll figure out a way to get rid of it." That was the only thing of the kind she ever said to me.[348]

And then came the hard time, of which my children, the two girls, have very bad memories.[349] We had to . . . and we were ordered by the NSDAP—I was expecting my fourth child—ordered to attach ourselves to a trek, in the middle of winter, a freezing cold winter. It was terrible.[350] In any event, my sister-in-law,[351] with her two[352] children, and[353] I, with my three little children and my mother, set off[354] with seven suitcases and all sorts of things[355] in a child's wagon, packed full up.[356] My mother and I had knitted little backpacks for the children from underwear. I had the baby in an old-fashioned quilted comforter with a little featherbed. And my mother had a rucksack and I had one too, each filled with underwear and some food.[357] So we made

---

* When Soviet forces reached East Prussia in October 1944, waves of refugees began fleeing west. Because the authorities refused to allow the civilian population to leave until the last minute, the refugees generally had to flee on foot or in horse-drawn carts just in front of the advancing Red Army in the middle of winter.

† By 20 February 1945, Soviet forces had reached the Oder south of Stettin, although in the north the Germans were able to halt the Russian advance. It was only by 31 March that the Red Army reached the Oder at Stettin.

our way through the German countryside.[358] Shortly before I had gotten sick somehow. I had a high fever, and my infant was also sick,[359] and there were low-altitude attacks from the English in those last days.[360] I really can't remember very much about this first attempt to escape. I had to struggle through.[361]

First we fled to Berlin to the sister of my mother, Aunt Luzi. She took us in with five children and was happy that we were there.[362] In the meantime my father had arrived from Danzig. He had been drafted into the Volkssturm* and had been sent to Danzig, and woe to anyone who didn't believe in the final victory, for that person would be locked up. My father simply shook his head and arrived with only a briefcase that contained all the things he thought valuable. It took him eight days to get from Danzig to Berlin, and he had terrible experiences. He arrived half starved and half frozen. What he related was horrible: how the women who were with him in the train, how their children froze to death, even though they were snugly wrapped in blankets and comforters. They threw their dead children out the window. My father said that only those who had kept their babies next to their bare stomachs, who had used their own body heat, managed to save their children.[363] After a short time we managed to settle in, but[364] we knew[365] that the Russians would make straight for Berlin.[366] That we knew, and[367] fortunately we had a place of refuge where we could go.[368] We had made arrangements to go to Neuhaus, just east of the Elbe, near Lüneburg.[369] My brother, my eldest brother, who later fell on 2 May 1945, had his in-laws in Lüneburg. They[370] lived on a [nearby] knight's estate[371] and had invited us to come there.[372] We tried to meet at this estate. That was our goal.[373]

We took the train from Berlin to Wittenberge.[374] There were all sorts of people in the waiting room. I had drummed into the children . . . You have to remember that it was 1945. It was prohibited to flee, for that would testify to the defeat. It was an experience my two daughters will never forget. We'd drummed the following story into them: "You are to say that your grandmother has suddenly gotten ill and she's all alone. We have to go and help her." You can't imagine what it's like to put little children under that kind of pressure. "You aren't to say anything else." What a burden.[375] Somehow or other, we made it. We landed in Neuhaus,[376] and of course there was quite a reception.[377] There I learned for the first time that my sister, who had a little son five years old, had been killed during a bombing raid. Her son had survived and was there. The men were all at the front.[378] So all of us who were still alive and could manage to get there collected in[379] this little nest,

---

* Created by order of the Führer on 25 September 1944, the Volkssturm was a sort of Nazi National Guard comprised of men between the ages of sixteen and sixty, generally unfit for military service, who had not been drafted into the Wehrmacht.

Neuhaus on the Elbe, near Lüneburg.[380] And it was there, in the beginning of April, that I was notified of the death of my husband.[381] I can still see myself sitting at the window. The mayor of the little town came from the village directly up the road, and I knew that he was bearing the news that my husband had fallen. I went out with him. I told him I knew where Burgkampen was. He brought me the official written news of my husband's death, and I went down to the milk collection point to get milk. We had no time to work that through, for we had to care for the children and my mother and by then our situation had become critical.[382]

We lived in[383] a former *Kindergarten* in a former barn [on the estate]. We were able to set up beds there, metal beds left over from some camp or other. There was no room for my father. He had to sleep in the corridor. We had a dark little kitchen, without electric light or windows, but we had our burners and my mother was blissful that she could cook.[384] We were actually renters, for the Kindergarten where we were staying belonged to the estate owner. She was a rich, self-confident woman, and we were beggars. We had come there as refugees. When there was an air raid, she had two cellars, and she wouldn't allow us into the cellar when we were under attack. She said that we could dig a ditch in the farmyard or in the garden and take shelter there. My father said, "The whole thing is nonsense. If a bomb lands on the house, they're in just as much danger as we are here." So we'd lie up against the wall, all together in the straw, thinking that if a bomb hits one of us, it hits us all. And thank God a bomb didn't hit us.[385] There was fighting until the bitter end. There were SS in the forest, and[386] my father stationed himself at the window and would say, "Look at those shots coming in." There was an antiaircraft gun a little way behind us, a hundred meters into the forest. They would shoot at that. My father would sit at the window and say, "Boy, do they shoot badly." He was never afraid. I was supposed to come and look. And I said, "For God's sake, no. I don't want to." So I stayed with the children. I simply pressed the children against me.[387] One experienced a lot at the end of the war.[388] I experienced the collapse, and the entry of the Americans into the town.* It was really an unforgettable experience, or rather many experiences. This entry occurred during April.[389] And then I also remember[390] sitting together listening to the radio. My father was there too. And we heard that Hitler was dead.† And my father said, "Oh, now he's dead." Just like that. We both looked at one another and didn't really know what to do. The news didn't make us very happy.[391] I didn't feel as if I had been freed from

---

* It seems likely that Neuhaus was occupied by units of the U.S. Eighteenth Airborne Corps. The Americans were subsequently replaced as occupiers, probably by units of the British Second Army.

† Hitler committed suicide in his bunker in Berlin on 30 April 1945.

Hitler. I felt as if we had lost the war.[392] And then on the 8th of May came the official surrender.[393]

Later the Russians would arrive, but the Americans were our first occupiers, and the way the Americans acted, it wasn't fine.[394] They had every woman between the ages of eight and eighty examined for venereal disease in the district hospital. That was obviously quite unpleasant. There was a German doctor there, however, and he treated us pretty gently. The Americans had declared that fraternization was forbidden because all German women had venereal disease or something like that. That wasn't exactly fine.[395] We did all have lice.[396] And along came the Americans to deal with that right away. We had to present ourselves. So there we all stood, the entire family, about fifteen of us, and they sprayed us, and that was the end of the lice.[397] Otherwise they didn't do anything to us.[398] When the British arrived, they conducted themselves better, but they didn't seem to love us very much either.[399] In those days you had to take what the foreigners did to you. Of course, with the Americans there were blacks. We had a terrible fear of the blacks back then. They gave the children candy. I told the children not to touch the candy, since it could be poisoned. The candies were lying on the table, and a white officer came in and looked at it and said, "What's going on in here, Kindergarten?" And I replied: "Yes, it's my Kindergarten." "And the candies, why are they lying on the table? Why aren't you eating them?" I can't remember anymore what excuse I came up with, but he was clearly suspicious. They meant well, but one didn't know. During the war we heard all sorts of things, such as "The Russians will rape all the women" and "The Americans and British will poison you or commit other scandalous acts." One didn't know and was frightened.[400]

Then one[401] afternoon, there were notices nailed to all the trees: "Comrades, the Russians are coming. Whoever has a clear conscience can remain. Nothing will happen to him."* The [German] soldiers knew already what was up, and those who could swam across the Elbe. I wanted to get over the Elbe too. I had a terrible fear of the Russians and wanted to go to the Elbe, but my father said, "You can't swim across the Elbe. The Americans are on one side, and the English on the other. There's no point in trying."[402] So, although we were frightened of the Russians,[403] we decided to stay where we were.[404] We formed a little circle of people, and all of them listened to what I had to say. I said that we should stay where we were. So we stayed[405] and let happen what would happen.[406] Perhaps we shouldn't have, given what happened later, especially to my sister-in-law, who had such strikingly blond hair and was constantly being pursued. But somehow or other I made up for that.

---

* Soviet forces occupied the lands east of the Elbe in the north of Germany, including Neuhaus, in July 1945.

I mean, there was nothing I could do about it, and she didn't blame me for it and wasn't angry at me. Fifty years have passed since then.[407]

So it finally came to pass that[408] the Russians arrived.[409] The others departed and then the[410] Russians marched in, that is, they came with their horse-drawn carts and everything. They didn't have tanks, at least not where we were.[411] There was a lot of fear, of course. And in the beginning a lot of [bad] things happened.[412] We gathered together in a cloister. There were twelve nuns, who were frightened and were glad that there were young people with them and above all children. Indeed, our children actually protected us from the worst dangers, since the Russian is incredibly fond of children.[413] Still, there were many difficult moments.[414] But then we made friends with our commandant, the Russian commandant, and with his translator and the others around him. And again and again he was able to protect us when there was danger.[415] It was an incredibly tumultuous time. I was just about to give birth, and somehow we managed the delivery with the help of those dear people who were with us.[416] He was the fourth. It was wonderful. Everything went smoothly. I had never had such an easy delivery.[417] In any event the very nice and attentive commandant was always ready to help us[418] and got milk for the children, but that was only for our small family circle. Others had a much rougher time.[419] There were Russians everywhere,[420] but the Russians didn't do anything to me.[421] At first I was still lying in, and then I was protected as a mother.[422] And later[423] they never really bothered me. I always wore a kerchief around my head and dressed simply.[424] One reason the Russians didn't do anything to me was because my father was there. He saved us countless times. He could speak a little Russian.[425] I remember once, it was summer, and I was wearing a white dress. One of them wanted to grab me, and he said to the man, "Hey there, watch it." The Russian noticed that there was a man with me. But that's how the Russians were. They could be terribly friendly, but at a moment's notice they could treat you in the opposite way. Above all they loved children. But it was not an easy time. Many things happened,[426] but fortunately nothing happened to me.[427] I had such nice friends in my youth movement group, and one unfortunately took her life after she with her children had been raped in Berlin.[428] And my aunt who had remained behind in her house with her dog took her own life when the Russians were there.[429]

So we spent two years[430] in the Russian occupation zone.[431] I tried hard to feed us.[432] I went out to the farmers,[433] way out past the villages, and exchanged foodstuffs, as long as we still had a little.[434] At first I exchanged coffee ration coupons and things that had existed during the German period: cigarettes, coffee, etc.[435] Then I'd bring home a sack of provisions.[436] But you know, we had bad experiences with Germans. There were farmers who weren't upstanding.[437] I'd go down to the people in the valley and beg or attempt to barter, but we didn't have much of anything. They'd always say, "Why do you come here? You don't belong here."[438] The farmers weren't good to us. I had gotten a case of cigars from one of them, so I'd always go with a cigar and ask, "Do you have milk for my youngest daughter?" I'd be pretty upset, standing there with three children. And there the farmers would sit, baking with fat. My children would stand in the doorway waiting for milk, and the farmers wouldn't give me any. That was very bitter.[439] And later, when we didn't have anything to barter with anymore, then I worked, I sewed. Thank God I could sew, and I mended things for farmers.[440] I was fortunate to land with a very nice family—Timmermann was their name, the Timmermanns in Krusendorf. They let me sew, mending one shirt after the other.[441] At first I also helped out at the farmstead. I got things more cheaply, but I still had to pay because they weren't doing so well either.[442] Otherwise we ate horsemeat. When the war was over, and the soldiers were gone and their horses were running around, then the horses were slaughtered and a horse butcher would sell the meat. I would get up at two in the morning to stand in the line that had already formed, and we'd get a piece of horsemeat. But we didn't ever get that much meat or get meat that often,[443] and we experienced a great deal of hunger.[444] The endless standing in lines. Only to survive. All one's energy and thought went into survival. That was the real misery. There were people who were starving, and we didn't actually experience starvation.[445] We didn't starve, but we froze.[446]

We had simply dreadful living conditions and this terrible winter [of 1945–46]. We froze wretchedly.[447] Shortly after the baby was born, we had left the cloister and[448] lived in a room in Neuhaus[449] and had nothing to heat with. We only had a hot plate, and we only had beets to eat, and we only had electricity at night. I'd wake up because of the overwhelming smell of [cooking] beets and immediately begin to feel nauseous. That was really a bad winter.[450] We were happy when we had something to put on our feet. I knitted really thick socks for the girls using yarn unraveled from other stockings. And in a way, it wasn't so bad. It's better when one has to make something out of nothing than when one simply goes to the store to buy what one needs today.[451] So one way or another, we managed to make it through together. There were other relatives who helped care for us so that we were able to survive. Finally the winter of 1945 came to an end, and[452] we knew we'd made it through.[453]

When I look back, the worst time in my life occurred[454] in the last period of the war and then[455] right after the war, when everything was completely different all at once. I mean no one laid a finger on me, and we had enough to eat since we were in the country. But this total collapse of everything . . . It was bad[456] the way everything collapsed.[457] I threw away my membership identification for the health insurance, for example. It had no meaning anymore. That was the first hard thing. The second was that one noticed how one was lied to and cheated,[458] the way people suddenly became completely different,[459] the way every ideal that one had . . .[460] It was the inversion of all values. Nothing made sense anymore.[461] Although I had always been more socially than politically oriented, I was naturally labeled a [Nazi] fellow traveler, quite appropriately, I have to say. At some point I had joined the Party. I was never one of those fanatical Nazis, but I believed in it with all my heart and soul, and I worked for it. Once we had a huge fight over a book attacking the Reich Work Service. "But it was *so* lovely!" That's what I said. "It *was* so lovely." Of course it was lovely. But one thing is certain. With all the good work we did—and no matter where we were, we did good work—we supported the state. I swam in my East Prussian Work Service camps and felt completely good about myself. I felt I was exactly where I ought to be.[462]

In any event, when it finally became[463] clear that the[464] children wouldn't achieve anything under this [Soviet] political system,[465] we went over to the West.[466] We gave away as many of our possessions as we could, but we couldn't tell anyone we were planning to go to the West. My father had already swum across the Elbe[467] and had managed to take one of the children with him.[468] So at five o'clock in the morning my mother and I[469] set off, with the three children, for the second eldest was already over, with two rucksacks, in which we had a couple of plates of Meissen porcelain that we hoped to sell to have a bit of money. We ended up crossing the border by the skin of our teeth[470] with the help of German farmers and boatmen. We[471] traveled along the Elbe, where the river divided into something like two ditches with water, and made it to an island covered with reeds. Suddenly I saw an East German policeman on my left and a Russian soldier on my right. Then from over on the other bank of the Elbe came farmers or boatmen, I don't know which. They had come to collect reeds. For whatever reason, they had the right to take as many of the reeds as they wanted. And I said, "Please, gentlemen, take us[472] back with you." "What?" they replied. "We don't even know who you are. Why should we do that?" I said who I was and asked, "Do you know farmer Timmermann in Krusendorf?" "Yes," they replied. "We know him, of course." "Well, I once worked with him." So they took us[473] back with them, and we[474] got over and went to my[475] father, who was waiting for us in Lüneburg.

As refugees, we were given a temporary apartment.[476] We all lived together in an attic room.[477] We were each given forty Marks as welfare.[478] And every so often someone would give us something: a cup and that sort of thing. We were so happy to be together again; we could finally sleep. We ended up living in that attic room for two years.[479] We were all healthy,[480] and I had my children with me. We lived there in very close quarters, but that made no difference.[481] I did my best to find work and a [bigger] place to live and had the good fortune to find a Protestant minister who had recently been asked by an elderly woman if he knew people who could move into spare rooms in her house. He told her about me. So that's how we got an apartment. We had three rooms, I think, and a kitchen, a lovely, big, live-in kitchen. We were so happy.

And so we managed to cobble our lives together. We could sit around a large wooden table on a bench in the kitchen, and my little family was there. I had been on the right track when I was able to get that apartment because the next thing was that I was able to get a job, at a weaving mill. I managed to get a residency permit. Everything I managed to get on my own. And so we all lived together, my four children,[482] and Vati and[483] Mutti, in these three rooms. Despite everything, we were a happy and fortunate family. I remember my daughter,[484] who was six years old, said as we all sat around the table, "Even if we are poor, we are still a fortunate family."[485] She doesn't experience it all as having been so terrible, like when we slept on the floor of the school, where the Negroes were.[486] So, if one didn't have faith and belief in the family, who knows if we could have mastered all that befell us. But we did master it,[487] and so our postwar lives began.[488]

5

ANALYSIS

Extending the Collective in the Community of the *Volk*

Those interviewed greeted the advent of the Third Reich in January 1933 with enthusiasm.[1] In no small measure their excitement was based upon the expectation that the National Socialists would carry forward the positive experiences of the youth movement while responding to some of its limitations. One interviewee uses *Aufbruchsstimmung* to describe the mood of anticipation at the beginning of the Third Reich, a word that captures the feeling at the outset of a youth movement excursion.[2] The interviewees had the sense that "something exciting was happening!" and did not want to miss out on the adventure.[3] To Germans the age of those interviewed, the NSDAP *was* a "youth movement," a party of and for German youth which, in the words of E. Günther Gründel, would sweep aside "the rule of the old men" to establish a "Reich of Youth."[4] The National Socialists were modern and "progressive" since they promised to combine nationalism and socialism, to abolish traditional class divisions, and to create a society that rewarded not ancestry but achievement.[5] In fact, it is in relation to National Socialism that echoes of generational conflict can be detected in the interviews. With their social snobbery and political conservatism, parents of the interviewees viewed the Nazis with contempt and the Nazi plan to create a populist Volksgemeinschaft with alarm.[6] Their children found these views old-fashioned, socially narrow, and timid.[7] By contrast, the Nazis were in tune with the needs of youth, presenting young people with the opportunity to be independent, to assume responsibility, and to take action.

The National Socialists, it seemed, would make the lived experience of the youth movement a national social reality. The intense collectivism of the

youth movement group would be carried forward and extended in the national "community of the people." Defining politics as self-interested and
divisive, the interviewees saw the creation of a homogeneous and harmonious Volksgemeinschaft as bringing "politics" as they understood it to an end,
and National Socialism seemed an apolitical movement of national regeneration and social unity that followed in the footsteps of the youth movement.[8]
In contrast to the youth movement, however, National Socialism offered not
hikes, games, and songs but rearmament and the open violation of the Versailles Treaty.[9] It offered not excursions to ethnic Germans living abroad but
their incorporation in the Reich. The National Socialists produced *visible*
achievement. Most obviously they eradicated the disturbing spectacle of the
unemployed loitering on German streets, an accomplishment due not only
to the economic upswing, which had already begun before 1933, and to
rearmament but also to the fact that unemployed people were put in work
camps.[10] The National Socialists also eliminated the very visible disorder of
the Weimar Republic, to which SA street violence had contributed so considerably.[11] The Nazis reduced the sense that one lived in an arbitrary and anar-
chic environment, instituting a regime where danger was apparently placed
under human agency, controlled and directed by state, party, and security
apparatus. Unpredictable disorder was replaced by Gestapo terror, but that,
if one obeyed and conformed, was readily negotiated.[12]

One woman denies that National Socialism had much of an impact on
her life and describes the Nazis as having created a system where the "insignificant" could flourish.[13] She clearly means to confirm that by accommodat-
ing oneself to the regime, one could live a comfortable life. And yet there was
significance in being insignificant in Nazi Germany. The National Socialists
glorified "the insignificant" not only to ensure popular obedience but also
to inspire popular enthusiasm. Just as the youth movement had made virtue out of necessity by transforming Weimar hardship into an elitist badge
of voluntary deprivation, now the National Socialists, by making ordinary
people into populist heroes, transformed the sense of being a little man or
little woman—which in Weimar had been such a humiliation for middle-
class Germans—into a source of honor and self-esteem. Another woman recalls meeting Hitler in Berlin after she won a national occupational competition; a picture of her being congratulated by the Führer appeared in German
newspapers the next day.[14] This "little person" became for a few moments
a national hero through her contact with the Führer, himself a "little man"
who had become a demigod. This sort of competition, along with the prolif-
eration of Nazi projects, programs, and campaigns, served to correct another
flaw associated with the Weimar period by enabling people to experience
mastery. Like youth movement excursions, the myriad National Socialist

competitions—athletic, musical, and occupational—gave young people, in the words of one woman interviewee, "challenges to meet and tasks to accomplish," opportunities to gain self-esteem and self-confidence.[15]

Although National Socialism provided these young people with unprecedented opportunities to assume responsibility, it exerted great pressure on them to conform, pressure to which most submitted willingly.[16] The Third Reich was a collective and a police state, and the two reinforced one another effectively. One interviewee sums up the essential connection between membership in the Volksgemeinschaft and its policing: "Well, there was always a kind of pressure. Each person had to look out for the other [in both the sense of spying and being spied on and the sense of taking care of one another]. It was practical that way."[17] Indeed, the effective functioning of the Gestapo was possible only with the active assistance of ordinary Germans who were willing to denounce those they deemed threats to the national community. Educational and career opportunities were blocked for those who did not belong to the appropriate Nazi organizations or who did not act appropriately at official Nazi functions.[18] Indeed, already in 1933 membership in the Hitler Youth (or being otherwise active in the NSDAP) appears effectively to have been a prerequisite for university study, and in more general terms, political reliability as measured by the appropriate political activism was an important factor in educational and occupational success.[19] In certain professions, party membership was a virtual necessity.[20] But perhaps the most effective pressure to conform was self-imposed. Gestapo terror and other, subtler forms of coercion were internalized by Germans, even those who opposed the regime and resisted incorporation into the collective, such that they became a living psychic presence inhabiting thoughts, feelings, and even dreams.[21] Conformity was enacted in small-scale rituals like the greeting "Heil Hitler" and in the festivals, ceremonies, and mass rallies that were so much a part of the landscape of the Third Reich.[22] These had the ability to create and sustain collective identity and conformity by dissolving the individual's rational connection to reality and integrating him or her into a "community of feeling."[23] To be sure, age-specific career concerns and family responsibilities made the interviewees particularly susceptible to National Socialist pressure to conform. Nonetheless, it was also crucially important for these Germans to subordinate themselves to the Gemeinschaft. The need to belong to an idealized collective that had defined their lives in the youth movement continued to define their lives in the Third Reich.[24] The youth movement group had simply been vastly enlarged and become more socially inclusive, its elitism given a racial cast.

One woman who went from the youth movement to become a leader of the Bund Deutscher Mädel (BDM) recalls how, during the Third Reich, she had tried to explain her enthusiasm for National Socialism to herself: "And then I had the idea, I had the idea myself, that it had something to do with the death of my father which, [since] we had lost the war, meant something like his death had been in vain. Everything had to do with our Volk. The Nazis managed to give us the feeling that we are all a little wheel, that we're finally needed, that we can participate somewhere, that we can help our Volk. That's what they managed to achieve. That was actually my main idea."[25] Although only two interviewees can be described as unrepentant Nazis, the vast majority concede that they turned against the regime only after its collapse in 1945 and remain convinced that there were significant positive aspects to National Socialism, aspects one would do well to imitate today. Despite its infamous historical reputation, virtually all of those interviewed have positive memories of the Third Reich and look back on the period from 1933 until at least the beginning of the war as "a wonderful, lovely, fulfilling time."[26] Their generation was in its prime. The experiences and values of the youth movement—togetherness, engagement, sacrifice, elitism—were being played out on the national stage. The losses of the past were apparently redeemed. It seemed to those interviewed that their time had come.

Despite the fact that the interviewees generally greeted the advent of the Third Reich with enthusiasm, the first action of the regime affecting most of them directly was the ban on the independent youth movement in May 1933 at the Munster Camp. Following the ban, most interviewees resisted the forced incorporation of the youth movement of the Bunds into the Hitler Youth. They resented the loss of independence and freedom, a resentment that manifested itself in clashes with the National Socialist leadership over its more authoritarian style.[27] Equally important in inspiring resistance was simple jealousy when members of the youth movement of the Bunds were not initially selected to lead the Nazi youth movement.[28] A few male interviewees found the proletarian character of the Hitler Youth off-putting.[29] One man put it bluntly: "We knew all about the Hitler Youth. We knew what sort of crew that was. It was a primitive crew, in our view."[30]

Nevertheless, a significant number of younger women moved easily from the independent youth movement to the Bund Deutscher Mädel, often becoming leaders of the Jungmädel, or the BDM proper.[31] They saw the Hitler Youth as a continuation of the youth movement and deny that the BDM was political.[32] Not only do they overlook the obvious political indoctrination in the Hitler Youth, more fundamentally, they fail to recognize that what attracted them to the BDM was central to the ideology of National Socialism: "the group experience," in the words of one; "being young and being together," in the words of another.[33] Many younger interviewees, after an initial period of resistance, soon became integrated into the Hitler Youth, their need to belong proving stronger than their resentment at the loss of independence. They contented themselves with trying to give the Hitler Youth as much of a youth movement character as possible,[34] and, in fact, the Hitler Youth adopted many of the activities and provided many of the satisfactions of the youth movement of the Bunds.[35] A few interviewees report maintaining a modest degree of illegal, independent youth movement activity, including secret meetings and excursions, although this activity appears to have been generally short-lived.[36] The majority of those interviewed, although they were indignant about the "coordination" of the youth movement and withdrew from the Hitler Youth, remained enthusiastic about the Third Reich.[37] Their move away from the Hitler Youth was, more than anything, age-related. By 1933 most interviewees had outgrown the youth movement and were ready to take on adult responsibilities and engage in adult activities.[38] Despite the pain the interviewees experienced at the Munster Camp,[39] the ban on the Bunds there brought a dramatic and "historic" close to this important chapter in their lives.

Although most interviewees were ready for adulthood in 1933, they still needed to find some age-appropriate successor to the youth movement "for," as one interviewee, who joined a National Socialist Student Bund following the ban, plaintively put it, "after all, one has to belong somewhere."[40] For a great many, the successor to the youth movement proved to be the Reich Work Service (Reichsarbeitsdienst) or, in a few instances, the related Country Year (Landjahr) program.[41] Virtually all responded to the Work Service with enthusiasm.[42] Women in particular describe their time in the Work Service as one of the happiest and most important periods of their lives.[43] This enthusiasm was doubtless connected to the fact that interviewees could regard the Work Service as "carrying on the spirit of the youth movement," and a significant number built on their youth movement experience to become Work Service leaders.[44] There was the same intense comradeship, and group cohesion was expressed and reinforced in music and song.[45] As in the youth movement, the Work Service presented the interviewees with tasks to master and challenges to meet. In the Work Service, toughness or hardness was also an idealized attribute, producing the same elitist satisfaction as it had in the youth movement.[46] As had been true of male youth movement groups, the Work Service was decidedly militaristic, even for women. And finally, those interviewed assert that, apart from the morning flag-raising ceremony, life in the Work Service was as apolitical as life in the youth movement had been.[47] Most failed to grasp that in fact they implemented a deeply political ideology in the Work Service, as they did not appreciate that ideology is most effectively transmitted through activities, songs, and symbols, expressed not in words but in action, in lived experience, in what the Nazis called the "socialism of the deed."

The ideological goal of the Work Service was set forth in the opening paragraph of the law of 25 June 1935 establishing it as a state institution and making six-month service obligatory for young German men: "The Reich Work Service shall educate German Youth, in the spirit of National Socialism, to be members of the Volksgemeinschaft and to develop a true conception of work, especially an appropriate respect for manual labor." Different social classes were brought together in the Work Service, and members of the upper and middle classes engaged in vigorous physical labor, often for the first time in their lives. Work Service projects also brought more privileged young people into contact with poverty and the poor, awakening or reinforcing a sense of social responsibility.[48] According to those interviewed, the National Socialist attempt to create and promote the "community of the people" in the Work Service, and in the other mass organizations to which interviewees belonged, was successful and overwhelmingly appreciated. Although, like the youth movement, these institutions were all populated by their generation, they were dominated by young people from lower-middle-class, proletarian, or peasant backgrounds. The women valued the experience of comradeship and equality with working-class and farm women.[49] The men appear occasionally to have felt threatened by the National Socialist melting pot, however.[50] Whereas the women seem to have welcomed the opportunity these institutions provided to prove themselves to *themselves*, the men appear to have felt the need more to prove themselves to *others*, to the proletarian men they encountered there. Nevertheless, the vast majority of interviewees, female and male, embraced the Volksgemeinschaft as experienced in these National Socialist mass organizations, and they remained deeply committed to the communal values they experienced in the Third Reich throughout the rest of their lives.[51]

Although a few women interviewees lament the fact that they were prevented from practicing their chosen professions during the 1930s, when combating male unemployment was at the top of the regime's agenda,[52] and others complain that they were forced to work when the regime conscripted women to work in vital industries during the war,[53] the vast majority of the women interviewed in this study describe their lives in National Socialist Germany in overwhelmingly positive terms.[54] The men—although by no means negative about their lives during the Third Reich—are more reserved in their descriptions, perhaps because they felt more threatened by the social opening of the Volksgemeinschaft, perhaps because they suffered more in the war. Despite the hardships and the losses this generation experienced, many women interviewees wax "nostalgic" about their lives in the Third Reich, including wartime.[55]

These positive memories on the part of the women can be attributed first and foremost to the fact that the women of this generation were given extraordinary opportunities to take responsibility and exercise independent authority in the Work Service and in other National Socialist organizations.[56] During the war, with the entire population mobilized and the men at the front, the opportunities for women interviewees to work and exercise authority in areas traditionally reserved for men increased still further.[57] The Volksgemeinschaft reached its culmination during the war, and these bourgeois women relished their exposure to people belonging to different social classes while doing war work.[58] Not only were the women of this generation freed from traditional class and gender roles during the Third Reich, they were also freed from the powerful ties to place that had existed in Germany before 1933, enjoying extraordinary mobility during the 1930s and especially during the war.[59] Finally, both the centrality of racism to National Socialist ideology and the desire to reverse the decline in the birthrate, which had been falling since the beginning of the century and reached its nadir during the Depression, meant that the Third Reich was, as one woman who had ten children put it, "a very 'children-friendly' state."[60] The regime offered monetary, physical, and moral support to pregnant women and mothers who met Nazi racial criteria. Programs like the marriage loan, increased financial allowances for children, programs for expectant mothers, generally improved welfare facilities, the "Leave of Absence to Uphold One's Duty to the Family," and the service-year girls significantly eased the burden of motherhood.[61] Given their age during the Third Reich, the high level of National Socialist support was particularly welcome to the women of this generation. At least until the war, it was a good time to bear and raise children.

When set between the emancipation achieved by women during the 1920s and after 1945, the emancipation experienced by women during the Third Reich can be seen as part of a historical development spanning the twentieth century. The same applies to social activism. Already during the Weimar Republic, economic hardship broke down class barriers and created interest in and opportunities for working with the unemployed; and a number of interviewees entered young adulthood hoping to do social and community work.[62] But if the seeds of social activism had been planted in the interviewees before 1933, those seeds blossomed during the Third Reich. The Nazis encouraged and provided ample opportunities for these young people, especially the women, to develop a sense of social responsibility and to engage in social work.[63] In fact, the interviewees who seem to have been the most committed National Socialists were generally the most socially active.[64]

And for many, that activism would continue after 1945.[65] The National Socialist populist project, combined with and enhanced by the mobilization of the population during the war, not only increased the social consciousness of younger middle-class Germans, it also accelerated the shift away from Christian charity to the conceptions of collective social responsibility that led to the creation of the postwar welfare state.

Most of those interviewed would deny that they were much affected by National Socialist ideology. Nevertheless, the interviews reveal the importance of that ideology generally and of Nazi racism and anti-Semitism specifically in their lives then and at the time of their interviews. Although only two interviewees appear unrepentantly anti-Semitic, and the vast majority would heatedly deny any animus toward Jewish people, racist phrases, categories, and stereotypes are prevalent in the interviews.[66] The interviewees generally define people with multiple identities by their racial identity. In particular, they refer to people who were among other things Jewish almost invariably simply as "Jews." Indeed, a number of the interviewees unwittingly accept the notion that Jewish Germans were not Germans at all but wholly and exclusively Jewish.[67] In various ways, anti-Semitism is a powerful presence in the interviews, and it is striking how eager interviewees were to talk about the subject. To be sure, racism and anti-Semitism were present in the lives of these people before 1933. The exposure given the Holocaust since 1945 has clearly increased the importance of racism and anti-Semitism in the consciousness of Germans generally and in the consciousness of this generation of Germans in particular. Nevertheless, anti-Semitism is so prominent in the interviews also because it was such a prominent part of everyday life in Nazi Germany, where "normality had become racialized."[68] The Nazi emphasis on "breeding" had a profound impact on the interviewees.[69] A number have a keen awareness of the precise proportion of "Jewish blood" possessed by contemporaries: which were "full Jews," which "half Jews," and which "quarter Jews."[70] Some report having had to engage in *Ahnenforschung*, or "ancestral research," in order to obtain a "Certificate of [Racial] Fitness to Marry."[71] Not only does the need to document one's Aryan status testify to the pervasiveness of racism in Nazi Germany, it also reveals the pervasive, often unacknowledged, threat of discovering that one had a Jewish ancestor and that, instead of being a member of the master race, one was suddenly a racial outcast.[72] The interviews testify to the importance of racial appearance in the Third Reich. Non-Jewish Germans who did not fit the Aryan racial stereotype were often painfully self-conscious about their appearance and rightly feared that conclusions would be drawn about their character and social value, that they would be viewed with suspicion, discriminated against, or reported to the authorities by their fellow citizens.[73] Thus one woman interviewee with dark hair was "always treated a bit as, 'Well, perhaps she is a Jew'—you know, in that way. But there was nothing to be done about it."[74] Not only appearance but other ethnic markers, such as accent, affected one's treatment.[75] The vital importance of appearance in the Third Reich, the privileges bestowed on those who reflected the National Socialist racial ideal and the prejudice and persecution directed against those who did not, would have been felt particularly keenly by this group of Germans, who so needed to fit in.

Four events are described in the interviews that, although they did not turn those interviewed into opponents of the regime, did cause them to question National Socialism. The first was the ban on the Bunds in May 1933 at the Munster Camp.[76] The second was the Röhm Putsch of 30 June 1934. A number of male interviewees found the purge of top SA and national conservative leaders to be an act of arbitrary violence.[77] Two women report being deeply distressed by Reichskristallnacht, the pogrom of 9 November 1938.[78] And finally, one woman recalls her dismay at learning during the war of the *Lebensborn* project (in which, it was rumored, Aryan women were sent to breed with SS men).[79] What connects these moments of opposition is an ability to imagine oneself in the place of the victims of National Socialism. Most of those interviewed were directly and personally affected by the ban on the independent youth movement. Many knew or at least could identify with the executed SA men, a significant number of whom had been members of the youth movement. The woman's outrage at the Lebensborn project clearly derived from her ability to imagine herself demeaned as one of the women in a Lebensborn facility. A close reading of the two interviews where distress over Reichskristallnacht is expressed reveals that the ultimate victims of the violence were not in fact Jews. Using virtually identical language and unwittingly testifying to their belief in the sinister power of international Jewry, both women see the ultimate victims of the pogrom to be non-Jewish Germans—in fact their own children, upon whom this act would be "avenged":

> And then I experienced Kristallnacht. My ——, my second child, had just been born. I became extremely depressed. Tears streamed down my face as I nursed her, and I said, "The poor child will be made to suffer for this. It's a cultural disgrace that the Germans have been the ones to do this." I always said, "The poor child will have to pay for this crime."[80]

> It was shortly before the birth of my third child, in November 1938. He was born on the fifteenth, ——, and at some point on the ninth this so-called Kristallnacht occurred. I was very much alarmed and told

my husband back then already, I can remember it today: "This will be avenged on us and on our children."[81]

It seems that Jewish people were one group of victims with which almost none of those interviewed could empathize. Despite centuries of assimilation, despite the fact that the Jews of Germany looked, talked, and acted liked the rest of the population, those interviewed could not imagine themselves in their place, either on 9 November 1938 or when they watched them being deported during the war or even when they spoke about them in their interviews. The Jews of Germany were simply "other," not Germans, not like "us," not people in whose place one could ever imagine being. There is a dramatic contrast between the vocal and effective opposition of the Catholic and Protestant churches to the regime's euthanasia program and their silence about the persecution and extermination of Jews (although church authorities were well informed about the genocide).[82] In the former case one could empathize with the victims, with the parents and other relatives of the mentally defective, the mentally ill, and the physically disabled.[83] But empathy with "Jews" was not possible and so, when confronted with their mistreatment, "one" simply "looked away." The basis of popular anti-Semitism during the Third Reich, then, was the inability or unwillingness of non-Jewish Germans to imagine themselves in the place of their Jewish fellow citizens.

Four interviewees break the pattern in being able to recognize "Jews" as human beings like themselves. The first and most impressive is one of the few interviewees who came not from the educated middle classes but from a lower-middle-class Social Democratic family. At one point in her interview, this woman describes bidding farewell to a friend who, it turns out, was Jewish. He was a "friend" first and a "Jew" secondarily:

> When I was in the Work Service a friend of mine from the SJV [Socialist Youth Association], from the leadership group there, emigrated to America, and he wanted to see me one last time before he left. . . . I knew the day he was leaving and at which railway station he would have to change trains. . . . So I went there, but I was wearing my Work Service uniform. We met one another in the waiting room. It was awful, because one could tell by looking at him that he was Jewish. And one could see, of course, how people stared and looked. And then he said, "Let's get out of here. I can't take it here anymore!" So we went to the railway platform and only spent an hour or two there together, and then his train came, and he was gone. It was awful, both for me, of course, and for him.

This same woman talks about three "children" abandoned in an apartment. Their mother had been arrested when she left to buy milk and had been confined in a cellar with twenty or thirty others to be transported to the East. The interviewee went to the cellar to get a key to the apartment from the mother, "who was beside herself with fear and terror." The mother begged the interviewee "for the love of God to go to her apartment and give her children the milk. So I did that. One was only three quarters of a year old. Another was two. And the third was five. They'd been there since midday. They were crying and waiting for their mother. It was just an awful experience."[84] For this interviewee, Jewish people were not simply "Jews." They were people. She could see their mistreatment and take action in response.

Another interviewee also expresses outrage at the mistreatment of Jewish people in the Third Reich. This is the man whose description of the atrocities committed against a village in the Ukraine by the Waffen-SS is quoted in the composite interview with "Franz Orthmann." He freely acknowledges visiting the concentration camp at Sosnowiec, where he saw "terrible things. . . . When I hear today again and again that there were never any concentration camps, well, it's a lie, is all I can say, for I saw with my own eyes how the people were brought to death by the people there." As a result of these experiences, "my pride in being a German was thoroughly driven out. For what was done back then, what I saw with my own eyes (others saw other things), is deeply shameful to me and doesn't allow me to be proud of being a German anymore."[85]

Another man's rejection of Nazi anti-Semitism was based upon his contact with a Jewish music teacher in childhood, a "half" Jewish classmate, and a "quarter" Jewish member of his youth movement group in adolescence, and Jewish professors at the University of Leipzig in young adulthood. Indeed, his attraction to blond Jewish girls appears to have played a role in his rejection of National Socialist racial stereotypes. Like the other two interviewees, this man was able to *see* the mistreatment of Jews: "Those are experiences that shape you, that push you in a certain direction. One can't simply go along with everything anymore. One sees, one has one's eyes wide open to see what is going on."[86] Finally, a woman who had extensive contact with several elderly Jewish women before 1933 recognized their importance to her, humanized them (they are not just "Jews"; they have names), and could acknowledge that the women were killed in the Holocaust.[87]

Two other interviewees provide a striking contrast. The first is a woman who concedes (the right word) that she has a "Jewish branch of the family." She describes her attitude toward the Third Reich as schizophrenic, with part of her enthusiastic about the achievements of the National Socialists, especially in foreign affairs, and with another part of her more reserved about the National Socialists, especially their lack of respect for the law and their persecution of Jews. She only grudgingly connects these reservations to her partial Jewish ancestry. Indeed, she expresses relief that, in contrast to Jewish classmates and relatives, her "Jewish blood" was thin enough not to interfere with her education. She claims to have participated in an effort organized by her local Protestant minister to help a married Jewish couple survive the war. Her role in this effort "never," in her words, constituted "resistance" to the regime. Instead, it was simply part of "her Christian duty." That is to say, her willingness to help these Jewish people was based *not* on an identification with them (which might have been expected, given her Jewish ancestry). Instead it was based on her *difference* from them, on her identity as a Christian. Similarly, despite her German-Jewish relatives, she still unwittingly contrasts "Jews" forced to flee the Third Reich with "Germans," as if the émigrés had voluntarily relinquished their national identity when forced to flee or, as Jews, had never really been Germans in the first place. This thoughtful, decent woman could not or would not see herself connected to the Jewish victims of National Socialism. She always implicitly and explicitly contrasts the "Jews" with "us" in her account. It is as if she remains psychologically trapped in the Third Reich, where her survival depended upon her ability to establish distance from the Jewish part of herself.[88]

The second interviewee is a man who had one-eighth "Jewish blood" and a readily identifiable Jewish name. He acknowledges that his name and racial background prevented him from becoming a leader in the Hitler Youth. Because he had a Jewish grandfather, the interviewee was designated a *Mischling zweiten Grades* according to the Nuremberg [Racial] Laws. He therefore needed Rudolf Hess's personal permission to study, which he was able to secure because his father had served and died in World War I, because he himself had completed voluntary military service, and because he was in good standing with the authorities.[89] At some point during the war, he had his stepfather adopt him so that he could exchange his "Jewish" name for a "German" one in order "to help him get ahead," according to his wife; but, she concludes, the adoption and name change "still didn't help him one bit." She reports that he was kept out of the Luftwaffe and experienced discrimination in the Wehrmacht, being sent on particularly dangerous missions because of his "blood."[90] The interviewee himself acknowledges that, despite his "years of military service" and "level of education," he never rose beyond the rank of corporal "on account of my ancestry." He confirms that his status as a "Mischling" meant that he had to serve as a forward artillery observer, well in advance of his own troops and close to enemy lines, at the battle of Monte Cassino in Italy in early 1941.[91] Despite being awarded a medal and wounded twice, he was tried for attempted desertion following an aborted reconnaissance mission in Italy. Although it seems clear that the military tribunal recognized his innocence, he was convicted of a lesser charge and sentenced to fourteen days in the brig, though he never served the sentence. Given the fact that he was the only one of the three soldiers on the mission to be put on trial, it is hard to believe that his ancestry played no role in this strange affair.

Nevertheless, despite these experiences, this man's wife acts as if she had been married to an ordinary German. She denies that National Socialism "much affected" her or her husband.[92] She heatedly denies knowing until after the war about the National Socialist extermination project or even about the regime's more draconian persecution of Jews.[93] Even more incredibly, her husband seems to have drawn no conclusions about the Third Reich based upon his experiences and, like his wife, claims to have been little affected by National Socialism during the Third Reich, including Nazi racial policies. He has kept the "German" name he adopted to avoid persecution during the war. He has never confronted the fact that his survival was threatened by Nazi racism. Most disturbingly, he, like his wife, launches into the "but we didn't know" justification about the persecution and extermination of Jewish people so typical of Germans of his generation. He seems unwilling or unable to identify with "Jews" as people in any way like himself or to recognize that he fought for a regime, with which he still clearly identifies, that regarded him to be less than fully human. His comments deserve to be quoted at some length:

Politically we were completely neutral. You know, we were *good Germans*, that's how I would describe us, you know. The fact that things were getting better with Adolf's help, if you will, pleased us. It's as simple as that and not one iota more. The instruction in racial science and that stuff we either cut or slept through or whatever. That was not something that appealed to us. It was absolutely not the case that I had difficulties because my name was ——, neither in the military, nor in the Work Service, nor in school. . . . National Socialism as politics scarcely reached us. The racial laws, although they should have affected me particularly, or did affect me, they scarcely interested us. How we . . . produced the Holocaust, I don't know either, I must honestly confess. Then as a German I really feel ashamed—especially when I'm together with foreigners—that that was really done by Germans, the Holocaust. . . . I want to emphasize, since it's so gladly and frequently laid upon our generation—for having seen nothing, heard nothing, etc.—that I am ashamed of what happened. I fully concede that I am ashamed that what happened could have been done by Germans or done under the German name. But I don't feel guilty. I simply won't accept a sense of guilt. . . . I reject talking about guilt, that we were supposed to have known, that there were concentration camps, especially to that extent. I want to distance myself from that. I do acknowledge that on leave I could have worried about such things, perhaps, but on leave one has other things to do than that. You know. I wanted to say that. Good.[94]

The interviewees seem to have experienced the Third Reich in an intensely visual way: what was seen and, crucially, what was *not* seen in Nazi Germany take on particular importance. As in other oral histories, forced laborers brought to the Reich during the war were a visible presence to the interviewees.[95] By contrast, they generally did not perceive the persecution of Jewish people and the entire extermination project, although they speak at length about this absence. Numerous examples of "not seeing" or "looking away" from the persecution, deportation, and extermination of Jewish people have been included in the composite interviews (particularly with "Magdalene Beck"), such as the woman who "saw" and "looked away" from the deportation of the Jews of Hamburg-Altona and "already after taking three steps," "thought about something else. I continued on my way and didn't get upset about it."[96] The act of "looking away" goes to the heart of the anti-Semitism of the interviewees. It was an act that eliminated the possibility of empathy, severing the bond of shared humanity connecting them to the persecuted Jews. It was an act of dehumanization, an eradication of Jewish people from consciousness, that mirrored and facilitated their physical annihilation.

Of course it is difficult to overemphasize the degree to which those interviewed had developed the capacity for denial, for "looking away" from potentially distressing or conflict-producing situations. It was the strife of the Weimar Republic that interviewees found particularly distressing. In the youth movement, they had avoided anything that might provoke tension or discord. During the Third Reich, interviewees not only looked away from the persecution of Jewish people; one woman "preferred not to look" at SA street violence either.[97] In the Free German Circle after the war, "tolerance" was upheld as the highest ideal in part because it enabled them to avoid conflict.[98] The persecution and extermination of Jewish people was incompatible with the interviewees' need to experience good feelings and therefore "one simply looked away. Of course one didn't want to see it, you know."[99] As evidenced by this statement, interviewees continue to distance themselves from the persecution they observed and closed their eyes to during the Third Reich by using the third-person impersonal pronoun in speaking to interviewers about the mistreatment of Jews: "I" did not witness the mistreatment; "one" did.[100]

Another interviewee not only uses the third-person impersonal pronoun, she also uses the passive voice to describe the deportation of Jewish people to extermination camps in the East: "In reference to the Jews, one saw in Frankfurt that the people were being transported away. They had to collect at the East Railway Station and then were transported away, and one thought they were being taken to the East. One didn't think any more closely about it. They were supposedly being resettled there."[101] Indeed, interviewees in this study as well as those in other oral histories frequently use the passive voice in recalling the persecution and deportation of Jewish people during the Third Reich. It is as if the mistreatment of Jews occurred of its own accord, without human agency, will, or coercion. The Jewish acquaintances of the interviewees in this and other oral histories simply "suddenly vanished" from their world.[102] Jewish classmates "suddenly disappeared" from interviewees' schools.[103] Jewish neighbors were "gone all of a sudden" and "no one knew where" they went.[104] When a "half Jew" who had belonged to one interviewee's youth group "disappeared one fine day, we noted he was gone but neither inquired where he had gone nor attempted to maintain contact with him. We simply noted it. Today this attitude is unintelligible to me, but I must concede that that's how it was back then."[105] Even one woman whose depressed sister was euthanized during the war also eliminates the violent act committed against her sister, stating first that "she was gone all of a sudden" and then, not that she was "murdered" or even "killed," but simply that "she died."[106] In order to maintain good feelings, the physical, violent mistreatment of human beings by human beings had to be denied.[107]

These two factors—that the interviewees sought to avoid anything that could make them feel uneasy and that they had no capacity or inclination to empathize with Jewish people—help account for the fact that so many interviewees are certain that not one "Jew" they knew personally actually perished in the Holocaust. The four interviewees described earlier in this chapter who were able to recognize Jews to be people like themselves provide a striking contrast. All were aware that their acquaintances suffered persecution and that some did not survive the genocide. Other interviewees insist that every Jew they knew emigrated.[108] Even one of the women who lived in an apartment expropriated from a Jew has managed to convince herself that he survived the Holocaust: "When I looked over the apartment in order to rent it, there sat the Jew in his apartment, everything packed up in crates, quite cheerful. He was picked up with all of his belongings. He went to Holland. So things didn't go badly with him. I don't have his address, but I know that he arrived safely in Holland. One does need to make that clear. There were such cases."[109] She fails to reflect on what happened to Jews in Holland, of course. Although the interviewees accept the historical reality of the Holocaust, they become in effect "Holocaust deniers" when discussing the fate of Jews on the level of personal experience.

In the same way that those interviewed "looked away" from "vanishing" Jewish people and deny the reality of extermination as far as anyone they actually knew is concerned, so too most "look away" from the Holocaust by denying that they knew about it until the collapse of the Reich in 1945.[110] Despite their denials, a significant number also reveal in their interviews that they did in fact have knowledge of the genocide before that date. I have tried to convey this contradiction in the composite interviews.[111] Still, because this phenomenon is so striking and so widespread, it merits further illustration.[112] Thus the wife of the "one-eighth Jew" described above denies knowledge of the Final Solution, asserting that only the higher-ups were in the know.[113] But then, in the same breath, she concedes that she saw the notorious concentration camp Bergen-Belsen on a Wehrmacht tour as well as Jews in cattle cars outside of Hamburg.[114] A woman BDM leader was kept in the dark and informed exactly: "As leaders, we were separated from the rest of the population. No one told us anything or brought anything to us. As crazy as it sounds, we had really from the inside . . . [sic] Once at the Reich Leadership School I heard about the extermination . . . [sic] I thought about it a lot later: 'Why doesn't one go into that?'"[115] A similar contradiction characterizes the following statement by a former nurse: "Yes, we didn't know about it. The same was true with the concentration camps. A patient also explained to me once [some years before the end of the war] that so many Jews were being gassed. I said: 'I don't believe it. Something like that can't possibly be true.' And then he said: 'I've seen it with my own eyes.'"[116] Another woman enlists an English newspaper columnist to defend her father and the German people from the charge that they knew about the Holocaust before the end of the war and then goes on to concede that knowledge seeped through long beforehand and that her father had in fact learned about the Final Solution as early as 1942.[117] Even the woman able to empathize with and help Jewish people in Berlin fits this pattern. Despite her firsthand experience of the persecution and deportation of Jewish people (described above), her awareness of what happened to a Jewish neighbor who was divorced by her Aryan husband and to her neighbor's daughter (quoted in the composite interview),[118] her explicit admission that "we knew exactly what was going on,"[119] and her discussion with a soldier on leave about the killing of Jews in the Flossenbürg concentration camp (quoted in the composite interview),[120] she claims that she did not know about the Final Solution, that everything was kept secret from the German people (quoted in the composite interview), and concludes by citing examples of the ubiquity of Nazi terror in the Third Reich (quoted in the composite interview), as if fear of the Gestapo explains her and her contemporaries' ignorance of the genocide.[121]

One way to characterize the interviewees' knowledge of the Holocaust before the end of the war is that they knew facts that should have led them to conclude that atrocities were being committed against Jewish people, including that they were being subjected to systematic extermination. Indeed, given what these interviewees concede they knew, it took an act of will for them *not* to have known what was going on. In a sense they had to avert their eyes to avoid seeing what was right in front of their noses. Thus one woman denies knowing about "these concentration camps, not to speak of the extermination of the Jews. . . . I know it sounds unbelievable, but it's so." She is the same woman quoted in the composite interview (a portion of which is also quoted above) who observed the deportation of the Jews of Hamburg-Altona in 1941 and "already after taking three steps" was "thinking about something else."[122] Another woman, whose description of the deportation of the Jews of Frankfurt to the East is also quoted above, goes on after "they were supposedly being resettled there" *immediately* to say: "And about, about mistreatment and that sort of thing, perhaps that seeped through near the end of the war. But we had no *specific* knowledge. No, we didn't get that."[123] For those interviewees who knew and yet did not know, it seems as if knowledge of the Final Solution before the end of the war was conscious but set off from the main sector of awareness, which remained blissfully ignorant: a vertical split of consciousness. For those who knew enough to have known absolutely, it seems as if the Final Solution was discerned but then immediately repressed: a horizontal split of consciousness.

There are several ways "not knowing and yet knowing" (the vertical split of consciousness) or "knowing enough to have known absolutely" (the horizontal split of consciousness) can be understood. It seems possible that interviewees knew about the Final Solution before 1945 and only now, in defensive reaction, deny knowing about the Holocaust before the end of the war. Nevertheless, one should not simply dismiss the claims of interviewees that they saw what was in plain sight but looked away so quickly that they were able to prevent the knowledge from registering in their consciousness completely. It is not that they did not want to know because knowledge would have forced them to take action that put them in danger or would have caused them to feel guilt for failing to do so. Taking action was never a plausible option for these people. Instead, they did not allow themselves to acknowledge the reality of persecution and genocide because they were unwilling to recognize "Jews" as human beings like themselves. And they were unwilling to recognize "Jews" as human beings like themselves because to have done so would have caused them to experience unpleasant feelings. They did not empathize with Jewish people, and they did not want to empathize with them.

There is a difference between perception and knowledge. When interviewees looked away from the persecution of Jews and forgot what they had seen "after taking three steps," they perceived, but they could not or would not integrate the perception into the structure of consciousness. They did not "know" what they had seen, and as sociologists, psychologists, and philosophers have made clear, knowledge is a social phenomenon and knowing is a social act. For something to be "known," it must be shared and validated by others. As Kai Erikson points out, without social affirmation, perception remains ungrounded, uncertified, and ultimately without meaning. Knowledge held in common is a condition of community, and a community conditions what its members know. The role played by society in integrating perception into consciousness is especially significant in a community as intense, as controlling, and ultimately as tenuous as the National Socialist Volksgemeinschaft. That is to say, there was a mutually reinforcing relationship between social consensus and knowledge during the Third Reich. What Germans "knew" was, in part, the product of social consensus, and accepting what was commonly known was a condition for membership in the community. By the same token, social consensus and community were affirmed and strengthened by common knowledge. And for those like the interviewees who needed so powerfully to belong to the collective, the ability to know what was unacceptable to and invalidated by the "community of the people" was extremely limited. Acknowledging the Final Solution would have asserted the "I" against the "we" and alienated the knower from the Volksgemeinschaft, a racial community in which the Jews and their persecution were to be eliminated from consciousness. For if the persecution of Jews was acknowledged, then Jews were acknowledged. And if Jews were acknowledged, then they could be experienced as human beings. But Jews were not to be experienced as human beings. They were to be rendered invisible.[124]

Instead of "seeing" the mistreatment of Jewish people during the 1930s and early 1940s, instead of "seeing" the extermination camps during the Third Reich, those interviewed "see Jews" in their memories of the period before 1945 as a way to defend themselves against self-reproach or the reproach of others after that date.[125] Some interviewees describe having had the wish to help Jewish people during the Third Reich. Although almost none of them apparently ever did anything, they seek to demonstrate their good intentions to the interviewers and to themselves.[126] A significant number describe how friendly they were with "Jews" before 1933 in order to demonstrate their lack of anti-Semitism.[127] One woman recalls her friendship with a little *Judenkind* during the last years of the Weimar Republic, "who would tell me about his family, about the Feast of Tabernacles. . . . And this little *Judenjunge* would tell me what he wanted to be when he grew up, a streetcar conductor and all sorts of other things. . . . And sometimes we'd exchange pieces of bread with one another. It was so sweet, the dependence of this little child on an older girl. I was fifteen or sixteen years old then." She goes on to acknowledge: "I was for him, for Hitler, during that period, you know."[128]

The fact that the woman could apparently overlook the glaring contradiction between her friendship with a little Jewish boy and her commitment to National Socialism during the Weimar Republic and throughout the Third Reich reflects the fundamental passivity of those interviewed. The interviewees appear generally to have accepted the received wisdom of the times. During Weimar Germany, this meant accepting the version of the world presented them by their parents and teachers. During the Third Reich, this meant accepting the version of the world presented to them by the National Socialists. The Weimar Republic was bad because "that's what was always being said." Jews were bad because "that's what was always being said." Post-1945, the interviewees adapted themselves to the new community consensus, as did the woman who had befriended the little Jewish boy: "My attitude toward National Socialism only changed after the war, when it was always being asserted that everything had been wrong."[129] This passivity is manifest in what one woman proudly presents as a powerful anti-Nazi dream from early 1944 in which Hitler is condemned not by human beings but by a disembodied God, while the dreamer looks passively, neutrally on, accepting the judgment of something outside and above herself: "I found myself in a wonderful Romanesque church with two entrances to the crypt. And in the chancel there was something like the Last Judgment. I saw God, not as a form but as an eye into which I could look. And everything was clear in this eye, in the view of the eye and in the eye. And I saw Hitler. It was a traditional depiction of the Last Judgment, with those on one side accepted by God and those on the other side rejected. I saw Hitler on the side of those rejected. There was no hatred, but simply that was the way it was. I had the feeling it was right that way."[130]

As suggested above, interviewees implicitly present fear of the Gestapo as an explanation for why they "looked away" from the persecution of Jews and from the Final Solution.[131] It needs to be emphasized, however, that Nazi terror did not prevent the interviewees from taking action to protect the persecuted. Nazi terror is presented by the interviewees not as an explanation for why they did not *act* but as an explanation for why they did not *know*. Indeed, the interviewees' attempt to use fear of the Gestapo to justify their lack of knowledge actually undermines the claim that they were unaware of the persecution of Jews or of the Final Solution, for if they really did not know then they obviously would have had nothing to fear.

The interviewees describe the pervasiveness of Nazi terror during the Third Reich. During the 1930s, this took the form of SA violence, of reports of children denouncing parents on advertising columns, of the local newspaper editor "shot trying to escape," of servants questioned about the family's political views.[132] In the interviewees' accounts, the consequences of the terror became dire during the war, as in the case of those involved in the wrong sort of office joke, of those interrogated by the Gestapo for having "conducted a church service–like action" in a private home, of those arrested for listening to foreign radio broadcasts, or of those knowing someone connected with the failed plot to assassinate Hitler in July 1944.[133] Although only one interviewee appears to have had direct contact with the Gestapo,[134] a good many claim to have lived in fear of the secret police. Unlike the Jews, people arrested by the Gestapo did not simply "disappear" from view, and the secret Gestapo arrest was very much a public event, "visible" to society through rumor, gossip, and whispered discussion. In fact, it was less the arrest itself than what the Gestapo called "whisper propaganda" about the arrest that made National Socialist terror effective.[135] As the woman who described the terrible consequences of an office joke put it: "All that built on itself and simply terrified people."[136] Arresting someone and then later releasing him or her further encouraged popular compliance and conformity, for the released prisoner was now a walking and visible reminder of what could happen to those who defied the regime or set themselves apart from the community.[137]

These memories of Nazi terror are vivid, even dramatic. Of course, Germans who lived through the Third Reich have a vested interest in playing up their fear of the secret police and, as we shall see, recent historical research has revealed that ordinary Germans who conformed politically, socially, and racially had little to fear from the Gestapo (see the essay "National Socialist Terror and the Germans" in chapter 6). Nevertheless, given the self-policing nature of the Volksgemeinschaft, the readiness of ordinary Germans to denounce fellow citizens whom they deemed threats to themselves or to the community of the people, fear of the consequences of opposition or nonconformity may not have been entirely misplaced.

From the beginning of the Third Reich, interviewees could sense that Germany was heading toward war.[138] Numerous interviews testify to the militarization of daily life and the preparation of the population for war.[139] In retrospect, the lives of the men in adolescence and young adulthood can be seen as preparing them for service in the Wehrmacht.[140] Following on the group experience in the youth movement and (for many) in the Work Service, the military was a collectivist organization, offering young men a sense of place and purpose.[141] It was also the institution where they experienced the National Socialist Volksgemeinschaft most intensively.[142] Unlike in the Work Service, however, in the Wehrmacht, the male interviewees were not faced with the need to prove themselves to their working-class contemporaries, since virtually all became officers, leaders of the military collective. As a result, perhaps, they seem generally to have experienced military service, in the words of one man, "in a social sense as a kind of liberation."[143] Like women Work Service leaders, the men, as officers, were able to exercise authority and take responsibility at a very young age, with one twenty-three-year-old commanding a unit of a thousand men on the Polar Sea.[144] Like the youth movement excursion, the war, in the words of one man, was "a special situation" where the rules of bourgeois civilization no longer applied.[145] It gave them the opportunity to overcome hardship and meet elemental challenges.

In fact, a number of those interviewed explicitly attribute their success as officers in the Wehrmacht, their ability to take the initiative and lead by example, to the youth movement, which they also credit with giving them the skills, toughness, and idealism to enable them to persevere and survive under extraordinary battlefield situations.[146]

Some of the military experiences of the interviewees are astonishing.[147] As far as I can tell, the man on whom the military career of the composite "Franz Orthmann" is largely based served on nearly every German front in World War II and was involved in nearly every major battle.[148] And he is convinced that it was the youth movement that enabled him to keep doing his "duty" even when he had lost faith in the justice or ultimate success of the German cause.[149] In the youth movement, singing or philosophical discussion had no purpose beyond itself. The destination of the youth movement excursion was relatively unimportant. What mattered was how the excursion was conducted. Means were privileged over ends. In the same way, these men fought not to conquer, not for the cause, but for the sake of fighting, for the sake of the group, for their own sake—in order, ultimately, to feel good about themselves.[150] The desire to be the ideal soldier who does his duty kept them fighting in a lost war.[151] One interviewee explains that he was attracted to Hitler and the National Socialists because he was a "dream dancer," able "to repress that which one thought worth repressing." He states that it was "a good thing" he "didn't see coming what ultimately did occur."[152] Another man expresses happiness that he learned about the extermination camps only during the very last phase of the war. Had he known sooner, he would have been deprived of the basis on which to keep doing his duty. He was and remains pleased that he could preserve his illusions about the Third Reich in order to fight with a pure heart.[153] For these men, it was better to kill and to die for an illusion than face the reality that the cause they were fighting for was immoral and lost.

In part because it threatened to destroy the illusion on which their self-esteem was based, the interviewees recall the attempt to assassinate Hitler on 20 July 1944 not as a noble act of resistance but as treason, even though a number of the conspirators had been in the youth movement of the Bunds and were celebrated after 1945 as heroic resistors to fascism.[154] Indeed, most Germans were outraged at the coup and relieved at its failure.[155] This reaction reflects the fact that, despite the impending defeat, the Third Reich and the Führer still enjoyed considerable popular support.[156] It also reflects the importance of doing one's duty in time of war and, in the case of the interviewees, at least, the need to preserve an idealized image of the Third Reich and Hitler as a way to preserve an idealized image of themselves.

Although the interviewees cannot be characterized as particularly self-reflective or open about their feelings, the men, once they begin to describe the war, become even more factual and unemotional than usual. They generally report what happened and not how they experienced it.[157] In some instances the laconic reportage appears to represent a form of masculine boasting. Their exploits become all the more heroic for being understated.[158] And yet it is also clear that the flat, reportlike quality of these reminiscences derives from the fact that the experiences of many of the men at the end of the war were wretched. Defeat and captivity presented them with few opportunities to feel good about themselves. Perhaps as a result, they have little to say about this period of their lives. It is as if they cannot bring themselves to speak about their suffering. Indeed, the men's experience of imprisonment is mostly described by their wives, as is their physical deterioration when they returned home.[159] Only a handful of men speak about captivity. One man, who is unusually open about his feelings, describes his experience in an American POW camp as having been so traumatic that he was "tortured" by terrifying "dreams of imprisonment" for a long time afterward.[160] With the exception of one younger interviewee, none of the men describe their experiences in Soviet POW camps.[161] These camps represented the inversion of the youth movement. They presented no opportunities for self-idealization, for autonomy or freedom, for merger with a collective, for accomplishment or adventure. Instead there was only confinement, degradation, despair, and grim survival.[162] In the brutal dog-eat-dog existence of the camps, all vestiges of the National Socialist and wartime Volksgemeinschaft were obliterated.[163] The camps were simply demoralizing. As a result, the men remain silent about their experiences—but silence can be eloquent testimony to suffering.

By contrast, the women's memories of the war and even of the period of the Reich's collapse are energized and vital—even, on occasion, romantic. Most interviewees married just before or during the war, but only the women describe falling in love, engagements, weddings, and honeymoons.[164] There is nothing remotely comparable in interviews with the men. They almost never mention their wives. One of the few descriptions of marriage by a man contrasts strikingly with those by the women: "It was 1939. In 1940 we got married, during the advance into France. During a pause [in operations] we got married in Salzufen."[165] On the subject of love and sexuality, the men remain largely silent—as on so much else.[166] A certain romance even creeps into the women's descriptions of fallen husbands, to whom several women seem to have maintained a sentimental loyalty throughout their lives: idealized figures from an idealized past.[167]

Despite the suffering and the losses, the war and the period of the Reich's collapse contained intense and even exhilarating experiences for the women. The bombing was where most women interviewees experienced the violence of war directly.[168] Certainly the air raids were terrifying, and images of the

bombing haunt the memories and, in two instances, the dreams of those interviewed.[169] It produced devastating losses of life and property. And yet for
some, there are positive memories associated even with the bombing. Women
express pride in performing tasks under extraordinary circumstances, such
as giving birth or getting an Abitur in a cellar during bombing raids.[170] They
describe the spectacle, even the beauty, of the bombing, and the intensity of
the joy at having survived.[171] It is the period of the Reich's collapse that the
women seem to remember most vividly and coherently.[172] A number of them
simply rushed to get to this period in their interviews. Even when they try to
talk about other topics, they seem to return inexorably to their experiences
during the *Zusammenbruch* (collapse), a time when many felt keenly alive.[173]
In their accounts, it seems almost as if the youth movement and the National
Socialist mass organizations to which they belonged during the 1930s had
been training camps that enabled these women to meet the challenges of this
period.[174] Flight before the advancing Red Army in a refugee trek is often
presented almost like a youth movement excursion, except that now survival
was the goal and the group had generally been replaced by members of the
interviewee's immediate family.[175] They also proudly describe their ability to
master hardship in eking out an existence for themselves and their families
once the trek was over and they had arrived at their destination.[176] The loss
of possessions is transformed into a virtue connected with the youth movement and made the basis for a critique of postwar materialism.[177] They give
triumphant accounts of their courage and resourcefulness in overcoming obstacles, including marauding Russians or hostile local inhabitants, to earn
money or get food for themselves and their families.[178] Indeed, it is almost as
if the women seek to protect the Zusammenbruch from anything that could
compromise its positive aspects. The women only vaguely allude to rape or
censor it out altogether, and when the fear of rape is mentioned, it always
proved in the interviewee's case to be unfounded.[179]

And yet a world collapsed along with the Third Reich in 1945, a world in
which the interviewees had flourished for the most part, a world to which
they had been ideologically and emotionally committed, a world they had
risked their lives to support and defend. The interviewees, like Germans generally, lost the familiar, the "fixed points" in their lives: now, in the words of
one woman, "everything was completely different all at once."[180] They lost
the Third Reich: its social networks and institutional supports; its worldview
and cognitive structures; the raison d'être it had given its citizens; the psychological compensations and emotional sustenance it had provided. The
National Socialist and wartime "community of the people" fell completely
apart during the last months of the war. People were suddenly unhelpful and
greedy, looking out for themselves as they fought to survive in the period of

the Reich's collapse.[181] The total defeat in the war seems to have been particularly hard on the men, who were imprisoned and now realized that the fighting, suffering, and dying had been in vain. And the generational unity that had defined this group broke down, as those interviewed looked not to peers but to families for strength and support (see the essay "Men, Women, and the Reassertion of the Family in Postwar Germany" in chapter 9).[182] Finally, on a most basic level, the collapse of the Third Reich was accompanied by a sudden sense of alienation from the lives the interviewees had lived until 1945.[183] With the Zusammenbruch, Germans were faced with the "rubble" not only of their ideals but also of their suddenly discredited autobiographies and expectations for the future.[184]

And, of course, there were the devastating losses experienced by those interviewed in the last years and especially months of the war, not just in terms of lost values and ideals, habits and worldview, but of possessions, homes, and neighborhoods, family members and friends. Interviewees living at war's end in Eastern Europe or in the eastern parts of the Reich fled before the advancing Red Army or were forcibly expelled immediately after the war, along with approximately 12 million other ethnic Germans, thereby losing not only home but homeland. In a few instances, the family home was destroyed by advancing Allied armies; in many more, by Allied bombing.[185] Monetarily valuable and psychologically precious heirlooms were lost or destroyed. And, of course, most devastating of all were the losses of loved ones, losses affecting virtually every interviewee. Those who died were brothers and sisters, brothers-in-law, beloved uncles, fathers, mothers, and husbands.[186] Some of the husbands who managed to survive the war and imprisonment returned with their health so impaired that they did not long survive. A number of interviewees had children who died, became seriously ill, or suffered psychological trauma.[187] Male interviewees lost friends and comrades at the front. Six and a half million non-Jewish Germans died in the war, five and a half million of them soldiers. One out of every eight German men, regardless of age, died in the war. For soldiers belonging to the generation of the interviewees, the mortality rate was a staggering 56 percent.[188] The loss of the men at the front affected the women. The dead and missing men left more than 1.7 million German widows and, with two German women of marriageable age for every man, many women were deprived of an opportunity to marry as a result of the war: "Everyone whom I could have married fell in the war. Also those in my [youth movement] group fell. When we were in West Prussia in the Land Year camp, there we had soldiers billeted with us, officers. In the evening we'd play music with them; it was wonderful. But they all died. They would have been possibilities, but they all died. There was a pastor who wrote me passionate letters. He fell. All of them gone. That's why I've remained single. It was at a critical age. Those who were a little bit older than I in the group, they all got married. They all have a child or two. And then their husbands all fell. All of them are gone. It's simply the fate of this generation."[189] Although the generation of the interviewees derived many benefits from National Socialism, it paid an especially heavy price for those benefits in the war.

Thus the defeat of Germany in World War II brought catastrophic losses to those interviewed. As we have seen, these were not the first such historically engendered losses the interviewees had experienced, for the losses they suffered at the end of World War II followed on those they had suffered after World War I. In contrast to the earlier losses, which were experienced indirectly through their impact on the parents, these were experienced directly by the interviewees. Nevertheless, the interviewees adopted strategies in the 1940s that they had adopted as adolescents to deal with the losses of the 1920s. And just as they had failed to accept and work through the losses that they had experienced as adolescents, they failed to accept and work through those they experienced as adults. Although it was the defeat in the war that led most interviewees to reject National Socialism, few appear to have come to terms with Nazi Germany—with the role they had played in it or with the role it had played in their lives.

Instead, as in adolescence, the interviewees dealt with this new set of losses through idealized memory, membership in an idealized collective, and activity. After World War I, they had compensated for losses in the family and society with an idealized memory of an idyllic childhood and with membership and activity in the idealized collective of the youth movement. After 1933, the role that the youth movement had played in bolstering the self-confidence and self-esteem of those interviewed was taken over and in a sense amplified by the idealized collective of the Nazi Volksgemeinschaft. Indeed, the collapse of 1945 may have been particularly difficult for those interviewed because the Third Reich had built on the youth movement in helping them to cope with the earlier losses they had experienced. After World War II, women interviewees appear to have again clung to idealized memories: for some, of their courage and resourcefulness during the period of the Reich's collapse, transforming what must have been one of the darkest periods of their lives into a sustaining memory linked directly to the youth movement. For the rest of the women and for the men, the more wholly negative experience of the war rendered it unsuitable as a memory that could sustain them in the face of the losses they had suffered. What had to sustain them emotionally were the more distant memories of the youth movement during adolescence. Indeed, the interviewees, both men and women, sought to restore the idealized collective that had been lost by re-creating the youth movement in 1947 in the form of the Free German Circle. This organization of those active in the youth movement during the 1920s provided the same psychological functions for those interviewed as the youth movement had before it and compensated for what they had lost along with the Third Reich: experiences of belonging, togetherness, and elitism; self-idealization through membership in an idealized collective comprised exclusively of their generational peers. Finally, as in adolescence, the interviewees denied loss by engaging in activity, attempting first simply to survive and then to rebuild their lives. And, as during the 1920s, this strategy was promoted by society at large, where the economic reconstruction of West Germany and the achievement of prosperity took the place of mourning what had been lost in the war.

6

ESSAYS

THE POPULARITY OF NATIONAL SOCIALISM AND THE *VOLKSGEMEINSCHAFT* WITH YOUNGER GERMANS

It is impossible to determine with any certainty popular attitudes toward National Socialism during the Third Reich, a time before public opinion polls and a place where dissent was suppressed by state, society, and individuals themselves. Obviously, different Germans had different opinions about National Socialism, and even the same Germans had different opinions at different times. Nevertheless, despite the necessarily speculative and oversimplified nature of the conclusion, many historians would probably accept Norbert Frei's recent verdict that Hitler and the National Socialists were supported "by the vast majority of Germans." Even the Nazis were surprised at the speed with which the German public rallied behind the Führer, according to Frei, and at least until the German defeat at Stalingrad the National Socialists enjoyed widespread popular support during what Germans recall as the "good years" of Nazi rule.[1]

Although one would expect Germans looking back to distance themselves from National Socialism, oral histories confirm Frei's verdict.[2] Since most oral history interviews were conducted after 1980, they tended to be with Germans who were relatively young during the Third Reich, those belonging to the "war youth" and subsequent "Hitler Youth" generations, who may have been more sympathetic to National Socialism than their elders.[3] Interviewees old enough to recall the Weimar period compare it unfavorably to the Third Reich.[4] They describe how the National Socialists brought order and tranquility after the political conflicts and civil unrest of the last years of the Republic, how they improved living standards and brought unemployment to an end, how they elevated the status of women and mothers and provided support for the family, and how Hitler restored Germany's honor following the humiliation of the Versailles Treaty.[5] They recall the enthusiasm generated by Nazi parades, rallies, and festivals, by Hitler's foreign policy successes of the 1930s, and by the military victories during the first years of the war.[6] Like the interviewees in this study, they recall the period of the Third Reich as having been a "lovely," "carefree," "wonderful" time.[7]

Approximately 68 million Germans were members of National Socialist mass organizations like the Hitler Youth, the Work Service, or the Frauenschaft. They were mostly young, and about one in three were women. Belonging and contributing to the Volksgemeinschaft was central to their experience in these organizations.[8] When interviewed for oral histories, they recall their service to the Volksgemeinschaft with enthusiasm, a response transcending class, gender, and region.[9] The intense collectivism of these organizations, created and reinforced in uniforms, rituals, and sacrifice on behalf of the collective, was essential to their appeal. Women in particular report experiencing a powerful sense of belonging, security, and empowerment as members of their group and of the overarching collective of the Volk.[10] Looking back, Melita Maschmann, who would become a leader of the BDM, recalled her experience in an East Prussian Work Service camp with other young women as "a miniature model of what I had imagined the Volksgemeinschaft to be. It was a wholly successful model." For Maschmann, "this model of a Volksgemeinschaft was connected" with "intense feelings of happiness," a "sense of optimism," and a commitment to National Socialism that would last until 1945.[11] These organizations enabled young women to escape "the narrow and restrictive milieus" from which they came, with one woman describing the Work Service as having represented "a little bit of freedom" in her life.[12] Young women were encouraged to become active and self-reliant and were exposed to "new experiences and responsibilities very much outside of the domestic sphere." Young people generally were able to interact with members of the opposite sex and enjoyed a degree of sexual freedom away "from the prudish moral codes of the parental household."[13] They discovered new places, increasing the geographical mobility of German youth. And finally, and most significantly, young people discovered new social territory. Looking back on their interaction with peers from every social class in the Hitler Youth or the Work Service, Germans, including those from working- or lower-middle-class backgrounds, insist that social differences in these organizations, in the words of one woman, "had *absolutely no* significance. It *really* was wonderful."[14] By expanding their social horizon and increasing educational and career opportunities, these organizations enabled young women and working-class Germans to transcend boundaries that previously would have blocked their way;[15] many took on leadership positions that served as springboards for professional careers after the war.[16] Partially as a result of the social activism promoted by these Nazi organizations, Germans no longer assumed, as they had before 1933, that class conflict was deep and intractable.[17]

In the face of the condemnation of the Third Reich after the war, those who had served in these organizations as adolescents and young adults sought to preserve the valuable "social side" of National Socialism from the taint of National Socialist "politics."[18] Indeed, despite the fact that the Hitler Youth or the Work Service sought to transform young Germans into Nazis and to create the Volksgemeinschaft through what Peter Fritzsche calls the "community of the camp,"[19] those interviewed in oral histories insist that, apart perhaps from the morning flag-raising ceremony and some of the songs that were sung, these National Socialist mass organizations were, like themselves, apolitical.[20] Because National Socialist ideology was transmitted "through experience" in "apparently apolitical forms," many simply did not recognize that their activities in these organizations had a political dimension.[21] Indeed, National Socialism itself seemed apolitical, and the Nazis actually sought to bring "politics," as Germans understood the concept, to an end.[22] In the Third Reich conventional distinctions between a political public realm and an apolitical private realm were dissolved, and actions that seemed private and apolitical were in fact infused with ideological significance and political efficacy.[23] Finally, the claim of interviewees that they and the organizations in which they served were apolitical protected them retrospectively from the charge that they had been ideologically committed Nazis and protected their overwhelmingly positive experiences in these organizations from being associated with National Socialism.[24] In response to the collapse of the Third Reich and the exposure of its crimes after 1945, Germans generally dealt with the Nazi past and their own disillusionment by becoming "apolitical." Apolitical in the present, Germans who were young during the Third Reich could look back on their past in the Hitler Youth or the Work Service as having been apolitical as well.[25]

NATIONAL SOCIALISM AND WOMEN

There is considerable disagreement among historians over how National Socialism's relationship toward women should be characterized, let alone understood. Some historians follow Sebastian Haffner in believing the emancipation of women made "great leaps forward" in the Third Reich, especially during the war, "with the full approbation and often vigorous support of party and state."[26] Others see the Nazis as simple misogynists and include Aryan women among the victims of National Socialism. Perhaps the most frequently made argument is that, although National Socialism was basically reactionary and sought to restrict women to the roles of wife and mother, the effort first to promote economic recovery, then to expand industry and the military in preparation for war, and finally to conduct the war itself had consequences for women that the National Socialists never intended, propelling women out of the family and into the workplace and the public sphere.[27] This view is generally compatible with "modernist" interpretations of the Third Reich (considered in the following essay), which focus less on the motives of the Nazis and more on the effect of their policies and of the war on German society.[28] Historians subscribing to the view that National Socialism had unintended benefits for women (primarily in the area of employment) differ in their assessment of the degree of autonomy and authority that women enjoyed outside the home, primarily in mass organizations like the BDM, the Work Service, or the Frauenschaft. According to Claudia Koonz, National Socialist misogyny paradoxically empowered women: Nazi men cared so little about women or women's issues that they "inadvertently gave Nazi women a unique opportunity" to create and shape autonomous spaces in gender-segregated National Socialist organizations where women could exercise authority.[29] Other historians regard women's autonomy and empowerment during the Third Reich to have been extremely limited. Thus, according to Jill Stephenson, "the only 'space' allowed" women "was a political backwater" and their activities within that space had virtually no influence on anything or anyone beyond it.[30] Ute Frevert adopts a position between Koonz and Stephenson. Because women simply carried out the directives of their male Party supervisors and because their activities were restricted to areas relating exclusively to women within exclusively female organizations, the regime cannot be said to have offered women "true equality," according to Frevert. Nevertheless, women in these organizations were able to exercise power at "the grassroots level of National Socialism's mass movements" and service in these organizations "meant involvement in public life and recognition to a far greater degree than ever before."[31]

Clearly, in making these judgments, historians are influenced by the perspective they adopt. Historians who conclude that Aryan women were oppressed under National Socialism generally adopt the perspective of the outside observer able to see and understand things about the past that the historical participants either missed or misunderstood, for they reach this conclusion in spite of the testimony of women who lived through the period. The assessment of women interviewed in oral histories that they had liberating experiences in mass Nazi organizations and in the Third Reich generally therefore needs to be dismissed or at least sharply contextualized. In addition to the problem posed by oral history evidence, some historians who see National Socialism as fundamentally oppressive of women make Nazi ideology more consistent than it actually was. To be sure, one of the principal tasks of the historian is to make an incoherent and ultimately incomprehensible past coherent and comprehensible. And in performing this task, historians necessarily oversimplify, making people, groups, actions, and ideas more consistent than they actually were. In the case of the Third Reich, historical oversimplification can be particularly problematic because National Socialism and the National Socialists were—as historical ideas and groups go— particularly incoherent and contradictory. Indeed, any model of Nazi theory no matter how nuanced will be considerably complicated by Nazi practice. The government of the Third Reich was what Martin Broszat characterized as a "plutocracy" of competing agencies and individuals.[32] The outcome of shifting rivalries, at the local and the national level, helped determine which element of Nazi ideology would dominate in any given circumstance, including those relating to women. In addition, as noted above, Nazi policies toward women were influenced by the exigencies created by the regime's own agendas and those created by the war.

Nonetheless, although the following paradigm oversimplifies, three strands of National Socialist ideology can be identified relating to women: a conservative strand that emphasized the home and family and the woman in her role as mother; a radical racist strand that emphasized breeding, a strand compatible with the woman as mother but potentially incompatible with the conservative emphasis on the family; and a radical populist strand that sought to mobilize younger women as activists on behalf of the Volksgemeinschaft, a strand at least partially compatible with the radical racist strand, for it was a community defined by race, but incompatible with the conservative emphasis on the family.[33] Furthermore, the Third Reich was situated in the midst of a profound social and cultural transformation affecting gender roles that spanned the first half of the twentieth century in Europe. As Dagmar Reese points out, "The transition from one prevailing notion of sexual roles to another is never clear cut or instantaneous. At any one time, several different 'images' or 'constructs' of gender will compete for predominance."[34] These different constructs of gender were present within National Socialism. The "received wisdom of the times" that women were to marry and have children was reflected in the conservative ideological strand, which sought to elevate and strengthen the family and, in harmony with the radical racist ideological strand, provided women with incentives to have children and with significant moral and material support once they had them.[35] Whereas state support for pregnant women and mothers was fully compatible with the radical racist strain of National Socialism, support for the traditional family was not, necessarily. This incompatibility is perhaps most strikingly illustrated by the Lebensborn project, a network of residential homes for expectant and nursing mothers who met National Socialist racial criteria. Designed to prevent abortions of racially valuable babies, the Lebensborn homes were primarily places where unmarried pregnant women went to receive support and have their babies. The Lebensborn homes also provided shelter and care for illegitimate Aryan children and orphans and, during the war, for racially valuable children abducted from families in Eastern Europe. Heinrich Himmler hoped that the Lebensborn project might ultimately serve to promote the breeding of genetically superior children by SS men and Aryan women outside of wedlock or indeed of any personal relationship. Nevertheless, even in its existing form, with its support for the bearing of children outside the institution of marriage, the Lebensborn project represented a radical departure from conservative veneration of the traditional family. The radical populist strain of National Socialism also worked against the family as a rival of the Volksgemeinschaft. The family was a source of social authority and an object of affective attachment that—along with other traditional institutions and institutional loyalties—potentially stood in the way of the National Socialist effort to forge popular identification with and commitment to the "community of the people."[36] The populist assault was directed against the family not as the place where children were produced but as the place where they were raised, and the National Socialists sought to draw young people away from the family to mobilize them on behalf of the Volk.

The challenge to the traditional family posed by the radical racist and populist strains of National Socialism and by the regime's need for women workers, then, contributed to the emancipation of women by weakening a patriarchal institution that had traditionally confined and inhibited them. The National Socialists also contributed to the emancipation of women in a positive sense by bringing women out into the workplace and by mobilizing mainly younger women in mass organizations where they enjoyed considerable independence and responsibility, a process of mobilization and emancipation that was radically accelerated by the war.[37] In postwar Germany, according to Ulrich Herbert, the "potential for activism" that had been "liberated" by the Nazis "made it impossible for many women to restrict themselves over the long term to the roles of housewife and mother or led them to experience those roles with deep frustration."[38] Dagmar Reese also concludes that, "contrary to popular opinion, National Socialism did *not* represent a return to outdated gender roles. On the contrary, the aim of the National Socialist state was to mobilize young women and exploit to the full their productive and reproductive capacities. This in turn required the removal of the patriarchal, regional, religious, and social restrictions that had traditionally confined the female role."[39] Nevertheless, it was only by defining themselves as "youth" that women were able to break through traditional gender restrictions. As a result, they experienced their emancipation as having come because they were young (and, I would add, "Aryan") and not because they were women (see the essay "Sexuality, Identity, and Equality in the Youth

Movement" in chapter 3). "But this flight from their own gender identity into the freer category of generation could only be partially successful and, indeed, the price was that they undermined at least part of their claim to be treated as equal individuals." As a result and because their emancipation was imposed on them by a criminal regime, these women remained, in Reese's view, "in a sort of limbo land," free of the bonds of the past but unable to participate in the liberation of postwar Germany.[40]

NATIONAL SOCIALISM AND MODERNIZATION

Historians have long debated whether the Third Reich should be treated as a historical period sharply delineated from what came before and what came after or whether it should be understood as reflecting historical continuities within a European context. Closely related to this historiographical debate is the disagreement among historians over whether National Socialism should be seen as reactionary or as a manifestation of modernization. Historians who emphasize the distinctiveness of the Third Reich tend to see National Socialism as reactionary; those who emphasize continuity and the European context tend to see National Socialism as an agent of modernization.[41]

The first scholars to claim that the Third Reich should not be seen as wholly reactionary were Ralf Dahrendorf and David Schoenbaum in the 1960s. Both believed that, although the Nazis did not set out to modernize German society, their policies had unintended modernizing effects.[42] Dahrendorf in particular argued that, by destroying the authoritarian structures and relationships that had prevented democracy from taking root in Germany, the National Socialists created the preconditions for democracy in postwar West Germany. Although the claim that National Socialism contributed to the modernization of German society was extremely controversial in the 1960s, over the course of the 1980s doubts about the inevitability of historical progress and the association of modernity with the catastrophes of the twentieth century, as well as the increased tendency of historians to view the Third Reich within a context that transcended Germany between 1933 and 1945, led a number of historians to connect National Socialism to modernization.[43]

The historian most closely associated with the modernization argument is probably Detlev Peukert. Like those who challenged the notion that Germany had followed a unique historical path (a German *Sonderweg*) leading ultimately to National Socialism,[44] Peukert argued in the early 1980s that National Socialism should be seen as a specific, if fatal, response to the crises that accompanied the modernization of all twentieth-century European societies.[45] The Third Reich both came in reaction to the "crisis-wracked, modernizing society" of the Weimar Republic and continued the process of modernization in a totalitarian and racist form.[46] Thus, Peukert did not see the Final Solution as "an atavistic breakthrough of primitive barbarism into a modern, humane civilization." Instead the National Socialist extermination project was simply a radical and racial form of the effort, characteristic of modernization, to establish social norms and impose social discipline.[47] Following Foucault, Peukert argued that the Holocaust reflected the dark side of the modernizing process:[48] "Both in its use of terror against 'community aliens' and its creation of an atomized society normalized by force, National Socialism demonstrated, with heightened clarity and murderous consistency, the pathologies and seismic fractures of the modern civilizing process."[49] Intentionally and unintentionally, according to Peukert, the National Socialists promoted the modernization of German society by weakening traditional institutions, authorities, cultural forms, and class barriers that had prevented the creation of a more egalitarian political and social order.[50] Michael Prinz and Rainer Zitelmann follow Peukert in arguing that "changes associated with postwar Germany had been introduced and promoted already before 1945 by the National Socialists."[51] Building on the social welfare initiatives of the Weimar Republic, the National Socialists created a welfare state, which in turn laid the foundation for state welfare in the two postwar Germanys.[52] The rearmament-driven economic boom and especially the Nazi mobilization of the population empowered the young, contributed to the emancipation of women, revolutionized sexual morality, and broke down traditional geographical barriers by bringing people out of villages and towns through organizations like the Work Service and the armed forces, a mobility that would characterize postwar West German society.[53] Indeed, Peukert and others have argued that, ultimately exhausted by the regime's mobilization efforts, Germans rejected politics and retreated into the private sphere, a rejection and a retreat that led to the social isolation and the mass consumer culture characteristic of West Germany.[54] "Looked at from a long-term perspective, the 1930s and 40s in Germany were," according to Prinz, "only a brief episode in the secular process of social modernization."[55]

Most historians would probably accept that National Socialism combined "modern" and "reactionary" elements and expressed both historical continuities and distinctiveness. Nevertheless, some scholars argue that any modernizing tendencies in National Socialism were overwhelmed by its retrogression to the archaic and that any continuities discernable in the Third Reich pale beside its ghastly distinctiveness. Thus Hans Mommsen concludes that "all measurable social-scientific evidence speaks against accepting the theory that the National Socialists gave an extensive thrust in the direction of modernization." He sees no significant progress in urbanization, occupational structure, or social mobility. Indeed, he even argues that the losses in the war, the hordes of refugees, and the Allied air raids produced no "relevant changes in the social structure of Germany. The decisive steps toward the modernization of German society occurred only in the period after 1945." Although Mommsen concedes that "a mobilizing and integrating function can be ascribed to the subjective factor, whereby National Socialism was experienced by broad sections of the population as a 'modern force,'" ultimately, National Socialism "possessed an exclusively destructive character" and produced nothing viable. "It all had to end in a monstrous marasmus." Although "the epoch of the Third Reich cannot be taken out of the context of German history as a whole," for Mommsen, it still represented "an unparalleled descent of a civilized western culture into barbarism."[56] Norbert Frei critiques the modernization theory from a different perspective. He argues that its proponents have divorced "modernization" from all ethical and political values to the point where the concept is emptied of meaning. To see Hitler or the Third Reich as manifesting modernizing tendencies can also serve as a dangerous retrospective rationalization of the irrational. Either one interprets National Socialism simply as a manifestation of underlying economic forces or one splits off "the impact of an anti-rational and immoral racist ideology and systematically applied extermination policies from the history of Germany in the twentieth century. . . . The result, in both cases, like it or not, is the historical and political leveling of the singular catastrophe that was National Socialism."[57]

Crucial to this debate is whether "modernization" is seen explicitly or implicitly as equaling "progress" or is regarded as making possible a more sophisticated, pervasive, and effective form of social control and oppression and whether one looks at National Socialism as a set of ideas and policies or focuses only on its effects, including especially the changes and destruction wrought by the war.[58] For the most part, the debate over modernization involves "social scientists," who compare empirical observations of Nazi Germany with an abstract model of modernization. From the perspective adopted here, a perspective that focuses on the subjective experiences of people, the case for historical continuity seems more clear-cut. Lutz Niethammer makes the simple but brilliant point that historical continuity is provided inevitably by human beings. The continuities that connect the Weimar Republic to the Third Reich and the Third Reich to the two postwar Germanys exist because people continued to live their lives after 1933 and after 1945, bearing the past into the present to create future historical realities.[59]

THE EXPERIENTIAL AND RACIAL REALITY OF THE *VOLKSGEMEINSCHAFT*

National Socialist ideology was conveyed not only in words but in sounds and images designed to appeal less to the intellect and more to the emotions, for the Volksgemeinschaft would be established not by economic restructuring but by transforming consciousness.[60] In and through the Volk, the individual would be given identity, power, and purpose. In and through the Volk, class conflict and political discord would be overcome. In and through the Volk, racially suitable Germans would be equal, or at least of equal value. National Socialism was based on the transcendent value of Gemeinschaft, on the belief that the subordination of the individual to the collective enhances and empowers both, that self-sacrifice is superior to self-interest, that unity brings harmony and strength whereas pluralism brings discord and weakness.

The first historian to draw attention to the psychological nature of the Volksgemeinschaft was David Schoenbaum, who argued in the mid-1960s that it represented a transformation of "subjective" and not of "objective" social reality. In his book *Hitler's Social Revolution: Class and Status in Nazi Germany, 1933–1939*, Schoenbaum claimed that the Nazi regime was characterized by tension between ideological ends and practical means.[61] The National Socialists resolved this conflict by producing a subjective social revolution, a revolution of consciousness, which reflected the movement's ideological goals while leaving objective economic and social conditions essentially intact in order to realize their political, economic, and military objectives. Specifically, by revolutionizing status, the Nazis were able to create, "at least psychologically, a classless society" while leaving wages and the class character of German society much as before 1933.[62] Viewed "objectively," then, no social revolution occurred; viewed "subjectively," the Volksgemeinschaft was an experiential reality.[63]

With the rise of social science history in the 1970s, historians tended to dismiss the Volksgemeinschaft as a "myth." However, beginning in the 1990s, as history came to focus less on an objectively observable social reality and more on people and their subjective experiences, historians rediscovered the experiential reality of the Volksgemeinschaft. Thus, following Martin Broszat, who saw Germans drawn to National Socialism primarily by "the vague attraction of its populism,"[64] Peter Fritzsche has argued that the Nazis' ability to respond to the widespread desire for a populist national community that would overcome the bitter political and social divisions of the Weimar Republic was crucial to their rise to power.[65] For Fritzsche, the Volksgemeinschaft stands squarely at the center of National Socialism and of its appeal to Germans during the Third Reich.[66] As we have seen, younger Germans were particularly enthusiastic about the ideal of the Volksgemeinschaft as well as about its reality as experienced in National Socialist mass organizations where young people from different classes and regions came together to work on behalf of the Volk. Not just Germans belonging to the "war youth" and "Hitler Youth" generations but, according to Norbert Frei, "broad segments of the population, including the working class," found "the ideology of the 'Volksgemeinschaft'" to be "both viable and attractive." Germans welcomed its egalitarian dimension, the idea that achievement should count more than ancestry, class, or rank, and social equality (measured empirically) appears to have increased during the Third Reich. More important than any tangible material benefits that came from the social opening and the revival of the economy, however, was "the widespread *feeling* of social equality" created by the National Socialists. The "constant social activism and the propaganda of egalitarianism . . . transformed social consciousness on a massive scale, the arrogance of class and estate were delegitimized and mental barriers were swept aside."[67] The "affective integration" of German society[68] was only increased by the mobilization of the population during the war.[69] Given its experiential "reality," then, the Volksgemeinschaft "was more than a myth."[70]

Although some have argued that the popularity of the Volksgemeinschaft with ordinary Germans led them to countenance National Socialist measures against the Jews, anti-Semitism specifically and racism in general were essential to the Volksgemeinschaft. The establishment of social consensus was based upon "ethnic homogenization," the exclusion—if necessary, the violent exclusion—of racial undesirables from the community.[71] "Racism was the foundation of the Volksgemeinschaft,"[72] and it was a racial "community of the people" whose existence depended equally on who belonged and on who did not. As a result, it makes more sense to understand Nazi anti-Semitism within the context of Nazi racism than the other way around. Whereas "anti-Semitism" determined who was to be excluded from the Volksgemeinschaft, "racism" also determined who was to be included in the community of the people. Moreover, if Nazi racism is seen simply as "a rationalization of Jew hatred,"[73] it becomes difficult to account for the German mistreatment of Poles, Russians, and above all gypsies. Finally, "anti-Semitism" conveys fear and especially hatred of Jews and employs the psychological mechanisms of scapegoating and projection. However, the term fails to convey the emotional satisfactions captured by the more comprehensive "racism," the intensely narcissistic experiences of belonging, superiority, and power. For National Socialist racism, with its attendant anti-Semitism, allowed Germans not only to belong to the Volksgemeinschaft but also to see themselves standing atop the evolutionary ladder—indeed, at the pinnacle of creation. And in order for Germans to experience themselves as *Übermenschen*, *Untermenschen* had to exist or be created. Racism allowed Germans "to raise their self-esteem," to experience feelings of superiority and dominance in mistreating people deemed racially inferior or in watching others mistreat them.[74] During the war, the occupied territories provided Germans with a stage on which to enact their role as members of the master race.[75] Gerhard Paul and Klaus-Michael Mallmann sum up the deadly racial essence of the Volksgemeinschaft and the experience of racial superiority it afforded Germans: "The equally inclusive and exclusive Janus face of a nation conceived of and realized as a Volksgemeinschaft found its most horrible expression during the war. Under its auspices not only was the 'Final Solution,' the Shoah of European Jewry, carried out; it also brought the collective elevation of the 'Master Race,' which was a very real—even if short-lived—experience for the Germans, as soldiers in the occupied territories, at home in relation to the slave army of foreign workers and prisoners-of-war."[76]

"LOOKING AWAY" FROM JEWS IN NAZI GERMANY

Like the interviewees in this study, Germans interviewed for other oral histories manifested the same inability to "see" Jewish people and "looked quickly away," "without thinking," from their mistreatment.[77] Some claim to have overlooked the persecution of Jews during the Third Reich altogether; they report not experiencing Reichskristallnacht, Jews wearing the yellow star, or the deportations.[78] According to Hans Dieter Schäfer, Germans, in relation to the persecution and extermination of the Jews, were like small children who put their hands over their eyes when confronted with something unpleasant or frightening in the conviction that what is not seen does not exist.[79] Gabriele Rosenthal understands the effort of her interviewees to "push away" the persecution of the Jews by not putting it into words or even allowing it to register in their consciousness as an effort to maintain emotional "distance" from "the suffering of the victims." Rosenthal's interviewees generally do not mention the degradation and the brutalization of Jews during the early years of the Third Reich. Similarly, they describe "the burning synagogues and the broken windows" on Reichskristallnacht in 1938 but not the violence done to human beings, "the arrested, beaten, and humiliated Jewish people." In striking contrast, Jews who experienced the pogrom recall not the property damage but their fear of being beaten or arrested. In Rosenthal's view, her interviewees sought to "evade the victims because they produced 'uncomfortable' feelings." The reaction of a woman interviewee who, as an adolescent, encountered Jews wearing the yellow star during the war is typical: "One avoided seeing the people, looking at them, or meeting them. One felt extremely uneasy."[80]

The effort to avoid feeling "uneasy" both grew out of and contributed to the exclusion of Jews from German society and ultimately from the human race in the consciousness of Germans, according to Rosenthal. "In this way the non-Jewish population began to deny the existence of Jewish people even when they 'shyly' went along the streets wearing the star. . . . It is typical that they speak indirectly about 'them,' referring to them in the third person. . . . It is always 'they,' whose only characteristic is that they do not belong to the 'we' of the Volksgemeinschaft."[81] Jewish people experienced the evasion, the "looking away," the "not seeing," as a dehumanization. Frau Meissner, who worked as a forced laborer at a concentration camp near Reichenbach in Silesia after 1944, recalls how the inhabitants of the town "*never, ever* looked at us" as she and her fellow inmates passed by on the way to work. She noticed how "they somehow or other managed to turn their heads away, for one wasn't supposed to see us. It wouldn't have been *pleasant* for them to have done so. If one didn't see us, why then we didn't exist, and then there were no concentration camps in the neighborhood. If one didn't see us, then one also couldn't see what people looked like, how they were dressed, what sort of people they were. If one doesn't look, then one doesn't witness, that's what I think."[82]

GERMAN KNOWLEDGE OF THE "FINAL SOLUTION" BEFORE 1945

The inability of Germans interviewed here and in other oral histories to "see" the persecution and deportation of their Jewish fellow citizens relates directly to their claim that they learned about the systematic extermination of the Jews only after the end of the war in 1945.[83] Indeed, the plaintive statement regarding the Holocaust, "But we didn't know," has been described as a postwar "national German refrain."[84] And yet recent historical research, most of it published since 1990, gives reason to doubt this assertion. Certainly, ample evidence of the genocide was available to ordinary Germans. Concentration camps were well known and well publicized as the places where the regime's political opponents and those deemed threats to the social and racial health of the Volksgemeinschaft (including especially Jews) were sent (see the essay "National Socialist Terror and the Germans" below). It was also, according to Robert Gellately, "virtually impossible" for people living in areas where there were Jews to avoid witnessing their persecution.[85]

The mass deportations of Jews from greater Germany, which began in the fall of 1941, took place in full public view and in front of crowds of onlookers. Indeed, the deportations aroused considerable public interest, out of a desire both to witness the spectacle and to acquire the possessions of those deported. As a result, without any official announcement, news of deportations spread across communities like wildfire. Jews were often collected at some central location (like the market square in Heidelberg) and then sent to the main railway station to be shipped to the East.[86] Any Germans who observed the trains filled with the deportees either at railway stations or as they waited on sidings for regular passenger trains to go by had to have a clear idea of what the fate of those inside was likely to be. As Volker Ullrich has pointed out, given that these were cattle cars crammed with human beings, barbed wire covering the air vents, it would have been difficult for anyone to believe that those inside were being taken to labor camps, since people whose work was of value would scarcely be transported in such a manner.[87] Finally, the deportation of millions of people from the Reich and the conquered territories was an enormous logistical undertaking involving large numbers of German civilians, from local town administrators to railway employees, who generally knew what would happen to the deported Jews.[88]

Given the scale of the killing and the number of people directly involved (including between two hundred thousand and five hundred thousand Germans and Austrians), the Final Solution was not a well-kept secret, and news of it leaked out of numerous sources and then circulated throughout the Reich via word of mouth.[89] Particularly, the activities of the *Einsatzgruppen* in the occupied territories in the East could not be kept secret.[90] These mobile killing squads, comprised of members of the Security Police and the Security Service supplemented by regular police and Waffen-SS military units, followed the victorious Wehrmacht first into Poland and then, after June 1941, into the Soviet Union, with orders systematically to kill Jews and gypsies as well as Soviet political commissars. The Einsatzgruppen were responsible for the death of as many as 1.3 million Jews and 200,000 Sinti and Roma in Eastern Europe. Hundreds of thousands of regular army soldiers witnessed and at times participated in these killings and communicated what they knew in letters and while on leave to the German civilian population.[91] Indeed, a stream of information not only about these killing actions but about the genocide in general flowed into the Reich from German soldiers—many of whom, according to the author of a recent study, had an "astonishingly detailed knowledge about the Holocaust"—as well as from family members of the occupying authorities in Eastern Europe.[92] Numerous sources confirm that, already by 1943, rumors and information about the genocide being carried out in the East had become widespread in Germany, including that gas was being used to kill Jews.[93] Auschwitz, the principal killing center, was not, as is usually assumed, some remote outpost in the distant East. It was located in the Warthegau, a newly incorporated part of the Reich, and was a vibrant rail hub through which large numbers of German soldiers and civilians routinely passed. The camp employed about seven thousand people, and the town of Auschwitz became home to many Germans over the course of the war, with a population of about twenty-eight thousand by 1943. Norbert Frei estimates that tens of thousands of Germans who either lived in the town or stopped there in transit would have known what was going on at the camp.[94]

But Germans did not need to rely on information and rumor coming from the East to learn about the Holocaust. Over the course of 1942, the BBC and other Allied radio stations broadcast detailed information to Germany about the genocide. Listening to these foreign radio broadcasts was a widespread practice—the BBC estimated that between 10 and 15 million

Germans tuned to its broadcasts daily.[95] In addition, the Allies dropped leaflets over Germany detailing the killing.[96] Finally, leading National Socialists, including Hitler, as well as the German press openly referred to the "Final Solution," even if details of the genocide were not discussed publicly either by the Nazi leadership or in the press.[97] Indeed, according to a recent study of the press during the Third Reich by Peter Longerich, the regime was actually far more publicly explicit about what was being done to the Jews than has been appreciated heretofore. Before the war, the press focused on the incompatibility of Jews with the creation of the Volksgemeinschaft in Germany.[98] After the invasion of the Soviet Union in June 1941, it presented the "Jewish Question" as the central issue of the war. Between October 1941 and mid-1943, during the phase of the deportations and when mass murder was in full swing, the regime, while not publicly mentioning the former and giving no details of the latter, openly proclaimed its intention to achieve "a radical, a final 'solution to the Jewish Question,'" using words like *Vernichtung* (annihilation) and *Ausrottung* (extermination) as euphemisms for genocide.[99] Speeches by top National Socialist officials and newspaper articles during this period proclaimed the general plan to "eliminate" the Jews, frequently referring to Hitler's "prophecy" of January 1939 that world war would bring "the extermination of the Jewish race in Europe" and stating openly that his prophecy was now coming to pass.[100] With the tide turning against Germany after the defeat at Stalingrad in 1943, the war was increasingly presented in the press as a racial *Endkampf*, or struggle for survival between the Germans and the Jews.[101] The Germans would either prevail or they would face extermination at the hands of their enemies and the Jews who were behind them.[102] Now the regime began making targeted references to the murder of the Jews in order to make the German people accessories to and complicit in the Final Solution. It appears that by raising the specter of punishment and vengeance for the genocide, the Nazi leadership sought to mobilize the German people behind the war effort and keep them fighting.[103] Although after 1943, the press campaign against the Jews abated somewhat, the theme "that the war had been forced upon Germany by 'the Jews' and must therefore end with the elimination of the Jews" was, according to Longerich, "repeated again and again until the bitter end."[104]

So, if evidence of the Final Solution was amply available to Germans, did they draw the obvious conclusion and "know" about the genocide before 1945? Some scholars seek to answer this question quantitatively. Postwar surveys conducted in West Germany between 1961 and 1998 consistently showed that between 32 and 40 percent of the population knew about the mass murder of the Jews before the end of the war. Accepting the essential accuracy of these figures, several historians conclude that a sizable minority (at least 20 to 25 million Germans) knew in some form about the Holocaust.[105]

Focusing less on how many Germans knew and more on what they knew, a number of leading historians conclude that most Germans had heard rumors about the mass shootings of Jews by the Einsatzgruppen in the East and knew about the deportations, but that the "majority" did not know that the latter meant death to the deported Jews in extermination camps.[106] Although most Germans knew that Jews had been mistreated and even murdered, Auschwitz and "the industrial mass annihilation" of the Jews was, in the words of Hans Mommsen, "simply beyond people's conception."[107] He and historians like him basically accept that the "mass of the population only learned about the existence of the extermination camps and of the systematic mass exterminations after the collapse" of the Third Reich.[108]

By contrast, historians like Saul Friedländer argue that, although "knowledge of 'Auschwitz' was limited until late in the war . . . information about the mass atrocities and wholesale extermination of Jews spread to the Reich soon after the beginning of the campaign against the Soviet Union" and became, in the words of Otto Dov Kulka, "general public knowledge."[109] Indeed, Friedländer thinks that the difference between knowing about "huge massacres" of Jews (such as were carried out by the Einsatzgruppen at Babi Yar) and "total annihilation" (such as occurred at Auschwitz) is not as decisive as some historians imagine. In any event, he concludes that "knowledge about the extermination centers was probably more precise than was thought until recently" and that "massive repression of knowledge, if it existed at all, took place after 1945, and probably much less beforehand."[110] Bernward Dörner, the author of a recent comprehensive study of German knowledge of the genocide, reaches a similar conclusion: "There can be no place for the claim that the German people 'knew nothing' about the systematic murder of the Jews. . . . Examination of contemporary sources establishes without doubt that the extermination of the Jews was not a secret in Germany. . . . At the latest by the summer of 1943, the vast majority of Germans had at a minimum assumed that all Jews living in German-occupied territory would be killed."[111]

Somewhere between these two positions is the view that the Holocaust was "an open secret."[112] In using this phrase, historians generally mean to convey that—with information about the mass murder "so plentiful, so detailed, and so credible"—"anyone who wanted to know could know" that the extermination of the Jews of Europe was being carried out in the East.[113] But, in this view, very few Germans "wanted to know" about the Holocaust. Just as interviewees in oral histories report having "looked away" from the persecution of Jews on German streets, Germans looked away from genocide before 1945. In the words of David Bankier: "There is no doubt that those who wished to know had the means at their disposal to acquire such knowledge. Those who did not or could not believe reacted so because they did not want to believe. In one sentence: They knew enough to know that it was better not to know more."[114] Thus a great many Germans knew individual details or aspects of the genocidal process (the deportations, the ghettos, the massacres), but relatively few had a comprehensive picture of the Final Solution—or wanted to have one. In the view of a number of historians, Germans repressed knowledge of the Final Solution by refusing to put the partial information, individual observations, and rumors together in order to draw the obvious conclusion.[115] Volker Ullrich cites a particularly vivid example of this form of not wanting to know. He quotes the testimony of SS-Unterscharführer Oswald Kaduk, one of the principal defendants at the Auschwitz trials in Frankfurt in the mid-1960s: "A flame rose five meters up into the sky when the ovens were going and could be seen from the [Auschwitz] railway station. The entire station was filled with civilians. Nobody said a thing about it. Passenger trains with vacationers were also there. Passenger trains often stopped at Auschwitz, and the entire station was shrouded in a fog. Wehrmacht officers would look out of the windows of the train and ask why the fog smelled as it did, so sweet? But no one had the courage to ask: What's going on here? There is no sugar factory here. What's the purpose of those smokestacks over there?"[116]

Scholars frequently attribute the repression of knowledge about the Holocaust to guilt.[117] Thus, according to Bankier, Germans cognitively withdrew from the extermination of the Jews "in the belief, whether conscious or not, that they could absolve themselves of collective guilt by dissociating themselves from the social consensus that had sanctioned a horrible crime." The claim not to have known about the Holocaust was, in Bankier's view, "a laborious pretence to deny guilt"—and to avoid punishment.[118] Indeed, the fact that Germans began to fear retribution and punishment after 1943, as the tide of the war began to turn against Germany after Stalingrad, is interpreted by a number of historians as revealing not merely the effectiveness of Nazi propaganda but, in the words of Volker Ullrich, "that underneath the cover of not knowing there was widespread awareness—or at least grounded suspicion—about the mass murder of the Jews."[119] Indeed, the popular claim of ignorance about the Holocaust was, in this view, a strategy developed by Germans already during the last years of the war to defend themselves against expected punishment in the event of a German defeat.[120]

Obviously, determining what it means to "know" is crucial in attempting to answer the question: What did the Germans know about the Holocaust before 1945?[121] In seeking to produce a more nuanced account of knowledge of the genocide, historians, explicitly or implicitly, often break the population down into discrete categories, such as those who knew a little, those who knew a great deal but did not have comprehensive knowledge, and those who were fully informed about the Final Solution.[122] And yet it seems clear that these distinctions existed not only between Germans but within them. Recognizing that knowing takes place on many levels, from the completely conscious to the deeply unconscious, and that one can simultaneously not know and know something, makes the attempt to draw distinctions between Germans based on their knowledge of the Holocaust problematic. Given the enormity of the genocide, the scale of the killing and depth of the horror, virtually every German with an awareness of the outside world must have known about the Final Solution on some level. In order to repress knowledge, one needs to know what it is that one does not wish to know. In order to look away, one needs to know what it is that one does not wish to see.

GERMAN ANTI-SEMITISM DURING THE THIRD REICH

In examining German attitudes toward Jews during the Third Reich, historians have tended to distinguish between the prewar period, which saw discrimination, persecution, and the relentless exclusion of Jews from German society, and the period of the war, which saw the mass deportations from Germany and the systematic extermination of European Jewry.[123] Despite some differences, historians generally agree that the 1930s saw the gradual establishment of what Frank Bajohr calls an "anti-Jewish consensus" between the regime and its citizens that Jews should be excluded from the Volksgemeinschaft, preferably legally and without violence.[124] By 1938/1939 the belief had been established, according to Bajohr, that Jews and Germans were fundamentally different, that a Jew was not a German but an alien presence "no longer belonging to the 'Volksgemeinschaft.'"[125] On the one hand, this consensus grew out of popular anti-Semitism that predated 1933 but that was given political will and force through the regime's actively anti-Semitic policies.[126] On the other hand, this consensus was fostered by National Socialist propaganda, by the adaptation of the population to the norms and expectations of the National Socialists, by the material, social, and political benefits that came to Germans as a result of the persecution, and by the affiliation of anti-Semitism with a popular and successful regime.[127] There were limits to this consensus, however. Anti-Semitic measures that Germans saw as working against their interests met with only modest success, such as the boycott of Jewish businesses in April 1933. Moreover, while there appears to have been little disapproval of attacks on Jews that did not affect non-Jews or sully the Reich's reputation abroad, there was considerable popular distress at brutal, public outbursts of violence against Jews, such as occurred on Reichskristallnacht in November 1938. The negative public reaction to the pogrom appears to have been based less on principled opposition to anti-Semitic persecution or on sympathy for the Jewish victims and more on the disorder and the destruction of property.[128] It was seen as an act of "hooliganism" and a "cultural disgrace."[129] Testifying to the deep-seated anti-Semitic belief in the sinister power of world Jewry, many Germans (including two interviewees quoted in this study) feared that the violence would lead to retribution against them or their families.[130]

In marked contrast to Reichskristallnacht, racial legislation, particularly the Nuremberg Laws and the abolition of Jewish citizenship in the fall of 1935, met with widespread popular approval because it "legally established" the "exclusion of Jews from the 'Volksgemeinschaft'" while promising to protect public order from extralegal acts of violence against Jews.[131] This legislation, along with countless ordinances at the national and local level and other forms of persecution from above and from below between 1933 and 1939, led to the occupational, sexual, social, physical, and psychological isolation of Jews from the rest of society.[132] Comprising less than 1 percent of the population in 1933, the half a million Jews living in Germany were already something of an abstraction to most Germans.[133] After 1933, in part out of anti-Semitic conviction and in part out of adaptation to the expectations of an anti-Semitic regime, most Germans broke off what contacts they had with Jewish acquaintances. Indeed, according to Bajohr, Jews discovered to their dismay that their isolation surpassed that decreed by law. Moreover, fear of rejection or persecution encouraged Jews to withdraw voluntarily from general society.[134] It seems clear that the isolation of the Jews of Germany fanned popular anti-Semitism, which was directed for the most part not at people one knew and interacted with but at "the Jew" who had been depersonalized and, in the words of Ian Kershaw, "reduced to an ideological anti-symbol."[135]

Although historians generally agree that from 1933 to 1939 most Germans wished to see Jews excluded from the Volksgemeinschaft, that they disapproved of brutal acts of violence but approved of legal discrimination against Jews, and that by the outbreak of the war Jews had been effectively isolated from the rest of the population, historians disagree strongly over the attitude of Germans toward Jews after 1939, the period that saw their deportation and extermination. This disagreement can be attributed to the national cultural, political, psychological, and ethical stakes involved, to the status of the Final Solution as an "open secret" in Germany, and to the lack of information in historical sources on popular attitudes toward the genocide. In particular, the Gestapo's *Stimmungsberichte*, or reports on the mood and attitudes of the population during the war, are characterized by what Otto Dov Kulka describes as "almost total silence regarding the Jews." Not just the Gestapo reports but the German public appears to have responded to the persecution, deportations, and readily available information about the mass killings of Jews in the East with an eerie silence, a silence all the more striking in light of the willingness of Germans to voice criticisms of the regime on virtually all other topics, including the conduct of the war, official corruption, or food and economic policy. Indeed, public protest brought the regime's effort to remove crucifixes in Bavaria and its euthanasia program to a halt.[136]

Given the silence of the sources and the silence of the Germans, historians have been forced to speculate on German attitudes toward Jews during the war by using what little evidence is available to reconstruct those attitudes and by interpreting the meaning of the silence.[137] A widely held view is that, although most Germans were anti-Semitic and wished to see the Jews removed from German society, even to vanish, very few actually wished their physical annihilation. In the words of Hans Mommsen, "The mass of the population had no sympathy for the genocidal policies" of the Nazis.[138] In this view, Germans were "latently" or "passively" anti-Semitic but did not share what Ian Kershaw calls the "active-dynamic hatred" of the Nazis and did not want to see the Jews brutalized, let alone killed.[139] The silence of the sources and of the Germans regarding the Final Solution is interpreted, in this view, as reflecting the passivity, the apathy, and above all the "indifference" of the overwhelming majority of Germans to the persecution, deportation and, to the extent that they knew about it, extermination of the Jews.[140] With Jews already "excluded from the 'real world' of daily life" by the time of their deportation in October 1941, popular indifference toward their fate was increased by the war, with its growing impact on the civilian population and brutality after that date.[141] During the years when the Jews were being systematically exterminated, Allied bombs rained down on Germany, the fighting at the front intensified, casualties mounted, and an ultimate German victory became less and less certain. As a result, to quote Kershaw, "the vast majority of Germans had plenty of other things on their mind."[142] Moreover, the ferocity of the fighting increasingly inured Germans to violence and death.[143] The mass killings of Jews in the East were simply "submerged" in the war of annihilation raging on the eastern front.[144] Although most Germans did not wish the Jews to be exterminated, their "indifference" was nonetheless "lethal," according to historians like Kershaw. By passively observing the persecution and deportation of their fellow citizens, by looking away from the evidence of mass killing in the East, and by failing to protest at any point along the way to the Final Solution, ordinary Germans enabled the Nazis to carry out genocide.[145] In Kershaw's famous phrase: "The road to Auschwitz was built by hate, but paved with indifference."[146]

In marked contrast, Otto Dov Kulka and Aron Rodrigue see the Germans as complicit in the genocide.[147] Thus "the absence of a pronounced reaction and the general passivity toward the physical annihilation of the Jews" on the part of Germans are understood as reflecting "a broad consensus on the government's policy, a kind of tacit agreement that there was no need to take an active stand on the subject."[148] Finally, a few scholars seek to bring "indifference" and "complicity" together by seeing the Germans as secretly and silently supportive of the regime's anti-Jewish policies and at the same time generally disinterested in the fate of the Jews.[149]

The view that the general populace wanted Jews to be persecuted and perhaps even killed and yet was simultaneously unconcerned about their fate reveals the fundamental problem created by the choice of the word "indifferent" to characterize the relationship of the Germans to the Jews and to their persecution, deportation, and extermination. For anti-Semitism (hostility toward Jews), not to speak of the wish to have them killed, means having a strong emotional response to Jews, whereas "indifference" means having little or no affective response to Jews at all. In order to use "indifference" in this context, one must posit a categorical difference between the perpetrators, who hated Jews, and the bystanders, who were indifferent to them. That is to say, one must follow historians who make a sharp distinction between "the Nazis" (a category that generally goes undefined) and "the Germans."[150] On the basis of this distinction, "the Nazis" were the hate-filled killers and "the Germans" were the indifferent onlookers. But of course, most Nazis were Germans and a great many Germans were Nazis or at least sympathetic to National Socialism; and in any event, it is difficult to see how a clear boundary can be drawn between the two.[151] The use of "indifference" to characterize the attitude of ordinary Germans toward Jews, then, presumes too sharp a distinction between leaders and led and fails to take account of the part played by German society in the persecution.[152] For, as Frank Bajohr points out, "The Nazi regime was no simple top-down dictatorship" that imposed its will on the Germans through force and terror "and condemned the society to play a strictly passive role. Instead the 'Third Reich' was more a plebiscitary dictatorship that took full account of 'popular opinion.'" According to Bajohr, "The creeping exclusion of the Jews, their gradual loss of civil rights after the coming to power of the National Socialists in 1933, their isolation, and finally their deportation and murder was not only a political process carried out by the state and the party. It was also a social process in which German society participated in many different ways."[153] State persecution of the Jews was rooted in "societal anti-Semitism" and effective because it resonated with popular anti-Jewish sentiment in Germany.[154] As Michael Wildt puts it, persecution of the Jews "'from below' was just as necessary as the decrees, laws, and measures 'from above' in creating the Volksgemeinschaft."[155]

If instead of "indifference," which creates too wide a gulf between state and society and a false categorical distinction between Nazi perpetrators and German bystanders, one speaks instead of a "lack of empathy" for Jews on the part of Germans, then the perpetrators and the bystanders do not become qualitatively different human beings but can be seen as connected to one another, standing at different points on a continuum. Whereas indifferent human beings do not carry out genocide, people lacking in empathy can persecute, deport, and exterminate or stand by, wordlessly, silently, passively, watching the persecution, deportation, and extermination. Neither perpetrators nor bystanders could imagine themselves in the place of the Jews. Jews were for both, to quote an *anti*-Nazi German schoolteacher in 1937, "another world."[156]

Although several historians have defined "indifference" in a way that suggests an inability or unwillingness on the part of Germans to recognize Jews as human beings like themselves,[157] only a handful of scholars have directly addressed the lack of empathy of Germans for Jews and its consequences for both groups of people. Thus Peter Fritzsche, in contrasting the reaction of Germans to the persecution and deportation of the Jews with their reaction to the euthanasia program, has written that in 1941 Germans "could imagine living off a meager pension, or suffering incapacitating wounds in battle, or growing old and infirm. But they could not imagine being Jewish."[158] And Claudia Koonz has described the creation of what she calls a "Nazi conscience" in ordinary Germans that "disabled empathy against outcasts," mentally excluded Jews from the Reich and ultimately from the human race entirely, and made popular acceptance of genocide possible.[159] Similarly, Gabriele Rosenthal argues that "before the German-Jews were taken aboard the 'transports' after 1941, they had already been dehumanized in the consciousness of many non-Jews to the point that one can speak of their having been psychologically murdered even before their arrival at the extermination camps. Thereby people were killed in the concentration camps who, in accordance with Nazi ideology, had already been transformed in consciousness into vermin, for whom one cannot experience empathy."[160] Finally, although using the word "indifference" to characterize the attitude of Germans toward Jews during the Third Reich, Carolyn Dean nonetheless unpacks and redefines the term in a way that makes it compatible with the dehumanizing absence of empathy. Following Saul Friedländer, she does so by focusing not on the "indifferent" reaction of the Germans but on how Jews experienced that reaction. Again citing Friedländer, Dean argues that the bystanders were only semiconscious of their "desire that Jews disappear." Neither unconscious nor in the forefront of consciousness, the wish had become "so deeply embedded in social reality" that only the Jews noticed it. Anti-Semitism had become "structural" for Germans, simply a "part of the way things should be," and their manifest "indifference" was "nothing more and nothing less than anti-Semitism" that had become "normalized prejudice." Because anti-Semitism had been "assimilated" or internalized by Germans, it could be fully experienced only by its victims. Thus it is only from the point of view of Jews like Frau Meissner (quoted on page 162) that the "indifferent" reaction of the Germans could be recognized for what it was: a brutal "symbolic erasure." For Dean, then, the bystanders share an "active . . . complicity" with the perpetrators, a complicity that took the "form of symbolic rather than literal murder." And she insists that we avoid minimizing the "agency" of the bystanders, their "responsibility" for the genocide, by chalking it up to an "'understandable,' . . . all-too-human response," one that transcends the specific context of Nazi Germany.[161]

To be sure, the Holocaust occurred at a particular time and in a particular place. Nevertheless, it must be remembered that while those who carried out genocide and those who simply acquiesced to it were connected by a lack of empathy for Jewish people, there are also connections between them and us, connections we might prefer not to face. By splitting off Nazi perpetrators from ordinary Germans, we also split the perpetrators off from us. We can imagine ourselves in the place of—empathize with—the ordinary Germans, perhaps, but we would prefer not to imagine ourselves in the place of—empathize with—the Nazi perpetrators: thus we interpose "indifferent" bystanders to stand between us and the "hate-filled" killers. Paradoxically, through our unwillingness to think our way inside the experience of those who carried out the genocide, we demonstrate that the closing off of empathy, which made the genocide possible, is a universal (though, to quote Dean, "understandable") human response. If a shared lack of empathy brings Nazis and Germans, perpetrators and bystanders, closer together, it implicitly brings the Nazi perpetrators closer to us as well. For the Holocaust was not simply a dehumanizing and murderous German response; it was also a dehumanizing and murderous "all-too-human response."

NATIONAL SOCIALIST TERROR AND THE GERMANS

It is in relationship to Nazi terror that a rare—and striking—discrepancy emerges between historical memory and historical research. The interviewees in this and other oral history studies present themselves as having lived in fear of the Gestapo, particularly during the war years, a fear they allege prevented them from voicing criticism of the regime generally and of the persecution of Jews in particular.[162] Recent historical scholarship presents a very different image of the relationship of the general population to the secret state police and the National Socialist terror network.

When asserting that they had no knowledge of the genocide of the Jews before 1945, interviewees in oral histories frequently claim that they did not know about the existence of concentration camps. It is possible that they are simply confusing concentration camps with extermination camps. Although the distinction is artificial to a degree and a great many Jews were murdered in concentration camps (often in gas chambers), some Germans may not have known about the extermination camps or at least about the full extent of the mass killing that went on in them. It is impossible, however, for anyone not to have known about the concentration camps. In fact, the regime publicized the existence of concentration camps as the place where racial and social outsiders and political troublemakers were sent by the Gestapo.[163] Not just concentration camps but concentration camp inmates, "dressed in the pathetic striped garb of the camp, right down to the well-known badges signifying nationality and 'crime,'" were a visible presence in the Third Reich, particularly during the war, working in factories, clearing city streets of rubble, and being transported in appalling conditions from one place to another.[164]

The regime publicized the concentration camps and the vigilance of the Gestapo not merely to intimidate potential opponents and to cow the population but also to win popular support.[165] Recent research suggests that Germans less feared than approved of the Gestapo and supported its effort to send criminals, the asocial, and other "community aliens" to concentration camps.[166] Indeed, Germans actively collaborated with the Gestapo by denouncing coworkers, neighbors, friends, and even family members they deemed a threat to the regime, the Volksgemeinschaft, or their own self-interest. Given the relatively small number of police officials, the Gestapo was dependent upon the willingness of Germans to denounce their fellow citizens.[167] Whereas Robert Gellately sees the Gestapo as generally "reactive," waiting to take action until it received information from the public,[168] Eric Johnson argues that in relation to those belonging to groups deemed political, social, or racial threats, "the Gestapo acted with conviction and might" while generally overlooking the "indiscretions" of ordinary Germans, who were "never the focus of the Nazi terror apparatus."[169] As a result, "people's comrades" (Germans who accommodated themselves to the regime, conformed to the community, and met Nazi racial criteria) had little to fear from the secret police. As Richard Evans points out, however, those designated as "enemies of the people" (Communists, Socialists, and other political opponents of the regime) and as "community aliens" (Jews, gypsies, Jehovah's Witnesses, and the asocial) numbered in the millions.[170]

The Gestapo's strategy of focusing on target groups and leaving ordinary Germans alone continued during the war, although the pressure on "enemies of the people" and on "community aliens," especially Jews, was increased. In part as a result and because the number of agents decreased during the war, the Gestapo was, if anything, even more dependent on denunciations from the public and even less concerned with offenses committed by ordinary Germans.[171] The most common of these was listening to foreign radio broadcasts.[172] Although the designated enemies of the regime were severely punished for this offence, ordinary Germans generally suffered nothing more than a reprimand and virtually none were sent to a concentration camp.[173] Similarly, the crimes of spreading "malicious gossip" (including criticism of Hitler and the Nazi Party) and "defeatism" (including complaints about the economy or the conduct of the war) were either ignored or only mildly punished by the authorities when committed by ordinary Germans.[174] In the words of Eric Johnson, "Although many German citizens belonged to one or more of the targeted groups, most did not, and consequently most Germans suffered not at all from the terror. There was no need to target them because most Germans remained loyal to the Nazi leadership and supported it voluntarily from the beginning to the end of the Third Reich, if to varying degrees."[175]

In attempting to reconcile the conclusions of historians with the testimony of oral history interviewees, it is important to keep in mind that the boundary separating "people's comrades" from "enemies of the people" and "community aliens" may have appeared more permeable during the Third Reich than appears to historians in retrospect. Moreover, although recent historical research suggests that ordinary Germans had little to fear from the Gestapo directly, it confirms they had good reason to be afraid of their fellow citizens, who were ready and willing to denounce them to the authorities. The obligation of Germans described by the interviewee in this study to "look out for one another" during the Third Reich, in both benign and malign senses of the phrase—to look after those who belonged to the Volksgemeinschaft and to watch out for those who were to be excluded from it—was what made the pressure on the population to obey and to conform ubiquitous and effective: the Gestapo was an instrument of a terror exercised in no small measure by the community.[176]

MEN AND WOMEN DURING THE WAR AND IN ITS AFTERMATH

Men interviewed in oral histories have overwhelmingly negative memories of the period of the war.[177] They do not have much to say to interviewers about their wartime experiences, and women report that their husbands have told them little or nothing either.[178] When men do speak about the war, they tend to censor its horrors, their suffering as well as the suffering of others. Killing, being killed, and the dead are generally left out of their accounts, as is all mention of criminal actions on the eastern front, or they are merely alluded to with phrases such as "One can't talk about such terrible things."[179] Despite the psychological centrality of the war for the German men who fought in it, they appear unable to integrate their experiences from this time into their life histories.[180] And what makes the war especially difficult for these men to come to terms with and hence to talk about, according to Gabriele Rosenthal, is its association with National Socialism. She sees these men as traumatically repressed. They cannot face the losses they suf-

fered, and they cannot face the crimes against humanity that were associated
with those losses. Hence for Rosenthal, as for other scholars, loss and guilt
become intertwined and mutually reinforcing (see the essay "The Mitscherlichs' 'The Inability to Mourn'" in chapter 9). The unwillingness or inability
of men to speak about these issues either to interviewers or to loved ones is
"an indication of how unresolved and therefore contemporary the suffering
they experienced remains."[181]

In marked contrast, women interviewed in oral histories generally are
eager to talk about their wartime experiences. Despite the hardships and the
horrors, many German women look back fondly on the period of the war,
often describing it as the most lovely time in their lives.[182] They appear to
have flourished during the war, working in the Work Service or for the BDM,
in field hospitals or for the Red Cross, in armament industries or in agriculture, in the military auxiliary or as streetcar conductors. The mobilization of
women in support of the war effort provided them with opportunities to engage in activities and assume responsibilities that would have been unimaginable in peacetime and to gain self-confidence and a sense of fulfillment.[183]
Even the period of the Reich's collapse is frequently recalled with an excited
nostalgia. Like several women in this study, women interviewed for other
oral histories, when asked to tell the story of their lives, leap to the period of
the Zusammenbruch. They describe repeatedly and extensively their experiences at the end of the war, and during the war generally, devoting more of
their interview to this time in their lives than to any other.[184] As in this study,
their accounts of this period are coherent narratives: alive, vivid, and visual.
They often read like adventure stories.[185] And finally, the women's descriptions of this period likewise brim with pride at what they had been able to
accomplish under difficult circumstances.[186] Just as the self-confidence that
women gained through their mobilization by the National Socialists in the
1930s laid the foundation for their effectiveness during the war and the period of the Third Reich's collapse, so the self-confidence that women gained
in mastering the challenges of the Third Reich's collapse laid the foundation
for their success in dealing with the hardships of the immediate postwar period.[187] Indeed, the years 1944 to 1947 have come to be known as the "hour
of the women" after the title of a book by Christian Graf von Krockow in
which he described the ability of his sister, Libussa, to survive the collapse of
the Reich in Pomerania and, with parents and newborn child, to make her
way to the West.[188]

Even the experience of rape, one of the principal horrors endured by
German women at the end of the war, serves to demonstrate their strength
and the weakness of German men. Recent historical research has revealed
the extent of the mass rape of German women by Allied soldiers, primarily
members of the Red Army. In Berlin alone, Soviet soldiers raped more than

one hundred thousand women, 40 percent of them multiple times. The vast majority of these rapes took place during the last week in April 1945, when rampaging Soviet soldiers raped women regardless of age, appearance, or infirmity; many women were raped to death. A thirty-two-year-old woman living in Berlin described in her diary the experience of rape, her own and others, with the arrival of the Red Army in the city during that April week. Some days later, in an entry on 8 May 1945, she wrote: "But here we're dealing with a collective experience, something foreseen and feared many times in advance that happened to women right and left, all somehow part of the bargain. And this mass rape is something we are overcoming collectively as well. All the women help each other by speaking about it, airing their pain, and allowing others to air theirs and spit out what they've suffered."[189] Indeed, in May 1945, it appeared that, because of its ubiquity, the trauma of rape would be worked through collectively. Women spoke openly with one another, with doctors, and with local authorities about having been raped and, like the woman quoted above, recorded the experience in diaries and memoirs.[190]

Nevertheless, the subject quickly became taboo, in the family and in society, as the rubble of the war, both literally and figuratively, began to be cleared away.[191] Indeed, the memory of rape appears to have been expunged from the life histories of women who lived through this period. Like the interviewees in this study, German women generally do not acknowledge having been raped when recalling their experiences at the end of the war, even though statistics suggest that many of them must have been. Instead they deal with the topic by describing the rape of others and their own dramatic escape from situations where rape was likely to have occurred.[192] To be sure, the silence of the women can be attributed to their experience of having been *geschändet*, violated and degraded by what had been done to them.[193] And yet the shift from speaking to silence that took place immediately after the war on the part of German women seems to have coincided with the return of the German men, many of whom experienced the rape of the women as a blow to their honor.[194] According to Atina Grossmann, "With the return of prisoners of war and the 'remasculinization' of German society, the topic was suppressed, not as too shameful for women to discuss, but as too humiliating for German men and too risky for women who feared . . . the reactions of their menfolk."[195] Years later, rape victims recalled that they had not wanted "to 'bother' their male partners with this experience." In the words of Andrea Pető, "Loyalty to their men was stronger than their wish to come to terms with the horror."[196] Women did not speak about being raped because men could not bear to hear about it.[197] And when men did learn that their wives had been raped, it often led to divorce or years of sexual abstinence.[198] The rape of the women was so difficult for the men to bear because it literally brought home their defeat as Germans and as men—and on a most basic, atavistic level. They had failed to defend and protect German women, in the eyes of the women and, especially, in their own eyes.[199] The rape of the women emphasized the men's helplessness, humiliation, and sense of emasculation at the end of the war.[200] Ultimately, women did not speak of having been raped to protect their defeated, demoralized, and weakened men.

III

Postwar Germany

7

INTERVIEWS

Maturity

VOLKER SEBASTIAN

When I was released from Russian captivity, I planned to make for Hamburg.[1] That was the only good solution. I was advised against returning to Thuringia, where I had my father's land and house. I'd counted on those, but I couldn't go there.[2] My parental household had completely fallen apart,[3] and besides, it was too risky. I didn't want to fall into the hands of the Russians again. I'd already been in Russia long enough.[4] But then I heard that I shouldn't go to Hamburg either because it was too badly damaged, too expensive, and impossible to find housing.* I learned this from "my man," the one who had recruited me into the youth movement, who lived in Hamburg.† He advised me and my wife[5] to make for Eckernförde instead.[6] I was able to travel through the Soviet zone to Eckernförde,[7] making it secretly over the border.[8]

So in June 1947[9] I returned to my family in Eckernförde, actually to a village near Eckernförde,[10] and there I began to rebuild my life.[11] I returned, I like to say, "beaten down and battered in body and soul."[12] Those were hard, hard years, without question.[13] When I was released from Russian captivity, I owned only a wooden crate and a cotton wool jacket, and thus equipped, I made it to Eckernförde.[14] My wife and children[15] were already there.[16] She had arrived from Halle a few weeks before with only a rucksack on her back

---

*Hamburg was one of the cities most heavily damaged by Allied bombing. After the war, seventy-seven thousand citizens of Hamburg lived in cellars.

†The act of recruiting someone into the youth movement was of considerable significance to those involved.

and the children[17] along with my father-in-law.[18] Unfortunately, my mother-
in-law had died young, and he had been living all alone. So he moved in
with us and helped out as much as he could.[19] We lived together on a little
farmstead and were as poor as church mice.[20] We lived in a region northwest
of Kiel[21] that had been declared a disaster area because of all the refugees
from East Prussia and Schleswig-Holstein who were there.[*,22] So things were
pretty lousy,[23] and I had to start from zero, but somehow we managed to
suffer our way through.[24] I worked very hard[25] as an agricultural laborer[26] at
the farm where my family had taken refuge.[27] Then, after a quarter of a year,
I went to a farmer in Osterby[28] and helped him out—I brought in the entire
harvest! Do you know what I got for doing that? A couple of liters of milk,
ten eggs, and two pounds of flour. That was it! He was stingy, and he was
the richest farmer in the whole village.[29] Those are things you get through
without a lot of "Juppheidi and Tralala" you know;[30] but with the help of
my wife, who threw herself into the task magnificently, we managed to eke
out an existence.[31] Still, for our children it was wonderful that they could be
in the countryside. As a result, they did not die and are alive today. What it
must have been like for my wife in the days when I was locked up, you can't
imagine.[32]

The years after I returned from imprisonment were not hard years only
in a material sense.[33] Suddenly we had to recognize—all of us—that everything we had done, often with great enthusiasm or out of a sense of duty—
everything had been in vain.[34] The Zusammenbruch not only meant the collapse of a state but also the collapse of values and ideals I'd believed in, values
and ideals that had simply become a part of me without my being aware of
it. They were the values of loyalty, comradeship, all those hackneyed words.
Suddenly water was splashed in our faces, and we realized that everything
had been abused in the service of certain political goals. Those values had
provided us with orientation, a real, very human orientation. We had *lived*
those values.[35] Not only[36] were we totally disoriented initially,[37] but we were
also always presented as bad people back then, especially those of us who
had been officers. If there was a play broadcast on the radio in 1947–48 and
they wanted to depict a bad person, then he was always an officer. My son
was three years old when I first saw him after the war. If I had fallen in battle,
what would he have thought of me?[38] Young women too condemned us, the
returning veterans, as war criminals and turned their attentions to the soldiers of the occupying armies. It was a wholly bitter time. We felt completely
abandoned.[39] And on top of it all there was the pure, naked fear about simple

---

* As of April 1947, there were approximately 10 million refugees in western Germany,
generally resettled in rural areas. As of 13 September 1950, 856,943 refugees had been resettled in Schleswig-Holstein, comprising one-third of the state's population.

survival.[40] So it was a *complete* collapse, and I just wanted to wipe it all away. I wanted simply to say, "That was all a bad period in my life, which can only be rectified by forgetting about it." That was my attitude.[41]

And it was when I was at absolute bottom that my wife helped me so much, for she had more confidence in the future than I did.[42] Nothing of what I had so often experienced and seen in other women applied to her.[43] I married her just after she had moved to Plauen. She went on to study to be a meteorologist at the university in Saxony. If she'd become one, she probably would only have been permitted to work in Saxony, as a civil servant.[44] But she gave it all up for the sake of our marriage.[45] Looking back, I'd have to say that without my wife I'd be worth half of what I am.[46] Without her, so much would have been utterly impossible for me to accomplish. She has a calm ability to persevere. We have very different temperaments, and I was always able to find calm and comfort in her.[47] Throughout our lives, we have discussed every difficult situation we faced and based many tough decisions on those calming conversations.[48] Today we live well together. Because of tensions in the family, we weren't able to celebrate our golden anniversary with all the children. So we celebrated outside the family, and then afterward drove to our daughter in Geneva. She asked how we had managed to stay together for fifty years. I replied, "Well, you have to want to a bit. But wanting to isn't always enough. You also have to have a bit of luck. And you can't allow disagreements to put you in a state. And you can't fight over trivial matters. That's how we managed it."[49]

So, as I said, I returned beaten down in body and soul[50] after the war, and of course I immediately sought to reestablish contact with members of our youth movement group and then beyond the group.[51] Those who had survived took us into their circle.[52] As I said, I had been in correspondence with the man in Hamburg who had recruited me. I traveled to Hamburg to visit him, and he took me along to a gathering of the Free German Circle.* Someone said to me, "Listen, if you are staying in Eckernförde, then you absolutely must go to Kiel. Dieter Busse is organizing the Free German Circle there." I went and visited him, and from then on, whenever I could, I attended meetings from Eckernförde.[53]

So we quickly reestablished our contacts and wondered what would happen next.[54] Well, Dieter Busse used numerous channels to help the two of us, my wife and me, so that we went from the rucksack and the list of returnees from Russia to getting back on our feet again. You don't forget something like that.[55] In addition, I suddenly found myself in a circle of people I felt I knew, which was so important given that I'd returned from captivity. And it wasn't just the imprisonment. We'd also been driven out of our homeland.

---

* The Free German Circle had been founded in late spring 1947.

It meant so much to have acquaintances around us who could serve as role models, people who had lived longer in the West[56] than we had and were able to tell us: "If you want to do thus and so, go there and there." In a practical sense,[57] the Free Germans helped me out immeasurably.[58] But finding a spiritual and emotional home, recognizable surroundings, was even more important.[59] The people in the Free German Circle had traversed exactly the same path in life in the Bunds as I had. You didn't need to explain things in order to have them understand what you wanted or to understand what they wanted.[60] That was the most important aspect of joining the Free German Circle for me.[61]

Through various means, Dieter Busse in Kiel was able to find me a job[62] and that's how I was able to rebuild my life after the war and become something again.[63] We moved immediately[64] from the country to Kiel,[65] where my wife and I were able to find an apartment. We lived in two barracks' rooms along with my father-in-law.[66] It was still the time of rubble during which you had to build, scrabble, and beg a new home together, for we had lost everything.[67] I took a position as manager of a small leather business. It had been founded by a former member of the youth movement[68] who owned many pieces of discarded leather. There was a lot you could do with pieces of discarded leather back then.[69] And in those days you didn't need an income, you needed things to barter.*,[70] At first I didn't know how to operate in the black market, even though I was sitting on a treasure trove. But over time you learn to play the game, you are forced to play the game. I would go out into the countryside and trade leather articles.[71] So, in the period before the currency reform, conditions were certainly bad for us, but we were able to secure the bare necessities.[72]

When the era of the Reichsmark came to an end,[73] I decided[74] to study to become an engineer.[75] There was a tradition of engineering in the family, and I thought I'd enjoy the work.[76] But in order to be admitted to civil engineering school, I had to complete a training period. Through various means, Dieter Busse was able to find a job for me[77] as a construction trainee with a building contractor near Osnabrück.[78] I didn't find the work very difficult, for in the first place, I'd been in the military and secondly, I had worked in a mine when I was in Russian captivity.[79] In the meantime, we had moved to Melle, which is near Osnabrück. It wasn't hard to move, since we didn't have a lot of possessions.[80] Anyway, I started working on a bridge over the Mittelland canal, which had been blown up by the SS. I mixed cement and

---

* Until the Currency Reform of June 1948, Germany effectively had a barter economy. The official currency, the Reichsmark, was essentially valueless, and therefore having an income was much less important than having things that one could exchange on the black market.

did whatever else was needed. When I started, I asked the building contractor not to let it be known on the construction site that I had held the rank of
major. I didn't know the people working there, and I feared that this information might not go over well. It turned out that the opposite was the case.
I was embraced by the others at the site. One man brought me special ration
cards to enable me to get things that weren't otherwise available or that one
could only get illegally, like china. Another brought me a pot of syrup. Nothing was too good for me.[81]

Then I began my studies at a school of civil engineering. Originally I
had wanted to study at the technical university in Hanover. I still have their
letter of rejection. The rejection was based on the fact that I first needed
to prove myself for a half a year by helping remove rubble from the city of
Hanover. I thought that was simply outrageous. I had already proved myself long enough during the war, and I didn't need to prove myself again by
shoveling out Hanover. I told them, speaking plainly, to piss off.[82] After my
rejection, I discovered that I could study at a specialized university in Lippe,
near Dortmund.[83] Following the currency reform, I had received a small loan
granted to soldiers who had been released from Russian captivity. It wasn't
more than two hundred Marks, but it made a difference during those semesters in Lippe.[84] Still, I had to work during vacations as well as during the university semesters in order to earn my keep.[85] After the currency reform it was
important to have some form of income, for the "trade and commerce" that
had gone on[86] during the period of the Reichsmark[87] had come to an end.*
Now you had to earn money, which above all else took up time, time you had
to find outside of your studies, time you didn't have if you wanted to finish
as quickly as possible. We had to work really hard.[88] Initially I had problems
concentrating, but very quickly I was able to produce good work and establish myself at the university.[89] I attended the school of civil engineering for
two and a half years, passed my examinations, and became a civil engineer.[90]

With the help of a friend,[91] I was able to land a job with an English firm,
Gerryson Engineering, in Bad Oeynhausen. I had gone to Gerryson Engineering with my final thesis project under my arm. It was a design for some sort
of bridge of a particular weight-bearing class. The man there looked at my
thesis. I could see that he didn't have a clue about it. He only asked if I could
speak English. I replied, "A little." Then he asked when I could start working. I replied, "Immediately." So three days later I began working there and
earned my first real income. With my first paycheck we were finally able to

---

* The barter economy came to an abrupt end with the Currency Reform of 20–21 June
1948, which saw the introduction of the German Mark in the Western zones of occupation
by decree of the Western Allies. The economic impact was dramatic, with a surge in demand
for consumer goods.

pay off our debts to the grocery store. So I lived in Bad Oeynhausen while the family stayed on in Lippe.[92]

Although I didn't much like working for the English,[93] I worked with them for three years and nine months.[94] Then I met[95] a member of the Free German Circle, an old Junabu man* and former officer who was working at[96] a construction firm in Wanne-Eikel.[97] As had been true in the past, after very brief initial contact, we had recognized one another [as former youth movement members] and talked about what we had done in the youth movement.[98] Then he asked me, "Would you like to work here?"[99] So I had the good fortune to have as my superior someone who had been in the youth movement of the Bunds.[100] Unfortunately, the firm was only able to pay low salaries, and I had to support my family, which remained in Lippe,[101] as well as myself in Wanne-Eikel,[102] where I rented a room from some people. So I looked around for a better-paying position[103] and ended up at the Hösch-Gesellschaft in Dortmund.[104]

So we moved to Dortmund.[105] I couldn't stand the constant commuting back and forth. My family had grown to five children in the meantime,[106] and it wasn't great for my wife to have a weekend marriage. We were only able to find a rather small apartment in Dortmund,[107] but we were glad to be together.[108] Of course it takes a while in any marriage before one really knows how to get along with one another. As a result of the war, we had been separated from one another, through the war and then during the postwar period. Again and again there were separations. We lived apart from one another for six or seven of the most important years of our lives, with all the disadvantages coming from that.[109] As a result, especially once I became active as a civil engineer, I left the raising of my children completely to my wife.[110] I was so committed professionally that I was never there.[111] It's hard to imagine today, but I would spend up to eighteen hours a day on a construction site. And when that site was away, then I wasn't around at all.[112] I would leave early Monday morning and return late Friday evening.[113] My wife did essentially all the childrearing. We both agreed that they needed to learn how to *work* and that was it. And we also tried to create an environment in which they could cope and feel comfortable.[114] I don't want to say it too loudly, otherwise she'll become full of herself,[115] but she did it so well.[116] She raised the children. Today they reproach me with that fact. They say, "We grew up without a father." I have to acknowledge that they're right. But it's often the case with fathers who are professionally engaged that the family gets short shrift.[117] The man isn't at home; the woman is, you know,[118] and that certainly was the case with me.[119]

---

* A member of the Jungnationale Bund during the Weimar Republic.

So we moved to Dortmund.[120] The move wasn't hard on me because I was immediately accepted into the youth movement Circle there.[121] And then we built our house in Schönau.[122] I worked as an engineer for Hösch in Dortmund from age forty-three to fifty-seven.[123] And at the end of my career, I worked in Soest for one of the ten biggest Autobahn-building companies.[124] When I retired, we moved to Bonn,[125] and we immediately joined the chapter [of the Free German Circle] here.[126] We don't regret the move at all. Our daughter lives next door. She's a child psychologist and has a sixteen-year-old son. She's divorced. It's wonderful for us to be able essentially to live with her.[127]

And that's how it was.[128] It is almost unbelievable when I describe it all so succinctly after the fact.[129] My wife had fled from East Germany, from Halle, and arrived with only a rucksack on her back in Eckernförde. So together we owned a box and a rucksack. I repeat that only to indicate just how much effort it took for us to attach ourselves to the economic miracle that was beginning in [West] Germany. But we did it. We were successful by working really, really hard.[130] You know, my generation, which lived through the whole of the war, was very much attuned to hard work. Soldiers as well as those on the home front who worked in defense industries or as engineers, they were all oriented toward work. They were uncannily good at making something out of nothing. Those in charge of businesses didn't know anything about forty-eight-hour workweeks. No, they worked fifty or sixty hours. Everything was achieved through incredible hard work. During the war we developed enormous strengths in the area of improvisation. And when the war was over, all those skills and attitudes weren't lost but carried over into the postwar period.[131]

Which brings us to our government today.[132] The best thing one can say about the politicians of today is that they didn't have the hard experiences of our time. All they have ever experienced is continuous progress and success. And where else should they have found their standards but in their own experience?[133] Still, based on those standards, what's going on politically is in my view largely false and bad.[134] Now the political parties have become the masters of politics, whereas it is the government that should be serving the people.[135] The Basic Law* wasn't bad, but the way it has been applied is miserable.[136] It was never written in the Basic Law that the political parties should have a monopoly on power in Germany.[137] The way the entire political establishment is fixated on itself and on political rivalries instead of focusing on the problems that need to be solved reminds me of the Weimar Republic. Everything is only a battle for political position.[138] So I don't have

---

* The Basic Law, or Grundgesetz, is the constitution of the Federal Republic, which established West Germany as a parliamentary democracy on 23 May 1949.

much use for political parties, whatever their orientation.[139] This Federal Republic has managed to make us all into the crassest, most materialistic egoists.[140] We don't ask, "What can I do for my country?" We only ask, "What can my country do for me?"[141]

I often wonder whether the traditional values and ideals that I continue to hold and that come from the time of my youth—values and ideals that were largely perverted by National Socialism—have lost their meaning today. I'm not yet ready to reach that conclusion. But it does mean that I'm considered a conservative person. I have nothing against that. For some people, I would probably even be considered reactionary.[142] I still feel myself deeply connected and obligated to the German people, beginning already in the youth movement, in the house of my parents, in the Work Service, and in the war.[143] It really is hard on me that we are no longer allowed to speak about Germany, about the Volk, about our homeland, about our fatherland, let alone about patriotism. Now "society" is the vocabulary we're meant to employ.[144] When I talk with my children, they say, "What is the 'Volk'? The word, the concept of the 'Volk' has no meaning for us. Now, 'society'—that concept means something." You see, I come from a totally different world.[145] Nowadays people lack a sense of responsibility for the well-being of the community. It's my view that in the youth movement the individual developed a sense of the collective, the sense that I can only exist when I am supported by the group, out of which I live, in which I live, this group experience, in a small, comprehensible circle. We had that sense in our youth movement groups. Where can you experience something like that today? Today people live in isolation; there is no community for people to feel part of.[146] I know that in expressing these sentiments I'm revealing that I'm outside the mainstream, and I know that only a few people take the line I do and that they are generally elderly, of course. I doubt whether these values will ever be realized again. I think that liberalism, with all its manifestations, from emancipation to libertinism, is here to stay.[147] But you will find my attitude to be widespread among the Free Germans, thank God![148] The sense of community was at the heart of the youth movement and is now again at the heart of the Free German Circle.[149]

Naturally, after my release from confinement, I went directly to the Free Germans,[150] and the Free German Circle has been a spiritual home for me.[151] I missed the first Altenberg meeting, but I attended all the important meetings on Burg Ludwigstein* over the years.[152] Although I wasn't present at the founding of the Free German Circle, I know that well-known figures

---

* Burg Ludwigstein, a castle in the state of Hessen, is the spiritual and administrative headquarters of the German youth movement. It also houses the archive of the German youth movement.

made the appeal "Let's come together again!" They said, "Let's be rid of the fragmentation and come together."[153] The youth movement hadn't been united [during the 1920s], when there were the various youth movement Bunds. But over time the fragmentation gradually disappeared, and as we got older, those distinctions became unimportant.[154] The common experience of the youth movement, the common experience lived out in so many different youth movement groups, is so binding, far more binding than what colleagues at work experience, decisively more binding.[155] You know, what's remarkable is that, whether I was in the Work Service or the military or later in my professional life, I was always able to tell quickly who had belonged to the youth movement of the Bunds.[156] In a railway car, you know, an accidental encounter, after exchanging ten sentences, you know. It's in how he expresses himself, in how he presents himself, in the appearance. You figure it out quickly,[157] and from then on you stay in contact with that person.[158]

When I joined the Free German Circle, I felt I belonged because I knew that all the members were in some form connected to the youth movement. Their fundamental attitude is related to my own, and I have grown ever more integrated into the Circle.[159] I have belonged and contributed to the Free German Circle for over forty years.[160] I've assumed responsibility and helped where I could.[161] I was active in the governing council at the district level,[162] and at the county level, I initiated convention themes and secured convention speakers.[163] Our goal is always to make every get-together a positive experience, where something special happens that everyone can remember afterward.[164] It's not difficult to find interesting lecture topics. They don't have to be highbrow, but it's good when once in a while we're challenged intellectually and then can talk about what we've heard.[165] We hear a lecture, and then there's an engaging discussion, which is always tolerant.[166] It's even not so bad if one doesn't exactly follow for a half an hour what the lecturer is talking about. Generally one says to oneself, "Even if the professor speaks so that I can't really understand what he's talking about, I'll still go." I'm drawn by being able to be together with my old friends—and by the music which, if you ask me, is a really powerful tie.[167] In fact, the singing circle probably creates a more powerful bond between people than when they listen to a lecture and then discuss it a bit.[168] We treasure the musical[169] in our Circles;[170] we sing songs.[171] It's sometimes a bit unfortunate that we always sing the same songs. We're never supposed to learn new ones. The group doesn't want that. They are happy when they can really cut loose.[172] We have a singing circle here [in Bonn].[173] We're down now to ten people out of a total membership of nearly thirty. And we sing a bit. The director of our singing circle, our conductor, has become so hard of hearing that he barely hears what's going on. It's pretty funny sometimes.[174] For the past six or eight years, I've been the spokesman of the Bonn District Circle, which still has twenty-nine members left.[175] We meet once every month,[176] although a not insignificant number can no longer attend our meetings anymore, either for reasons of health or because of where they now live.[177] We tend to go on sightseeing tours, visiting cloisters or other cultural sites,[178] attending performances and exhibitions and lectures.[179] In the past,[180] I'd take hiking trips with other Free Germans.[181] Now we only[182] make short trips in this area. One can't describe them as hikes, because not everyone is able to walk anymore.[183] Still, with older people, the most important thing is being together and exchanging old memories and experiences with one another. Being able to do that is of existential importance for older people, especially when they can find others who speak the same language they do, speak it from the beginning.[184]

Certainly for me, personally, the most important thing is to have true friends at my advanced age, something that is very difficult to achieve, of course.[185] My friends are *in* the Free German Circle. I don't have many friends outside.[186] And that's been possible because we share a common attitude toward life coming from the youth movement. It's easy to get close to one another.[187] My wife and I can travel to every corner of Germany and knock on a door and someone will open it up and embrace us and be glad to see us. We didn't plan that; it just fell into our laps as a result of our experience in the youth movement.[188] Of course, I don't get along with everyone. But that doesn't bother me. One still speaks with them, exchanges views.[189] We need to be tolerant, we need to be able to like someone even when he thinks a bit differently.[190] One learns to tolerate opinions different from one's own without destroying a friendship.[191] That's an art that doesn't flourish everywhere.[192] Our tolerance is a positive that characterizes us, Free Germans.[193]

I can remember after the Free German Circle was founded in 1947 how proud we were that we could all speak with one another. In the Hamburg Circle, to which I was closely connected, there were a couple of people who had held high positions in the SS and there were former Communists. Nevertheless, we were proud that we could still speak with one another. This openness is something we should hang onto.[194] We take the position that human beings are fallible. I don't have the right to accuse another person, a friend, of being fallible when I think of my own shortcomings.[195] So we were able to look past the fact that some members had been in the SS, and we were able to accept that they had made a mistake, providing that they had not committed injustices against anyone or harmed anyone.[196] Still, one is cautious. I once spoke with the longtime leader of the group here [in Bonn]. I asked, "How did you all deal with National Socialism?" "We were very cautious about approaching that subject," he replied. "We rarely, if ever, discussed it, except perhaps in personal conversation." In Hamburg they didn't have the confidence that they could keep the group together if the subject was raised at all.*,[197] Certainly politics doesn't play much of a role here. Although originally one had dreamed of accomplishing something politically, that never happened.[198] We defeated Wyneken's suggestion that we adopt a common political position.† That was a fundamental decision, and certainly the proper one. The Free German Circle would never have become what it has become or been a support for people in their old age if the organization had gotten itself mixed up with political parties. That would have been an immediate fiasco[199] because we would never have been able to agree on what political position to adopt,[200] and we never would have been able to be together with one another.[201] But naturally that interferes with our achieving anything politically on the outside.[202] What's positive is that we share a fundamental attitude.[203] We had the goal to live our lives honestly and honorably, to help our friends, to tell the truth, to love our fatherland, to love life. None of that was ever mentioned; it was somehow felt or grasped intuitively[204] in living this lifestyle until today.[205] Being honest in thought and action in relation to oneself and to others is one of the hallmarks of the youth movement,[206] and being unpretentious.[207] There are no phonies in our ranks, and there never have been. Such people would never have fit in.[208]

So it would be too much to say that the Free German Circle has produced achievements: achievements that last, achievements that are visible to the outside, achievements that have an effect on the outside. Of course we have sought to keep the spirit of the youth movement alive inside of ourselves and to embody that spirit, but not in order to have it noticed on the outside. Our conventions are internal affairs. In the past, the conventions were more impressive than they are now. Now we're all too old. The fact that our average age is eighty is certainly obvious. We're missing some of our old energy, our élan, our zest. Today it makes absolutely no sense to talk about achievement. We're a dying association,[209] an association condemned to extinction, like the refugee organizations when there are no more refugees and the older generation dies out or the groups of old war veterans.[210] You have to keep in mind that after the war, during the 1950s and '60s, the Free German Circle

---

* Although the theme of the convention founding the Free German Circle in 1947 was "Overcoming National Socialism Spiritually," in practice the Nazi past was rarely confronted in the organization.

† The effort of the educational reformer Gustav Wyneken (1875–1964) to give the Free German Circle a more political character was vehemently rejected by the organization. Earlier, in 1946, he and Knut Ahlborn, who had been a cofounder of the Freideutsche Jugend before World War I, had vainly sought to re-create the latter after World War II as a politically progressive and democratically oriented youth movement group that would bridge the generations. At the convention of the Free German Circle in October 1948, Wyneken's call for the Free Germans to develop an explicit political platform and to take positions on the political issues of the day was officially repudiated, whereupon Wyneken announced his resignation.

was large and still had many male members. There were some really brilliant people who elevated the intellectual level remarkably. Now only a few
modest exceptions remain.[211] Practically all that's left are old women, who
are certainly to be admired for how active they are, how intellectually alive
they are.[212] When I worked in Oeynhausen, I[213] joined the Bielefeld District
Circle. It doesn't exist anymore. The Bielefeld Circle has simply died out.[214]
There's no one left.[215] Who knows how much longer we'll be able to continue
to hold our conventions? Looked at from today's perspective, it was already
a weakness of the youth movement that we were content to remain closed as
a group, as a circle of friends. We've done exactly the same in the Free German Circle: kept ourselves a closed circle and, as a result, have ensured our
extinction. But we set off on that course already in our youth.[216]

The style of the younger generation is uniquely its own, and it's an alien
style to me. I sensed this when I was at the big convention on the Hohe
Meißner in 1988.* Of course I have positive memories of that occasion,
but when I left the Hohe Meißner in the evening to drive to my hotel, I
stopped for dinner at a restaurant only a couple of kilometers from the Hohe
Meißner. To my astonishment I found the restaurant filled with smoking,
beer drinking, singing, and in part rowdy participants from the Meißner
convention. Since I'd recently had a heart attack, I'm sure I didn't cut a particularly imposing figure. I was greeted in a friendly fashion but as an "old
geezer."[217] One of the characteristics of the prewar youth movement was
asceticism.[218] Living naturally and healthily is part of living life in the spirit
of the Bunds. One didn't smoke, one didn't drink, and that type of thing.[219]
Every elite—and I still believe in elites—every elite depends upon asceticism.[220] So I found it alienating to see the whole of the postwar youth movement sitting in a restaurant creating the atmosphere of a tavern with beer
and smoke and shouting.[221] I have remained abstemious,[222] and I think that's
why I'm in such good shape today,[223] although ever since my heart attack, my
ability to accomplish things has been somewhat restricted.[224] I still have my
old energy to do what I like to do, even if at a somewhat slower pace.[225] Of
course, tomorrow something can be found to be wrong with me—cancer or
something. No one is ever spared that.[226]

So I'm grateful, grateful. It could all have turned out differently, turned
out much worse. I'm grateful that so many good things happened to me.[227]
Taking everything together, I would say I look on my life positively,[228] for
there's nothing to be gained by being pessimistic.[229] Younger people today,

---

* After the war, the German youth movement was reborn and has flourished in the
Federal Republic, although its character is different from the youth movement of the Bunds.
In 1988 various German youth movement groups gathered on the seventy-fifth anniversary of
the original meeting of German youth on the Hohe Meißner in 1913.

including my five children and grandchildren, always express amazement at my optimistic attitude toward life.[230] I believe I can say that there were always lovely things even during those hard years when there were conflicts with the children.[231] They were influenced by the 1968 movement when they were university students.* Or perhaps it was during their earlier time in school when they learned to be ashamed of being German. It was at that point that their conceptions became fixed, conceptions I don't share. There were certainly disagreements that led to conflict, but I've given up trying to reach agreement with them.[232] They do what they want, not what one had expected them to do.[233] I've come to accept that they have to think differently because they live in a different era. They will have to see for themselves if they can get through life with the attitudes they hold, just as I had to get through life. It's their business, not my business. If I even raise the subjects that are contentious, it doesn't lead to anything. They are issues of faith and can't be resolved with argument. I didn't have such conflicts with my parents, and I get along much better with my grandchildren than with my children. My grandchildren ask me, "How was it back then?" They can't begin to imagine. They ask, "How was it back then during the Hitler period with the concentration camps and so forth?" They ask and want to know. My children never ask. They think they already know, but they don't know anything. And if they don't ask, there's no point in trying to explain anything to them. If I try, they think I'm trying to influence them, which would be pointless.[234] So yes, there were disappointments in my children.[235] One[236] of our children's marriages fell apart. We didn't think that ideal, and her son was the one[237] who did most of the suffering.[238] His mother, my daughter, is a psychologist and lives, as I said, next door to us in Bonn.[239] Another daughter lives in Geneva and has a child, but she's not married.[240] My eldest daughter[241] was born in 1938 and is fifty-five or fifty-six today. She is married to a Moroccan, a geneticist. They have a daughter. He would have preferred a son, perhaps.[242] My younger son has no children.[243] He's a missionary, mainly in Africa. He isn't married and has no children. My eldest son[244] is a technician. He has a flourishing business in Mainz. He has a good, hard-working wife helping him, which one can only welcome.[245]

Well, that's it.[246] You know, I didn't choose my life. I was born into this world, and I will die one day.[247] I don't fear death.[248] I accept that my life will come to an end. I'm not exactly delighted about the fact.[249] You can only hope to have a good death, a quick death, and that you don't have to suffer for a long time,[250] that it goes quickly and doesn't hurt.[251] I don't think about it constantly.[252] As someone who fought in the war and was imprisoned in Russia, I've lost some of my fear of death. I served in a burial detachment in

---

* The "1968 movement" refers to the student protest movement in Germany.

Russia and saw quite a lot in that regard. [To his wife, who has entered the room,] Maria, have you finished making supper?[253]

ILSE MÜLLER

The postwar years, along with the last years of the war, those were certainly bad times, hard times.[1] Although the period of reconstruction lasted for years,[2] life was especially hard right at the beginning because you simply didn't have the necessary physical strength and there was such deprivation and such hardship. I also had my parents, my father's health was not good, my husband was a POW,[3] and so very many had died. It was all so hard.[4] We had arrived in Bremen on a freight train.[5] The first car became so soaked with rainwater that we had to move to another car. I[6] sat in that freight car for eight days along with my two children, without a toilet.[7] And then, when we finally arrived in Bremen, the city[8] had been completely bombed out.[9] My parents had been bombed out three times.*[,10]

So I returned from the Bavarian Forest with my two children,[11] and we lived together with my parents in an apartment that[12] had two rooms, a toilet,[13] and no windows.[14] They had tried to start their business up again, for the third time, in the foyer of the building. The debris of four floors was lying on top of our ceiling, and when it rained, I had to open up my umbrella.[15] That's where the five of us lived.[16] But then my son developed ulcers. It was terrible. In exchange for some shoes, my father managed to get another place for the three of us to live in a recently restored building.[17] A family of old Nazis was living there. They had taken the best rooms for themselves, and there were only two rooms left for us, one room on the north side and an unattractive room without heat. The wife ran an extremely profitable black market business—the doorbell would ring all day long.[18] Every now and then we'd be given a cup by someone, and my father[19] got hold of a little oven on which I could cook our food.[20] I made all the children's clothes[21] myself. Out of a French [military] cape I made an outfit that my eldest still talks about.[22] There were many nights when I simply didn't go to bed.[23] There was no time for me to do anything other than housework with the little children, without hot water out of the faucet, without a refrigerator, without a washing machine. I spent hours standing in line to get bread.[24]

Of course the most pressing issue was finding something to eat.[25] Before my husband returned from the POW camp was the time of hunger, which we experienced acutely in Bremen.[26] It was bad in 1945 and 1946, especially

---

* Beginning as early as May 1940, Bremen was subject to frequent Allied bombing. Two major raids in August and October 1944 killed 1,365 people and bombed out 67,000 others.

with [two] little children.[27] We received one loaf of bread per person per week. As soon as I got a loaf, I made a notch, so that each of us would eat one slice in the morning and one in the evening.[28] We had our ration coupons,[29] but there was nothing to get with them.*,[30] So I went begging with the children. I always took the eldest along. She was born in 1940, so she was five or six years old then.[31] It was easier to beg if you had a child holding your hand.[32] Sometimes we got a little piece of bacon.[33] Later I went on "hamster" trips[34] out into the country.†,[35] But in the beginning[36] we had nothing to barter with, absolutely nothing. At times we had nothing to eat, no potatoes. It was really, really bad.[37] Things got so bad that[38] I went out to the countryside with a friend, who had nothing anymore either. She said, "Let's go out there and see if we can manage it." Well, it turned out we couldn't.[39] We went out and sat on the edge of a field with a rucksack and stole two or three stalks of rhubarb. Of course, the police or the field watchman caught us immediately and wrote our names down. It was awful. I could have just died.[40] A bit later we made our first[41] successful "hamster" trip.[42] Everything revolved around potatoes, potatoes in exchange for cigarettes.[43] First we traveled by train to Nienburg,[44] and then we took the highway until we reached a farmstead along the road right before the first village. We looked at one another and asked, "All right, who goes in?" Then we saw two men in the barn, and my friend went up to them. I waited at the road and watched. Then she waved to me, and she got a rucksack, not a very large one, full of potatoes, and I got a bag full of potatoes in exchange for our cigarettes. Then we went back. We had been gone for about two hours and wanted to take the next train back to Bremen.[45] But the railway station had been sealed off by the English. We had to watch from a distance as the trains traveled by. They were completely covered with people. They hung from the roofs and wouldn't let anyone else climb up from the railway station. But Nienburg had two railway stations,[46] so we went into the waiting room of the other station, which was filled with those "hamstering" like us and all of their "hamstered" possessions. We were barely able to squeeze in. We sat there throughout the whole night. In the morning they started checking everyone's papers. Thank God, they started at the other end of the room, and we were able to get out through a window.[47]

---

* At the end of the war, ration coupons issued by the Allied authorities gave people a diet of 1,200 calories per day, a total gradually increased over the course of 1945 to 1,550 calories.

† Hamster trips were typically taken by city dwellers out to the countryside by train, where they exchanged objects of value (like jewelry or silver) or cigarettes for food (generally potatoes). Because railway tickets were inexpensive, people would travel great distances to get a sack of potatoes, and trains were crammed with people on hamster excursions. These trips came to an end with the Currency Reform of 1948, when grocery store shelves became filled again with goods.

Those were bad times in our lives, and in order to survive you had to break the law.* You had to steal a rucksack full of wood or something from the railway embankment and that sort of thing.[48] It was awful.[49] But that's how we were able to live. We ate nothing but potatoes and beets, except on Sundays when we would eat the tiniest piece of meat.[50]

Still we were so glad to have survived those terrible times.[51] We made it through and succeeded under really primitive conditions.[52] We started with practically nothing. But you know, we had nothing more to lose, in a way,[53] and everyone was in the same boat.[54] There were other positives as well. The war was over, and you had the chance to start anew.[55] People turned to one another. You had *experiences* during the postwar period.[56] It was certainly exciting to meet my sisters again and my other relatives and friends, including my friends from the youth movement. It was fantastic. Unless you lived through the collapse, you can't imagine what that was like.[57] So although we always ate the same things or ate nothing at all, it was a fruitful time and I wouldn't want to have missed it.[58]

Then in the summer of 1946 my husband returned from captivity,[59] from an American POW camp, and came to live with me.[60] I must confess that it was difficult after my husband's return from captivity, just as it was difficult for 90 percent of all young marriages, at least for those who hadn't had the time to get used to being married. We already had two children, and they didn't know their father at all. It was so difficult that we actually considered separating, like so many of my acquaintances, but we didn't and after a while got used to being married. So it was a very difficult time. And in addition there were the economic problems one had to face. We got furniture from our relatives. It all fit together somehow, but then again it didn't. We lived in really cramped quarters,[61] and wanted to get out of there without landing in a refugee camp.[62] And my husband had returned[63] without a profession, really.[64] He had never learned how to do anything, and I hadn't learned how to do anything either.[65] He wrote little articles for a refugee newspaper or for youth work or something.[66] But the question was: What should we do next?[67]

Then, through the Youth Authority and people who had been in the youth movement, my husband was able to establish connections with the newly established Cultural Authority in Hamburg, which was under the jurisdiction of the English occupation. The English were looking for someone untainted [by National Socialism] to oversee the re-creation of civic life in the city as part of the attempt to establish democracy in Germany.[68] So he reported to

---

* On 31 December 1946, during the brutal winter of 1946–47, the archbishop of Cologne, Josef Frings (1887–1978), delivered a sermon declaring that under conditions where survival was at stake it could not be considered a mortal sin to steal food or fuel.

the Cultural Authority.[69] There he was asked, "Were you ever in the [Nazi] Party?" Well, yes, he had been in the Party and had a certificate: "People's Comrade Müller is entitled to wear the Party insignia pending the approval of the Reich Treasury." But for some reason he had never bothered to pay a penny [in Party dues]. So when de-Nazification* came along, and he was asked, "Did you apply for Party membership?" he answered, "Yes." "Was your application accepted?" "No." So it was a complete accident that he was as pure as the driven snow. Indeed, the man who was to hire him shook his hand and said, "Thank God! We can really use people like you."[70]

It was wonderful work for him. He was made responsible for the revival of civic organizations in Hamburg, from the rabbit breeders and professional magician associations to groups promoting amateur theater, folk dance, and Low German.[71] But the question then became: What would happen to us? because we didn't have permission to live in Hamburg,[72] of course. First those who had been evacuated had to be allowed back in.[73] We were only able to obtain permission to live in an outer district, which had been incorporated into Hamburg, but we weren't permitted to live in the center of the city or anywhere else. So we had to live in Moorwerder,[74] where my husband had found us emergency lodgings with a farmer who had just returned from the war. He had a son who was exactly the same age as our eldest. His wife was expecting a second child.

We had it relatively good with them.[75] We lived in the country. Because we had a garden,[76] we had ample amounts of vegetables but nothing else.[77] Still, we managed.[78] Every day, I collected milk from the village in exchange for ration coupons.[79] The farmers had everything, of course. And we were always able to smell what they prepared for themselves. They slaughtered pigs, once legally and once illegally, and then we were given a bit so we'd keep our mouths shut and occasionally a sausage or a pot of sausage broth, but otherwise nothing. Still, our relations with them were amicable.[80] The farmer had created a little lean-to that separated his quarters from ours, which was probably good. We had a larger, a smaller, and a tiny room. Actually, the tiny room would prove to be our salvation, because it only had one wall facing outside. The three other walls faced into the stable. We lived in these emergency quarters at this farmstead from October of 1946 until December 1948. My husband continued to work for the Cultural Authority, and I remained there with the family.

---

* De-Nazification was pursued by the Allies to punish individual Nazis for their crimes and to eradicate National Socialist attitudes from the German population and from state and local institutions. A vast, inconsistent, and frequently unjust bureaucratic process, de-Nazification left many former Nazis untouched or inappropriately rehabilitated and damaged the careers of Germans whose connection to National Socialism was more nominal than substantive.

It was a very bad time. The winter of 1946–47 was terrible, dreadful. December 17th was the last day you could take a boat across the Elbe to the town on the other side. From that date until the middle of March, the Elbe was uninterruptedly frozen.* We didn't have enough wood to burn.[81] In the morning[82] there was ice on the ceiling,[83] the whole ceiling was covered with ice from our[84] frozen breath, and we had no heat.[85] Also—I didn't know any better; after all, I'm not from the countryside, and the farmer didn't tell us either—he had stacked all of his vegetables and his potatoes, but we hadn't. We had an old bunker where we kept our potatoes, and they froze completely in there along with our vegetables. What food we had, we got with our ration coupons, bread and so forth. But we lacked what we really needed. And the worst was the cold. I rearranged everything. My husband had the little room that didn't have any external walls. That's where he'd go when he wanted to work. And then one day in the cold I rearranged everything. I put myself and the children in the tiny room, where the temperature never went below freezing, thanks to the warmth of the stable.[86] Finally, my husband never came out anymore. It was simply too cold. He lived with his sister, who had a little apartment with some heating. He could survive there and continue to work with the Cultural Authority.[87] But for us it was really, really bad. For several weeks, I never let the children leave the room. We only lit the little portable oven we'd gotten from the farmer in the evening. We had an electric cooking burner,[88] but there were constant blackouts. We had access to water, and when it finally ran, say, for an hour at a time, then we'd fill up every possible, miserable container we had, and in the evening we'd heat up a pot on the little oven for me and for the children. I'd stand in a bowl along with the children and rub hot water over their bodies. Later a doctor told me, "That was crucial. By doing that you enabled your children to survive."[89] But then one day the little one threatened simply to pack it in as a result of the lack of warmth. In January 1947, the child simply sat there passively in my lap, his hands fallen to his sides, not wanting anything, not speaking, not doing anything. Fortunately I[90] had some bean coffee and cooked up a little coffee out of five of the beans and gave it to him. Then suddenly he said, "Na!" I'll never forget it. "Na!" And he slid off my lap and ran around the room again. That's what saved him, and somehow we managed to get through that winter.[91] But that winter was terribly, brutally cold.[92]

---

* The winter of 1946–47 was the worst winter of the century to that date. Undernourished and generally physically and psychologically debilitated, the population was in poor condition to withstand the bitter cold. In addition, with most buildings destroyed or damaged in Germany's bombed-out cities, shelter was inadequate for millions, and there was a shortage of coal, the principal source of heat, as snow-blocked roads and frozen railroad tracks prevented coal from being transported from the mines to the cities.

Then our third child was born,[93] and having babies really made you hold your breath.[94] But little Richard came into this world, and Fritz was always in Hamburg. For two years we were apart, which was not a good thing.[95] Our [older] son was over four or five years old[96] by that time, and the eldest had just started school. Although nothing much else was, the school was functioning again.[97] So I went to the newly installed school principal and asked whether I might work in the village as a schoolteacher as long as there was a shortage of teachers. For the refugees had arrived. Refugees. Refugees.* During the winter of 1945–46 between 45 and 46 pupils had come to this little village school, adding to the 360 pupils who were already there. There were three teachers, including me.[98] I began working at the Volksschule in 1948.[99] After about a year I applied for[100] a position as a Latin teacher in Hamburg,[101] but when the school director heard that I had children—for I felt I owed her the truth—she was as cold as ice and said, "I'm sorry, but then you won't have any energy and time for my school, and I can't take you on, unfortunately." So I looked everywhere. I even went back to Bremen[102] to visit my former school director. Things were as bad for him as they were for me. While I was there I met the old upper-school principal. He had become a night watchman and couldn't help me either.[103]

Finally I realized that I couldn't continue[104] living in Moorwerder with the children while my husband worked and mostly stayed in Hamburg.[105] But we found ourselves[106] in a vicious circle familiar to many back then.[107] In order to obtain permission to live in the city,[108] you had to be able to demonstrate that you had a place to live and a job.[109] But you could only get work if you had a place to live.[110] So with courage born of despair we found ourselves a little house. It was very little but very nice.[111] Looking back, [the years we spent in that house] turned out to be a lovely period in our lives.[112] We moved into the house in the winter of 1949[113] and after four years, finally became citizens of Hamburg.[114] Things slowly began to get better after that.[115] We were gradually able to acquire possessions and to eat decently again.[116] The financial situation in general had been clarified by the Currency Reform [of June 1948]. Everyone was given forty Marks. You knew what money was worth. You knew what the prices were. The black market was gone. Suddenly there were goods on the shelves, goods not seen for years,[117] and if you wanted to buy something, you could now.[118] We were actually quite well dressed when we finally moved into Hamburg.[119] My husband actually had a suit. As long as we had lived in Moorwerder,[120] he always wore a heavy jacket made out of military fabric.[121]

---

* By April 1947, the population of the British and American zones had increased 25 percent compared to 1936 through the influx of refugees. By September 1950, those who had fled to West Germany constituted 16 percent of the population.

The years before we moved to Hamburg[122] were the hard years, I have to say,[123] and without the Free Germans, I don't know how things would have gone.[124] My husband, through old youth movement friends, had been able to find work. These people found one another and helped one another. That's how connections were established[125] and groups were formed. My husband attended those first meetings and[126] was involved in the founding of the Free German Circle.[127] Indeed, it was in 1947, when we endured such a miserable existence, when we suffered so from the cold—that was the time when the Free German Circle was founded, initially in Hamburg. I once went to a meeting during that terrible winter, when it wasn't quite so cold. Along with my husband, I walked to the meeting on foot for an hour from Moorwerder across fields of vegetables through Wilhelmsburg to Hamburg.[128] It was wonderful to be together with the Free Germans again. I felt at home again. I felt safe and secure again.[129] A package of coffee beans had just arrived, sent from Kurt Bondi in exile, and we all drank the coffee together. It was the first time I felt really warm, from the bean coffee. The trip back was nothing. I was warm as toast.[130]

After Hamburg[131] we moved to Düsseldorf and were quickly integrated into the Free German Circle there. Once again we had difficulty finding a place to live, since housing was still in short supply.* My husband moved first and took a furnished apartment and then tried to find a place for the rest of us. We'd had to wait an entire year before we were able to find an apartment in an old building. There had been absolutely nothing available during that whole time.[132] It was after we had moved to Düsseldorf and the children had gotten a bit older that I began to be professionally active again.[133] When the shortage of teachers was really great, in 1962, I returned to my profession and worked in secondary school teaching, between half and two-thirds time.[134]

I've lived here, in this house, for thirty-five years now. Although we had saved, we had constant anxiety over whether we would ever manage to pay for it. Now I can laugh,[135] but building the house was quite a strain. It took quite a while even to begin construction.[136] The house reflected all of our special requirements. It had an oil-burning furnace, for example. Because of my professional activities, I didn't want to have to worry about the heating. The oil-heating furnace cost seventy thousand Marks. Because all three of our children were in school, we received low-interest loans and had a

---

* With one-fifth of the housing destroyed or rendered uninhabitable by the war and with 10 million refugees trying to find places to live, there was a severe housing shortage in Germany. In 1946, there were 14 million families and only 8 million available dwellings. By 1958, however, 4.5 million new housing units had been constructed in West Germany, alleviating the housing shortage.

low mortgage rate. So in the end, we managed to pay for it after all.[137] The neighborhood is wonderful. Mainly older people live here. Five years ago we celebrated the thirtieth anniversary of the neighborhood. There were only two younger families at the festivities. It's sweet to have them included in the group, but most everyone else has lived here for thirty-five years, and they are elderly just as I am.[138]

By the time we had finished building the house, our eldest was finishing her Abitur.[139] It was really too bad that we couldn't have built earlier. You should build when the children are little and can play in the garden, in the sandbox, on the swings, and so forth. Our eldest studied at the university in Cologne. During the first two years, when she was preparing for her preliminary examinations, she lived at home and commuted to Cologne. It's not far from Benrath to Cologne; it's easy to get there. Our second finished his Abitur[140] two years after she had, so the two children left home at the same time. Suddenly, after only two years, our new house was considerably emptier.[141]

Once my husband was sorting through old things, and we found a letter we'd received after the war when none of us had anything. We lived in the country and had potatoes. Back then I had sent a box of potatoes to some friends in Dresden so that they wouldn't starve to death. We found their letter thanking us for the potatoes. The man had written that he would never find better friends.[142] Today young people are brought up so that they get everything they want.[143] Today you can't give anyone anything anymore. Our grandchildren already have everything. Isn't that sad?[144] Their parents, who had to do without after the war, now give their children everything. My grandchildren have lived their lives without ever having had limits imposed on them. They've never heard, "There's nothing more to be had."[145] There's too much consumption. Today young people aren't challenged enough, and things have gone so easily for them. Most have too few responsibilities and too much prosperity.[146] We experienced the 1920s and the period after 1945, and as a result have a completely different attitude toward possessions. My generation can easily imagine that the things we possess today will be gone or worthless tomorrow. By contrast, the next generations have only experienced progress, and they are convinced that progress will continue. People's expectations have risen, expectations that my generation learned to relinquish after experiencing two wars.[147]

Today young people are more egotistical.[148] I have observed again and again that our children and grandchildren no longer say thank you, either in writing or over the telephone, when you have sent or brought them something. And children no longer stand up when the teacher enters the classroom.[149] In a sense it's a backlash against the Third Reich. Then the youth was controlled far too much; now they are left completely free—and that's not good either.[150] Individualism plays a larger role with younger people than it did with us,[151] and there are fewer groups.[152] Still, I can't accept a sweeping condemnation of the younger generations. We were very socially engaged, and I don't think social activism is any less important to the younger generations. If anything, they are more honest, more open, and they say what they think. Because of our upbringing, there were limits to our honesty. In fact, we protested against those limits in the youth movement. I believe that our protest has been carried further by the members of the current generation, even if they never belonged to the youth movement. The youth movement is dying out, you know, but continues on in this openness and honesty, and I regard that positively. I've experienced it in my own family, in my own grandchildren. When I arrive, for example, they say, "Grandma, there you are again in that old dress, the one we don't like in the least." I'll never visit them in that dress again. It's a small episode but it's revealing. I would never have dreamed of saying something like that to my grandmother. My respect for her was far too great, and for my grandfather even more. He could be wearing his tie at the wildest angle, and I would have bitten my tongue. When I hear what is said to the teachers today—well, there's certainly no ambiguity as far as clarity and truthfulness are concerned. We would never have dared to speak to adults in that way, even though we were much freer and more open than our parents had been. In the youth movement we put a great deal of emphasis on truthfulness, so I think this honesty is something to be applauded. Still, from the perspective of old age, one does have to be able to tolerate a certain crudity in order to get at what's behind it.[153] And I also don't really expect the younger generation, not to speak of the generation of my grandchildren, to be particularly interested in what I am doing, even though I am interested in what they are doing and attempt to understand their perspective. But it doesn't function in the other direction. That's simply the way it is, and that's fine.[154] And in the end[155] you live not with the generation of your children but with your own generation.[156] So it's appropriate perhaps that the Free German Circle has no new blood. Occasionally my children have attended a convention. I remember taking my daughter, the physician, along to the convention in Freiburg. She said, "What a fabulous atmosphere *you* have." It was not something for her or for the generation of my children, who were born during the war.[157]

I really don't know whether I did everything right in raising my children. I now have a good relationship with all four,[158] although the eldest is a bit difficult.[159] She's very critical, and we've often gotten into conflict, although I must admit that, as a child, she didn't have the easiest time with me.[160] My daughter has childhood memories of my husband and me fighting constantly. She told us once that we had always bickered. As far as I can recall, that's a distortion. We were always open about our disagreements, but there wasn't constant conflict.[161] I'm also never sure what she's thinking. She says, "Yes, yes. Uh-huh." But I don't know what she really thinks. Perhaps my eldest daughter would say, "With your first child you experimented in childrearing." When I look around, I see that the first child in many families is somewhat more difficult, while the second one has an easier time.[162] When my first baby was born, I had the book *The Mother and Her First Child*.* I followed the prescriptions in that book religiously. Today I question what I did. The book stated that "the child must be fed at precise intervals" and "if the child cries, you must simply allow it to cry until it becomes accustomed to the rhythm of the feeding schedule." That was the opinion of the experts for a long time, and that's how we did things. Perhaps it was a mistake. It's certainly different today. My daughters picked up their children, and they were fed immediately when they were hungry.[163] It's more of a strain for the mother, and our children certainly adapted themselves to the feeding rhythm very quickly and no longer cried at night but slept through. Our grandchildren, by contrast, were always awake at night when I took care of them.[164] Perhaps [my daughters'] method was psychologically better, and that's probably most important. Still, from the perspective of daily life, my clever little book was more practical. So maybe I made mistakes, but I only did what I was told to do.[165]

I get along wonderfully with my grandchildren, but it was difficult with my children. We had a difficult time[166] especially during the 1968 period;[167] the years 1968 and 1969 were really a strain.[168] Although my eldest didn't, my next[169] two children went to Berlin to study in 1967.[170] So many of the 1968ers studied in Berlin.† All the leading figures of the 1968 movement were there.[171] So my children found themselves in the middle of the whole uprising of the 1968 generation and participated in it passionately. As a result, their studies fell by the wayside, and they ended up dropping out. There were communes and drugs; they tried everything.[172] My second oldest is a

---

* The book *Die deutsche Mutter und ihr erstes Kind* by Johanna Haarer appeared in 1934 and achieved enormous popularity in Germany. The book reflected the precepts of National Socialist ideology and was aggressively promoted by the state as a way to shape the development of children in the spirit of National Socialism. The book continued to be sold after 1945 under a slightly altered title, *Die Mutter und ihr erstes Kind*. The last edition (heavily revised) appeared in 1987.

† West German universities and the Free University in West Berlin in particular were the centers of the so-called 1968 movement. Dissatisfaction with their educational experience, worries about job prospects, and a more diffuse rejection of the "establishment," consumer society, and American "imperialism" sparked a series of student protests in Germany, beginning with a mass demonstration against the Vietnam War in Berlin in 1966. Although similar protest movements existed in other European countries, most notably France, and in the United States, the protests in Germany were also directed at the older generations for their complicity in National Socialism. Student unrest in Germany, as elsewhere in Europe, reached a climax in the spring of 1968. At its peak, one-third of all students in Germany were active in the 1968 movement. By the early 1970s, the 1968 movement had run its course.

real 1968er,[173] along with his former wife.[174] They met in Berlin, in a student commune.[175] Rainer had gone there to study art history at the university, where the left-wingers and the 1968ers had really taken hold. As a result, he was more involved in politics than in the history of art.[176] And there were times when I really worried that my third son would become a part of the RAF scene.* I could readily imagine my third one doing that, and I didn't want him involved in any criminal activity.[177] My [youngest] daughter followed in the footsteps of her brothers. She had her wild years as well[178] and was also politically engaged,[179] but then she returned to Düsseldorf. I always thought that the girls who lived in these communes were a lot more realistic about things than the boys were, and when things started to go badly they tended to leave sooner than the boys did. So our daughter returned here and got her training as an occupational therapist. She had a long-term relationship with a boy and had a daughter with him. But they simply couldn't live together, so she's raised the daughter on her own. The father is present as a father, but they don't live together.[180] You know, they could have gotten married. It would have been quite nice. But women today don't want to subordinate themselves. They want to be independent, which is fair enough.[181] She's now the director of a rehabilitation center connected to the university hospital in Berlin.[182] That's the one daughter. The other, the eldest, is completely normal. Well, not completely, but the most normal anyway.[183]

So those were really difficult times. We had a lot of worry and grief regarding our children[184] and got to hear quite a lot as parents about how wrong everything was.[185] From our point of view we swallowed it all, although with some difficulty, and tried to maintain connections to them. I certainly tried very hard to understand them. Of course it was completely impossible to exert any influence on them, but they couldn't get rid of me. I always went to visit them in Berlin, initially with my husband. Finally, he said that he couldn't take it anymore, because what he saw going on made him too upset.[186] I remember when,[187] on her birthday, I went to the occupied house [where my daughter was living] but found it all closed up.† I couldn't get in or see in. Suddenly someone came out, and I slipped inside.

---

* The Rote Armee Fraktion, or Red Army Faction (RAF). As the 1968 movement began to lose momentum, a hard-core minority, led originally by Andreas Baader (1943–77) and Ulrike Meinhof (1934–77), turned to terrorism in 1968–70 in an effort to foment violent revolution. After their arrest in 1972, the terrorist movement was taken over by the Red Army Faction, which targeted West German business and political leaders as well as individuals and institutions associated with "U.S. imperialism." RAF terror reached a peak in 1977 with a series of spectacular assassinations, abductions, and murders.

† In the mid-1970s, students occupied vacant houses and apartments that were being held empty as objects of speculation, frequently by German banks.

Then someone appeared and asked me what I was doing there. I said, "I am looking for my daughter and have brought her something for her birthday." Well, she wasn't there at the moment, but I found her room and had a good conversation with the people there.[188] They put a mattress in a corner for me to sleep on.[189] Later I had a discussion with Petra, and she was right in much of what she said but also wrong.[190] That's how I was able to gain insight into their lives. It was important for me to do. Later they repaid me for my efforts, for my not having dropped them as they had hoped I would at the time. Once they brought many of their friends along, whose parents had said, "That's it! You're out the door. Don't bother coming back here again." And my boys brought them all here to our house. I said that I would hang a sign on the door: "Home for children who have been thrown out by their parents." It was a wild time. The police came and searched the house for hashish. Coming from the idealistic youth movement and a strictly conservative parental household, it was all pretty hard for me to swallow.[191] Still, I learned from my children.[192] Theirs is the first generation which didn't simply accept the traditions that were passed down to them, which called those traditions into question. But it wasn't easy.[193] Those were pretty difficult years, but they passed, and today we can laugh about them.[194]

We had to deal with four children, and we have nine grandchildren[195] in the meantime. They are scattered in every imaginable direction.[196] The eldest, Irmgard, is a physician, and her husband is a neurologist with a large private practice.[197] She works with autistic people and their families. She has four children herself. All are socially engaged,[198] working with asylum seekers.[199] My second child is a quite different type. He went off to the place where he really belongs, to Finland. He married a girl he met in a commune [in Berlin]. She had been thrown out by her parents, and so I helped support her financially. They had two children and then separated. I've always maintained contact with Jutta on account of the children. Although she had been rather wild, after several years she settled down and now leads a quite bourgeois life. The children live with her in Berlin. My son so wanted to live in Finland, which she didn't want to do, and besides, she had a boyfriend. So they got divorced, and she stayed on in Berlin. As always, the children were the ones to suffer. They visit my son in Finland during their school vacations, but it's still painful for him not to be with his children. He did various odd jobs and tried to save money to buy land, knowing that we would always try to support him financially. Initially he was unable to obtain a residency permit, so he had to leave Finland after half a year and return to Berlin, where he lived with friends. He drove a taxi, mostly at night, to earn money for the next half year in Finland. Finally, after six years, he was able to obtain a residency permit, and now he lives up there permanently and has made a go of it. He makes furniture there. Although I have two dropout sons, both work very hard physically. After the death of my husband, I gave them both a portion of their inheritance to help them out. My son up in Finland used it to buy a carpentry workshop. So he now is set, and I don't worry about him anymore.[200] The other dropout,[201] my third child, traveled for two or three years after finishing his university studies. He was always an adventurer. I don't know exactly what he did, and I really don't want to know. He had a girl from Düsseldorf with him. They bought property in Portugal and are still living down there. They live from hand to mouth. He has two children and imagines himself a large landowner, but he has a hard time holding onto money. But he does own property and ten or eleven horses, a herd of sheep, and quite a lot of land. His children live a good life in Portugal, but he is no longer together with his wife. Actually they were never married, but they separated two or three years ago. She lives nearby, and the children go back and forth between them.[202] As I mentioned,[203] our youngest daughter, Petra, runs a rehabilitation center in Berlin and has a little boy. Petra is not married but was together with a Greek man for years.[204]

In any event, we've had considerable worry and grief regarding our children,[205] and I get along best with my oldest grandchildren—better than with my children.[206] You can't talk about the Nazi past with your own children, but you can with younger people. We always used to be in conflict with our children[207] about the past.[208] My children never talked with me about it—in the first place, because I had been a Nazi, and secondly, because they felt they simply couldn't talk to me about anything.[209] So we held back at home, which was perhaps a mistake.[210] Now we are able to talk with one another;[211] now that they are older, I can speak with the children about these things.[212] But I still avoid certain topics,[213] topics they simply don't want to hear about. The generation of my grandchildren is so much more eager to listen.[214]

Of course, I've had to wrestle with my Nazi past myself. It took a while, but I have wrestled with it.[215] I'd never wanted to be one of those who remain silent until the grave, never speaking about the past, and I've never thought it was a good idea to lie, as so many do, about what we did.[216] Something happened recently that I found almost humorous—and others noticed it too. For the eighty-fifth birthday of a Free German, a little pamphlet was handed lovingly around on which the various stations in the person's life were depicted in a photomontage. It was clear that the photographs of the engagement or wedding had been retouched. The husband was depicted there, obviously originally in a brown [Nazi Party] uniform, but now that was gone and something harmless had been glued over it. Everyone noticed. Today we should be able to speak openly about the past. Nevertheless, I can understand when others find it difficult to do. And women, many women, had experiences that are difficult to bear, whether of being bombed at night or driven from one's home.[217] It takes courage to face your past honestly, and facing your past sets the whole mourning process in motion, which many people of my generation don't want either.[218] It's hard to do that even under the best of circumstances. Last year in January the whole Nazi business was brought up again, and I became physically ill. I couldn't sleep.[219] But it's bothered me or, perhaps better, I've missed that these experiences aren't reflected upon, the experiences of the Third Reich and what surrounds it. One needs to take a position on the past,[220] even when it's bitter.[221]

I always tried to find opportunities to face up to my Nazi past, even if for a long time I didn't do it. My first opportunity to put my thoughts into words occurred on the fiftieth anniversary of 1933. There were various public occasions to commemorate the anniversary, and there was an open-minded gymnasium here that held an assembly entitled something like "Eyewitnesses Speak to Young People." I decided to go because I wanted to hear what the eyewitnesses had to say.[222] The auditorium was filled to the rafters. Five elderly gentlemen sat up on stage and talked about the past. One after the other would say that he had been there back then but had never been a supporter of anything the Nazis did, he'd only observed what went on. "Well," I said to myself, "they are eyewitnesses, all right, but not the sort these young people want to hear." The audience became restless. I had drunk a bit too much coffee before the event. Normally I never open my mouth in public. In fact, until then, for all those years I'd never planned to say a word about the Nazi past in public. But as I sat there, I thought to myself, "This can't go on." The students started asking questions, and their questions simply got no response. They wanted to hear the other eyewitnesses. So I stood up and said that I had the impression that the students wanted to hear from those who had been supporters of the Nazis. "You can ask me," I said. "I did support them.[223] I can honestly tell you that I was a supporter of the Nazis."[224] My goodness, what did I precipitate? The questions started flying: "How did you become a Nazi?" "Did you read *Mein Kampf*?" One after the other. I described the atmosphere,[225] the atmosphere with the German Nationalists, and anti-Semitism, which we had experienced as young people. The five men who sat on the stage had been forgotten. Finally, one of them got up and said that he had been in the Hitler Youth. Afterward we all went out together to a pub.

And that episode set quite a lot in motion in me. My husband had come to terms with the Nazi past very quickly. He always said, "You simply have to delete those years." I would say, "I can't delete those years. I can't."[226] I once spoke with a student, a young woman who had grown up in the German

Democratic Republic and was bitter about her experiences in school there. When I tried to explain how people had ended up in the SED* and how one should treat them, she replied, "No! I want to avenge myself on my teachers, who treated me so unfairly." But I *can* imagine what it's like. I've experienced myself what it's like to believe with passionate enthusiasm, with heart and soul, that something is right, only to discover later that one had committed nothing but crimes.[227]

You know, for old people like me the world seems completely changed.[228] So much has changed over the course of my life.[229] All you need to think of are the technical innovations of the modern era, the things we didn't have when I was a child. It started with washing machines and then radio and television and trips to the moon.[230] Now it's a computer world.[231] And the change is not only technological but also cultural and historical.[232] We've experienced *fundamental* changes. Previously the world didn't change as rapidly as it does today. During our youth, change came more slowly.[233] Until 1933 things were pretty much as we had known them before, but then everything was completely different.[234] We have experienced a transformation that no generation ever had to face.[235] It's been difficult for people to process such profound change,[236] but you know, I've never found it irritating.[237] I was born in 1915.[238] Just think of all that has changed since then, especially for women. There are so many more possibilities for women today, possibilities that would have been unthinkable for us when we were young. The way women are raised in the family and educated at school has changed fundamentally.[239] I found my mother to be an extraordinarily capable woman. She managed a large household. Even if we did have someone to help with the housework, there was a lot for a housewife to do. I would almost say there was too much, because she didn't have time to help us develop intellectually. But we had a nice family life, and I regret the fact that women now leave the house early and become independent. Of course women can achieve every bit as much as men do,[240] and I think I've always been an emancipated woman.[241] But I'm not a complete feminist because I still think the family is so important.[242] It still makes me sad when children have to return to empty houses. And I can't let go of the idea that family and woman are connected.[243] Of course I can understand when someone who has an Abitur and has studied at the university wants to take up her professional life again once the children have become more independent. I can understand that. But I don't think it's right if you never stop working in order to achieve professional success and the children are neglected as a result.[244] Still, my children, my daughters, have professions as well as children. It's a different era, you know.[245]

---

* The Socialist Unity Party of Germany was the state-sponsored Communist party of the German Democratic Republic.

When I look back and try to make sense of my life, I have to say that I have always sought to merge with the collective [Gemeinschaft] as much as it has been in my power to do so. And now I have this community composed of members of the Free German Circle. We are all on the same experiential level through hiking and through the *collective*, which holds and which endures.[246] Actually, we have all, always, sought the collective.[247] There is mutual support. There is the feeling that there is someone you can count on, someone who is concerned about you.[248] That was my "youth movement" life and remains so to this day. Similar genuine connections also existed, although rarely, during the war.[249] When my husband died,[250] the Free Germans stood by me,[251] and they still stand by me today. When something happens, the Free Germans are *there*.[252]

And what's inside me has also made my life fulfilling, happy, and above all content.[253] I'm often described as a happy person.[254] Recently one of my grandchildren said to me, "Grandma, you have so many grooves in your face." Sweet. "Grooves." I said, "When you get older, you will get grooves in your face too." And recently someone said to me, "You look so good." "Yes," I said, "I'm content."[255] I've always been content.[256] There are so many disgruntled people. You have to learn always to find the bright side of things.[257] You have to make do with the life that's presented you. The meaning of life is to make the best out of every situation.[258] Even though I'm not optimistic in an exaggerated sense, optimism dominates my outlook.[259] Despite the fact that we were born into terrible times, everything has gone incredibly well for our generation.[260] Even the bad times have been good for me. Things can't always go well in life, and you really only grow in the bad times.[261]

So, for me, there were really no bad years,[262] and I've had a great deal of good fortune in my life.[263] I've been lucky.[264] It was lucky that I got to know my husband. He was capable and worked hard. He was knowledgeable and successful.[265] I learned an incredible amount from my husband.[266] He encouraged and loved me, and I loved him. What more can one ask?[267] I'm still grateful to him long after his death. He's always around me somehow.[268] When my husband was so ill, he once told an acquaintance, "Don't tell my wife how badly I'm doing. She worries too much as it is." Despite his illness, my husband kept his sense of humor, even when it got so bad that I had to pack him in cotton wool, so bad with his ankles and head. Those were certainly very hard times, but you know, I was always glad to care for him. I never had the feeling that too much was asked of me. It would have been nice if things could have been different, but what is one supposed to do?[269] I had powerful dreams about the illness of my husband, dreams that haunted me. In my dreams I'd always see a long avenue. And I would walk down that avenue all alone. It must have been in the fall. I had this dream often. It probably was connected with my fear that something would happen to him, and then you are all alone. And in some ways that's how it turned out.[270] I can still remember when I came into his room in the morning. I always had to turn him over in the night; he couldn't do it himself anymore. I'd come in at seven. We always left the doors open. I didn't hear him breathing. So I went in and closed his eyes. And I was so thankful. The sun shone. It was Sunday. Later the bells started ringing in the bell tower here in front of my window. I sat on his bed and accompanied him on his way to heaven. That was a powerful experience for me for which I can only be thankful. At noon the doctor came, one I didn't know, because it was Sunday. And he spoke with us and said, "If people would think about death as you do, many would find solace."[271]

I can't remember anymore whether my husband was already dead, but I had the loveliest dream of my life sometime back then. I dreamt about going on hikes, hikes mainly with my husband, and I went into strange medieval cities, which I would swear I had never seen before in reality. But the last dream, the one I remember most clearly, is very personal. I think he was already dead. Yes, he was already dead. I dreamed that he was climbing up the steps in our house and that many steps were missing and that I could grasp hold of his foot and, if I could have grasped his foot, he would be there again.[272] Now I can almost never remember my dreams. I sometimes regret that. I sometimes have the feeling, the vague feeling that I've somehow or other dreamt about my husband. But it's gone. I simply can't remember anymore. Sometimes it could have been quite a lovely dream. But I simply can't remember anymore.[273]

8

ANALYSIS

Resurrecting the Collective in the Generational "Circle"

The themes of loss and perseverance in the face of loss, so central to the interviewees' lives before the end of the war, continued to characterize their lives after 1945. In the immediate postwar period women interviewees persevered through loss that took the form of deprivation. Virtually all recall having experienced, directly and profoundly, the loss of the basic necessities of life. They describe how desperately difficult it was to find shelter in bombed-out Germany for years after the end of the war, given the housing shortage and the number of refugees and evacuees.[1] And they describe the constant search for food for themselves and their children. Facing starvation, the women had to resort to begging, trading on the black market, and even theft to survive in the period before the Currency Reform of June 1948.[2]

Women generally overcame these hardships without their husbands, who either had been killed in the war or were in prisoner of war camps. And even when their husbands finally were released from imprisonment, many of the women still had to face these hardships on their own, for the men, in an effort to rebuild their lives and support their families, were frequently absent, often until the 1960s.[3] Indeed, over a period of twenty years beginning in 1940, it would seem that many married couples spent relatively little time together. A significant number of the children of this generation, then, grew up without fathers or with fathers who were at best an inconsistent presence in their lives, a fact to be considered in attempting to understand the 1968 generation psychologically.

The women had to cope with the loss of the basic necessities in the absence not only of husbands but of the traditional institutions and social networks that had previously supported them. As we have seen, the National

Socialist Volksgemeinschaft broke down in the last months of the war period and was replaced by an ugly, selfish, often brutish struggle for survival.[4] Not only did those interviewed lose the support of their fellow Germans, they lost the sustaining myth that the individual, when faced with loss, would always find support and a home in the group.[5] Indeed, the generational collective that had sustained the interviewees since early adolescence appears temporarily to have lost much of its significance for them. Instead, in the immediate postwar period, the family became the basic unit of survival.[6]

Despite the catastrophic defeat, the loss of life and the destruction, the deprivation and the suffering, many of the women recall the immediate postwar period positively.[7] Their accounts reflect their pride at the self-reliance, resourcefulness, and courage they displayed immediately after the war and carry forward the sense of adventure and excitement that characterized their descriptions of their lives during the period of the Reich's collapse.[8] These positive experiences came both despite and because of loss. The breakdown of traditional institutions and social networks, the suspension of old rules and ways of doing things, and the absence of husbands and of men generally gave women an opportunity to stretch their wings.

By contrast, male interviewees have more negative memories of the immediate postwar period.[9] It is probably difficult to overestimate the traumatic impact of defeat and imprisonment on the men, and they emerged from the prisoner of war camps not only psychologically demoralized but also, in many instances, with their physical health seriously impaired.[10] These losses were not made good for the men upon their release, for they returned to an unfamiliar, even alien, world. The people and the places they had known were gone or had become unrecognizable. *Heimat*, physically and psychologically, had been lost. And the men returned to women who seemed to have flourished in their absence. In what had been a profoundly patriarchal society, the success of the women only increased the men's sense of inadequacy. Feeling alienated, irrelevant, and insignificant, several of the men credit their "faithful" wives with having helped them overcome feelings of hopelessness and desperation.[11] The losses accompanying the collapse of the Third Reich appear, then, to have been significantly harder on male than on female interviewees,[12] in part because the losses experienced by men were probably more physically and psychologically damaging, and in part because the men's losses, unlike the women's, lacked compensating positive aspects. As a result, perhaps, male interviewees were more inclined to repress their Nazi and wartime past,[13] whereas female interviewees were more inclined to come to terms with it.[14]

The men appear to have felt ideologically adrift in postwar Germany. The collectivism of the Right had been destroyed in the war and discredited in its aftermath and, given their social class and experience in Soviet POW camps, the collectivism of the Left was never a viable option.[15] Nor did the pluralistic, democratic values represented by the Federal Republic provide male interviewees with a sustaining ideological alternative to what they had lost with the Third Reich. Western individualism and political and economic liberalism felt too much like egotism and hedonism and was alienating to men for whom collectivist experiences and self-sacrifice had defined their lives since adolescence. A handful openly regard it as "tragic" that the "many positive aspects of the Hitler period, which on reflection were worth preserving, perhaps," were simply "tossed overboard in 1945."[16] They regret the loss of German national pride and cultural traditions and the country's new slavish dependence on American power and eagerness to adopt "cheap and garish" American culture.[17] A striking number of the men seem critical or at least unenthusiastic about the Federal Republic which, to the extent it embodied anything valuable, simply carried on earlier German traditions.[18]

Unable to find ideals to replace those that had been lost, most of the men plunged themselves into rebuilding their lives, which they achieved, as one man notes with a certain grim pride, through nothing but "hard work."[19] Indeed, "hard work" became the one value men could cling to when so many of the ideals that had provided them with orientation in the past had been discredited.[20] The idealization of hard work also carried forward the youth movement tradition of making the means an end in itself. It was more the *achievement* of material prosperity than prosperity itself that appears to have produced the greatest satisfaction for people who proudly rejected materialism. Despite that rejection, however, in reaction to the turbulence, deprivation, and suffering of the 1940s, the interviewees, along with most other Germans, yearned for prosperity as a sign that normality had finally been achieved, with a settled life, "orderly work," and a stable family, something the interviewees and those belonging to their generation had experienced only briefly, if at all, during the mid-1930s.[21] The achievement of material prosperity gave Germans a sense not only of security and stability but also of agency and hope. At least until the advent of the Third Reich, most working-class Germans as well as Germans living in the countryside had the sense that they were powerless to change lives determined by class, gender, and geography. During the war virtually all Germans felt at the mercy of forces beyond their control. By contrast, material prosperity seemed attainable through discipline and effort after the Currency Reform and the revival of the West German economy. Defined in material terms, personal progress was tangible and measurable and took the form of increased income, the possession of modern consumer goods, and home ownership.[22] Finally, for the interviewees, at least, working hard to achieve prosperity represented a strategy for coping with loss that went back to adolescence. As they had dealt with losses in the family during the 1920s by engaging in activity in the youth movement, so too after the war they, along with their fellow West Germans, turned away from the catastrophic losses they had suffered by "working hard" to rebuild their lives and achieve prosperity.

Although the Currency Reform of 1948 marks the beginning of West Germany's economic recovery, those interviewed, as well as their contemporaries, generally experienced significant improvement in their personal situation, and with it the sense that "normality" had been achieved, only by the mid-1950s or even later.[23] The symbol and substance of prosperity and normality was owning and especially building a house, generally in the late 1950s and 1960s.[24] On a practical level, home ownership reflected the fact that the housing shortage in Germany, created by the destruction of the war and the influx of refugees, had finally been overcome.[25] Psychologically, home ownership represented security and stability for people whose lives had been characterized by movement and disruption. The mobility that the interviewees had experienced during the Third Reich and in the period of the Reich's collapse continued, first in the immediate postwar period, as they struggled to survive, and then in the Federal Republic of Germany (after its founding in May 1949), as they sought to attach themselves to the West German economic miracle.[26] After the war, one interviewee lived in six different places in fifteen years in order to further her husband's career. For her, buying land and then building a house on it represented "finally finding and hanging onto a place you can call home."[27]

Nevertheless, disappointments accompanied the achievement of normality and prosperity. In some cases, prosperity simply came too late for the interviewees and others of their generation. History and biology had been in synchrony for the interviewees during the Third Reich, when Nazi support for childbearing and childrearing met the needs of a generation ready to have and to raise children. In postwar Germany, however, biology dictated settling down long before most interviewees were able to do so. By the time the members of this generation were in a position to establish a "normal family life," they were in their forties or fifties and their children were young adults.[28] Thus, the house of the woman quoted above was finally finished just as her children were ready to move out and establish independent lives.[29] For this woman, the beautiful new house—now empty—symbolized not only the loss of her children to adulthood but also the hollowness of prosperity.

Indeed, the achievement of normality and prosperity brought with it a new set of losses for those interviewed. For women, the establishment of a male-dominated nuclear family, a household and family routines, and the general return to traditional gender roles inside and outside the family meant a loss of autonomy and authority. For both women and men, the establishment of a stable, orderly society and reemerging social divisions restricted the scope for individual imagination and initiative.[30] And prosperity brought new pressures that some found overwhelming.[31] As in other oral history interviews with members of this generation, when the interviewees come to their lives in the Federal Republic, their descriptions seem to lose intensity, energy, and coherence.[32] Their accounts break down and flatten out, spreading like water over a flat surface, reflecting that, with the attainment of prosperity, the interviewees' lives became duller—routine, uniform, unexceptional.[33]

It is against this background of loss that the enduring success of the Free German Circle should be understood. One woman, whose father was largely absent from the family and whose mother died when she was an adolescent, who remained unmarried after her fiancé fell at Stalingrad and whose best friend had died shortly before the interview, claims that she was able to convert each of these losses into something positive. She attributes her ability to make the best of personal misfortune to the fact that throughout life she has been able to "merge with the collective."[34] One finds in the group what has been lost to the self, and the group protects against further loss, for one is dependent not on any single individual—who may disappoint, leave, or die—but on the group as a whole. As this interviewee puts it, one is supported "through the *collective*, which holds and which endures."[35] Or, in the words of another woman who was also helped by the Circle in dealing with a series of personal losses, "The Free Germans are *there*, you know."[36] Thus, the youth movement group, which had helped those interviewed cope with loss in adolescence during the 1920s, was resurrected in the Free German Circle to help them cope with loss after 1945. And the collectivist values that had sustained the interviewees in the youth movement and in the Third Reich were reaffirmed and rehabilitated in the Free German Circle.

So, once basic survival had been secured with the help of the family, the generational unit resumed its central place in the lives of those interviewed.[37] Informal links between former youth movement members were established immediately after the war.[38] These connections were institutionalized in the late spring of 1947 with the official founding of the Free German Circle.[39] The organization not only provided practical support, helping people find work or housing, it also offered psychological support, helping people find meaning and purpose in lives that had been disrupted by war, defeat, captivity, and dislocation. As one interviewee puts it, the Free German Circle began as "a collecting basin" for refugees "who found their way to one another" after the war "in search of a sense of belonging and togetherness."[40] And it remained a source of comfort and security throughout their postwar lives. Whenever and wherever those interviewed moved in the mobile society of the Federal Republic, the Free German Circle was there to help them get settled.[41] As the interviewees aged, the support provided by the Free Germans if anything increased in importance. Although aging is frequently accompanied by isolation and loneliness, the Free German Circle provided these elderly people with a remarkable number of close friends.[42] And the Free German Circle helped the interviewees deal with the final losses of their lives, the loss of physical and mental capacities and of friends, as the members of the generational unit on which they had depended throughout their lives gradually and inevitably departed.[43]

Well into old age, the Free Germans remained impressively active people, hiking, going on sightseeing excursions, and traveling to distant parts of the world.[44] As in the youth movement, these activities engendered self-esteem and a sense of superiority in relation to the more sedentary members of their generation, as did the group's cultural and intellectual pursuits. They no longer sat around the campfire, but they still sat in a circle discussing a selected topic at local chapter meetings, or they listened to presentations on the contemporary world by academics, politicians, and public intellectuals at their annual national conventions.[45] As in the youth movement, it was less important what was discussed than the fact of the discussion itself, which was designed not to reach conclusions or adopt positions but to create a sense of self-satisfaction and, through that shared experience, of heightened group cohesion. It seems, in fact, that, through these intellectual and cultural activities, the Free German Circle reasserted the youth movement's educated, upper-middle-class character after the leveling populism of the Third Reich, and in so doing reflected the social hierarchies that reemerged in the Federal Republic after the war.

Beyond the shared experience in the youth movement, the interviewees find it difficult to articulate exactly what characterized the Free German Circle in their interviews. They either claim that what defined the youth movement and the Free German Circle cannot be explicitly stated but only sensed and felt or they describe it vaguely as a "spirit," a lifestyle, or an outlook on life.[46] The belief of those interviewed that what characterized the Free German Circle can be grasped only intuitively is manifest in their conviction that former youth movement members can instantly recognize one another based on appearance or a few sentences or on what one woman calls the "smell of the nest."[47] When pressed by their interviewers, a number of interviewees, mostly men, attempted to spell out what distinguished the Free German Circle but managed only to produce what seems a quite generic list of attributes, including: to live life "honestly and honorably," to be genuine and unpretentious, to love nature, to endure hardship, and to lead an ascetic life.[48] The value most often cited by interviewees as characterizing the Free Germans, however, is their tolerance.[49] The importance placed on tolerance testifies to the fact that the cohesion of the Circle remained quite simply its raison d'être.

From the youth movement in adolescence though the Work Service and the Wehrmacht in young adulthood to the Free German Circle in maturity, the collective played a vital psychological role in the lives of those interviewed. Intolerance would have threatened what one woman called the *Zusammenhalt* (literally, the "holding together") of the group.[50] Hence, it was crucial that the Free German Circle remain apolitical.[51] As we have seen, politics seemed intrinsically divisive to those interviewed. Moreover, the presence of "politics" in the Free German Circle would not only have produced tension and conflict over contemporary Germany but would have inevitably led to a confrontation with National Socialism, a divisive and traumatic subject that the Free German Circle was in part designed to avoid.[52]

Although a number of interviewees claim to have learned lessons from the past, most seem relatively unaffected by the history through which they have lived. They generally maintain their apolitical orientation,[53] criticizing the National Socialists for having turned out to be "political" after all.[54] Few appear to have become politically engaged after 1945. Two of the men regard the Federal Republic with skepticism because of its thoroughly political nature, its party politics, and the fact that the common good has apparently been sacrificed to narrow political self-interest.[55] As they had in adolescence and young adulthood, the interviewees still yearn for apolitical times, which they associate with sacrifice on behalf of the collective and social harmony. Although professing to be forward looking, most interviewees, then, remain deeply conservative. This conservatism should hardly be surprising given the fact that the focal point of their postwar lives, the Free German Circle, was rooted deeply and self-consciously in the past—an institution that, by excluding younger people from its ranks, remained their generational preserve. The topics discussed by the Free Germans may have changed along with their means of transportation and the length of their hikes, but the discussions, the excursions, and the hikes remained the same, as did the songs that they sang.[56]

Although many interviewees look back on their lives in the Third Reich with fondness, virtually all condemn National Socialism and anti-Semitism. Nevertheless, it does not appear that they experienced much guilt over the Third Reich or the Holocaust. Instead, their attitude is best described as *defensive*.[57] The interviewees cannot afford to experience guilt because guilt is incompatible with the feelings of harmony and self-esteem on which they depend. Being defensive about the Third Reich, however, is fully compatible psychologically with trying to preserve the space inside the circle (both the individual circle of the psyche and the communal Circle of the Free Germans) as a place where only good feelings are experienced. Moreover, the interviewees cannot afford to experience guilt because to do so would force them to confront the even more threatening sense of loss. In order to feel guilty about the Third Reich, the interviewees would need to take psychological ownership of it, to reinvest emotionally in that period in their lives—an ownership and reinvestment that would bring home all they had lost with its collapse. And finally, the fact that the interviewees feel themselves reproached by others for the Third Reich discourages them from reproaching themselves and encourages them to react defensively.

The first attempt to force Germans to face their National Socialist past was the de-Nazification program conducted by the Allies immediately after the war in the Western zones of occupation. It was experienced as a slipshod and meaningless process by the interviewees, which disposed them neither to confront the Third Reich nor to embrace democratic values.[58] But even if conducted with rigor and psychological sensitivity, it seems unlikely that de-Nazification would have succeeded in bringing Germans to come to terms with the Third Reich and to accept their guilt for its crimes. The situation in Germany was so desperate in the first years after the war and the losses were so fresh and so extensive that people simply lacked the physical and emotional wherewithal to confront Nazi Germany and what it had meant to them. All their energies were devoted to survival, and they plunged themselves into rebuilding their lives and reconstructing their country. For nearly two decades the Nazi period was largely repressed. It was only later, after prosperity had been achieved and normality established, that West Germans belonging to the generation of the interviewees might have been able to confront guilt over the Third Reich, and with it the perhaps more threatening sense of what they had lost with its collapse. But then, in the later half of the 1960s, the generation of their children came of age to raise the issue of the relationship of the parental generation to National Socialism, and to raise it with a vengeance. Faced with the accusations of their children and their children's intellectual representatives, the interviewees generally responded with a sullen, defensive silence to what one calls "the guilt that was laid on us."[59]

A significant number of interviewees experienced intense conflict with their children. Latent tension, present throughout the relationship, erupted into open strife in the later 1960s, generally when the parents had finally established a normal life for themselves and their families. The interviewees were repudiated by their children—for their way of life, for their values, and especially for their National Socialist past.[60] It is ironic that babies "born for the Führer" during the war would comprise the "1968 generation" in Germany, denouncing their parents as former Nazis and becoming, apparently, the opposite of all their parents stood for socially, culturally, and politically.

The conflict with their children was the most painful experience in the lives of those interviewed after 1945. It was also threatening. Whereas the interviewees consistently sought to cast themselves in an ideal light, their children were ashamed of them. Whereas the interviewees idealized the past, their children repudiated that past as criminal. Whereas the interviewees consistently sought to preserve harmony, their children presented them with strident and unavoidable conflict. Whereas the interviewees' stoicism covered a lifetime of repression, their children were psychologically minded and emotionally open. Whereas the interviewees had suppressed disappointment and anger in relation to their own parents during the 1920s and had made consistent efforts to realize their parents' dreams, their children showed no such consideration and loyalty and openly rejected what they stood for.[61] It is only in reference to the way they raised and related to their children that the interviewees seem to have experienced self-doubt or self-reproach.[62] In adolescence, the interviewees had lost their parents as figures whom they could idealize; in maturity they were de-idealized by their own children, whom they lost partially as a result.

Their children's rejection represented yet another loss for those interviewed, but unlike previous losses, this was a loss that could not be denied, romanticized, or transformed into a positive. One woman and her children never discussed her Nazi past because "we are all silent in relation to difficult topics." She associates from this lack of communication to her greatest disappointment. With considerable effort she had finally built a house, thereby achieving the stability, security, and success she had yearned for and felt she owed her children. But they repudiated it and her: "It was a bitterly painful experience for me when I had finally finished building this house and I thought to myself just how happy my children would be about it. Well, they weren't happy at all about it. I should have been concerned with other things. The slogan of the day was to reject consumption. It was a lovely, comfortable house, but it did not represent a success to my children. Can you imagine that? Our little dedication ceremony was really fraught."[63]

A number of the children of those interviewed rejected their parents by physically abandoning them and Germany itself,[64] and a number married or were in serious relationships with non-Germans.[65] Moreover, their children were often not professionally successful in a traditional sense.[66] And finally, to the interviewees' dismay, a good many of their children were either divorced or separated or unmarried with children.[67] Feeling rejected by their children, interviewees see their grandchildren as more appreciative and understanding, even curious and nonjudgmental about their National Socialist past.[68] According to one woman, "The generation of my grandchildren is much more eager to hear" about the National Socialist period. She told her youthful interviewer: "I would *never* tell my own children the stories about my experiences in the Third Reich that you have listened to so patiently today because they don't want to hear them."[69]

Despite their positive comments about their grandchildren, however, the interviewees seem generally critical of the contemporary world and alienated from the younger generations.[70] Their criticism is generally directed at contemporary affluence and its deleterious impact on people generally and on the young in particular. They see postwar prosperity as having produced selfishness and egoism, undermining the communal values so central to their lives.[71] Whereas the women seem more concerned about the moral and social consequences of postwar materialism, the men's criticisms of the younger generations and of contemporary Germany tend to be more explicitly political. They lament the lack of devotion to "Germany," "the Volk," and "the fatherland" and the privileging instead of the vague and bloodless concept of "society."[72]

Yet not all those interviewed were negative about the contemporary world, and a striking number of women have positive things to say about the young.[73] They see the directness and honesty of the younger generations as carrying on the spirit of the youth movement and the social and cultural rebellion of youthful dropouts as connected with their own adolescent rejection of bourgeois society.[74] Indeed, the interviewees testify to the fact that, although their children overtly and often violently rejected them, those children, in sometimes subtle and indirect ways, also carried on the values, traditions, and activities of the interviewees. Like their parents in the early 1930s, the 1968ers rejected democratic liberalism and the bourgeois social order for a totalizing collectivism—if of the socialist Left and not the National Socialist Right. Indeed, despite their intensely political Marxist rhetoric, the 1968ers can still be seen as following in the apolitical footsteps of their parents. The 1968ers rejected political engagement within the system for the apolitical politics of the street. Although some of the 1968ers eventually returned to politics, by supporting the Green Party, for example, others simply rejected politics altogether, as their parents had done. Not only did the 1968ers and their parents generally embrace collectivism on the national political level, both adopted a collectivist lifestyle: the parents in the youth movement and the children in the communes of the counterculture, carrying on their parents' back-to-nature and back-to-basics lifestyle as well as their devotion to music.[75] Like the interviewees during the 1930s and early 1940s, their children were socially conscious and socially active, concerned with the less fortunate and the environment. Although her children and grandchildren rejected the youth movement, one woman is convinced that their extraordinary level of social engagement carries on the tradition of the youth movement—although in fact this activism carries on the tradition less of the youth movement than of National Socialism.[76]

Even if the children of the interviewees can be seen as following in their parents' footsteps, this seems to have occurred more in spite than because of their parents. For although the interviewees avow that they are concerned about the survival of the values of the youth movement, it is striking how little effort they appear to have made to transmit those values to the next generation. Ultimately these people seem more concerned with themselves than with their children, about whom they have surprisingly little to say. Indeed, as one interviewee puts it, "We live in isolation from the next generation. We live for and among ourselves."[77] Feeling reproached or ignored by their children and those belonging to their children's generation, the interviewees see no reason to include them in the Free German Circle.[78] And yet there is one last reason why those interviewed keep their distance from those younger than themselves. As one interviewee puts it, "You live not with the generation of your children but with your own generation."[79] After all, parents grow old and die and children grow up and leave; loss is inevitable on both generational sides. By contrast, one's own generation remains, until at last its members depart as well.[80]

Given the losses the interviewees had faced in the past and the losses they were facing at the time of their interviews, perhaps the most striking characteristic of these aged people is their relentless optimism. By transforming loss into ultimate gain or, where that proved impossible, by simply remaining silent, they recalled lives that experienced considerable suffering as more or less consistently positive.[81] And despite the fact that most interviewees were well into their eighties at the time of their interviews, they remained hopeful about the future.[82] This optimism can be understood in part as an attempt to come to terms with the physical and mental deterioration that is a part of the aging process by taking life as it comes and accepting the "natural course" of things.[83] But the optimism expressed again and again in interview after interview reflects not only how the interviewees coped with their present difficulties, it also reflects how they coped with difficulty throughout their lives. Adapting to the vicissitudes of old age by looking "on the bright side of life" merely represents the latest installment in a lifetime of adaptation to the environment on the part of the interviewees.[84] Indeed, the intimate relationship between optimism and adaptation helps to explain the general passivity of these people. Making the best of every situation means accepting things as they are; there is no frustration, no anger at the way things have turned out, and hence no desire to adapt the environment to oneself. In attempting to deal with the extraordinary losses they experienced over the course of their lives, the interviewees consistently respond with adaptation and optimism—that is to say, they respond with denial, for denial of loss is a form of psychological adaptation (or maladaptation) that encourages—perhaps demands—optimism.[85]

Loss and its denial are the central themes of the interviews and of the lives of these people. From their memories of an idyllic childhood during

World War I to their optimism in the face of death at advanced old age, the interviewees transformed loss into something positive, even ideal, in order to deny suffering and unhappiness. And yet there are places in the interviews where the sadness slips out. Although they rarely remembered their dreams, in *every* dream that is recalled in the interviews either the interviewee is alone or the dream otherwise conveys abandonment, loneliness, and loss. There is the "youth movement" dream of the man alone in a starry sky.[86] There is the wartime dream of the woman, alone with the eye of God, looking on passively as Hitler is condemned to eternal damnation.[87] There is the recurring postwar dream of the woman standing alone on a deserted boulevard in the fall, a dream she associates with the premature death of her husband, whose health had been compromised by war and imprisonment.[88] There are the two dreams of another woman after the premature death of her husband. The first, which she describes as the most beautiful dream of her life, was of strange and beautiful medieval cities, lovely and bygone. The second was of her dead husband climbing the stairs of their new house and of her futile attempt to grasp his ankle, to hold on to him, to restore him to life.[89] Finally, there are the recent dreams that one woman can never remember but vaguely feels were about her husband, who died in the war. She thinks that "sometimes it could have been quite a lovely dream" but "it's gone" and she "simply can't remember anymore."[90]

And there are enduring memories that convey powerful images of loss. One memory, which has haunted the interviewee, comes from the immediate postwar period. It is a memory about trying to get home and having to say good-bye. It is a memory about the collective and about who is allowed to belong and who is forcibly to be excluded. And it is a memory about the ethical choices that faced this generation of Germans over the course of the twentieth century.

A bit later the trains began to run again. I tried to get through, of course, back to my mother, who still lived in Dortmund-Kirchhürde-Schanze. But the trains were all filled up. Even the roofs of the trains were covered with people. Everything was full of people. And you tried to get into the station. And when you managed to get in, it was the same on every railway platform, always more people trying to get onto the trains. There were always those who reached out their hands to the people trying to get on board and others who pushed the people away. I don't know which group was in the majority. In such an exceptional situation, so much out of the ordinary—that's when people show themselves for what they are. Their essential nature comes to the fore. They don't even realize what they are doing. I've often wondered what human beings are capable of. And all those many, many good-byes. To this day, I can't bear to watch when people say good-bye to one another on a railway platform.[91]

The interviewees had reached out their hands to bring others on board, in the youth movement during the Weimar Republic, in organizations like the Work Service during the Third Reich, and in the Free German Circle after the war. But they also pushed people away or stood by passively while others did so, and therein lies the moral failure of a generation. Not everyone could be a member of their collective, whether it was that of the youth movement, of the National Socialist Volksgemeinschaft, or of the Free German Circle. If *anyone* could belong to their group, it would lose its exclusivity, its harmony, its identity, its purpose. So some people had to be excluded in order to give life and power to the collective on which their lives depended. And that desperate need to belong—and with it, inevitably, to exclude—came in part from "all those many, many good-byes" they had experienced over the course of their lives, good-byes they could not "bear to watch."

9

ESSAYS

MEN, WOMEN, AND THE REASSERTION OF THE FAMILY IN POSTWAR GERMANY

Writing immediately after the war, the middle-class feminist Gertrud Bäumer noted that, despite National Socialist rhetoric praising the family and the mother, National Socialist policies had actually reduced the significance of both in favor of the Volksgemeinschaft. Through the "collectivization of motherhood," the role of individual mothers had been reduced, and children had been pulled out of the family into generational collectives. Indeed, the National Socialists regarded all intimate personal relationships as "useless and dangerous," according to Bäumer, for they "inhibited the formation and reduced the power of the Gemeinschaft." Although the "atmospheric power of the family had faded" during the Third Reich, she noted with relief that with the defeat of Nazi Germany the family had been restored to its proper, central place in the lives of people, especially in the lives of the young.[1]

The restoration of the family after 1945 came within the context of the devastation and disruption wrought by the war, which Germans had to face in the absence of the collectivist institutions and ideals that had collapsed along with the Third Reich. In an effort to find orientation, Germans turned initially to the extended family and then to the nuclear family as the site of support, security, and stability.[2] In the chaos of the war's end and immediate aftermath, the family became what Lutz Niethammer characterized as a "magnet" for Germans. Refugees, prisoners of war, children evacuated to the countryside, civilians conscripted into the military auxiliary, people of every sort were on the move, under the most difficult and dangerous conditions, all trying to get "back" to "the family." Although Germans hoped that the family would help them master the dire economic situation at the end of the war, their determined and frequently desperate effort to "return home through the collapsed society was not about economics but about a regressive utopia, the protection and simplicity of the world of childhood," according to Nietham-mer. Given the appalling conditions of postwar Germany, the fact that most families contained numerous relatives needing assistance, the absence of ad-equate extrafamilial social support, and the unrealistic expectations placed on it, the idealized family was bound to disappoint in reality. Nevertheless, although the emergency constellations of relatives that constituted "family" in the immediate postwar period generally failed to provide the physical and emotional support its members craved, that yearning laid the foundation for the ideological and social preeminence of the nuclear family in the 1950s. Despite and because of the disappointment, "family" remained an ideal as-sociated with "normality," and its resurrection became, in Niethammer's words, "a duty, a phantom, and a project" for individuals, society, and the West German state.[3]

A central obstacle to the restoration of the traditional nuclear family after 1945 was the disruption of traditional gender roles that had occurred during the war and immediately thereafter. Indeed, probably for the first time in its long patriarchal history, Germany was defined by its women at the end of the war. The so-called *Trümmerfrauen*, or "women of the rubble," who cleared away the tons of debris left primarily by Allied bombing, became "a central symbol of the era," according to Elizabeth Heineman. "A single im-age linked women in rags and ruined cities on the one hand, Germans' resil-ience and the promise of reconstruction on the other." Indeed, the immediate postwar period was characterized as the "hour of the women," reflecting the fact that women, largely without the help of men and displaying excep-tional resourcefulness and pluck, "pulled their families and German society through . . . the 'hunger years.'"[4]

These two postwar images conveying the resiliency and strength of women and their role in the reconstruction of postwar Germany contrast sharply with the predominant image of men in the first years after 1945, the "dystrophic" returning war veteran. Already before the release of the first POWs, however, German men presented a picture of demoralization and las-situde strikingly different not only from the fortitude and energy displayed by the women but also from the heroism and masculinity supposedly char-acteristic of the warrior at the front. "These days I keep noticing how my feelings toward men—and the feelings of all the other women—are chang-ing," a thirty-two-year-old woman living in Berlin recorded in her diary on 26 April 1945, just one day before the arrival of the Red Army in the city. "We feel sorry for them; they seem so miserable and powerless. The weaker sex. Deep down we women are experiencing a kind of collective disappointment.

The Nazi world—ruled by men, glorifying the strong man—is beginning to crumble, and with it the myth of 'Man.'"[5] The image and self-image of German men was further damaged with the arrival of the Soviet frontline troops. The inability of the men to prevent the rape of wives, sisters, daughters, and mothers by their victorious enemies exposed their utter helplessness and transformed the loss of the war into a humiliating personal defeat.[6] Four weeks after the Soviet occupation of Berlin, the woman noted in her diary, "Once again it's clear that we women are dealing with this [defeat and its attendant horrors] better [than the men]; we're not as dizzy from the fall."[7] Gabriele Strecker, an opponent of the Nazi regime who worked for an American-run radio station in 1945, reached the same conclusion: "In the period of complete collapse, women seemed to be the only ones who were still psychologically intact." She quoted a colleague, recently returned from the ruins of Frankfurt, who had told her that there "'the men all make such a tired, weak, defeated impression. By contrast, the women seem to me to be better, fresher, stronger.' And so it was."[8]

Whereas the women experienced themselves as "survivors" and grew more independent and self-assured in meeting the challenges they faced, the men experienced themselves as "defeated," and their self-esteem and self-confidence plummeted. Their sacrifices and suffering had been in vain. They had lost the war and were imprisoned by their former enemies, who now exercised complete power over them. And whereas the activism and effectiveness of the women carried over from the war into the postwar period, the men were transformed from heroic fighters and members of the "master race" into humiliated and degraded POWs.[9] The experience in POW camps, particularly those in the Soviet Union, often did lasting physical and psychological damage.[10] The returning POWs were frequently found to be suffering from a physical and mental condition called "dystrophy," whose symptoms, according to Frank Biess, included "apathy, depression, underachievement, and a tendency to become easily agitated, any and all of which persisted even after their initial somatic cause—malnutrition—had ceased to exist."[11] In fact, Biess reads the postwar medical and psychiatric literature on dystrophy as implying that the "sexual identity" of the men had been "destroyed" in the camps and "that the unconditional surrender of the Wehrmacht was followed by a complete emasculation of its former soldiers in Soviet captivity."[12]

Not only were the men weakened physically and psychologically as a result of their experiences at the end of the war, they were further traumatized by their return to a home and a homeland that had become alien to them. As we have seen, given conditions in postwar Germany and the unrealistic expectations of the returning veterans, "home" was bound to disappoint. And, given their demoralization and debility and the unrealistic expectations placed on them to live up to the ideal of manhood held by wives, by society, and above all by the men themselves, they were bound to disappoint as well.[13] Moreover, the liaisons that had frequently developed between German women and the occupying Allied soldiers increased the men's sense of inadequacy and humiliation. In general, "women's independence and autonomy (including sexual autonomy) became a huge problem" for the veterans, according to Hanna Schissler. The very strength and independence of the women, their success in coping with the chaotic conditions of postwar Germany, only underscored the weakness and disorientation of the men.[14]

The sense of emasculation, bitterness, and alienation experienced by returning veterans was captured in Wolfgang Borchert's play *Draußen vor der Tür* (The Man Outside) written in 1946 and performed for the first time in Hamburg in November 1947, one day after the death of its twenty-six-year-old author from liver failure brought on by alcoholism. The play is about the crippled veteran Beckmann, who returns home to find his wife with another man. Beckmann realizes that he is "one of those who come home but then don't come home because there is no home for them to return to. Their home is then outside the door. Their Germany is outside, at night in the rain, on the street. That is their Germany."[15] Upon being released from POW camps, the men "returned" to a civilian life that many of them had never actually experienced, for they had spent most of their lives outside the family in military organizations (for most, the Hitler Youth and/or the Work Service and for all, the armed forces). In the absence of the hierarchical structures, clear-cut orders, and well-defined objectives that they had come to depend upon, the men found themselves disoriented and floundering, unable to adapt to the unfamiliar and chaotic postwar world.[16] With their self-esteem and self-confidence deeply shaken by defeat and captivity and unable to get their bearings in postwar society, many men experienced what Biess calls "a sense of existential uncertainty," and there was a high incidence of suicide among returned veterans.[17]

Already bearing a disproportionate share of responsibility for ensuring the survival of the family, women were now called upon to cure the "dystrophy" of the returning veterans.[18] As Ursula von Kardorff put it in 1945, "The hardest task for women in this war is the one they are only now facing: to furnish the understanding, the emotional balance, the rebuilding of confidence, the encouragement needed now by so many totally beaten and desperate men."[19] As they had with the rubble left by the war's physical destruction, German women were now charged with "clearing away the rubble of the men's psyches" and psychologically "rebuilding" them.[20] Their ability to perform this task was considerably complicated, however, by the severe tensions that erupted in families with the return of the veterans from POW camps.[21] Indeed, "familial conflict became almost the order of the day" after 1945, and the divorce rate soared.[22]

The difficulties that couples experienced can be partially attributed to the fact that a great many had married either right before the war or during it and had had little chance to know or live with one another. In the absence of actual experience, under the conditions of wartime and then with the men in POW camps, marriage, like the family, became the focus of idealized hopes and expectations that could never be fulfilled.[23] And husbands and wives became reacquainted after having had intense, traumatizing, and vastly different experiences. The men had lived through the horrors of battle, defeat, and captivity and saw themselves as the ones who had suffered. They did not understand that their wives had also lived through horrors—and they did not want to understand.[24] As we have seen, men could not bear to hear about the rape of their wives, which destroyed married life "as an imaginary idyll," placing "the war and the victor permanently in the marital bed."[25] Moreover, as a result of their experiences, the people who came together after 1945 were different from what each partner remembered or expected. Again as we have seen, despite hardship and suffering, the women had become strong and self-confident, while the men had become weak and demoralized. Many were ill and/or disabled. Hardly the heroic figures of memory, the returning veterans were often bitter disappointments to their wives, and the forceful and independent women were often alienating to their husbands.[26]

There was tension not only between husbands and wives but also between fathers and children. Most returning veterans were close to complete strangers to their children, who generally regarded the fathers as unwelcome intruders and often responded with hostility and defiance or, like the five-and-a-half-year-old Ingeborg Bruns, with "shame" at the "man in the torn uniform" who had returned home.[27] Women also resented the returning husbands for disrupting a family unit that had learned to function and even flourish under exceptionally difficult circumstances and for seeking to reassert their authority in the family. For their part, the already vulnerable men felt excluded and unwanted by wives and children, and when they sought to take their "rightful" place as the head of the family, struggles for power frequently broke out between the marriage partners.[28]

Initially, the woman tended to prevail in this domestic "war in miniature," since the family generally depended on her income and ability to function in the chaotic conditions of postwar Germany.[29] Nevertheless, within a few years, the traditional nuclear family, with the man at its head, had been generally reestablished in West Germany. By the early 1950s, most husbands had regained a measure of self-confidence and most wives had decided that the preservation of domestic harmony and family cohesion took precedence over maintaining their independence and authority.[30] And, perhaps most important, society at large as well as individual men and women were eager to return to "normality," defined as the reinstatement of traditional social norms and gender roles. Indeed, a broad social and political consensus emerged that the restored nuclear family, with the man at its head and the woman returned to the home in her traditional role as wife and mother, should become "the anchor" of postwar West German society.[31]

Based on a study of 167 families between 1949 and 1950 in Hamburg, the noted sociologist Helmut Schelsky acknowledged in 1953 "that the events of the war and the postwar years" had posed an "exceptional danger to the family." He concluded, however, that the family had emerged from this period of crisis strengthened, revealing itself to be "the ultimate place of safety" and "the last stable structure remaining in society." Nevertheless, although "the old familial order and way of life" had reasserted itself, Schelsky and other contemporary observers concluded that the experiences of women during the war and the immediate postwar period had resulted in long-term "changes in the structure of the family." Specifically, the independence and self-confidence that women had gained made them less willing to "subordinate themselves" to their husbands, and their autonomous authority and involvement in decision making, particularly relating to the family, increased.[32] Moreover, the organizational abilities and work ethic that women had developed, coupled with the introduction of technology into daily life over the course of the 1950s, allowed women to do more than provide the basic household necessities (which had consumed the lives of most women during the Weimar Republic), giving them more time for family, children, and activities outside the home.[33]

Although women were progressively pushed out of the workplace to make room for the returning veterans after 1947, and the percentage of married working women in West Germany dropped from 33.8 percent in 1939 to 26.4 percent in 1950, it had risen to 36.5 percent in 1961 and would climb steadily thereafter.[34] Even when women stopped working after the war, their experience during the 1940s was transformative. They had been responsible outside of the family and had learned "to shape their lives through employment and occupation."[35] They had discovered that individual initiative and activity led to results and that a woman could exert control over her destiny. Partly as a consequence, women, including working-class women, tended to place a high value on education in raising their children, especially their daughters, so that their children would realize the occupational dreams that had been frustrated for them with the "return" to "normality" during the 1950s.[36]

Still, by the fall of 1955, "the hour of the women" was over in West Germany, the return of the last German POWs from the Soviet Union symbolizing the return of German manhood after the war.[37] And the return of German men brought losses to German women. Indeed, Gabriele Rosenthal interprets the eagerness of women belonging to the generation of the interviewees to talk about their experiences during the war and the Reich's collapse as a reaction to those losses: "For the women of the Weimar-youth generation, the return of husbands who reclaimed the right to be the 'head of the family' and the loss of responsible jobs during the postwar period spelled the end of a relatively autonomous period in their lives. As a result, the war took on retrospective biographical significance. The women experienced the war not only as a time of suffering but also as a time when they were able to take independent action to meet the challenges of daily life in time of war, thereby increasing their self-esteem and self-confidence. It was only after they had lost a measure of the autonomy they had experienced that this period in their lives became in retrospect so significant to them."[38]

THE MITSCHERLICHS' "THE INABILITY TO MOURN"

In 1967 Alexander Mitscherlich, a physician and psychoanalyst who had opposed the Nazis, and his wife and colleague, Margarethe, published an extraordinarily influential essay entitled "The Inability to Mourn—And Connected with It: A German Way of Loving." In the essay, the Mitscherlichs argued that postwar Germany and postwar Germans were burdened by a powerful sense of unconscious guilt over the Nazi past. According to these two West German psychoanalysts, Germans had been unable "to mourn" the loss of Hitler and the Third Reich after the war because to have done so would have confronted them with their guilt over the crimes they had committed. In the view of the authors, the effort to avoid facing their guilt prevented Germans not only from mourning their own losses but also from mourning the millions who had been killed or otherwise victimized by Germans.[39]

Although generally ignoring the complexities of the Mitscherlichs' argument and their arcane psychoanalytic theorizing, historians, intellectuals, and members of the educated general public in the Federal Republic have come to accept—indeed, to take for granted—that the central psychohistorical problem for West Germans in the first two decades after the war was an inability to confront their guilt over the National Socialist past.[40] Until recently, with the notable exception of the conservative philosopher Hermann Lübbe, few academics have challenged the Mitscherlichs' argument.[41] In fact, over the last ten or fifteen years, a number of particularly thoughtful and psychologically sensitive works have implicitly or explicitly assumed that the culture of the Federal Republic of Germany during the 1950s developed partially in response to a widespread and largely unconscious sense of guilt over the crimes committed by Germans and in their name during the Third Reich. In this view, the prevailing ideologies, the defining myths, the self-representations of West Germany and of its citizens during the 1950s and early 1960s sought in part to assuage or defend against that buried sense of guilt. Specifically, historians have called attention to the fact that Germans, as a result of their experiences at the end of the war—during retreat, flight, and expulsion, and in the POW camps and the ruins of occupied Germany—regarded themselves as victims. Although acknowledging that these were indeed horrific, even traumatizing, experiences, historians have argued that, by casting themselves as victims, Germans also implicitly sought to evade responsibility and guilt for those victimized by Germans, for, as Annemarie Tröger puts it, "a victim of war cannot be responsible for it."[42] Similarly, historians frequently also follow the Mitscherlichs in interpreting the "desperate" or "manic" quest of West Germans for "normality" and prosperity during the 1950s as an attempt, in part, to ward off buried guilt.[43]

Whereas the Mitscherlichs argued that the inability of Germans to face their unconscious guilt prevented them from mourning the loss of the Third Reich, I would invert their formulation to argue that the inability of Germans to mourn the overwhelming losses they had suffered, including the loss of the Third Reich, prevented them from experiencing guilt over its crimes. And whereas the Mitscherlichs argued that the inability of Germans to face their unconscious guilt prevented them from mourning the victims of National Socialism, I would argue that the inability of Germans to mourn their own overwhelming losses prevented them from mourning the losses of others— including those inflicted by Germans.[44] Although many Germans undoubtedly experienced guilt after the war and more wrestled with guilt feelings that were not altogether conscious, the fundamental psychohistorical problem facing Germans in the 1950s and early 1960s was not guilt, in my view, but loss. Amending Dagmar Herzog's formulation slightly, I would argue that the political, social, and sexual conservatism of the 1950s was less a "strategy for mastering the Nazi past" and more a strategy for mastering the *loss* of the Nazi past.[45] The psychohistorical problem of guilt in West Germany emerged only later, in the mid-1960s, with the Auschwitz trials of 1963–65 and the coming of age of the children of those who had lived through the Third Reich. Indeed, in rejecting the politically, socially, and sexually conservative culture of the 1950s (along with their parents), the rebels of the 1968 generation (along with the Mitscherlichs) interpreted that culture as created in reaction to repressed feelings of guilt—as opposed to repressed feelings of loss. The members of the 1968 generation needed and wanted to believe that their parents experienced guilt, for they themselves felt guilty over what their parents had done or enabled. They therefore tended to project their own guilt over the Third Reich onto their parents, in the process avoiding having to empathize or even sympathize with their parents' suffering and helping to establish the myth (defined as a belief whose truth is accepted uncritically) that the parental generation experienced buried guilt over the National Socialist past.

The Mitscherlichs' 1967 "The Inability to Mourn" can be seen as marking the generational shift from the earlier psychohistorical problem of loss (the burden borne by those who lived through the Third Reich) to the later psychohistorical problem of guilt (the burden borne by their children) and, associated with that generational shift, the emergence of a new West German attitude toward the National Socialist past and a new West German identity developed in reaction against it.[46] The transitional position of the Mitscherlichs' essay is reflected in the fact that, while the title announces that the essay will consider historical loss and the inability of Germans to come to terms with it, the contents actually focus on collective German guilt, thereby failing to acknowledge and to empathize with the losses that Germans had suffered.

To be sure, feelings of guilt and of loss are not mutually exclusive, and the two may well have reinforced one another in ways that made it difficult for Germans to experience either after 1945. Coming to terms with the loss of Hitler and Nazi Germany was difficult for Germans not only because of guilt over National Socialism they may have experienced, but also because the total defeat of the Third Reich and the exposure of its crimes, as well as the conduct of the Nazi Party and its leaders during the last months of the war, had discredited most of what National Socialism had represented for them.[47] The condemnation of a horrified world also made it difficult for Germans to mourn the loss of the National Socialist past openly. From the Allied program of "de-Nazification" in the late 1940s to the reproaches of the younger generation and those like the Mitscherlichs in the late 1960s, the lack of empathic responses from the environment for the losses suffered by the Germans who had lived through the Third Reich worked to cut off their empathy for themselves—or for the victims of National Socialism—and simply put them on the defensive.[48] Indeed, the ineffectiveness of the program of de-Nazification immediately after the war had to do not only with the incompetence of the Allied authorities but also with the fact that Germans needed to mourn the loss of the National Socialist past, not to reject it. And they needed to come to terms with the losses they had suffered at the end of the war, losses so profound and extensive, so psychologically overwhelming, that Germans were "unable," in the Mitscherlichs' phrase, "to mourn" them.[49]

It is striking how the far less catastrophic losses of 1918 were openly experienced as a national trauma by Germans and have subsequently been interpreted as such by historians.[50] After 1918, Germans, like Europeans generally, "found memorable words and cultural expressions" that helped them to process the horrors they had experienced; after 1945, however, "it seemed impossible to depict and interpret the suffering," and people merely wanted to forget what they had been through. One turned "one's back on death," in the words of Richard Bessel and Dirk Schumann, and sought "to rebuild, in a strangely anesthetized state, 'normal' life." The "desperate flight into normality," which characterized all European countries after the war but none more than Germany, came in response to the catastrophic losses that people had suffered.[51] Although Bessel and Schumann may well be right to conclude that "the shock of the 1940s was so profound and so deep that perhaps there simply was no other way to deal with it other than to move on and not look back," Germans appear to have paid a heavy psychological price for turning their backs on the past.[52]

To be sure, Germans regarded themselves as victims after 1945, and as a number of historians have pointed out, "German suffering" along with "German well-being" (in the form of the economic miracle) became the twin foundational and integrative myths of the Federal Republic during the 1950s.[53] According to Robert Moeller, West Germany was conceived as "a nation of victims, an imagined community defined by the experience of loss and displacement during the Second World War. The stories of German victims, particularly expellees and POWs in Soviet hands, were central to shaping membership in the West German polity."[54] Therefore, Moeller argues that Germans repressed the past not completely but selectively, recalling the traumas they had experienced at the end of the war vividly and "with extraordinary passion and emotion" but not the traumas they had inflicted.[55] If most Germans failed to acknowledge "their responsibility for the crimes of the Third Reich or the extent of their identification with Hitler and National Socialism" during the 1950s and, as a result, did not "engage in the therapeutic 'work of mourning' called for by the Mitscherlichs," Moeller concludes that "there was much else for which Germans demonstrated a striking ability to mourn."[56] It is important to emphasize, however, that the Germans' sense of victimization related primarily to flight, expulsion, and imprisonment, experiences from the very end of the war and its immediate aftermath, and not as much to the massive losses they had incurred at the front or on the home front during the war itself. The Germans' sense of victimization after 1945 related, then, to a sense less of loss than of mistreatment and injustice and to their general defensiveness in the face of the accusations leveled against them of complicity in the crimes of the Nazi regime. Ultimately a sense of victimization is not the same as "mourning," as working through and coming to terms with loss. Indeed, it can be argued that casting themselves as victims worked to prevent Germans from fully accepting what they had lost. As the psychoanalyst Gerard Fromm points out, victimization has more to do with "grievance" than with "grief." It implicitly contains the notions of restitution, compensation, and repair and, at its core, defends the person who feels victimized against accepting the fact that something has been lost and will never be regained.[57] All of which is to say that we should not simply presume

that Germans who lived through the Third Reich subsequently struggled with
guilt over their National Socialist past either consciously or unconsciously,
nor should we overlook their experiences of loss in our haste to assume their
struggle with guilt. Instead we should take the title of the Mitscherlichs' essay more seriously than its authors did to focus attention on the inability of
Germans after 1945 to come to terms with the overwhelming losses they had
suffered.

THE NATIONAL SOCIALIST PAST IN WEST GERMAN FAMILIES

Germans continued to deal cognitively and emotionally with the Holocaust
after 1945 as they had dealt with the Final Solution during the Third Reich.
Just as Germans had looked away from the persecution, deportation, and extermination of the Jews during the 1930s and early 1940s, they looked away
from the Holocaust after the war by simply not thinking or speaking about
their lives during the Third Reich. Germans were encouraged to adopt this
strategy by the deplorable conditions of postwar Germany, which focused
attention on surviving the immediate present. The Nazi period could not be
repressed completely, however, for, as Gabriele Rosenthal points out, human
beings need a past to anchor them in the present and give them direction for
the future. Therefore, following the immediate postwar period, Germans,
individually and collectively, tried to create an unproblematic, usable past
by "de-politicizing" their lives during the Third Reich. Specifically, Germans
"attempted to disentangle their own life histories from the Nazi regime"
and above all from the genocide which, in the version sanctioned by West
German society, was the responsibility of "the indicted Nazi bigwigs" while
ordinary Germans "knew nothing" and learned of the Holocaust only after
1945. Although the crimes of the Nazis could be discussed in general terms,
"any life experience in which one had been directly or indirectly confronted"
with those crimes had to be censored out of one's personal life history.[58]

  With the tacit support of West German society, parents and children invested enormous energy in repressing any past personal family connection to
National Socialism, including even family history about which one might expect people to feel proud.[59] Following the psychologist Dan Bar-On, Rosenthal argues that a double barrier blocks access to memories of the Third
Reich and of its crimes in West German families. The first is the wall erected
by those who lived through the period; the second is the wall erected by those
who might potentially hear those memories were they ever to be recounted.
Those who lived through the Third Reich do not want to talk about it, and
younger Germans do not want to listen.[60] Thus, instead of learning about
their family during the Third Reich, children and grandchildren "learned
which questions to ask and which to avoid and which questions they can use

to attack their parents and grandparents," attacks that are actually designed to prevent parents and grandparents from speaking about that time in their lives.[61] Although many of those who lived through the Third Reich are now ready to talk about their personal experiences of National Socialism, including its crimes, they are discouraged from doing so by what Rosenthal calls "the community of silence" in Germany, a community that includes their own children.[62]

The children seek to silence the parents about the National Socialist period both to maintain their relationship with the parents and to distance themselves from National Socialism, according to Rosenthal. On the one hand, the children fear that if their parents talk about their Nazi past, they will learn something so alienating and monstrous that all empathic contact with their parents will be broken. On the other hand, by silencing their parents, the children actually ensure that they never have to empathize with their parents and are never confronted with the possibility that they might have acted as their parents did during the Third Reich.[63] Thus Gabriele von Arnim, in her book *Das große Schweigen* (The Great Silence), acknowledges that she really did not want to understand the experience of her parents in Nazi Germany. Rather than asking, "How was it?" she asked only, "How could you?" By denouncing them into silence, she sought to maintain her position of moral superiority in relation to her parents and to keep National Socialism at emotional arm's length.[64] Following Arnim, the psychoanalyst Tilmann Moser notes that the children of those who lived through the Third Reich have been unable to confront the family past and sees those belonging to the 1968 generation, in particular, as frozen in a position of outrage and accusation that has prevented them from understanding their parents or their own relationship to National Socialism.[65]

Because the National Socialist past has never been confronted or worked through in any personally affecting way by the members of the generation that lived through the Third Reich, it lives on, unprocessed and unmastered either intellectually or emotionally, in the generation of their children.[66] Specifically, Rosenthal and other sociologists and psychologists argue that, despite their ostentatious rejection of their parents, the children of those who lived through the Third Reich unconsciously identify with their parents and seek to protect and even to exonerate them. Thus, the inability or unwillingness of the older generation to empathize with the victims of National Socialism is maintained, according to Rosenthal, by the next generation which, in the effort to avoid encountering those victims emotionally, continues to "de-realize and dehumanize" them.[67] Whereas the "de-realization and dehumanization of Jews in the generation that lived through the 'Third Reich' primarily takes the form of not speaking of Jews or the genocide, in the next generations it reappears again in a manifest anti-Semitism" that takes the form of anti-Zionism and "allows the younger generations to continue to condemn the victims of their parents and grandparents," thereby implicitly absolving their relatives of responsibility for the Holocaust.[68] Thus in the children and grandchildren of those who lived through the Third Reich "a secondary anti-Semitism emerges 'because and not in spite of Auschwitz.'"[69]

Despite the fact that young people across Europe and the United States took to the streets in protest during the late 1960s, scholars generally see the rebellion of the 1968ers in the Federal Republic as coming at least partially in response to the failure of West Germans to work through the National Socialist past. Frank Biess, for example, argues that the traumatic issues created by the loss of the war, including the crimes of National Socialism, were not dealt with collectively in West German society but were instead "privatized" in families, where they festered unresolved only to erupt in bitter conflict with the rebellion of the 1968 generation against their parents and the society their parents had created.[70] While Biess connects the 1968 rebellion with the transfer of the trauma of Nazism from West German society to the family, the sociologist Heinz Bude follows Rosenthal in connecting the 1968 rebellion with the transfer of the trauma of Nazism from those who lived through the Third Reich to their children. Specifically, Bude argues that those who lived through the Third Reich were too weak and traumatized after 1945 to deal with National Socialism and its loss themselves. They therefore passed the burden of the Nazi past on to their children, whose rebellion in 1968 represented in part a delayed outburst of resentment at having to shoulder what should not have been theirs to bear.[71] And yet, despite the fact that it was manifestly directed against their parents and their parents' values and society, the rebellion of the 1968ers was based on an unconscious and unresolved identification with the parents, according to Bude and Rosenthal. Although resentful of the burdens their parents had laid on them, those born in the late 1930s and the 1940s had made those burdens their own, becoming "containers" for the parents' sense of loss and guilt. As a result, the rebellion of the 1968ers came partially in response to the loss and guilt they experienced on behalf of their parents. Thus, for Bude (as for Rosenthal), theirs "was a proxy rebellion, designed in a way to protect and 'clear' a parental generation which could no longer bear its own history."[72]

CONCLUSION

The Authority of Historical Experience

When I began writing this book, virtually all of those interviewed for it were alive. As I write this conclusion, virtually none are.[1] Not only the interviewees but their generational peers have died or soon will, including their counterparts in the United States, now commonly known as "the greatest generation" after the book of that name by the television newscaster Tom Brokaw. It would be difficult to find two generations with more contrasting historical reputations than the "German generation" represented in this book and what Brokaw confidently describes as "the greatest generation that any society has produced."[2]

In attempting to understand how these two contemporaneous generations came to have such radically different reputations, one could look to the German and the American national character or, more plausibly, to long-term historical developments in the two countries. Indeed, according to the so-called Sonderweg interpretation of modern German history, National Socialism, and by implication the generation of Germans that is the subject of this book, was the end product of a unique and fateful path of German historical development extending back well into the nineteenth century and perhaps even beyond. Although some of the wind has gone out of the sails of this interpretation in recent years, the American version of the Sonderweg, the view that the United States has undergone a long-term and exceptional historical development, of which Brokaw's "greatest generation" is an end product, still enjoys widespread acceptance, certainly in the political arena. Unlike Germany's "special path," however, American "exceptionalism" is not to be repudiated and overcome. It is to be celebrated and carried forward.

Less separates these two twentieth-century generations than their contrasting historical reputations might suggest. Based on Brokaw's celebratory oral history at least, "the greatest generation" and its comparatively infamous German counterpart seem remarkably similar to one another. In childhood or adolescence both experienced economic hardship (primarily the Depression), directly and indirectly through its impact on their families, and learned to succeed "despite" a childhood of "deprivation."[3] Both generations fought doggedly and heroically in World War II, experiencing the terror, the exhilaration, the killing, and the losses of combat. The conditions of wartime gave members of both generations unprecedented opportunities to assume responsibility at a young age and broke down traditional gender roles, enabling young women, in Brokaw's words, to raise "the place of their gender to new heights."[4] And the war—like the Depression—broke down traditional class barriers, exposing middle- and upper-middle-class members of each generation to people lower on the social ladder.[5] Using the organizational and leadership skills, the ability to improvise, and the discipline acquired in the war, both generations played key roles in establishing flourishing economies and stable societies in their respective countries after 1945.[6] Frequently absent from their families during the 1940s and '50s and emotionally withdrawn as a result of their traumatic wartime experiences, many male members of both generations appear to have been somewhat distant from their children, laying the groundwork, perhaps, for the subsequent tension that would characterize their relationship.[7] Indeed, in the late 1960s both generations were denounced by their children: the one over the Vietnam War, the other over the National Socialist past. Like the interviewees in this study, the members of "the greatest generation" "hated the long hair, the free love, and, especially, what they saw as the desecration of the flag," the fact that "the concepts of duty and honor" were mocked by the young.[8] "If there's a common lament of this generation," Brokaw writes, "that is it: where is the old-fashioned patriotism that got them through so much heartache and sacrifice?"[9] Having worked hard and valued hard work throughout their lives, members of both generations had the sense that the young have been "victimized" by affluence, that "everything comes too easy" nowadays, and that younger people do not appreciate what they have because they did not have to "work" for it.[10] Concerned about the breakdown of the family, both sets of interviewees worried about children's and grandchildren's divorces and that daughters and granddaughters frequently left the children at a young age to work.[11]

In general, the values, attitudes, and outlook of "the greatest generation" in the United States seem much the same as those of their generational peers in Germany. Brokaw summarizes those shared values: "duty, honor, country, personal responsibility and the marriage vow."[12] Both generations took the obligations and difficulties that came their way and did what was expected of them without complaint or the sense that life owed them a favor.[13] Indeed, qualities celebrated by Brokaw in "the greatest generation" enabled the members of "a German generation" to create and sustain the Third Reich and kept them fighting in an immoral war until its bitter end.

This is not to suggest, of course, that nothing separates these two generations beyond historical reputation. The belief in God and the role evidently played by religious faith in the lives of the members of Brokaw's "greatest generation" find no parallel in the life stories related by the members of "a German generation" for this study.[14] Indeed, the absence of expressions of religious faith in the interviews is all the more striking given that the interviewees were asked explicitly about the role of religion in their lives by their interviewers. By contrast, the overriding importance of Gemeinschaft to the interviewees and the central role played by collective experiences in their lives and in the lives of other Germans of their generation finds no real parallel in "the greatest generation" as presented by Brokaw. Indeed, although those Americans interviewed for Brokaw's book appear to have developed a sense of generational identity as a result of the war and the rebellion of their children in the late 1960s, the interviewees and many of their German peers had a keen generational consciousness already in adolescence, which the war and the 1968ers merely served to strengthen.

The differences between these two contemporaneous generations should not, in my view, be attributed to national character or even to long-term historical developments. What distinguishes these two generations is the fact that they had different historical experiences beginning in childhood. And they lived in different cultural contexts that defined the options for processing and responding to their historical experiences. Unlike "the greatest generation," the members of "a German generation" experienced defeat in World War I and the political unrest and economic hardship (particularly the inflation of 1923) that came in its wake, both directly and through the impact of these events on their families and on other institutions that supported the young. In response to these historical experiences and in a country without a long-standing tradition of democratic government, bourgeois adolescents in Germany turned to the generational collective for support; rejected the Weimar Republic, with its party politics, its liberalism and pluralism; and, in many cases, embraced National Socialism and the collective of the Volksgemeinschaft. Despite certain similarities between the Civilian Conservation Corps in the United States and the Work Service in the Third Reich, "the greatest generation" never experienced anything like the mass mobilization of youth by the National Socialists during the 1930s.[15] Whereas "the greatest generation" was victorious in what was ultimately a just war, its generational counterpart in Germany was defeated in a war that was unambiguously unjust. Germans of the interviewees' generation suffered incomparably greater losses in the war and at its bitter end, and they also had to live for the rest of their lives with the consequences of having supported National Socialism. In sum, "the greatest generation" did not suffer a lifetime of loss comparable to that experienced by "a German generation," nor did it turn to the collective as a way to repair those losses as "a German generation" did.

What distinguishes "the greatest generation" from its German counterpart, then, is perhaps less than Americans might like to imagine: different concrete historical experiences processed and responded to within different cultural contexts. And what accounts for the similarities in values, attitude, and outlook between these two contemporaneous generations are similar concrete historical experiences, their different cultural contexts notwithstanding. Indeed, the similarities between "the greatest generation" and its German counterpart and the differences in identity, values, and outlook between "a German generation" and other twentieth-century German generations (outlined in the introduction to this book) suggest that the role played by cultural context in creating and giving shape to these generations was comparatively limited. Given the authority of historical experience, we should focus attention less on long-term historical developments, let alone on national character, in attempting to understand the failure of the Weimar Republic, the rise of National Socialism, and the popularity of the Third Reich for much of its brief existence, and more on the concrete experience of Germans during the period between 1918 and 1933, on their responses to the loss of the war, the political disorder, and the economic hardship.

Not only are the last members of "the greatest" and of "a German" generation now dying away, so too are the victims of National Socialism, including, of course, those who survived the Holocaust. At this point of generational transition it seems important to remind ourselves that what ultimately separates us from those who carried out and enabled the genocide is historical experience. We share human nature with the perpetrators and their complicit bystanders. Two specific aspects of human nature seem particularly relevant in the context of National Socialism and the Holocaust. Although its intensity may vary from person to person, or indeed from culture to culture, all human beings have the need to belong to the group and to exclude others from it, a need that centrally motivated the genocide, in my view. And all human beings have the capacity to dehumanize others by closing off empathy for them, a capacity that enabled the genocide to be carried out. Moreover, the similarities between "the greatest generation" and "a German generation," as well as the differences between the German generation described here and other twentieth-century German generations, suggest that we should not count on cultural context to distance us from the Nazis. What separates us from those who carried out the worst horror in the history of modern Europe is nothing intrinsic to them or to us. What separates us from them is "the grace" of historical experience.

As historical experience exercises authority over human beings, determining in no small measure what they think, feel, and do, it exercises authority over their memories. Of course, it is possible that the centrality of loss in the life stories related by the interviewees in this study reflected their present circumstances more than their past experience. Having reached the end of their lives, the interviewees were confronted with a series of age-related losses, not least their own impending death. Thus, it is possible that the interviewees simply recalled and recast their life histories in terms of the losses they were facing at the time of their interviews. Readers must ultimately judge for themselves, based on the evidence presented over the course of this book, whether the prominence of loss in the interviews reflects retrospective reconstruction or whether the losses of old age represent the latest and ultimately last installment in lives characterized by loss.

In relation to our own memories, of course, we are convinced "that particular past experiences are not just the object, but in some vital sense, the source, of our present recollections."[16] We do not need to rely solely on introspection, however, to feel confident that memory is determined by past experience more than by present-day concerns. The limited influence of the present over memories of the past is demonstrable. Thus Germans from East and West Germany who were interviewed for oral history studies, generally in the early 1980s, gave the same account of their experiences in the Hitler Youth and in the Third Reich despite having lived most of their lives in very different societies and finding themselves in very different circumstances at the time of their interviews. According to Alexander von Plato, their memories and judgments, myths and images "were the same whether the respondent was from the FRG or the former GDR."[17] Indeed, as the essays sections of this book have presumably made clear, Germans of varying ages and in varying circumstances interviewed about their lives during the twentieth century related similar experiences in similar ways, not because they shared a common present (which they often did not) but because they shared a common past. It is also testifies to the authority of the past that those interviewees described experiences not in their present-day self-interest to recall, such as their enthusiasm for National Socialism during the 1930s or their having regarded the plot to assassinate Hitler in July 1944 as an act of treason.

Readers must judge for themselves whether the memories of the interviewees should be read as elderly people recalling and recasting their life histories in light of the losses of advanced old age. They must also judge whether my interpretations of the interviewees reflect more my life experience than theirs—whether my own family history, for example, led me to impose loss and suffering on people who led, as so many claimed, fulfilled and happy lives. I would argue, however, that my own experiences did not so much distort my understanding of the interviewees as make it possible. Just as the position of the observer determines what he or she is able to observe, so we use our life experiences to see and understand historical phenomena that would otherwise remain invisible to us. Our own experiences enable us to empathize with the experiences of others, experiences different from our own but sufficiently related or comparable to enable us to imagine our way, to think our way, inside them. Thus, my own experiences of loss, the loss of my parents and of their generation, helped me to appreciate and understand the losses of the interviewees and the impact that those losses had on their lives. Similarly, my own generational consciousness enabled me to appreciate and understand the generational consciousness of the interviewees, the sense of connection, identity, and place in history that it provided them.

This book, then, testifies to the authority of historical experience. In no small measure, it determines who we are, what we do, and what we re-member of it all. And yet human beings are not only constituted by history, they also make history "as a result of the apparently private experiences of thousands and millions of individuals," experiences like joining the youth movement, devoting oneself to the National Socialist ideal of the Volksge-meinschaft, doing one's duty as a soldier in the Wehrmacht until the bitter end, looking away from Jews as they were being persecuted and deported, or plunging oneself into the achievement of prosperity in the wake of the war—experiences that changed the world. History flows through every "accidental and private individual person," and in the process its course is altered. [18]

NOTES

INTRODUCTION

1. See my first published article, "Kaiser Wilhelm II and His Parents."

2. For the role played by historical experience in shaping not a group but the self of the individual, see Annemarie Karutz's sensitive depth-psychological study, *Von der Idealisierung*.

3. Haffner, *Geschichte eines Deutschen*, 170–71.

4. Jürgen Reulecke, "Vorwort" to the final project report, "Die Freideutschen: Seniorenkreise aus jugendbewegter Wurzel—Ein Modell für sinnerfülltes Alter," November 1996, 4.

5. Ibid., 3.

6. Two of the three interviewers have written monographs on the Free German Circle: Heinrich Ulrich Seidel's *Aufbruch und Erinnerung* is a history of the Circle, and Sabiene Autsch's *Erinnerung-Biographie-Fotographie* studies the relationship between lived and remembered experience as mediated and shaped by personal photographs.

7. The advisory board consisted of Insa Fooken and Georg Rudinger, psychologists specializing in gerontology; Annette Niederfranke, a psychologist; Irene Woll-Schumacher, a sociologist; Imbke Behnken, Norbert Schwarte, and Jürgen Zinnecker, professors of education and social pedagogy; Gerhard Hufnagel, a political scientist and historian; Christa Berg, a professor of the history of education; Alexander von Plato, director of the Institute for History and Biography and a historian with expertise in the practice of oral history; and Gabriele Müller-List, a historian representing the Federal Ministry for Family, Senior Citizens, Women, and Youth.

8. For a model collective biography of a generation, see Wierling's *Geboren im Jahr Eins*, a study of East Germans born around 1949.

9. Zinnecker, "'Das Problem der Generationen,'" 44.

10. Mannheim, "The Problem of Generations," 289–90.

11. Ibid., 290–91.

12. Ibid., 298, 300.

13. Ibid., 303, 310–12.

14. Ibid., 288, 304–9.

15. Pinder, *Problem der Generation.*

16. Rusinek, "Krieg als Sehnsucht," 129; Zinnecker, "'Das Problem der Generationen,'" 39.

17. Reulecke, "'. . . und sie werden nicht mehr frei,'" 129–30, 132; Reulecke, "Einführung"; Jaeger, "Generationen in der Geschichte," 433, 450; Plato, "Nachkriegssieger," 351.

18. Reulecke, "Generationen und Biografien," 33–36; Rosenthal, "Zur interaktionellen Konstitution," 64–66.

19. Herbert, "Drei politische Generationen," 98.

20. Fogt, *Politische Generationen,* 129–30.

21. Ibid.; Herbert, "Drei politische Generationen," 97–102.

22. Schelsky, *Die skeptische Generation*; Plato, "Hitler Youth Generation," 223; Wierling, "The Hitler Youth Generation in the GDR," 307–8; Herbert, "Drei politische Generationen," 105, generally 102–9. Also Reulecke, "Generationen und Biografien," 35–36; Rosenthal, "Zur interaktionellen Konstitution," 66–68.

23. Bude, "The German *Kriegskinder*," 302–5; Rosenthal, "Zur interaktionellen Konstitution," 69–71; Wierling, "Mission to Happiness," 110–18.

24. Herbert, "Drei politische Generationen," 109–11.

25. Ibid., 113–14.

26. Ibid., 111–12.

27. Babett Lobinger, "'Soziale Netzwerke' und 'Support-Bank': Alltagsbewältigung durch die Freideutschen heute," in final project report "Die Freideutschen," 145.

28. I recognize the circularity of the reasoning here. I claim that I could create the composite interviews because the interviewees lived and related similar lives. And I claim that the interviewees lived and related similar lives because I was able to create the composite interviews. Nevertheless, the argument has validity. Originally I had considered ignoring gender difference to blend the interviews of men and women. Such a "transgendered" composite interview would have been possible to create for the first part of this book. Its creation was not possible for the second two parts of the book, however: the paths of the men and women diverged too much for me to bring them together.

29. Niethammer, "Fragen—Antworten—Fragen," 405–6, 418.

30. Personal communication from the sociologist John Downey.

31. It is striking, however, that the interviewees tended to speak more about their lives during the Third Reich, the war, and the immediate postwar period than about the youth movement or the Free German Circle.

32. Rosenthal, *"Als der Krieg kam,"* 17.

33. Ibid., 22; Cubitt, *History and Memory,* 234–35.

34. Remark at a conference presentation and personal communication.

35. Cubitt, *History and Memory,* 98–99. Even in the case of people far more disparate than those interviewed for this study, the memories recounted in oral history interviews always express individual and collective experience and it is virtually impossible to distinguish one from the other. Tröger, "German Women's Memories," 288.

The more homogeneous the group, the more coherent the narrative contents and structures of interviews with its members will tend to be. Niethammer, "Fragen—Antworten—Fragen," 412.

36. Halbwachs argued that an experienced past becomes articulated memory (including to the self) only when it is communicated to others. While individuals remember, memory itself is collective. Welzer, "Das gemeinsame Verfertigen," 166, and "Das soziale Gedächtnis," 16–17.

37. Halbwachs, *Collective Memory*, 78, 86–87. Also Cubitt, *History and Memory*, 132–40, 154–71.

38. A104.

39. Personal communication from the historian Robert Dalzell; Lobinger, "'Soziale Netzwerke' und 'Support-Bank,'" in final project report "Die Freideutschen," 145.

40. Most are between fifteen thousand and twenty-five thousand words, and a significant number exceed thirty thousand words.

41. Nonetheless, I would hope that readers might reach conclusions about the interviewees very different from mine based upon their reading of the composite interviews.

42. Lessing, *Geschichte als Sinngebung*, 6.

43. My interpretation of the interviewees emerged from the evidence of the interviews; my presentation of the interview evidence emerged from my interpretation of it.

44. Oral history breaks down the traditional distinction between subject and observer, for the historical subjects are also the observers of their lives, and their observations of those lives are the basis of what the historian has to say about them. Niethammer, "Einführung," 8; Grele, "Ziellose Bewegung," 205; Rosenthal, *"Als der Krieg kam,"* 242.

45. Grele, "Ziellose Bewegung," 200–201.

46. Daniel, *Kompendium Kulturgeschichte*, 306–7.

47. Cubitt, *History and Memory*, 71.

48. Rosenthal, *"Als der Krieg kam,"* 235, 242; Tröger, "German Women's Memories," 288.

49. Plato, "Oral History als Erfahrungswissenschaft," 108.

50. Niethammer, "Fragen—Antworten—Fragen," 401.

51. Rosenthal, *"Als der Krieg kam,"* 215.

52. One historian who effectively and sensitively compares remembered experience based on oral history interviews with more traditional but no less subjective contemporary sources is Mark Roseman in his biographical study, *Past in Hiding*.

53. Niethammer, "Heimat und Front," 218.

54. Rosenthal, *". . . wenn alles in Scherben fällt,"* 14–15.

55. Niethammer, "Fragen—Antworten—Fragen," 415.

56. Ibid., 420, 428; Plato, "Oral History als Erfahrungswissenschaft," 97–98, 104; Eley, Foreword; Eley, "Labor History, Social History, Alltagsgeschichte."

57. As Alon Confino aptly puts it, "One can understand without forgiving and forgive without understanding." "Prologue," 10. An example of empathy used for a hostile purpose was the attempt by the Germans "to create disintegrating panic in those they were about to attack" by attaching sirens to the wings of dive-bombers during World War II. "It was empathy (vicarious introspection) that allowed them to predict how those exposed to the mysterious noise from the skies would react." Heinz Kohut, "From a Letter to a Colleague," 580.

58. As my father wrote in reference to the Nazis, "If the depth psychologist [or the historian, for that matter] is to make a contribution to the understanding of man's role in history and his control over his destiny, then he must try to extend his empathic observation not only to the victims but also to the persecutors, not only to the martyrs but also to their torturers. He must discover the human, the all-too-human, whether in the normal . . . or in the psychopathological, in the good and in the evil." Heinz Kohut, "On Leadership," 119.

CHAPTER 1. INTERVIEWS: YOUTH

Heinrich Rath

1. *S104.* Each interview cited in this study is identified by a letter or letters and a number. The letters refer to the interviewer or interviewers: A for Autsch, B for Baumgarten (now Lobinger), S for Seidel. Three interviewees were interviewed twice, which is indicated by the hyphen in their interview designation: A110-A121 (interviewed twice by Autsch), AB102-B106 (interviewed first by Autsch and Baumgarten and then again by Baumgarten), and S102-A107 (interviewed first by Seidel and then by Autsch). Italicized interview designations indicate those conducted with men; nonitalicized interview designations were with women. Each change made in the interviews is indicated in the endnotes except for brief deletions. Ellipses in the text do not indicate deletions but reflect the speech of the interviewees. When the same interview is cited in successive notes, this indicates that the statements come from two different parts of the same interview. When two different interviews are cited in the same note, this indicates that both interviewees used exactly the same phrase.

2. *S104; A118.*

3. *S104; A118.*

4. *A118.*

5. *S111.*

6. *A118.*

7. *S104.*

8. *B104.*

9. This date has been changed from 1916. The interviewee is older than most of the others, and most interviewees date the end of a "happy" childhood to the early 1920s.

10. *S122.*

11. This sentence is an amalgam of two interviews, *S101* and *S106.* *S101* went with his mother to live with his maternal grandfather in Brandis in the Nieder Lausitz. *S106* was sent to live with his aunt and uncle in the Ober Lausitz.

12. Changed from "1914 to 1921."

13. *S106.*

14. *S101.*

15. *B107.*

16. *A117.*

17. *A117.*

18. *A118.*

19. *S101.*

20. *S107.*

21. Phrase added.

22. *S101*. The interviewee is referring here to his step-grandmother.
23. *S106*.
24. *S107*.
25. *S106*. "1921" has been changed to "1919."
26. *S101*. The interviewee is referring to his step-grandmother.
27. Phrase added.
28. *S106*.
29. *S106*.
30. Phrase added.
31. *S106*.
32. *B104*.
33. Changed from "Frankfurt."
34. *B103*.
35. *A118*.
36. *B103*.
37. *S115*.
38. *S115; S118*.
39. *S115*.
40. *S115*.
41. *S115*.
42. These two sentences have been added.
43. *S106*.
44. *B111*.
45. *S104*.
46. *B111*.
47. *A118*.
48. *S106*.
49. *S107*.
50. *S104; B107*.
51. *A118; S107*.
52. *A118*.
53. *S107*.
54. Changed from "Frankfurt an der Oder."
55. Changed from "two large sawmills."
56. *B107*.
57. *S106*.
58. *S107*.
59. *S118*.
60. *S106*.
61. Phrase added.
62. Changed from "a group of Altwandervogel, Gruppe Steglitz."
63. *B104*. "We" has been changed to "I."
64. *B104*.
65. *S117*.
66. *S104*.
67. *S119*.
68. *A117; S117; B104*.

69. *B104.*
70. Changed from "home evenings."
71. *A118.*
72. *S117.* The order of this sentence has been slightly altered.
73. *S124.*
74. *S118.*
75. *S107.*
76. *B104.*
77. *B111.*
78. *B104.*
79. *B104.*
80. *S115.*
81. *S117.*
82. *S106.*
83. *S102-A107.*
84. *S106.*
85. *A118.*
86. *S106.*
87. *A118.*
88. *S119.*
89. *A118.*
90. *S119.*
91. *A118.*
92. *A123.*
93. *S118.*
94. *A123.*
95. Sentence added.
96. *A117.*
97. *A117.*
98. *A117.*
99. *S107.*
100. *S107.*
101. *S102-A107.*
102. *S104.*
103. *S107.*
104. *S104.*
105. *S107.*
106. *S102-A107.*
107. *S117.*
108. *S104.*
109. Changed from "Oppeln."
110. *S117.*
111. *S117.*
112. *S119.*
113. *S118.*
114. *S119.*
115. *S102-A107.*

116. *A117.*
117. *S107.*
118. *AB103.*
119. *B104.*
120. *S117.*
121. *S117; AB103.*
122. *S117.*
123. *S117.*
124. *S117.*
125. *AB103.*
126. *B104.*
127. Phrase added.
128. *B104.*
129. *B104.*
130. *S106.*
131. *S106.*
132. *B104.*
133. *S106.*
134. *S106.*
135. *A117.*
136. *S106.*
137. *S106.*
138. *S106.*
139. *S107.*
140. *AB103.*
141. *S107.*
142. *S117.*
143. *S117.*
144. *S117.*
145. *S123.*
146. *S123.*
147. *AB103.*
148. *S115.*
149. *S117.*
150. This phrase is an amalgam of *S117* and *S115.*
151. *S117.*
152. *S117.*
153. Phrase added.
154. *S117.*
155. *S107.*
156. *S104.*
157. Sentence added.
158. *S117.*
159. Changed from "Yugoslavia."
160. Changed from "Trau."
161. *S102-A107.*
162. Changed from "Rhine."

163. *S102-A107.*
164. *S102-A107.*
165. *S102-A107.*
166. *S104.*
167. *S104.*
168. *S104.*
169. *S104.*
170. *S117.*
171. *S104.*
172. *S117.*
173. *S104.*
174. *S117.*
175. *B104.*
176. *S117.*
177. *S104.*
178. *S117.*
179. Phrase added.
180. Changed from "the Black Forest."
181. Changed from "the Feldberg."
182. *S102-A107.*
183. *A117.*
184. *S117.*
185. *S123.*
186. *S117.*
187. *B104.*
188. *AB103.*
189. Sentence combines *AB103* and *B104.*
190. *AB103.*
191. *B104.*
192. *AB103.*
193. *S104.*
194. *S106.*
195. *S104.*
196. *S106.*
197. *S106.*
198. *S106.*
199. *S106.*
200. *S123.*
201. *S106.*
202. *S106.*
203. *S106.*
204. *S106.*
205. *S104.*

Margarete Schulte

1. *S116.*
2. Changed from "two years."

3. B109.
4. BS121.
5. B109.
6. BS121.
7. B109.
8. B102.
9. B114.
10. BS121.
11. Changed from "Dresden" and "1903."
12. A103.
13. A103.
14. A103.
15. A103.
16. S116.
17. S108.
18. A101.
19. B113.
20. A101.
21. B113.
22. A119.
23. A104.
24. A104.
25. B113.
26. A106.
27. A104.
28. Word added.
29. Phrase altered slightly.
30. A104.
31. B113.
32. S108.
33. S116.
34. A103.
35. S116.
36. S112.
37. A103.
38. S108.
39. B113.
40. Changed from "father." A105.
41. "Still" added. B114.
42. A115.
43. A116.
44. Changed from "my father." B112.
45. A109.
46. A108.
47. B115.
48. B112.
49. B115.

50. B114.
51. AB102-B106.
52. AB102-B106.
53. A120.
54. A104.
55. B114.
56. A104.
57. S116.
58. AB102-B106.
59. S110.
60. S116.
61. AB102-B106.
62. S116.
63. AB102-B106.
64. A120.
65. A103.
66. A104.
67. B114.
68. A104.
69. A103.
70. Changed from "Minden."
71. B114.
72. AB102-B106.
73. A103.
74. Changed from "1919" and "from Berlin to Hamburg."
75. BS121.
76. Changed from "Thüringen."
77. A105.
78. BS121.
79. Changed from "Dresden" and "an upper girls' school." A103.
80. Changed from "four."
81. A104.
82. B102.
83. S113.
84. B112.
85. S110.
86. B102.
87. "Still" added. A101.
88. A104.
89. A114.
90. Changed from "brother."
91. A104.
92. A101.
93. BS121.
94. Changed from "Altona outside Hamburg."
95. A114.
96. S116.

97. B110.
98. B110.
99. B108.
100. B110.
101. Phrase added.
102. S113.
103. Changed from "grandfather."
104. B108.
105. S113.
106. Changed from "uncle."
107. B108.
108. S113.
109. B110.
110. S110.
111. BS121.
112. AB101.
113. BS121.
114. B108.
115. S109.
116. S116.
117. A101.
118. S116.
119. A101.
120. A101.
121. A101.
122. A101.
123. BS121.
124. B115.
125. BS121.
126. B115.
127. BS121.
128. B115.
129. BS121.
130. S112.
131. S112.
132. B102.
133. S112.
134. B102.
135. S112.
136. B115.
137. A116.
138. A116.
139. S112.
140. B102.
141. S112.
142. B102.
143. BS121.

144. A116.
145. B102.
146. S114.
147. A112.
148. A101.
149. Changed from "mother."
150. A124.
151. B102.
152. Changed from "her" and from "mother."
153. B102.
154. A124; A101.
155. Changed from "three little children." A112.
156. B102.
157. B102.
158. Changed from "our house."
159. A112.
160. Changed from "Doberan in Mecklenburg." BS121.
161. S108.
162. "and" added. S113.
163. A104.
164. A105.
165. Changed from having her father die a half a year *after* the move. S108.
166. S114.
167. Changed from "changed schools" and "a girls' gymnasium."
168. S114.
169. S112.
170. A104.
171. A115.
172. Changed from "Ludwigsburg."
173. S108.
174. A105.
175. Phrase added.
176. B115.
177. A105.
178. A105.
179. S108.
180. S108.
181. Changed from "we weren't."
182. B112.
183. A101.
184. Changed from "Stuttgart."
185. A101.
186. S110.
187. B102.
188. A116.
189. B102.
190. S113.

191. AB101.
192. S120.
193. AB101.
194. S112.
195. BS121.
196. Changed from "he."
197. S112.
198. Changed from "they."
199. BS121.
200. S116.
201. Changed from "1929."
202. S113.
203. S113.
204. S113.
205. A115.
206. Changed from "Berlin." A109.
207. Changed from "Harn Heath." A115.
208. A109.
209. A106.
210. A115.
211. A115.
212. A116.
213. BS121.
214. A105.
215. S116.
216. A115.
217. S116.
218. A120.
219. A120.
220. Changed from "parents." A104.
221. B113.
222. BS121.
223. A106.
224. A109.
225. A115.
226. A109.
227. A115.
228. A109.
229. A115.
230. A109.
231. A115.
232. Changed from "thirteen."
233. A109.
234. S116.
235. A109.
236. A120.
237. S112.

238. A106.
239. B110.
240. A106.
241. A109.
242. A103.
243. A106.
244. A103.
245. A109.
246. B108.
247. S112.
248. B102.
249. A109.
250. S112.
251. Changed from "Dresden."
252. S112.
253. A115.
254. S112.
255. A115.
256. S113.
257. A110-A121.
258. S113.
259. A106.
260. B115.
261. B116.
262. A106.
263. BS121.
264. A106.
265. B112.
266. B109.
267. A116.
268. A109.
269. A109.
270. BS121.
271. A109.
272. "That happened later in Magdeburg" added.
273. A111.
274. S110.
275. "In that" added.
276. A119.
277. B115.
278. A110-A121.
279. A119.
280. A110-A121.
281. S110.
282. B115.
283. S110.
284. AB101.

285. Changed from "for academics." A110-A121.

286. A109.

287. A116.

288. S113.

289. B112.

290. A115; B112.

291. S113.

292. S116.

293. AB101.

294. BS121.

295. A101.

296. A116.

297. Phrase added.

298. BS121.

299. A109.

300. Changed from "parents."

301. BS 121.

302. BS121.

303. "In Berlin" added.

304. Changed from "Doberan."

305. Changed from "Rostock."

306. BS121.

307. A101.

308. A119.

309. B116.

310. A119.

311. A116.

312. A119.

313. B114.

CHAPTER 2. ANALYSIS: FINDING THE COLLECTIVE IN THE YOUTH MOVEMENT "GROUP"

1. *B107*; B115. Here and in the other analysis sections, interview designations in bold have not been quoted in the interviews; those not in bold have been. As indicated above, italicized interview designations are with men, nonitalicized designations with women.

2. **A103**; *A117*; **A120**; A124; AB102-B106; B114; **B115**; *S107*; S110; S116.

3. A103; A105; B104; S106.

4. A104; *A118*.

5. A104; *S101*; *S104*.

6. A104; *A117*; B114; S101; S106.

7. B115, *S118*, and *S119*, coming from proletarian backgrounds, also recall the period of the war as happy, secure, and nurturing.

8. A105; A114; **A116**; *A118*; AB101; AB102-B106; B102; *B104*; B113; B115; B117; BS121; *S104*; S108; S110; *S111*; S112; S120.

9. *B104*; B109; **BS121**; *S101*; S116.

10. The facts that the period of World War I is remembered fondly by the interviewees, that only a handful of their fathers were killed in the conflict, and that most of their fathers remained at home throughout the war fail to confirm the thesis, advanced first by the psychoanalyst Martin Wangh and subsequently by the historian and psychoanalyst Peter Loewenberg, that the attraction of National Socialism generally and of Adolf Hitler in particular for younger Germans can be attributed psychologically to the absence of their fathers during their early lives. Wangh, "National Socialism and the Genocide of the Jews"; Loewenberg, "The Psychohistorical Origins of the Nazi Youth Cohort." Nevertheless, this study *does* follow Wangh and Loewenberg in explaining the psychological susceptibility of this generation to the blandishments of the Nazis and Hitler as emerging in part out of an effort to compensate for the loss of the father—the physical loss of the father for many of those interviewed, the loss of the father as an admired figure for more. It merely assigns the moment of that loss not to World War I but to the Weimar Republic. And what Loewenberg writes about the veteran father after 1918, that he returned "in defeat and was unable to protect his family in the postwar period of unemployment and inflation" (1480), applies equally to the noncombatant fathers of the interviewees.

11. A120; S113; *S123* report fathers killed in the war; **A114** and **B117** report older brothers killed in the war.

12. A114; *A118*; *B111*; **BS121**; S116.

13. *A118*; B110; **BS121**; *S104*; *S106*; S113.

14. **S114**; A101; **A116**; AB101; **B105**; B116; *S111*; S116.

15. A101; **A103**; A104; **A116**; A116; A120; **BS121**; *S115*; S116; *S118*; *S122*.

16. *B104*.

17. **A104**; **A114**; *A118*; B117; *S107*.

18. A101; *A118*; BS121.

19. **B105**; B110.

20. A116; **B102**; BS121.

21. A116; *A118*; *B104*.

22. A105; BS121; *S106*; *S107*; S112; S113.

23. A104; **A109**; *S101*; **S116**; *S117*.

24. A101; A104; A119; *B103*; *S106*.

25. B108; S113; **S114**.

26. A101.

27. A112; A116; *A118*; **A119**; A120; **B102**; B115; *S107*; **S109**; S116; *S122*; *S123*.

28. **A112**; **B102**; *S101*; S108.

29. According to Bernd Hüppauf, Germans generally experienced the Weimar Republic as an arbitrary and meaningless time, governed by historical accident. "Langemarck, Verdun."

30. A103; **A104**; A116; *A118*; *B107*; B108; *BS101*; BS121.

31. B102; *S104*; S116.

32. A104; A116; BS121; *S104*; S112.

33. B102; **B108**; *BS101*; *S104*; S116; *S124*.

34. Personal communication from the psychologist Babett Lobinger.

35. It is possible that this strategy originated with the parents. The parents' oft-voiced contempt for people like President Ebert who were unable to maintain order or

uphold Germany's honor may thus have been an attempt to blame the politicians of Weimar for their own sense of failure and disgrace.

36. A116; B102; *BS101*; BS121; *S104*; S116; *S124*.

37. Their general characterization of the parents is almost always positive, although specific memories of the parents are often negative: A105; A115; A116; *A118*; A124; B102; B112; B113; **B114**; BS121; *S104*; *S107*; S110; S112; S116; *S124*.

38. A116; BS121; *S104*; S112.

39. A103; *A118*; *A123*; AB101; S110; S112; *S119*.

40. Suhrkamp, "Söhne ohne Väter," 689.

41. In childhood or adolescence the following interviewees lost a parent: A101; **A103**; A112; **A114**; A116; A124; **AB101**; B102; B108; B110 (lost both parents); *B111*; B112; B117; *BS101*; *S101*; *S107*; S108; S113; S114; *S115*; *S122*; *S123*; *S102-A107*. *S111* lost his father as a result of his parents' divorce. The following interviewees lost beloved parental figures: *S101*; S110; **S113**; *S123*. For A103, A104, A114, and B117, the loss of a sibling had a deleterious psychological impact not only on them but on their parents.

42. B102 and *S107* stand out because they express anguish at the loss of their fathers.

43. Personal communication from the sociologist Lerke Gravenhorst.

44. B115; *S115*; *S117*; S124.

45. A119; A110-A121; *S106*.

46. S113; S116.

47. **A114**; B112; **B115**.

48. Bessel, *Germany After the First World War*, 221, 223, 228, 251; Buck, *How It Happens*, 129, 142, 143.

49. *S101*; *S106*; *S118*.

50. Personal communication from the psychologist Phebe Cramer.

51. A101; A116; B102; **B110**; *S106*; *S107*; S113; *S115*; S122.

52. *AB103*; *B104*; B113; *S111*; S120. Stachura, *German Youth Movement*, 63.

53. *A118*; AB101; B102; *S104*; *S107*; S110; S112; *S115*; S120.

54. A104; A105; A106; A109; A116; *A117*; *A118*; A119; A120; B110; B113; B114; BS121; S110; S110; S112; S112; *S115*; S116; *S102-A107*.

55. A120; *A123*; *AB103*; *S104*; *S104*; S117; *S119*.

56. A101; A116; S110; S116; *S119*; *S119*; *S102-A107*.

57. A115; *B104*; *B111*; S110; S116.

58. AB101; *B104*; S113; *S117*.

59. Laqueur, *Young Germany*, 30, 134, 190; Stachura, *German Youth Movement*, 47–48.

60. A116; *A117*; *A118*; *A123*; *B103*; **B104**; BS121; *S107*; S110; *S117*; *S122*; S124.

61. A115; *S102-A107*.

62. A115; *A118*; *S107*; *S118*.

63. A109; *B111*.

64. Gründel, *Die Sendung*, 41–36; Matzke, *Jugend bekennt*, 7; Baumgarten, "Der sittliche Zustand," 75; Herbert, "'Generation der Sachlichkeit,'" 118.

65. *A118*.

66. *S106*.

67. **A101**; A109; *A117*; *S106*; S113; S116.

68. A103; **S120**.

69. B102; S112.

70. A103; BS121; *S106*; *S119*.

71. A103; A106; A109; *A118*; A123; B108; B110; ***BS101***; *S118*; *S119*; *S102-A107*. Linse, "'Geschlechtsnot der Jugend,'" 262–69.

72. A109; *A118*; *AB103*; *B104*; ***BS101***; *S107*; ***S115***.

73. A106; *S107*; *S117*; *S119*.

74. *A117*; *S102-A107*.

75. Personal communication from the historian Ute Daniel.

76. **BS121**; S110; **S113**; *S117*. In 1932, E. Günther Gründel was convinced that the "*ruin of the German middle class*" as a result of the hardships of the early 1920s had "awakened" the members of the youth movement and given them a sense of calling: "As an entire large class we were disinherited and exposed in order to make us ready to face the great challenges that awaited us." *Die Sendung*, 40–41. According to the historian Ulrich Herbert, young people like Gründel "glorified hardship" and transformed their "suffering, loss, and fear about the future" into positive attributes, which gave them "an almost avant-garde predisposition." "'Generation der Sachlichkeit,'" 117–18.

77. A120.

78. *B104*.

79. A123; *AB103*; *S117*; *S123*; *S102-A107*.

80. *S102-A107*.

81. **BS121**; *S106*; *S117*.

82. *AB103*; *B104*; *S117*. Janz, "Die Faszination der Jugend."

83. Reulecke, "'Wir reiten die Sehnsucht tot,'" 107.

84. *S118*.

85. Reulecke, "'Wir reiten die Sehnsucht tot,'" 107.

86. A106; A115; A116; *A117*; **AB101**; *AB103*; *S106*; *S107*; S113; **S116**; *S117*; *S119*; *S120*; *S102-A107*. Only **A109** and **B115** were members of more internationalist socialist youth groups.

87. *A117*; *S117*. Rusinek, "Krieg als Sehnsucht."

88. AB101; *AB103*; BS121; S116; *S117*; *S123*; *S124*.

89. A103; B112; S114.

90. **A101**; **A109**; *AB103*; *B104*; ***S106***; **S119**.

91. *B104*; *S117*.

92. Kater, "Bürgerliche Jugendbewegung," 153–55.

93. Ibid., 144.

94. A120; *S117*; *S123*. Stachura, *German Youth Movement*, 48–50; Raabe, *Bündische Jugend*, 48–53.

95. A101; A106; A115; *B104*; *S104*; S110, S112; S116; *S117*; *S119*; *S102-A107*.

96. *S107*.

97. A106; A109; A115; *S104*; S110; S112; *S119*. Kater, "Generationskonflikt," 222.

98. Raabe, *Bündische Jugend*, 191.

99. A116; *A118*; *B104*; **B111**; B112; *S117*. Stachura, *German Youth Movement*, 64.

100. A106; A115; A116; B110; *B111*; *S104*; *S106*; *S107*; S113; *S117*.

101. A101; B110; B116; S113.

102. Raabe, *Bündische Jugend*, 108; Mommsen, "Generationenkonflikt," 117–18.

103. A106; A109; **A120**; S114.

104. A109; A110-A121; *S106*.

105. **A103; A109; A111;** *A123;* **BS101;** *S117.* The one rebellion against school authorities, described by **S113**, was an anti-Semitic rebellion against a progressive school that sought to promote republican ideals. Stachura, *German Youth Movement*, 63.

106. *S104*.

107. A101; A109; **A115**; B115. According to AB101, B109, B112, and B115, although they tended to vote as their husbands or fathers did, the right to vote had a positive impact on them.

108. **A103**.

109. **A101; A103; A104; A106; A108; A109; A115; A119; B102; B113; B115;** S108.

110. *S106*; A109; A116; *S107*; *S124*.

111. **A103;** *S104; S107.*

112. A116; **B112; BS101;** *S106;* S112; S114; *S117; S118; S124*.

113. Herbert, "Drei politische Generationen," 98–99; Herbert, "'Generation der Sachlichkeit,'" 118; Kater, "Generationskonflikt," 225–26.

114. Gründel, *Die Sendung*, 40–41; *S123*.

115. A109; A116; **BS121;** *S107; S124*.

116. B114. At least three interviewees, B114, *S104*, and *S107*, were active at the end of the Weimar Republic in the Freiwillige Arbeitsdienst, the Volunteer Work Service, which developed out of the youth movement.

117. B114; also *A123*.

118. A116; **A120;** B114; S108.

119. For a fully compatible analysis of the interviewees, see Seidel, "'Wir waren so himmelblaue Idealisten,'" 58–61.

CHAPTER 3. ESSAYS

1. Haffner, *Geschichte eines Deutschen*, 19–20.

2. Klaus Mann, *Kind dieser Zeit*, 63; also Golo Mann, *Erinnerungen*, 56–57.

3. Gründel, *Die Sendung*, 31. Germans older than the interviewees—even by a few years—such as those represented in Ernst Glaser's semiautobiographical novel, *Class of 1902*, appear to have experienced the war very differently. Although Glaser's protagonist initially found the war an exciting adventure, he was soon disenchanted. For him the war became a time of suffering and death associated with the loss of innocence.

4. Haffner, *Geschichte eines Deutschen*, 22.

5. Bessel, *Germany After the First World War*, 259–60, 273; Rosenthal, *"Als der Krieg kam,"* 17–18, 20; Herbert, "Drei politische Generationen," 96–97. Herbert notes that two-thirds of the leadership of the Gestapo, of the *Einsatzgruppen* (mobile police units that carried out genocide), and of the security service were born between 1900 and 1915. Herbert, 100. Michael Wildt sees the members of this generation, who comprised three quarters of the leadership cadre of the Reich Main Security Office, as *the* crucial

perpetrators of the Holocaust. *Generation des Unbedingten*, 25, 28, 45, 49–52, 77. See also Mallmann and Paul, "Sozialisation, Milieu und Gewalt," 6.

6. Haffner, *Geschichte eines Deutschen*, 33.

7. Klaus Mann, *Kind dieser Zeit*, 125.

8. Gründel, *Die Sendung*, 31, 39.

9. Kruedener, "Die Entstehung des Inflationstraumas," 233–34.

10. Bessel, *Germany After the First World War*, 222.

11. Haffner, *Geschichte eines Deutschen*, 57; Klaus Mann, *Kind dieser Zeit*, 265–94.

12. Buck, *How It Happens*, 134–36, 140, 146–47. Also Feldman, *The Great Disorder*, 858.

13. Bessel, *Germany After the First World War*, 252; Baureithel, "Masken der Virilität." Two scholars have argued that visibly maimed veterans were a striking physical representation of the humiliation of the nation generally and of the German male in particular: Kienitz, "Body Damage," 189–90; Mosse, "Shell-Shock."

14. Koonz, *Mothers in the Fatherland*, 94.

15. Bessel, *Germany After the First World War*, 241, 249, also 232–38.

16. Schulz, Radebold, and Reulecke, *Söhne ohne Väter*, 131–32.

17. Reese-Nübel, "Kontinuitäten und Brüche," 225–27.

18. Prümm, "Jugend ohne Vater," 583–84.

19. Suhrkamp, "Söhne ohne Väter," 695.

20. Baumgarten, "Der sittliche Zustand," 71, 75, 76, 81, 84.

21. Reulecke, "Männerbund versus Familie," 214.

22. Ibid., 200, 204, 214, 218. See also Reulecke, "Neuer Mensch."

23. Fogt, *Politische Generationen*, 129–30; Rusinek, "Krieg als Sehnsucht," 129.

24. Gründel, *Die Sendung*, 31–32.

25. Herbert, "Drei politische Generationen," 97, 101–2; Wildt, *Generation des Unbedingten*, 63–67.

26. Stachura, *German Youth Movement*, 47–48.

27. Raabe, *Bündische Jugend*, 117–20; Stachura, *German Youth Movement*, 52–53; Benz, "Vom freiwilligen Arbeitsdienst."

28. Raabe, *Bündische Jugend*, 50–53, 117–20; Kater, "Bürgerliche Jugendbewegung," 139–41; Stachura, *German Youth Movement*, 47–48; Mommsen, "Generationenkonflikt," 117–18.

29. Fritzsche, *Rehearsals for Fascism*, 234; Fritzsche, *Germans into Nazis*, 7–8, 199, 205; Verhey, *Spirit of 1914*, 213–14; Bessel, *Germany After the First World War*, 281; Bessel, *Nazism and War*, 29; Wildt, *Volksgemeinschaft*, 26–68; Wildt, "Die Ungleichheit des Volkes."

30. Tönnies, *Gemeinschaft und Gesellschaft*. Tönnies's book was first published in 1887.

31. Raabe, *Bündische Jugend*, 44–45.

32. Reulecke, "Hat die Jugendbewegung?" 157–58.

33. Schade, *Weibliches Utopia*, 40, 194.

34. Busse-Wilson, quoted in Linse, "'Geschlechtsnot der Jugend,'" 266.

35. Busse-Wilson, "Liebe und Kameradschaft," 246–51.

36. Riegger, "Die Frau in der Jugendbewegung," 239–41, 243. The author Stefan Zweig, looking back on the German youth of the 1920s, reached a similar conclusion,

although the connection between androgyny and equality of the sexes was merely implicit. *Welt von Gestern,* 75, 80.

37. Frevert, *Women in German History,* 201–3.

38. Reese, "BDM Generation," 231–33.

39. Frevert, *Women in German History,* 201–3.

40. Schade, *Weibliches Utopia,* 200.

41. Ibid., 155–76.

42. Of the 3,616,000 overnight stays spent in German youth hostels in the year 1929, 68.19 percent were by males and 31.81 percent by females; in mixed boy-girl Bunds, with a total membership of 37,900 young people, 11,430 were girls. Riegger, "Die Frau in der Jugendbewegung," 241–42.

43. Schade, *Weibliches Utopia,* 194–99.

44. Hellfeld, *Bündische Jugend*; Raabe, *Bündische Jugend,* 152–78.

45. Raabe, *Bündische Jugend,* 155, 200.

46. Kater, "Bürgerliche Jugendbewegung," 174.

47. Stachura, *German Youth Movement,* 65–70.

48. Reulecke, "Hat die Jugendbewegung?" 157, 164, 166, 175.

CHAPTER 4. INTERVIEWS: YOUNG ADULTHOOD

Franz Orthmann

1. *B104.*

2. *BS101.*

3. *BS101.*

4. *S104.*

5. Changed from "the National Socialist Student Bund."

6. *BS101.*

7. *S124.*

8. *B104.*

9. *B104.*

10. *S115.*

11. *B104.*

12. *S115.*

13. *B107.*

14. *B104.*

15. Changed from "a student Bund."

16. *AB103.*

17. *B107.*

18. *S123.*

19. *B107.*

20. *B107.*

21. *B107* and *S123* use the same words to describe their Work Service experience.

22. *S123.*

23. *S102-A107.*

24. *S123.*

25. *B107.*

26. *S123.*

27. *S117.*
28. *BS101.*
29. *S107.*
30. *S122.*
31. *S107.*
32. *S102-A107.*
33. *S123.*
34. *A123.*
35. *AB103.*
36. Changed from "twenty-seven."
37. *B104.*
38. *A117.*
39. *B104.*
40. *S123.*
41. Changed from "Hamburger Singschar."
42. *A118.*
43. *S123.*
44. *S123.*
45. *A118.*
46. Phrase added.
47. *S102-A107.*
48. *S102-A107.*
49. Changed from "Russian."
50. *A118.*
51. *S102-A107.*
52. *S102-A107.*
53. *S104.*
54. *S123.*
55. *S102-A107.*
56. *S102-A107.*
57. Changed from "intelligence troop."
58. *B104.*
59. *B107.*
60. *B104.*
61. *S102-A107.*
62. *S102-A104.*
63. *B104.*
64. Phrase added.
65. *S102-A107.*
66. Phrase added.
67. Changed from "us who were officer candidates."
68. Changed from "Kattowice."
69. *A117.*
70. *A117.*
71. Two words added.
72. *A117.*
73. *A117.*

74. Changed from "when I was drafted."
75. *S122.*
76. Phrase added.
77. *A117.*
78. *A117.*
79. Phrase added.
80. *B107.*
81. *A123.*
82. *B107.*
83. Changed from "quite early on."
84. *A123.*
85. *B107.*
86. *B107.*
87. *B107.*
88. Changed from "after."
89. Changed from "after."
90. Word added.
91. *S115.*
92. Changed from "when I was a prisoner of."
93. *S115.*
94. *BS101.*
95. *A118.*
96. *B104.*
97. *B107.*
98. *B104.*
99. *A118.*
100. *B107.*
101. Phrase added.
102. *B104.*
103. *S102-A107.*
104. *S102-A107.*
105. *B107.*
106. *B107.*
107. *A118.*
108. *S102-A107.*
109. *A118.*
110. *S102-A107.*
111. *A118.*
112. *S102-A107.*
113. *B104.*
114. *S102-A107.*
115. *B104.*
116. *S102-A107.*
117. *S102-A107.*
118. *S102-A107.*
119. *B104.*
120. Changed from "the Crimea."

121. *B104.*
122. *S101.*
123. *S102-A107.*
124. *B104.*
125. *S123.*
126. Changed from "Thuringen."
127. Changed from "Stendal."
128. *B104.*
129. *B104.*
130. *B104.*
131. *B107.*
132. Changed from "Elbe."
133. *B104.*
134. *S122.*
135. Changed from "the Chiemsee."
136. *S122.*
137. Changed from "Stendal." *B104.*
138. *B107.*
139. *B107.*
140. This last phrase is not in the interview, but it clearly reflects *B104*'s experience.
141. *B104.*
142. *B111.*
143. *B111.*
144. *B111.*
145. *B107.*
146. Changed from "flight."
147. Changed from "through France finally made it to Mannheim." *S102-A107.*
148. *B111.*
149. Words added.
150. Changed from "my."
151. Changed from "in Schörderup."
152. Phrase added.
153. *B107.*

Magdalene Beck

1. Name changed.
2. Changed from "1909" and "Altona."
3. *A114.*
4. *B116.*
5. Phrase added.
6. *S120.*
7. *B116.*
8. *A119.*
9. *B116.*
10. *B110.*
11. *B116.*

12. B110.
13. AB102-B106.
14. S120.
15. Phrase added.
16. B110.
17. A110-A121.
18. This phrase is an amalgam of A106 and S113.
19. A106.
20. A110-A121.
21. S113.
22. B110.
23. A110-A121.
24. B110.
25. A110-A121.
26. B110.
27. A106.
28. B110.
29. A106.
30. A110-A121.
31. S113.
32. S113.
33. A110-A121.
34. B110.
35. A110-A121.
36. S116.
37. B110.
38. A106.
39. A110-A121.
40. B110.
41. B110.
42. A110-A121.
43. S113.
44. A106.
45. A108.
46. Changed from "Kassel."
47. A106.
48. A108.
49. A110-A121; A119.
50. A119.
51. B110.
52. S116.
53. B110.
54. B110.
55. B110.
56. A119.
57. B110.
58. A119.

59. A105.

60. Quotation slightly altered because it came in response to a question by the interviewer.

61. A120.

62. S120.

63. A119.

64. B110.

65. Changed from "a quarter of a year."

66. B116.

67. A110-A121.

68. A106.

69. S113.

70. A116.

71. A112.

72. AB102-B106.

73. AB102-B106.

74. AB102-B106.

75. S113.

76. AB102-B106.

77. S113.

78. AB102-B106.

79. AB102-B106.

80. A112.

81. S113.

82. A112.

83. S113.

84. S113.

85. S113.

86. S113.

87. S113.

88. S113.

89. S120.

90. S120.

91. S113.

92. S113.

93. S113.

94. S113.

95. B114.

96. B117.

97. B117.

98. B114.

99. S113.

100. S113.

101. B114.

102. A112.

103. A112.

104. A112.

105. B114.
106. A112.
107. A112.
108. A112.
109. A124.
110. A112.
111. S113.
112. A112.
113. B110.
114. A112.
115. Changed from "1938."
116. Changed from "a new."
117. A112.
118. A112.
119. A119.
120. A112.
121. Phrase added.
122. A112.
123. A120.
124. A112.
125. B115.
126. B115.
127. B115.
128. A120.
129. A111.
130. A120.
131. A111.
132. A111.
133. Changed from "Dortmund."
134. A119.
135. B116.
136. AB102-B106.
137. A111.
138. A124.
139. AB102-B106.
140. B113.
141. A114.
142. B113.
143. A111.
144. A124.
145. Changed from "the 1930s."
146. A111.
147. A111.
148. A111.
149. B117.
150. AB102-B106.
151. S110.

152. A111.
153. AB102-B106.
154. A111.
155. B113.
156. A111.
157. B113.
158. A111.
159. B114.
160. A111.
161. B115.
162. B115.
163. B114.
164. A119.
165. A119.
166. A110-A121.
167. A119.
168. A110-A121.
169. A119.
170. A103.
171. A110-A121.
172. A110-A121.
173. A110-A121.
174. A116.
175. A110-A121.
176. A110-A121.
177. A110-A121.
178. BS121.
179. A112.
180. Changed from "school service."
181. BS121.
182. A110-A121.
183. A110-A121.
184. A112.
185. BS121.
186. B117.
187. A110-A121.
188. B117.
189. Changed from "Lötzen."
190. A112.
191. B105.
192. B105.
193. B105.
194. A112.
195. A112.
196. A112.
197. A112.
198. A112.

199. BS121.
200. BS121.
201. Changed from "1934." B115.
202. Changed from "three years."
203. A114.
204. Changed from "on the 28th of January 1943." A112.
205. Changed from "November."
206. A112.
207. Word added.
208. Changed from "Haigerloch." A112.
209. Changed from "daughter."
210. A112.
211. B109.
212. A114.
213. A112.
214. Phrase added.
215. A112.
216. Changed from "four children and the fifth."
217. A104.
218. Changed from "children."
219. In this section the number of service-year girls has been changed from plural to singular. A109.
220. A106.
221. A109.
222. A112.
223. Phrase added.
224. A112.
225. Changed from "one and two-thirds children."
226. A112.
227. A103.
228. A112.
229. A103.
230. A112.
231. A112.
232. Phrase added
233. A110-A121.
234. A110-A121.
235. B110.
236. B110.
237. B112.
238. Changed from "another house."
239. S114.
240. B115.
241. S114.
242. B115.
243. B105.
244. A111.

245. B116.
246. S110.
247. B116.
248. S110.
249. Changed from "Kiel."
250. A110-A121.
251. A110-A121.
252. S114.
253. B116.
254. A108.
255. B116.
256. B116.
257. A108.
258. S116.
259. AB102-B106.
260. B115.
261. B117.
262. AB102-B106.
263. AB102-B106.
264. S114.
265. A111.
266. A124.
267. A111.
268. S114.
269. Changed from "Detmold."
270. A120.
271. B115.
272. A104.
273. A124.
274. A120.
275. A104.
276. B105.
277. A120.
278. B105.
279. A120.
280. B115.
281. B116.
282. B115.
283. B113.
284. B117.
285. B113.
286. AB102-B106.
287. A116.
288. B113.
289. B117.
290. B113.
291. A116.

292. Phrase added.

293. BS121.

294. B115.

295. A103.

296. B117.

297. BS121.

298. B108.

299. B115.

300. Changed from "in Wuppertal." B105.

301. B117.

302. B115.

303. A103.

304. A114.

305. S108.

306. Phrase added.

307. B108.

308. S108.

309. S108.

310. A103.

311. Changed from "early 1943."

312. B105.

313. A103.

314. A114.

315. Changed from "into the Rhineland."

316. Phrase added.

317. B115.

318. B116.

319. Changed from "Stuttgart."

320. B115.

321. Changed from "Winssen and Aßhausen are about thirty kilometers from Hamburg." A124.

322. A124.

323. Changed from "Kassel." AB102-B106.

324. AB102-B106.

325. A124.

326. Changed from "a quarter of a year."

327. A116.

328. A101.

329. A115.

330. Phrase added.

331. BS121.

332. A112.

333. A119.

334. BS121.

335. A119.

336. A105.

337. A105.

338. A105.

339. B105.

340. Changed from "Cottbus." B105.

341. A104.

342. A112.

343. A104.

344. B105.

345. Changed from "aunt."

346. A104.

347. Changed from "forty-three years old in 1944, and we were eighteen and twenty."

348. B105.

349. BS121.

350. A105.

351. Changed from "sister."

352. Changed from "three."

353. A105.

354. BS121.

355. B117.

356. A105.

357. BS121.

358. A105.

359. A105.

360. BS121.

361. A105.

362. A104.

363. A104.

364. A104.

365. BS121.

366. Phrase added.

367. BS121.

368. A104.

369. Changed from "Thüringen, near Altenburg, in Nobitz."

370. A104.

371. Changed from "owned a knight's estate." A105.

372. A104.

373. A105.

374. Changed from "our beloved Cottbus." B105.

375. BS121.

376. Changed from "Nobitz." A105.

377. A105.

378. A105.

379. A105.

380. A104.

381. Sentence added.

382. A112.

383. Phrase added.

384. A104.

385. A104.

386. S116.

387. A104.

388. S116.

389. A119.

390. Phrase added.

391. B109.

392. B105.

393. A119.

394. Sentence order slightly rearranged.

395. A104.

396. Wording slightly altered. B115.

397. B115.

398. A104.

399. A104.

400. A104.

401. Phrase added.

402. A104.

403. A104.

404. A105.

405. These sentences combine two separate statements relating to these events in the interview. A105.

406. A104.

407. A105.

408. A105.

409. S116.

410. S116.

411. A105.

412. S116.

413. A105.

414. A105.

415. A105.

416. A105.

417. A105.

418. A105.

419. A105.

420. A104.

421. A104.

422. A105.

423. Changed from "then."

424. A104.

425. A104.

426. S116.

427. S114.

428. B114.
429. B105.
430. Changed from "three."
431. A104.
432. A104.
433. A104.
434. A104.
435. A104.
436. A104.
437. A104.
438. A116.
439. A114.
440. A104.
441. A104.
442. A112.
443. A104.
444. B110.
445. B116.
446. B116.
447. B116.
448. Phrase added.
449. Changed from "Wedel."
450. B116.
451. B110.
452. A105.
453. A114.
454. A112.
455. A119.
456. A112.
457. A119.
458. A112.
459. A119.
460. A112.
461. A119.
462. A112.
463. A104.
464. Changed from "our."
465. A103.
466. A104.
467. A104.
468. Phrase added.
469. Changed from "we."
470. A103.
471. Changed from "I."
472. Changed from "me."
473. Changed from "me."
474. Changed from "I."

475. A104.

476. A105.

477. A114.

478. B110.

479. A114.

480. A114.

481. A114.

482. Changed from "three."

483. "Vati and" added.

484. Changed from "our son."

485. A105.

486. A114.

487. A105.

488. S113.

CHAPTER 5. ANALYSIS: EXTENDING THE COLLECTIVE IN THE COMMUNITY OF THE *VOLK*

1. A*111*; **A124**; **AB102-B106**; *B104*; *B107*; B110; **B111**; B113; *BS101*; *S104*; *S107*; *S124*.

2. A*111*.

3. A*111*; **AB102-B106**; *B104*; *BS101*.

4. Bude, *Bilanz der Nachfolge*, 83–84; Schmitt-Sasse, "'Der Führer ist immer der Jüngste,'" 145–46; Raabe, *Bündische Jugend*, 153; Reulecke, "'. . . und sie werden nicht mehr frei,'" 136; Gründel, *Die Sendung*, 70; Hopster and Nassen, "Vom 'Bekenntnis' zum 'Kampf.'"

5. Bude, *Bilanz der Nachfolge*, 84; Raabe, *Bündische Jugend*, 153.

6. A*111*; B113; S110; *S102-A107*.

7. A*111*; A120; B117; S120; *S124*.

8. A120; *B104*; *BS101*. Kater, "Bürgerliche Jugendbewegung," 138.

9. **A101**; **A111**; **AB102-B106**; **B111**; *BS101*; S110.

10. A114; A124; AB102-B106; B113; B117.

11. Johnson and Reuband, *What We Knew*, 342.

12. Ibid., 359–60.

13. **B116**.

14. S108.

15. B114; also A119. A woman interviewed in an oral history study conducted by Margarethe Dörr uses the same language to describe the attraction of National Socialism. "*Wer die Zeit nicht miterlebt hat,*" 3:202; Peukert, *Inside Nazi Germany*, 151.

16. *BS101*.

17. **A108**.

18. *S104*; **S114**.

19. A108; A*111*; B115; S113. Kohler, "'Irgendwie windelt man sich durch,'" 242–43.

20. A101; *A103*; *A117*; B108; B112; *S115*. Nolzen, "Inklusion und Exklusion," 67.

21. Peukert, *Inside Nazi Germany*, 237; Erdheim, "Die tryrannische Instanz"; Beradt, *Third Reich in Dreams*.

22. A105; A119; **A120**; **B102**. Fritzsche, *Life and Death*, 20–24; Bergerson, "Hildesheim in an Age of Pestilence," 114–20; Bergerson, *Ordinary Germans*, 146–58; Gerstenberger, "Alltagsforschung und Faschismustheorie," 41.

23. Möding, "'Ich muß irgendwo engagiert sein,'" 259–61.

24. A106; A108; A111; A119; B110; *S107*; S116.

25. **A120**.

26. **B115**; also A104; A108; A109; A110; A111; **A112**; A115; *A117*; *A118*; A119; A121; *A123*; **A124**; *B103*; *B104*; *B107*; B110; B114; **B116**; *BS101*; S110; S120. Even **B112** and **B115**, who present themselves as having opposed the regime, inevitably come back to their positive experiences during the Third Reich.

27. A106; A108; B110; S113.

28. B110; *B111*; *S123*.

29. *S123*; *S102-A107*.

30. *B111*.

31. A106; A119; **A124**; AB102-B106; B116.

32. A108; A112; **A119**; **A120**; B110.

33. A108; A119. These sentiments are echoed almost verbatim by one of the women interviewed by Margarethe Dörr. *"Wer die Zeit nicht miterlebt hat,"* 3:201.

34. *A117*; A119; B110; *B111*; S113.

35. Reese, "BDM Generation," 234, 239; Dörr, *"Wer die Zeit nicht miterlebt hat,"* 3:201, 216; Kater, *Hitler Youth*, 1–4; Peukert, *Inside Nazi Germany*, 15; Pine, *Nazi Family Policy*, 53–54.

36. *A118*; *AB103*; *B104*; S116.

37. Only *S115* claims that the ban on the Bunds turned him against National Socialism.

38. A110-A121; B110; B116.

39. A106; A110-A121; *B104*; B110; S113; *S115*.

40. *AB103*; also A106; A108; A111; A119; B110; *S107*; S116.

41. A106; A110-A121; B110.

42. A105; **A108**; A108; A112; A116; *A118*; A124; AB102-B106; **B105**; *B107*; B110; *B111*; B114; **B115**; S113; *S117*; S120; *S123*.

43. A108; A112; **A116**; A124; *B107*; B114; B117; S113; *S117*; S120; S123; *S102-A107*.

44. S113. At least one of the men (*S117*) and six of the women (A112, A120, **A124**, B110, B114, **S113**) became leaders in the Work Service or in the Landjahr program.

45. A105; **A112**; *B107*; S113; **B114**; *S123*.

46. **A112**; S113; *S123*.

47. A116; **B114**.

48. B114; B115.

49. A112; AB102-B106; B114; B117; S113; S120.

50. *S123*; *S102-A107*.

51. A109; A112; A119; A120; AB102-B106; *B104*; *B107*; B114; B115; B117; BS121; **S104**; S113; S120; *S123*; *S102-A107*. They defend the Volksgemeinschaft directly or by defending the collectivism of the German Democratic Republic (**A111**, **A112**, *B107*, B110). Rosenthal, *"Als der Krieg kam,"* 113–14.

52. The law against double wage earners meant that **A101** and **A104** had to abandon their teaching careers when their husbands found work; but once the war broke

out and the male teachers were drafted, they were both able—indeed, compelled—to work as teachers again.

53. **AB102-B106; B116**.

54. A104; A109; A111; A112; A119; A120; A124; AB102-B106; B105; B109; B110; B113; B114; B115; B116; B117; S110; S113; S120.

55. **A112**.

56. A111; A112; A119; A120; B110; **B114; B115**; S113.

57. A111; A112; **A116**; A119; A110-A121; AB102-B106; **B114**; S120.

58. Frei, "'Volksgemeinschaft,'" 122–26; Steinbacher, "Differenz der Geschlechter?" 100. **A103; A116; AB102-B106; B114; S110**.

59. **B113** lived in at least twelve different places during the Third Reich and its immediate aftermath; **B114** lived in at least eleven different places from around 1938 until the end of the war; also **A111**; A112; **A102-B106; A110-A121**; B105; B110; **B116**. Interviewees in the Work Service (A112; AB102-B106; **B110**; S113) were sent to every corner of the Reich. The number of Work Service camps where the composite "Magdalene Beck" worked is by no means extraordinary.

60. A106.

61. **A103; A104; A109**; BS121; S120.

62. **A112; A116**.

63. A106; A109; A111; A112; A116; A119; A120; A124; A110-A121; AB102-B106; *B104*; B110; *B113*; B114; B115; B117; BS121; S113; S120; and the husband of B108.

64. A103; A112; A119; A120; *B104*; the husband of B108; B113; B114; B115.

65. A112; **A119**; B108; B110; B113; BS121.

66. Margarethe Dörr notes in her massive oral history of over five hundred German women that "traces of anti-Semitism can also be detected in apparently harmless patterns of behavior, sensibilities, and forms of speech that the women use in part thoughtlessly." *"Wer die Zeit nicht miterlebt hat,"* 3:306.

67. **A101; AB102-B106**. Dörr, *"Wer die Zeit nicht miterlebt hat,"* 3:285.

68. Fritzsche, *Life and Death*, 81.

69. A103; A104; A106; A109; *A117*; *B107*; BS121; S120.

70. S102; *S101*; S110; A101.

71. *A117*; B105.

72. A101; *S123*.

73. Gellately, *Backing Hitler*, vii, 25; Beradt, *Third Reich in Dreams*, 79–80; Engelmann, *Im Gleichschritt*, 240–41, 79–90; Galinski, Herbert, and Lachauer, *Nazis und Nachbarn*, 167; Owings, *Frauen*, 205.

74. **B117**; also **B110**; B116.

75. **B113**, a Banta-Swabian (ethnic Germans whose ancestors had established settlements in Hungary during the Middle Ages; after 1918 this area became part of Romania), testifies to the hostility directed at her as a "foreigner" because she spoke accented German.

76. A106; A110-A121; B110; S113; *S115*; S123.

77. A107; S102; *S104*; *S107*; S122.

78. A104; B102.

79. S120.

80. B102.

81. A104.

82. Kershaw, *Popular Opinion*, 255–57, 334, 339–57.

83. Friedländer, "Wehrmacht," 25. Whereas the five hundred interviewees in Margarethe Dörr's oral history did not "see" the persecution and deportation of Jews, "nearly every one" of them was able to observe and observe critically the National Socialist euthanasia program. *"Wer die Zeit nicht miterlebt hat,"* 3:268–69.

84. B115.

85. *A117.*

86. *S101.*

87. B112.

88. A101.

89. *S123.*

90. B117.

91. *S123.*

92. B117.

93. B117.

94. *S123.*

95. A119; AB102-B106; *B107*; *S122*. Bergerson, *Ordinary Germans*, 217; Gellately, *Backing Hitler*, 151–82; Herbert, "Apartheid nebenan," 233.

96. B116; also A108; *A118*; *B104*; B117; S116; *S102-A107*. A110-A121 claimed that she has no memory of Reichskristallnacht. The fictional Magdalene Beck, who spent much of the 1930s in Work Service camps, is more justified in having overlooked the pogrom than the actual interviewee, who lived in Kiel.

97. S114.

98. Personal communication from the psychologist Babett Lobinger.

99. *S102-A107.*

100. Personal communication from the historian Peter Fritzsche.

101. A108.

102. Bergerson, *Ordinary Germans*, 96, 251; Dörr, *"Wer die Zeit nicht miterlebt hat,"* 3:256; Kempowski, *"Haben Sie davon gewußt?"* 47, 48, 54, 56, 70; Niethammer, "Juden und Russen," 120; Rosenthal, "Antisemitismus," 457–58, 460–61.

103. A110-A121; B110.

104. B112; A116; also B105; S114.

105. *S102-A107.*

106. B109.

107. Interviewees in a study conducted by Rosenthal recall Reichskristallnacht as if it were a "natural event," one without human beings either as perpetrators or as victims. "Antisemitismus," 464–65.

108. A110-A121; **AB101**; *B103*; B110; B112; *S102-A107*. Interviewees in other oral history studies also make the unexamined assumption that the Jewish people with whom they were personally acquainted somehow always managed to emigrate: Dörr, *"Wer die Zeit nicht miterlebt hat,"* 3:256, 296; Rosenthal, *"Als der Krieg kam,"* 35.

109. A103.

110. A108; A111; **A119**; **A124**; A110-A121; AB102-B106; B105; *B107*; B116; B117; **BS101**; S109; S110; *S115. A117, A123*, and *S122* openly acknowledge knowing about the Final Solution well before the end of the war.

111. Because the interviews are composite, the reader may not be persuaded that the very same interviewees both deny and acknowledge their awareness of the genocide before the end of the war. A close referencing of the endnotes will confirm, however, that this is the case.

112. Germans interviewed in other oral histories manifest the same striking tendency to deny knowledge of the Final Solution before 1945 and then, often in the very same sentence and without any apparent sense of contradiction, to acknowledge that they did know about the genocide before that date: Rupp, "Zur Herausbildung"; Unruh, *Trümmerfrauen*, 83; Rosenthal, *"Als der Krieg kam,"* 47, 218–19; Rosenthal, "Antisemitismus," 469; interview with "Ilse F," described in Bajohr and Pohl, "Einleitung," 7–9; Dörr, *"Wer die Zeit nicht miterlebt hat,"* 3:252; Kempowski, *"Haben Sie davon gewußt?"* 75.

113. B117.

114. B117.

115. A120.

116. A124.

117. A111.

118. B115.

119. B115.

120. B115.

121. B115.

122. B116.

123. A108; also *S107*.

124. This paragraph is based on an e-mail and conversations with the sociologist Kai Erikson.

125. Dörr, *"Wer die Zeit nicht miterlebt hat,"* 3:286–87; Owings, *Frauen*, 470; Rosenthal, *"Als der Krieg kam,"* 212; Rosenthal, "Antisemitismus," 458.

126. A110–A121; *S107*. A101, B115, and *S122* describe helping Jewish people. *S122*'s assistance was not entirely selfless, however. He explains that he took over a Jewish-owned business, a raincoat factory in Frankfurt in 1938, because he was a "friend" of "the Jews" and was able to keep Jewish employees working there "as long as they were productive."

127. A101; A103; A116; A110-A121; AB101; *B103*; B105; B110; B112; B115; *S101*; S102; S110; S114; *S122*; *S102-A107*.

128. S110.

129. S110.

130. BS121.

131. A108; A111; A120; AB102-B106; *B104*; B115; S114; S120.

132. A115; S114; B115; A120; *S102-A107*.

133. B115; B113; A120; S114; A103.

134. B113.

135. B115. Gellately, *Backing Hitler*, 205.

136. B115; also A116; S114.

137. AB102-B106; B117; *S115*.

138. AB101; *B111*.

139. S120; A120; *A117*; *A117*; AB102-B106; B114; *S123*.

140. *A123*; *AB103*; *S123*; *S102-A107*.

141. Gabriele Rosenthal claims that men born between 1906 and 1919 were socialized as a generation in the barracks of the military organizations in which most spent their lives beginning at age eighteen or nineteen and ending only in midlife. *"Als der Krieg kam,"* 18–19, 114–16.

142. *A118*; *A123*; *S104*; *S102-A107*. Frei, "'Volksgemeinschaft,'" 122–23.

143. *A123*; also *S102-A107*.

144. *S102-A107*.

145. *A123*; also *S102-A107*.

146. *A118*; *B104*; *S104*; *S102-A107*.

147. *A118*; *S102-A107*.

148. *S102-A107* participated in the Polish campaign, the invasion of France (albeit the so-called Second Wave), the Balkan campaign (Romania), the invasion of Greece, the airborne assault of Crete, the invasion of the Soviet Union, positional warfare on the Artic Ocean in Finland, the Courland Bridgehead, the retreat out of Italy, and then the last stand in Germany itself.

149. *S102-A107*.

150. Bessel, *Germany 1945*, 12, 20, 45.

151. *A118*; *S104*; *S102-A107*.

152. *B104*.

153. *B107*.

154. *A118*; *B107*; *S102-A107*. Even *AB102-B106*, a self-described anti-Nazi, was outraged by the plot.

155. Kershaw, *Hitler Myth*, 215; Frei, "Erinnerungskampf."

156. Mommsen, *Nationalsozialismus*, 343; Gellately, *Backing Hitler*, 253; Friedländer, *Years of Extermination*, 656–59.

157. Rosenthal, *"Als der Krieg kam,"* 119–30, especially 124–26.

158. *AB103*; *BS101*.

159. *A103*; *A104*; *A105*; *A116*; *S113*; *S116*.

160. *S107*.

161. *S111*.

162. *B104*; *B111*.

163. Rosenthal, *"Als der Krieg kam,"* 132, 182.

164. *A112*; *A116*; *A110-A121*; *B108*; *B117*; *B117*; *BS121*.

165. *AB103*.

166. Rosenthal, *"Als der Krieg kam,"* 123.

167. *A112*; *A113*; *A110-A121*; *B109*; *B113*; *S110*.

168. *A101*; *A103*; *A105*; *A106*; *A111*; *A114*; *A115*; *A123*; *A124*; *AB102-B106*; *B105*; *B108*; *B113*; *B115*; *B117*; *BS121*; *S108*.

169. *A116*; *B113*.

170. *B115*; *B105*.

171. *A111*; *A116*; *A124*; *AB102-B106*; *S108*.

172. *A104*; *A105*; *A112*; *A114*; *A116*; *A119*; *B110*; *B116*; *BS121*; *S116*.

173. *A106*; *A114*; *A115*. Also Dörr, *"Wer die Zeit nicht miterlebt hat,"* 3:196.

174. *A116*; *A124*; *AB102-B106*; *S110*; *S120*.

175. *A104*; *A105*; *B105*; *B110*; *B117*; *BS121*.

176. *A103*; *A104*; *B110*.

177. A105; A114; **B110**.

178. A103; A104; A116.

179. The composite interview may be misleading since virtually every reference to rape in the interviews was included in it. A104; A105; B116; S116.

180. Bessel, *Germany 1945*, 6; A112.

181. Bessel, *Germany 1945*, 38–68. A104; **A105; A112; A114; A116; A119;** B105; B117.

182. A104; A105; A114; A116; **B105;** B109; B115; B116; BS121; S116; *S102-A107.*

183. Dörr, *"Wer die Zeit nicht miterlebt hat,"* 2:536.

184. Rosenthal, *"Als der Krieg kam,"* 239.

185. A101; A103; **A105; A106; A111;** A114; A115; *A123;* A124; AB102-B106; B105; B108; B113; B115; B117; BS121; S108; *S102-A107.*

186. A103; **A104;** A105; **A108; A110-A121;** AB102-B106; B109; B115; S112; S116; S120. **B116** describes the family of her husband, in which four of six brothers were killed at the front, "one every month." **B117** lost seven cousins and her brother-in-law during the war.

187. **A104; A105;** A114; *B103;* **B112.** Schulz, Radebold, and Reulecke, *Söhne ohne Väter*, 116; Stargardt, *Witnesses of War*, 231–352.

188. Schulz, Radebold, and Reulecke, *Söhne ohne Väter*, 115; Bessel, *Germany 1945*, 8.

189. **B110**; also **B113**. Olick, *In the House of the Hangman*, 28; Frevert, *Women in German History*, 264.

CHAPTER 6. ESSAYS

1. Frei, "Epochenjahr 1933," 91; Frei, "'Volksgemeinschaft,'" 112–13; Frei, *National Socialist Rule*, 70–71; also Friedländer, *Nazi Germany and the Jews*, 115, 331; Gellately, *Backing Hitler*, 1–2; Lüdtke, "The Appeal of Exterminating 'Others.'" Ian Kershaw and Richard J. Evans have a very different view of the relationship of the Germans to National Socialism: focusing on dissent in Bavaria, Kershaw presents the National Socialists as deeply and pervasively unpopular (*Popular Opinion*, 295–96, 329, 385); Evans argues that German consent to National Socialism was to a considerable degree generated by National Socialist coercion ("Coercion and Consent," 71–81).

2. Oral history was developed in Germany during the 1970s by New Left historians who sought to give voice to those previously voiceless in historical writing and, it was assumed, to celebrate the resistance of the German working class to National Socialism. The celebration quickly foundered, however. According to Alf Lüdtke, these oral history studies "have been explosive in their impact" because they "reveal the degree to which the preponderant majority" of Germans were complicit in National Socialism. "Introduction," 4–5.

3. Evans, "Coercion and Consent," 72–73.

4. Aderhold and Nölleke, "'Es war eine ganz erbärmliche Zeit,'" 193.

5. Peukert, "Alltag und Barbarei," 147.

6. Lüdtke, "'Coming to Terms,'" 551; Aderhold and Nölleke, "'Es war eine ganz erbärmliche Zeit,'" 201–2; Dörr, *"Wer die Zeit nicht miterlebt hat,"* 3:361, 365, 366, 420; Johnson and Reuband, *What We Knew*, 387, 398; Szepansky, *"Blitzmädel,"* 10.

7. Dörr, *"Wer die Zeit nicht miterlebt hat,"* 3:193; Johnson and Reuband, *What We Knew,* 154, 225; Owings, *Frauen,* 9; Reinecker, *Die Illusionen der Vergangenheit,* 43, 52–53. The positive memories of the Third Reich consistently reported in oral histories are confirmed by opinion polls taken in West Germany in 1949 and 1951 and again in 1985. Herbert, "Good Times, Bad Times," 97; Bessel and Schumann, "Introduction," 6; Johnson and Reuband, *What We Knew,* 325–37.

8. Bajohr and Wildt, "Einleitung," 18; Steinbacher, "Differenz der Geschlechter?" 95.

9. Althaus, "Geschichte, Erinnerung und Person," 596; Dörr, *"Wer die Zeit nicht miterlebt hat,"* 2:100–101; 3:193, 368–77; Galinski, Herbert, and Lachauer, *Nazis und Nachbarn,* 191; Möding, "'Ich muß irgendwo engagiert sein'"; Kohler, "'Irgendwie windelt man sich durch,'" 244; Münkel, "'Volksgenossen' und 'Volksgemeinschaft,'" 168; Owings, *Frauen,* 57; Plato, "Hitler Youth Generation," 214; Reese, "BDM Generation," 228; Rempel, *Hitler's Children,* 152–53; Steinbacher, "Differenz der Geschlechter?" 96; Wilke, "Village Life in Nazi Germany," 21–22.

10. Möding, "'Ich muß irgendwo engagiert sein,'" 259–61, 265, 268–69.

11. Maschmann, *Fazit,* 35–36.

12. Möding, "'Ich muß irgendwo engagiert sein,'" 257.

13. Plato, "Hitler Youth Generation," 212–14; also Herzog, "Hubris and Hypocrisy," 17; Herzog, *Sex After Fascism,* 61.

14. Möding, "'Ich muß irgendwo engagiert sein,'" 267.

15. Ibid., 263–67.

16. Plato, "Hitler Youth Generation," 212–14.

17. Plato, "Nachkriegssieger," 352.

18. Plato, "Hitler Youth Generation," 212–14, 218–19; Bajohr and Wildt, "Einleitung," 22.

19. Fritzsche, *Life and Death,* 96–108; Patel, *Soldiers of Labor,* 243, 250, 324.

20. Dörr, *"Wer die Zeit nicht miterlebt hat,"* 2:100–101; 3:201, 204; Möding, "'Ich muß irgendwo engagiert sein,'" 258; Plato, "Hitler Youth Generation," 220; Reese, *Growing Up Female,* 59–60; Szepansky, *"Blitzmädel,"* 11; Kohler, "'Irgendwie windelt man sich durch,'" 244, 251.

21. Möding, "'Ich muß irgendwo engagiert sein,'" 259.

22. Paul and Mallmann, *Milieus und Widerstand,* 542.

23. Lüdtke, "'Coming to Terms,'" 571.

24. Rosenthal, *"Als der Krieg kam,"* 46, 235, 237; Möding, "'Ich muß irgendwo engagiert sein,'" 259.

25. Plato, "Hitler Youth Generation," 220. Also Wierling, "The Hitler Youth Generation in the GDR."

26. Haffner, *Meaning of Hitler,* 36.

27. Thus, despite the efforts of the National Socialists upon taking power to combat male unemployment and return women to home and family by reducing female employment and despite a campaign against married women workers, the number of working women, indeed of married working women, actually rose in Germany over the 1930s. Although the war did not significantly increase female employment, it did bring an increase in the number of women working in traditionally male occupations as well as in agriculture, the return of professional women to schools and clinics, and a striking increase in the number of women university students. Heineman, *What Difference*

Does a Husband Make? 40, 42–43; Stephenson, *Women in Nazi Germany*, 52–53, 55, 58, 65, 69; Frevert, *Women in German History*, 197–98, 218, 220, 223–26; Koonz, *Mothers in the Fatherland*, 396–97; Kohler, "'Irgendwie windelt man sich durch,'" 242.

28. Peukert, *Inside Nazi Germany*, 99, 151–52.

29. Koonz, *Mothers in the Fatherland*, 5, 6, 13–14, 55, 71–72.

30. Stephenson, *Women in Nazi Germany*, 133–36.

31. Frevert, *Women in German History*, 217, 241.

32. Broszat, *Hitler State*, xi.

33. Heineman, *What Difference Does a Husband Make?* 17–43; Reese, *Growing Up Female*, 44.

34. Reese, "BDM Generation," 231.

35. Schmidt, "Krieg der Männer," 133–34, 138–39, 158–61.

36. Kater, "Generationskonflikt"; Koonz, *Mothers in the Fatherland*, 388.

37. Möding, "'Ich muß irgendwo engagiert sein,'" 263–67.

38. Herbert, "Zur Entwicklung der Ruhrarbeiterschaft," 33–34.

39. Reese, "BDM Generation," 229; Reese, *Growing Up Female*, 44, 56.

40. Reese, "BDM Generation," 229, 245–46; Reese, *Growing Up Female*, 44, 56.

41. For a wonderfully lucid and sensible assessment of the historiographical debate over these issues, see Roseman, "National Socialism and Modernisation"; also Kershaw, *Nazi Dictatorship*, 161–82.

42. Dahrendorf, *Society and Democracy*; Schoenbaum, *Hitler's Social Revolution*.

43. Prinz and Zitelmann, "Vorwort"; Roseman, "National Socialism and Modernisation."

44. See, in particular, Blackbourn and Eley, *Peculiarities of German History*.

45. Peukert, *Inside Nazi Germany*, 11.

46. Ibid., 175.

47. Bajohr, "Detlev Peukerts Beiträge"; Peukert, *Inside Nazi Germany*, 234–35.

48. Roseman, "National Socialism and Modernisation," 204–5.

49. Peukert, *Inside Nazi Germany*, 248.

50. Ibid., 99, 174, 178–79, 182–83; Mommsen, *Nationalsozialismus*, 421.

51. Prinz and Zitelmann, "Vorwort," vii.

52. Prinz, "Die soziale Funktion," 304.

53. Frevert, *Women in German History*, 250–51; Haffner, *Meaning of Hitler*, 35–36; Heineman, *What Difference Does a Husband Make?*; Herzog, *Sex After Fascism*, 4–5, 10–63, 72, 79; Kater, *Hitler Youth*, 1; Peukert, *Inside Nazi Germany*, 99, 100, 151–52, 179; Prinz, "Die soziale Funktion," 303; Schäfer, "Das gespaltene Bewußtsein," 123–25, 139.

54. Peukert, *Inside Nazi Germany*, 77–80, 247; Prinz, "Die soziale Funktion," 316; Schäfer, "Das gespaltene Bewußtsein," 115–37.

55. Prinz, "Die soziale Funktion," 326.

56. Mommsen, *Nationalsozialismus*, 421, 423; Mommsen, "Nationalsozialismus als vorgetäuschte Modernisierung," 31–32, 37, 41–44, 46.

57. Frei, "Wie modern war der Nationalsozialismus?" 386.

58. Kershaw, *Nazi Dictatorship*, 161–62, 181–82.

59. Niethammer, "Einleitung des Herausgebers," 7–8.

60. Fritzsche, *Life and Death*, 15, 65–75; Möding, "'Ich muß irgendwo engagiert sein,'" 291.

61. Schoenbaum, *Hitler's Social Revolution*, xxii.

62. Ibid., 66.

63. Ibid., 296.

64. Martin Broszat, quoted in Mommsen, "Nationalsozialismus als vorgetäuschte Modernisierung," 32.

65. Fritzsche, *Rehearsals for Fascism*, 234; Fritzsche, *Germans into Nazis*, 7–8, 18, 184, 199, 205; also Bajohr and Wildt, "Einleitung," 8.

66. Fritzsche, *Life and Death*, 19–75, particularly 38–56.

67. Frei, "Wie modern war der Nationalsozialismus?" 382–84; Frei, "'Volksgemeinschaft,'" 113–14; Paul and Mallmann, *Milieus und Widerstand*, 542–43; Prinz, "Die soziale Funktion," 316–17; Bajohr and Wildt, "Einleitung," 8–9, 19.

68. Ian Kershaw's felicitous phrase is quoted in Frei, "Wie modern war der Nationalsozialismus?" 382.

69. Frei, "'Volksgemeinschaft,'" 110–12, 122–23.

70. Ibid., 110–12.

71. Paul and Mallmann, *Milieus und Widerstand*, 542–43; Bajohr, "Vom antijüdischen Konsens," 24, 36. Michael Wildt's book *Volksgemeinschaft als Selbstermächtigung* describes and analyzes the creation of the Volksgemeinschaft in provincial Germany as a process of racial inclusion and violent, public, ritualistic racial exclusion; see especially 12, 13, 63–68, 136–37, 144, 372–74; also Bajohr and Wildt, "Einleitung," 9, 17.

72. Frei, "Wie modern war der Nationalsozialismus?" 383.

73. Bauer, *The Holocaust*, 30.

74. Bajohr, "Vom antijüdischen Konsens," 33–34; Wildt, *Volksgemeinschaft als Selbstermächtigung*, 215, 373.

75. Frei, "'Volksgemeinschaft,'" 24.

76. Paul and Mallmann, *Milieus und Widerstand*, 542–43; also Lüdtke, "The Appeal of Exterminating 'Others,'" 171–77.

77. Dörr, *"Wer die Zeit nicht miterlebt hat,"* 3:266, 258; Rosenthal, "Antisemitismus," 468; Rosenthal, "Kollektives Schweigen," 24; Ullrich, "'Wir haben nichts gewußt,'" 45.

78. Niethammer, "Juden und Russen," 123; Johnson and Reuband, *What We Knew*, 147–48, 197–98.

79. Schäfer, "Das gespaltene Bewußtsein," 146.

80. Rosenthal, *"Als der Krieg kam,"* 238; Rosenthal, "Antisemitismus," 457, 464–65, 468; Rosenthal, "Kollektives Schweigen," 24, 25, 31.

81. Rosenthal, "Kollektives Schweigen," 24.

82. Rosenthal, "Antisemitismus," 457, 470–71.

83. Niethammer, "Juden und Russen," 121.

84. Johnson and Reuband, *What We Knew*, xvii.

85. Gellately, *Gestapo*, 101.

86. Bajohr, "Vom antijüdischen Konsens," 47; Bankier, *Final Solution*, 130–38; Friedländer, "Wehrmacht," 21; Friedländer, *Years of Extermination*, 296–98, 307; Johnson, *Nazi Terror*, 400; Johnson and Reuband, *What We Knew*, 305; Longerich,

"Davon haben wir nichts gewusst!" 198–200; Mommsen and Obst, "Die Reaktion," 401–2, 415; Stokes, "German People," 181.

87. Ullrich, "'Wir haben nichts gewußt,'" 25–26.

88. Johnson, *Nazi Terror*, 404; Mommsen and Obst, "Die Reaktion," 401–2.

89. Dörner, *Die Deutschen und der Holocaust*, 65; Johnson, *Nazi Terror*, 457; Mommsen and Obst, "Die Reaktion," 414.

90. Mommsen and Obst, "Die Reaktion," 403; Stokes, "German People," 186–87.

91. Bankier, *Final Solution*, 108; Friedländer, "Wehrmacht," 26; Fritzsche, *Life and Death*, 151–54, 250–56; Gellately, *Backing Hitler*, 254; Johnson, *Nazi Terror*, 457; Kershaw, *Popular Opinion*, 368.

92. Bajohr, "Vom antijüdischen Konsens," 59–60, 73; Dörner, *Die Deutschen und der Holocaust*, 93–135.

93. Bajohr, "Vom antijüdischen Konsens," 61; Bankier, *Final Solution*, 111–12.

94. Frei, "Auschwitz und die Deutschen," 170–73, 175.

95. Johnson, *Nazi Terror*, 322–23, 325, 328, 442; Bajohr, "Vom antijüdischen Konsens," 59–60; Bankier, *Final Solution*, 113; Dörner, *Die Deutschen und der Holocaust*, 194–242.

96. Dörner, *Die Deutschen und der Holocaust*, 242–54; Johnson, *Nazi Terror*, 457.

97. Dörner, *Die Deutschen und der Holocaust*, 157, 192–93; Friedländer makes this point throughout *Years of Persecution* and *Years of Extermination*; Gordon, *"Jewish Question,"* 128–36, 158; Gellately, *Backing Hitler*, 30; Johnson, *Nazi Terror*, 457; Koonz, *Nazi Conscience*, 269.

98. Longerich, *"Davon haben wir nichts gewusst!"* 313.

99. Ibid., 8, 314–315.

100. Ibid., 187–89, 191, 201–2, 207–10.

101. Ibid., 324–25.

102. Ibid., 203, 277.

103. Ibid., 266–67, 278, 281.

104. Ibid., 310–11.

105. Bajohr and Pohl, "Einleitung," 9; Johnson and Reuband, *What We Knew*, 369, 385, 393; Longerich, *"Davon haben wir nichts gewusst!"* 239–40.

106. Gordon, *"Jewish Question,"* 186; Kershaw, *Popular Opinion*, 364; Mommsen and Obst, "Die Reaktion," 403–5; Stokes, "German People," 185, 189.

107. Mommsen and Obst, "Die Reaktion," 420.

108. Ibid., 410.

109. Friedländer, "Wehrmacht," 24; popular German knowledge of the Holocaust is considered throughout Friedländer, *Years of Extermination*; Kulka, "German Population," 276.

110. Friedländer, "Wehrmacht," 27.

111. Dörner, *Die Deutschen und der Holocaust*, 417, 605, 608.

112. Bajohr and Pohl, "Einleitung," 13; Pohl, "Das NS-Regime," 128; Johnson, *Nazi Terror*, 381; Dörner, *Die Deutschen und der Holocaust*, 416, 472.

113. Johnson, *Nazi Terror*, 437; Niethammer, "Juden und Russen," 119.

114. Bankier, *Final Solution*, 114–15.

115. Bajohr, "Vom antijüdischen Konsens," 64–65; Frei, "Auschwitz und die Deutschen," 176; Johnson, *Nazi Terror*, 458; Mommsen and Obst, "Die Reaktion," 411, 416; Ullrich, "'Wir haben nichts gewußt,'" 32–33.

116. Ullrich, "'Wir haben nichts gewußt,'" 31.

117. Bajohr and Pohl, "Einleitung," 12; Niethammer, "Juden und Russen," 123; Rosenthal, *"Als der Krieg kam,"* 219; Ullrich, "'Wir haben nichts gewußt,'" 44.

118. Bankier, *Final Solution*, 146–47, 151.

119. Ullrich, "'Wir haben nichts gewußt,'" 42; Bajohr and Pohl, "Einleitung," 12; Fritzsche, *Life and Death*, 265–66, 285–86; Stokes, "German People," 189.

120. Ullrich, "'Wir haben nichts gewußt,'" 44; Bajohr and Pohl, "Einleitung," 13–14; Dörner, *Die Deutschen und der Holocaust*, 483–84.

121. Ullrich, "'Wir haben nichts gewußt,'" 12.

122. Thus Johnson and Reuband, in *What We Knew*, divide their interviewees into those "knowing little about," those "hearing about," and those "witnessing and participating in" mass murder.

123. Kulka, "German Population," 273.

124. Bajohr, "Vom antijüdischen Konsens," 18–19; Kershaw, *Popular Opinion*, 370–73; Kulka, "German Population," 273–74.

125. Bajohr, "Vom antijüdischen Konsens," 23, 42–43.

126. Kulka, "German Population," 273–74.

127. Bajohr, "Vom antijüdischen Konsens," 18–19, 34, 37.

128. Wildt, *Volksgemeinschaft als Selbstermächtigung*, 342–47.

129. Bajohr, "Vom antijüdischen Konsens," 37, 42–43; Bankier, *Final Solution*, 74–75, 85–88, 129; Friedländer, *Years of Persecution*, 269–305; Gellately, *Gestapo*, 121–22; Kershaw, *Popular Opinion*, 234–35, 262, 267–69; Mommsen and Obst, "Die Reaktion," 377–79, 381, 388–89, 391–92.

130. Bankier, *Final Solution*, 85–88, 129.

131. Bajohr, "Vom antijüdischen Konsens," 36; Bankier, *Final Solution*, 76–80; Kulka, "German Population," 273; Gellately, *Gestapo*, 110; Kershaw, *Popular Opinion*, 239; Mommsen and Obst, "Die Reaktion," 384–85.

132. Gordon, *"Jewish Question,"* 185–86.

133. Ibid., 8–10.

134. Bajohr, "Vom antijüdischen Konsens," 25–27, 29.

135. Kershaw, "Alltägliches und Außeralltägliches," 286.

136. Kulka, "German Population," 274.

137. Ibid., 277.

138. Mommsen and Obst, "Die Reaktion," 402, 380, 386–87.

139. Bankier, *Final Solution*, 68–70, 83–84, 155; Kershaw, *Popular Opinion*, 231.

140. Bankier, *Final Solution*, 81; Friedländer, "Wehrmacht," 26–27; Gellately, *Gestapo*, 102, 125; Gordon, *"Jewish Question,"* 5, 197, 206; Ullrich, "'Wir haben nichts gewußt,'" 34.

141. Kershaw, "Alltägliches und Außeralltägliches," 286; Mommsen and Obst, "Die Reaktion," 397–98.

142. Kershaw, "German Popular Opinion," 384.

143. Mommsen and Obst, "Die Reaktion," 412.

144. Bankier, *Final Solution*, 107.

145. Kershaw, "Alltägliches und Außeralltägliches," 286.

146. Kershaw, *Popular Opinion*, 277.

147. Kulka and Rodrigue, "German Population and the Jews," 434.

148. Kulka, "German Population," 277, 280.

149. Friedländer, *Years of Persecution*, 324–25; Heim, "German-Jewish Relationship," 320–21.

150. One historian who explicitly addresses the relationship between the two collective nouns *Nazis* and *Germans*, is Fritzsche in *Life and Death*, 6–7, 266–72.

151. According to Alf Lüdtke, oral history research has reduced "the gaping distance between rulers and ruled . . . a presumed gulf that has so often appeared to exonerate the majority of their guilt." "Introduction," 4–5.

152. Wildt, *Volksgemeinschaft als Selbstermächtigung*, 217–18, 372–73; Bajohr, "Vom antijüdischen Konsens," 16; also Dörner, *Die Deutschen und der Holocaust*, 362.

153. Bajohr, "Vom antijüdischen Konsens," 16–17.

154. Wildt, "Violence against Jews," 182; Bankier, *Final Solution*, 155.

155. Wildt, *Volksgemeinschaft als Selbstermächtigung*, 214, also 115–32, 138–75, 197, 268, 304, 318.

156. As reported by an informant for the Social Democratic Party in exile. Bankier, *Final Solution*, 70.

157. Ibid., 81, 120, 130, 156; Johnson, *Nazi Terror*, 458–59; Kershaw, "German Popular Opinion," 372; Ullrich, "'Wir haben nichts gewußt,'" 34.

158. Fritzsche, *Life and Death*, 119, also 93.

159. Koonz, *Nazi Conscience*, 256.

160. Rosenthal, "Antisemitismus," 455.

161. Dean, "Indifference and the Language of Victimization," 89, 94, 101, 104.

162. Dörr, *"Wer die Zeit nicht miterlebt hat,"* 3:307–21.

163. Gellately, *Backing Hitler*, 5–6, 257; Johnson and Reuband, *What We Knew*, 353; Peukert, *Inside Nazi Germany*, 197.

164. Gellately, *Backing Hitler*, 204, 212.

165. Ibid., 5–6, 259.

166. Ibid., vii, 51–69, 80, 87, 138, 204–23, 257, 259; Johnson, *Nazi Terror*, 20, 253.

167. According to Eric Johnson, there was something like one Gestapo officer for every ten thousand to fifteen thousand citizens in German cities and none at all in rural areas. Because ordinary Germans "were so often willing to watch over and denounce fellow citizens . . . relatively few secret police officers were needed to control a German population that was quite ready and able to control itself." *Nazi Terror*, 46–48; also Gellately, *Gestapo*, 72, 130, 136; Gellately, *Backing Hitler*, 261; Mallmann and Paul, "Omniscient, Omnipresent, Omnipotent?" 174–75, 178, 180.

168. Gellately, *Backing Hitler*, 188.

169. Johnson, *Nazi Terror*, 48, 254, also 19–21, 51, 253.

170. Evans, "Coercion and Consent," 58–64.

171. Johnson, *Nazi Terror*, 309–11, 388.

172. Gellately, *Backing Hitler*, 183–203; Johnson and Reuband, *What We Knew*, 358.

173. Johnson, *Nazi Terror*, 322–23, 325, 328.

174. Ibid., 310–11, 335–36, 341.

175. Ibid., 20–21.

176. Paul and Mallmann, "Die Gestapo," 629–33; Wildt, *Volksgemeinschaft als Selbstermächtigung*, 12.

177. Herbert, "Good Times, Bad Times," 110.

178. Schröder, *Die gestohlenen Jahre*, 273–317; Rosenthal, *"Als der Krieg kam,"* 125–28; Dörr, *"Wer die Zeit nicht miterlebt hat,"* 3:46, 48, 77.

179. Rosenthal, *"Als der Krieg kam,"* 8–10; Dörr, *"Wer die Zeit nicht miterlebt hat,"* 3:50–52.

180. Herbert, "Good Times, Bad Times," 110; Rosenthal, *"Als der Krieg kam,"* 18, 21.

181. Rosenthal, *"Als der Krieg kam,"* 8–10, 217–18.

182. Dörr, *"Wer die Zeit nicht miterlebt hat,"* 3:193–95.

183. Schwarz, "'During Total War,'" 137; Frei, "'Volksgemeinschaft,'" 123; Dörr, *"Wer die Zeit nicht miterlebt hat,"* 2:111; 3:169–87, 201, 449–51; Pine, *Nazi Family Policy*, 184–85; Heineman, *What Difference Does a Husband Make?* 44–74; Steinbacher, "Differenz der Geschlechter?" 99–100; Reese, *Growing Up Female*, 6–7.

184. Tröger, "German Women's Memories," 287, 299.

185. Dörr, *"Wer die Zeit nicht miterlebt hat,"* 2:451–72.

186. Ibid., 2:448–49, 486; Meyer and Schulze, "'Als wir wieder zusammen waren,'" 311; Heineman, *What Difference Does a Husband Make?* 80.

187. Reese, "BDM Generation," 239; Heineman, *What Difference Does a Husband Make?* 43, 72, 84.

188. Krockow, *Hour of the Women*; Bude, *Bilanz der Nachfolge*, 86–87.

189. *Woman in Berlin*, 147.

190. Ibid., 204–5, 220, 225; Dörr, *"Wer die Zeit nicht miterlebt hat,"* 2:426–27; Grossmann, "A Question of Silence," 39.

191. Grossmann, "A Question of Silence," 50; Grossmann, "Trauma, Memory, and Motherhood," 102, 122; Petö, "Narrative of Rape," 132.

192. Petö, "Narrative of Rape," 138, 146; Meyer and Schulze, *Von Liebe sprach damals keiner*, 26–27; Hoerning, "Frauen als Kriegsbeute"; Dörr, *"Wer die Zeit nicht miterlebt hat,"* 1:201–22; 2:385, 418, 420; Niethammer, "Privat-Wirtschaft," 28–29.

193. Dörr, *"Wer die Zeit nicht miterlebt hat,"* 2:420.

194. Ibid., 2:426–27.

195. Grossmann, "A Question of Silence," 50.

196. Petö, "Narrative of Rape," 140–41.

197. *Woman in Berlin*, 259–61.

198. Meyer and Schulze, *Von Liebe sprach damals keiner*, 134.

199. Grossmann, "A Question of Silence," 49; Erich Kuby, quoted in Schmidt-Harzbach, "Eine Woche im April," 55.

200. Rosenthal, *"Als der Krieg kam,"* 130, 140.

CHAPTER 7. INTERVIEWS: MATURITY

Volker Sebastian

1. *B111*. Changed from "the Pfalz." To protect the identities of the children of the interviewees, names, occupations, and other facts that could possibly be used to identify them have been changed. These changes have *not* been noted in the endnotes.

2. *A118*.

3. *S102-A107*.

4. *A118*.

5. "And my wife" added.

6. *S117*.

7. *S117*.

8. *B111*.

9. *A118*.

10. *B104*. Changed from "Stendal."

11. *S122*.

12. *A118*.

13. *S124*.

14. *S117*.

15. Changed from "child."

16. *B111*.

17. Phrase added.

18. *B111*. Changed from "mother-in-law."

19. *S101*.

20. *S107*; *A118* uses the same phrase to describe his situation.

21. Changed from "Gesacht near Hamburg."

22. *A118*.

23. *S123*.

24. *S106*.

25. *A118*.

26. *B107*.

27. *B104*.

28. Changed from "Kemnat."

29. *S123*.

30. *S124*.

31. *A118*.

32. *S106*.

33. *S124*.

34. *A118*.

35. *S102-A107*.

36. *A118*.

37. *S102-A107*.

38. *A118*.

39. *S102-A107*.

40. *S102-A107*.

41. *S102-A107*.

42. *S102-A107*.

43. *S102-A107*.

44. *S101*.

45. *S102-A107*.

46. *S102-A107*.

47. *S107*.

48. *S102-A107*.

49. *S107.*

50. *A118.*

51. *S107.*

52. *A118.*

53. *S117.*

54. *S107.*

55. *S117.*

56. Changed from "Federal Republic."

57. *S117.*

58. *S106.*

59. *S117.*

60. *S117.*

61. *S117.*

62. *S117.*

63. *S122.*

64. *S101.*

65. *BS101.* Changed from "Wuppertal."

66. *S101.*

67. *B111.*

68. Changed from "a friend of mine."

69. *B111.*

70. *S102-A107.*

71. *B111.*

72. *S102-A107.*

73. *B111.*

74. Changed from "started."

75. *S117.*

76. *B107.*

77. *S117.* The order of this quotation has been slightly rearranged.

78. *B107.*

79. *S117.*

80. *B107.*

81. *B107.*

82. *B107.*

83. *B107.*

84. *B111.* Changed from "Kiel."

85. *S102-A107.*

86. *S102-A107.*

87. *B111.*

88. *S102-A107.*

89. *S102-A107.*

90. *B107.*

91. *S123.*

92. *B107.* Changed from "Melle."

93. *B107.*

94. *S123.*

95. Phrase added.

96. *S123.*
97. *S117.*
98. *B111.*
99. *S123.*
100. *B111.*
101. Changed from "Lübeck."
102. Changed from "Kiel."
103. *B111.*
104. *B111.*
105. Changed from "Rieth."
106. Changed from "four children."
107. Changed from "Rieth."
108. *B107.*
109. *S107.*
110. *S117.*
111. *S117.*
112. *S117.*
113. *S104.*
114. *S117.*
115. *S117.*
116. *S104.*
117. *S104.*
118. *AB103.*
119. *S104.*
120. *B107.* Changed from "Bad Oeynhausen."
121. *S101.*
122. *S123.* Changed from "Volksdorf."
123. *B111.*
124. *S117.*
125. Phrase added.
126. *S101.*
127. *B107.*
128. *S101.*
129. *S106.*
130. *S117.*
131. *B111.*
132. *S107.*
133. *S107.*
134. *S104.*
135. *S107.*
136. *S107.*
137. *S104.*
138. *S107.*
139. *S104.*
140. *S104.*
141. *S104.*
142. *S115.*

143. *S104*.

144. *S115*.

145. *S104*.

146. *S104*. This passage is a slightly shortened and rearranged version of the original quotation.

147. *S115*.

148. *S104*.

149. *S104*.

150. *S107*.

151. *S115*.

152. *S107*.

153. *AB103*.

154. *S117*.

155. *AB103*.

156. *B111*.

157. *AB103*.

158. *B111*.

159. *B104*.

160. *BS101*.

161. *B104*.

162. *BS101*.

163. *BS101*.

164. *A118*.

165. *A118*.

166. *B107*.

167. *A118*.

168. *S101*.

169. *B107*.

170. *S104*.

171. *B107*.

172. *A118*.

173. *S101*.

174. *S101*.

175. *B104*.

176. *A118*.

177. *B104*.

178. *S104*.

179. *A117*.

180. Phrase added.

181. *A117*.

182. Phrase added.

183. *S104*.

184. *S117*.

185. *S104*.

186. *BS101*.

187. *S104*.

188. *S107*.

189. *S104.*
190. *A118.*
191. *S107.*
192. *S107.*
193. *B107.*
194. *S115.*
195. *S107.*
196. *S107.*
197. *S107.*
198. *S104.*
199. *S107.*
200. *S104.*
201. *S107.*
202. *S104.*
203. *B107.*
204. *B104.*
205. *S119.*
206. *S119.*
207. *A118.*
208. *B107.*
209. *S104.*
210. *B107.*
211. *B111.*
212. *B111.*
213. Phrase added.
214. Changed from "Duisburg."
215. *S104.*
216. *S102-A107.*
217. *S115.*
218. *S115.*
219. *B111.*
220. *S115.*
221. *S115.*
222. *S115.*
223. *B111.*
224. *S115.*
225. *A123.*
226. *B111.*
227. *S107.*
228. *S102-A107.*
229. *B111.*
230. *A123.*
231. *S124.*
232. *S104.*
233. *S107.*
234. *S104.*
235. *S107.*

236. Changed from "two."
237. Changed from "their children were the ones."
238. *S107.*
239. Sentence added.
240. *S107.*
241. Phrase added.
242. *B103.*
243. *S107.*
244. Phrase added.
245. *B103.*
246. *B107.*
247. *S107.*
248. *B107.*
249. *AB103.*
250. *B107.*
251. *B104.*
252. *AB103.*
253. *S117.*

Ilse Müller

1. *B115.* To protect the identities of the children of the interviewees, names, occupations, and other facts that could possibly be used to identify them have been changed. These changes have *not* been noted in the endnotes.
2. *A120.*
3. Changed from "brother."
4. *B115.*
5. Changed from "Nuremberg."
6. Changed from "we."
7. *AB101.*
8. Phrase added.
9. *B113.*
10. *B115.*
11. Changed from "daughter."
12. *B115.*
13. *AB101.*
14. *B115.*
15. *B115.*
16. *AB101.*
17. *AB101.*
18. *B115.*
19. Changed from "husband."
20. *A114.*
21. *A109.*
22. *A114.*
23. *A109.*
24. *A120.*
25. *A120.*

26. Changed from "Stuttgart."

27. A101.

28. A101.

29. A105.

30. AB101.

31. "He" has been changed to "she."

32. A101.

33. A110-A121.

34. A114.

35. A110-A121.

36. Phrase added.

37. S114.

38. A105.

39. S114.

40. A105.

41. Changed from "Once I made a."

42. S114.

43. S114.

44. Changed from "Lüneburg."

45. Changed from "Hamburg."

46. Changed from "Lüneburg."

47. S114.

48. A105.

49. S114.

50. A110-A121.

51. A114.

52. B108.

53. B115.

54. A120.

55. B115.

56. B115.

57. BS121.

58. B115.

59. Changed from "1947."

60. AB101.

61. A101.

62. AB101.

63. A115.

64. A110-A121.

65. A120.

66. A110-A121.

67. A120.

68. BS121.

69. Changed from "Youth Authority."

70. B110. Changed from "the woman who was to hire me, embraced me." This incident actually relates to the interviewee and not her husband, and the text has been altered to reflect that change.

71. BS121.
72. BS121; A110-A121.
73. A110-A121.
74. BS121.
75. BS121.
76. A109.
77. BS121.
78. A109.
79. AB101.
80. BS121.
81. BS121.
82. B113.
83. AB101.
84. B113. Changed from "my."
85. AB101.
86. BS121.
87. BS121.
88. BS121.
89. BS121.
90. Changed from "my mother still."
91. BS121.
92. B115.
93. A110-A121.
94. A120.
95. A110-A121.
96. Changed from "just over a year old."
97. BS121.
98. A115.
99. A115. Changed from "1950."
100. Phrase added.
101. Changed from "Lübeck."
102. Changed from "down to Hanover."
103. A104.
104. A115.
105. Phrase added.
106. Changed from "I found myself."
107. A115.
108. Phrase added.
109. A110-A121.
110. A115.
111. A110-A121.
112. AB102-B106; A110-A121.
113. A115.
114. A110-A121.
115. S110.
116. A114.
117. S114.

118. A114.
119. Changed from "Bieberstein."
120. Changed from "Hamburg."
121. A114.
122. Phrase added.
123. S116.
124. S116.
125. A106.
126. B115.
127. A106.
128. BS101.
129. S116.
130. BS101.
131. Changed from "Braunschweig."
132. AB102-B106.
133. Sentence added.
134. A101.
135. BS121.
136. AB102-B106.
137. Changed from "we've lived."
138. BS121.
139. Changed from "his."
140. Changed from "her."
141. AB102-B106.
142. A113.
143. S110.
144. A113.
145. S110.
146. B110.
147. S109.
148. S110.
149. A105.
150. B110.
151. S109.
152. S110.
153. S109.
154. S109.
155. S109.
156. B115.
157. BS121.
158. Changed from "three."
159. AB102-B106.
160. B102.
161. AB101.
162. AB102-B106.
163. Tense changed.
164. Tense changed.

165. AB102-B106.
166. A108.
167. A101.
168. A101.
169. Changed from "other."
170. A120.
171. A119.
172. A120.
173. Changed from "my oldest."
174. Changed from "current wife."
175. A101.
176. A119.
177. A120.
178. A120.
179. A101.
180. A120.
181. A104.
182. A119.
183. A120.
184. A105.
185. A101.
186. A120.
187. Phrase added.
188. A104.
189. A120.
190. A104.
191. A120.
192. A101.
193. A101.
194. A108.
195. Changed from "five."
196. A110-A121.
197. A109.
198. A109.
199. A109.
200. A120.
201. Phrase added.
202. A120.
203. Phrase added.
204. A110-A121.
205. A105.
206. A101.
207. A120.
208. S120.
209. A119.
210. A106.
211. A119.

212. Changed from "we." A106.
213. Changed from "we."
214. A119.
215. A120.
216. S120.
217. A101.
218. A101.
219. A120.
220. A101.
221. A120.
222. Changed from "we."
223. A120.
224. S120.
225. Changed from "we."
226. A120.
227. A119.
228. S109.
229. S116.
230. A101.
231. S109.
232. BS121.
233. S109.
234. S116.
235. BS121.
236. A101.
237. BS121.
238. Changed from "1910."
239. S116.
240. B114.
241. S110.
242. B114.
243. B114.
244. S110.
245. A106.
246. A111.
247. A114.
248. A111.
249. A111.
250. Phrase added.
251. A116.
252. S116.
253. A113.
254. S110.
255. A113.
256. A103.
257. A113.
258. A114.

259. S110.
260. B105.
261. A120.
262. A101.
263. B108.
264. S120.
265. B108.
266. A113.
267. B108.
268. A113.
269. S116.
270. S116.
271. A113.
272. A115.
273. S112.

CHAPTER 8. ANALYSIS: RESURRECTING THE
COLLECTIVE IN THE GENERATIONAL "CIRCLE"

1. **A114**; A110-A121; *AB101*; **B113**; **B115**; BS121.

2. A101; A105; A109; A114; A120; A110-A121; *AB101*; *B111*; B115; **S110**; S114; *S102-A107*.

3. A101; *A123*; *AB103*; A110-A121; AB102-B106; *B107*; *B111*; B115; BS121; *S104*; *S107*; *S117*.

4. A105; **A119**; *AB101*; B115; B117; BS121; *S123*.

5. **A110-A121**.

6. **A114**; **A115**; A110-A121; *AB101*; *B107*; B115; BS121; *S101*; *S107*; **S110**; *S117*; *S102-A107*.

7. A111; A120; **A110-A121**; B115; BS121.

8. A105; A109; A114; A115; A120; A110-A121; *AB101*; B108; B113; BS121; *S101*; S114.

9. Only *S107* recalls the immediate postwar years as "among the happiest" of his life.

10. The husbands of A114, A115, A119, A122, B102, B116, S109, S113, and S116 died prematurely. Biess, *Homecomings*, 71–74.

11. *A118*; *S106*; *S107*; *S102-A107*.

12. **A114**; *A118*; **B104**; *S104*; **S115**; *S124*; *S102-A107*.

13. **A116**; A120; *S102-A107*.

14. A101; A109; A119; A120; B116; **S120**. Women were generally better able to bring their experiences during the Third Reich and the war into psychotherapy than men. Müller-Hohagen, *Verleugnet, verdrängt, verschwiegen*, 114.

15. *A118*; *B111*; **S117**.

16. **S104**. Also *B103*.

17. *S104*; *S115*; **B103**.

18. *A118*; **B103**; *S104*; *S107*; *S115*.

19. *S117*.

20. Biess, "Men of Reconstruction," 349.

21. Niethammer, "'Normalization,'" 239.

22. Ibid., 241, 259.

23. **A114; A120; S110;** *S123*. Measured in material terms, West Germans achieved normality in the late 1950s and early 1960s. Wildt, "Continuities and Discontinuities," 215, 216, 221.

24. A115; *A118;* **A119;** A110-A121; **AB102-B106;** BS121; *S101; S107*.

25. **A114; A115;** A110-A121; *AB101;* **AB102-B106; B113;** BS121; *S101*.

26. A104; *A107;* A109; *A118;* A110-A121; *AB101;* **AB102-B106;** *B104; B107; B111;* **B113; B115;** *BS101;* BS121; *S101; S107;* S110; S116; *S117; S123; S124; S102-B114*.

27. **AB102-B106.**

28. Meyer and Schulze, *Von Liebe sprach damals keiner,* 220; Schulz, Radebold, and Reulecke, *Söhne ohne Väter,* 128.

29. AB102-B106.

30. B115; BS121; S110; **S114.**

31. Thus **A110-A121** experienced her new house as overwhelmingly large, and, in general, plenty seems to have oppressed her.

32. Sabiene Autsch, who conducted many of the interviews for this study, reaches the same conclusion about them. "'Zeit hat Zeit,'" 210. Niethammer, "'Normalization,'" 239; Rosenthal, *"Als der Krieg kam,"* 77–79.

33. As Lutz Niethammer points out, "Normality cannot be narrated as history." "Privat-Wirtschaft," 19. Although oral history is often characterized as "the history of everyday life," oral history interviews generally relate anything but the everyday.

34. A111.

35. A111. Also A116.

36. S116.

37. Whereas the interviewees resurrected the Gemeinschaft in the form of the Free German Circle, other Germans found collective sustenance in reunions of former members of National Socialist organizations, sports clubs, churches, or trade unions. Möding, "'Ich muß irgendwo engagiert sein,'" 277–81.

38. *S106; S107; S117.*

39. **A106;** *A118;* **B113; B115;** *BS101;* BS121; *S106; S107;* S116; *S117; S122; S123.*

40. **A120.** Also *S104;* S116.

41. **AB102-B106;** *BS101; S101; S104; S107; S115;* **S116;** *S117.*

42. **A111;** *BS101; S104; S107;* S117.

43. **A111.**

44. **A111;** *A117;* S104; *S107;* **S109; S116.**

45. *A117; A118;* **AB102-B106;** *B107;* **BS121;** *S104;* **S109;** S116.

46. *B104; S104; S119.*

47. **B113.** Also *AB103; B111;* **BS121;** *S101;* S117.

48. *A118;* **A119;** A110-A121; *AB103; B104; B107; B111; S104; S107; S115; S119.*

49. **A115;** *A118; AB103; B107; S104; S107; S115; S102-A107.*

50. **A111.** Also A114; *AB103; B104; B107; BS101; S104; S107;* **S119.**

51. *S104; S107; S115.*

52. *S104; S107; S115.*

53. There are few exceptions: **B116**; **A110-A121**; **S120**.

54. *A106*; **A119**; **B113**; **B115**; *S102-A107*.

55. *S104*; ***S107***.

56. *A118*; *B107*; *S101*; *S104*; **S116**; *S122*.

57. **A116**; **A119**.

58. *A101*; **A115**; **A120**; *B104*; *B110*; *S107*.

59. *A101*. Also A115; **A116**; **A119**; *B110*; *S109*.

60. *A101*; *A105*; *A106*; *A108*; **A109**; *A119*; *A120*; *AB101*; AB102-B106; *B102*; **B115**; *BS101*; *S104*; *S107*; **S110**; *S120*; *S124*. Seidel, "'Wir waren so himmelblaue Idealisten'"; Reulecke, "'In Unruhe Leben.'"

61. *S104* explicitly contrasts his lack of conflict with his grandparents and parents to the conduct of his children toward him.

62. A104; *AB102-B106*; *B102*; *S104*; *S107*; *S117*.

63. **A119**.

64. A105; *A106*; *A120*; **A110-A121**; *B103*; *S107*; S110.

65. A105; *A123*; **A110-A121**; *B103*; **B115**; *S107*. B114 and S110 have nieces who are or were married to non-Germans.

66. A105; A113; A120; **A110-A121**; *AB102-B106*; *B103*; *S104*; *S107*; **S110**; *S102-A107*.

67. A104; A105; A113; A120; **A110-A121**; *AB102-B106*; *S104*; *S107*; S110; *S102-A107*.

68. A101; **A119**; *S104*. Dörr, *"Wer die Zeit nicht miterlebt hat,"* 3:475.

69. **A119**. Meyer and Schulze, *Von Liebe sprach damals keiner*, 221; Dörr, *"Wer die Zeit nicht miterlebt hat,"* 3:466.

70. A103; A105; **A109**; A113; *A120*; *A123*; *B103*; *B110*; *S104*; *S109*; S110; *S115*.

71. A103; A104; A109; **A113**; A120; *B110*; S110.

72. **A109**; *B103*; *S104*; *S115*.

73. A101; A104; A120; **B113**; *S109*; S110; *S120*.

74. A101; **A104**; A120; **B113**; *S109*; *S120*.

75. A104; A105; A119; A120; *B103*.

76. **A109**. Also A119.

77. **S109**.

78. **B115**; *BS121*; *S104*; S109; *S102-A107*.

79. **B115**.

80. *B104*; *B107*; *B111*; ***BS101***; *S101*; *S104*; *S107*; *S115*; *S117*; *S102-A107*.

81. A101; A103; A111; A113; A114; A120; A121; *A123*; *A110-S110*; *B105*; B108; *B111*; *S107*; S116; *S120*; *S124*; *S102-A107*.

82. Only ***B104*** and ***S104*** seemed somewhat negative about the future.

83. Personal communication from the gerontological psychologist Insa Fooken.

84. **B115**. Also A113.

85. **A111**; **A113**; *A120*; *B105*.

86. *S118* (see chapter 2, "Analysis: Finding the Collective in the Youth Movement 'Group'").

87. **BS121** (see chapter 5, "Analysis: Extending the Collective in the Community of the *Volk*").

88. S116 (interview with Ilse Müller).

89. A115 (interview with Ilse Müller).

90. S112 (interview with Ilse Müller).

91. **A119.**

CHAPTER 9. ESSAYS

1. Bäumer, *Der neue Weg*, 47–48.

2. Meyer and Schulze, *Von Liebe sprach damals keiner*, 9–10; Bessel, *Germany 1945*, 277.

3. Niethammer, "Privat-Wirtschaft," 39–40, 46–49, 54.

4. Heineman, "Hour of the Woman," 33–34.

5. *Woman in Berlin*, 42–43.

6. Grossmann, "A Question of Silence," 49.

7. *Woman in Berlin*, 206.

8. Strecker, *Überleben ist nicht genug*, 56.

9. Meyer and Schulze, "'Als wir wieder zusammen waren,'" 312–13.

10. Smith, *Heimkehr*, 107; Dörr, *"Wer die Zeit nicht miterlebt hat,"* 3:39.

11. Biess, "Men of Reconstruction," 338.

12. Biess, "Survivors of Totalitarianism," 59, 61; Biess, "Men of Reconstruction," 340, 342–44.

13. Biess, "Men of Reconstruction," 350.

14. Schissler, "'Normalization' as Project," 361–62. Also Wierling, "Mission to Happiness," 115.

15. Quoted in Benz, "Schwierigkeiten der Heimkehr," 17.

16. Rosenthal, *"Als der Krieg kam,"* 18–19; Frevert, *Women in German History*, 262; Meyer and Schulze, "'Als wir wieder zusammen waren,'" 313–22.

17. Frevert, *Women in German History*, 262; Biess, "Men of Reconstruction," 347; Smith, *Heimkehr*, 109. Also Herzog, *Sex After Fascism*, 86–87.

18. Biess, "Men of Reconstruction," 345.

19. Frevert, *Women in German History*, 262.

20. Möding, "'Ich muß irgendwo engagiert sein,'" 290; Moeller, *Protecting Motherhood*, 11.

21. Heineman, *What Difference Does a Husband Make?* 115–25.

22. Ibid., 108.

23. Ibid., 108, 115–16; Rosenthal, *"Als der Krieg kam,"* 19; Meyer and Schulze, "'Als wir wieder zusammen waren,'" 313–22.

24. Dörr, *"Wer die Zeit nicht miterlebt hat,"* 3:32–34; Schissler, "'Normalization' as Project," 361–62.

25. Heineman, *What Difference Does a Husband Make?* 119; Meyer and Schulze, *Von Liebe sprach damals keiner*, 134; Meyer and Schulze, "'Als wir wieder zusammen waren,'" 314.

26. Dörr, *"Wer die Zeit nicht miterlebt hat,"* 3:32–34; Heineman, *What Difference Does a Husband Make?* 115–16, 119–20; Schulz, Radebold, and Reulecke, *Söhne ohne Väter*, 128, 132; Wierling, "Mission to Happiness," 115.

27. Bruns, *Als Vater aus dem Krieg heimkehrte*, 8, 105.

28. Dörr, *"Wer die Zeit nicht miterlebt hat,"* 3:32–34, 76–77; Frevert, *Women in German History*, 263; Heineman, *What Difference Does a Husband Make?* 119–20;

Meyer and Schulze, "'Als wir wieder zusammen waren,'" 313–22; Schissler, "'Normalization' as Project," 362; Smith, *Heimkehr*, 110–11.

29. Meyer and Schulze, "'Als wir wieder zusammen waren,'" 313–22; Frevert, *Women in German History*, 263.

30. Dörr, *"Wer die Zeit nicht miterlebt hat,"* 3:36, 170.

31. Moeller, *Protecting Motherhood*, 5, 34.

32. Frevert, *Women in German History*, 265–66; Meyer and Schulze, *Von Liebe sprach damals keiner*, 216–17; Meyer and Schulze, "'Als wir wieder zusammen waren,'" 321; Einfeldt, "Zwischen alten Werten und neuen Chancen," 182–83; Möding, "'Ich muß irgendwo engagiert sein,'" 285.

33. Herbert, "Zur Entwicklung der Ruhrarbeiterschaft," 44.

34. Frevert, *Women in German History*, 333; Möding, "'Ich muß irgendwo engagiert sein,'" 285.

35. Schmidt, "Krieg der Männer—Chance der Frauen?" 159.

36. Einfeldt, "Auskommen—Durchkommen—Weiterkommen," 292; Einfeldt, "Zwischen alten Werten und neuen Chancen," 182–83; Dörr, *"Wer die Zeit nicht miterlebt hat,"* 3:76–77, 187, 189.

37. Moeller, "Last Soldiers," 132–33.

38. Rosenthal, "Erzählbarkeit," 17.

39. Mitscherlich and Mitscherlich, "Die Unfähigkeit zu trauern," 27, 34–35.

40. Following the Mitscherlichs' essay, Germans have come to accept the psychoanalytic notion that the past needs to be "worked through" and in some sense "mourned." Rabinbach, "Response to Karen Brecht," 316.

41. Lübbe, "Der Nationalsozialismus im deutschen Nachkriegsbewußtsein."

42. Tröger, "German Women's Memories," 299.

43. Mitscherlich and Mitscherlich, "Die Unfähigkeit zu trauern," 30; Herzog, *Sex After Fascism*, 101–40.

44. Moser, "Die Unfähigkeit zu trauern," 210–11.

45. Herzog, *Sex After Fascism*, 181.

46. Rabinbach, "Response to Karen Brecht," 316.

47. Bessel, *Germany 1945*, 38–68.

48. Moser, "Die Unfähigkeit zu trauern," 216–17; Confino, "Traveling as a Culture of Remembrance," 237.

49. Bessel, *Germany 1945*, 4–7, 389, 397. An Allensbach Institute poll in 1952 revealed that more than half of the German population could be said to have suffered one or more traumatic losses. Förster and Beck, "Post-traumatic Stress Disorder and World War II," 30. Whereas Förster and Beck see Germans suffering from post-traumatic stress disorder after the war, Atina Grossmann sees Germans "in the grip of what one today might identify as mass clinical depression." "Trauma, Memory, and Motherhood," 109–10.

50. Biess notes "the discrepancy between the rich historiography on the political, social, economic, cultural, and psychological consequences of the First World War and the virtual absence of a similar literature for the post-1945 period." *Homecomings*, 2.

51. Bessel and Schumann, "Introduction," 1–3; Niethammer, "'Normalization,'" 239.

52. Bessel and Schumann, "Introduction," 3.

53. Moeller, "Remembering the War," 101.

54. Moeller, *War Stories*, 6–7.

55. Ibid., 12, 16; Moeller, "Remembering the War," 84–85, 99.

56. Moeller, *War Stories*, 174, 18.

57. Personal communication.

58. Rosenthal, "Kollektives Schweigen," 23, 27; Rosenthal, *"Als der Krieg kam,"* 238–39.

59. Hartmann, "Spuren des Nationalsozialismus," 236; Rosenthal, "Antisemitismus," 476; Rosenthal, "Kollektives Schweigen," 23, 27; Rosenthal, *"Als der Krieg kam,"* 220; Stierlin, "Der Dialog," 39.

60. Rosenthal, "Kollektives Schweigen," 29–30.

61. Rosenthal, *"Als der Krieg kam,"* 240; Rosenthal, *" . . . wenn alles in Scherben fällt,"* 16–17.

62. Rosenthal, "Kollektives Schweigen," 29, also 22–23; Rosenthal, *"Als der Krieg kam,"* 218–19, 221.

63. Rosenthal, *"Als der Krieg kam,"* 220–21.

64. Arnim, *Das große Schweigen*, 6.

65. Moser, "Die Unfähigkeit zu trauern," 215–18. Also Confino, "Traveling as a Culture of Remembrance," 239.

66. Massing and Beushausen, "'Bis ins dritte und vierte Glied.'"

67. Rosenthal, "Antisemitismus," 477.

68. Rosenthal, "Kollektives Schweigen," 30–31.

69. Rosenthal, "Antisemitismus," 478. Also Herzog, *Sex After Fascism*, 177–82, 251–52.

70. Biess, "Men of Reconstruction," 344–45, 350–51; Biess, *Homecomings*, 120–25.

71. Bude, *Bilanz der Nachfolge*, 88–89; Bude, "The German *Kriegskinder*," 302–3.

72. Bude, "The German *Kriegskinder*," 304–5.

CONCLUSION

1. When the last of the interviewees has died, their interviews, the recordings and the transcripts of the recordings, will be available to scholars at the Archiv der deutschen Jugendbewegung in Burg Ludwigstein.

2. Brokaw, *Greatest Generation*, xxx; also vii, xxvi, 11.

3. Ibid., 319.

4. Ibid., 282, 12; also, 97, 146, 171, 306, 385.

5. Ibid., 282.

6. Ibid., xx, 45, 51, 92.

7. Ibid., xviii, 69, 71, 72, 111, 242.

8. Ibid., xx, 66.

9. Ibid., 159; also 83, 212.

10. Ibid., 44, 66, 82, 92, 110, 161, 248.

11. Ibid., 161, 231.

12. Ibid., 321; also xx, xxx, 24, 34, 37, 75, 159, 232, 247, 248.

13. Ibid., xix, 20, 61, 67, 388.
14. Ibid., xx, 34, 55, 336.
15. Patel, *Soldiers of Labor.*
16. Cubitt, *History and Memory,* 78.
17. Plato, "Hitler Youth Generation," 212.
18. Haffner, *Geschichte eines Deutschen,* 170–71.

BIBLIOGRAPHY

Aderhold, Cornelia, and Brigitte Nölleke. "'Es war eine ganz erbärmliche Zeit,' Bürger aus Hamburg-St. Georg erzählen von ihrem Alltag während des Nationalsozialismus." In *Terror und Hoffnung in Deutschland, 1933–1945: Leben im Faschismus*, edited by Johannes Beck et al., 191–220. Reinbek: Rowohlt, 1980.

Althaus, Claudia. "Geschichte, Erinnerung und Person: Zum Wechselverhältnis von Erinnerungsresiduen und Offizialkultur." In *Erinnerung, Gedächtnis, Wissen: Studien zur kulturwissenschaftlichen Gedächtnisforschung*, edited by Günter Oesterle, 589–609. Göttingen: Vandenhoeck und Ruprecht, 2006.

Arnim, Gabriele von. *Das große Schweigen: Von der Schwierigkeit, mit den Schatten der Vergangenheit zu leben*. Munich: Kindler, 1989.

Autsch, Sabiene. *Erinnerung-Biographie-Fotografie: Formen der Ästhetisierung einer jugendbewegter Generation im 20. Jahrhundert*. Potsdam: Verlag für Berlin-Brandenburg, 2001.

———. "'Zeit hat Zeit'—Beobachtungen über unterschiedliche Zeitdimensionen im biographischen Interview." *SOWI, Sozialwissenschaftliche Informationen* 23 (1994): 207–13.

Bajohr, Frank. "Detlev Peukerts Beiträge zur Sozialgeschichte der Moderne." In Bajohr, Johe, and Lohalm, *Zivilisation und Barbarei*, 5–16.

———. "Vom antijüdischen Konsens zum schlechten Gewissen. Die deutsche Gesellschaft und die Judenverfolgung, 1933–1945." In Bajohr and Pohl, *Der Holocaust als offene Geheimnis*, 15–79.

Bajohr, Frank, Werner Johe, and Uwe Lohalm, eds. *Zivilisation und Barbarei: Die widersprüchlichen Potentiale der Moderne*. Hamburg: Christians, 1991.

Bajohr, Frank, and Dieter Pohl. "Einleitung." In Bajohr and Pohl, *Der Holocaust als offene Geheimnis*, 7–14.

———, eds. *Der Holocaust als offene Geheimnis: Die Deutschen, die NS-Führung, und die Alliierten*. Munich: C. H. Beck Verlag, 2006.

Bajohr, Frank, and Michael Wildt. "Einleitung." In Bajohr and Wildt, *Volksgemein-schaft*, 7–23.

———, eds. *Volksgemeinschaft: Neue Forschungen zur Nationalsozialismus*. Frank-furt: Fischer Verlag, 2009.

Bankier, David. *The Germans and the Final Solution: Public Opinion under Nazism*. Oxford: Blackwell, 1996.

———, ed. *Probing the Depth of German Antisemitism: German Society and the Per-secution of the Jews, 1933–1941*. Jerusalem and New York/Oxford: Yad Vashem and the Leo Baeck Institute with Berghahn Books, 2000.

Bartov, Omar, Atina Grossmann, and Mary Nolan, eds. *Crimes of War: Guilt and Denial in the Twentieth Century*. New York: New Press, 2002.

Bauer, Yehuda. *The Holocaust in Historical Perspective*. Seattle: University of Wash-ington Press, 1978.

Bäumer, Gertrud. *Der neue Weg der deutschen Frau*. Stuttgart: Deutsche Verlags Anstalt, 1946.

Baumgarten, Otto. "Der sittliche Zustand des deutschen Volkes unter dem Einfluß des Krieges." In *Geistliche und sittliche Wirkungen des Krieges in Deutschland*, edited by Otto Baumgarten et al., 1–88. Stuttgart: Deutsche Verlagsanstalt, 1927.

Baureithel, Ulrike. "Masken der Virilität: Kulturtheoretische Strategien zur Überwin-dung des männlichen Identitätsverlustes im ersten Drittel des 20. Jahrhunderts." *Die Philosophin* 8 (1993): 24–35.

Benz, Wolfgang. "Schwierigkeiten der Heimkehr: Eine Einführung." In *Heimkehr 1948*, edited by Annette Kaminsky, 13–21. Munich: C. H. Beck Verlag, 1998.

———. "Vom freiwilligen Arbeitsdienst zur Arbeitsdienstpflicht." *Vierteljahrshefte für Zeitgeschichte* 16 (1968): 317–46.

Beradt, Charlotte. *The Third Reich in Dreams*. Chicago: Quadrangle, 1968.

Bergerson, Andrew Stuart. "Hildesheim in an Age of Pestilence: On the Birth, Death, and Resurrection of Normality." In *The Work of Memory: New Directions in the Study of German Society and Culture*, edited by Alon Confino and Peter Fritz-sche, 107–35. Urbana: University of Illinois Press, 2002.

———. *Ordinary Germans in Extraordinary Times: The Nazi Revolution in Hildesheim*. Bloomington: Indiana University Press, 2004.

Bessel, Richard. *Germany After the First World War*. Oxford: Clarendon, 1993.

———. *Germany 1945: From War to Peace*. London: Simon and Schuster, 2009.

———, ed. *Life in the Third Reich*. Oxford: Oxford University Press, 2001.

———. *Nazism and War*. London: Weidenfeld and Nicolson, 2004.

Bessel, Richard, and Dirk Schumann. "Introduction: Violence, Normality, and the Construction of Postwar Europe." In Bessel and Schumann, *Life After Death*, 1–13.

———, eds. *Life After Death: Approaches to a Cultural and Social History of Europe during the 1940s and 1950s*. Cambridge: Cambridge University Press, 2003.

Biess, Frank. *Homecomings: Returning POWs and the Legacies of Defeat in Postwar Germany*. Princeton, NJ: Princeton University Press, 2006.

———. "Men of Reconstruction—The Reconstruction of Men: Returning POWs in East and West Germany, 1945–1955." In Hagemann and Schüler-Springorum, *Home/Front*, 335–58.

———. "Survivors of Totalitarianism: Returning POWs and the Reconstruction of Masculine Citizenship in West Germany, 1945–1955." In Schissler, *The Miracle Years*, 57–82.

Blackbourn, David, and Geoff Eley. *The Peculiarities of German History: Bourgeois Society and Politics in Nineteenth-Century Germany*. Oxford: Oxford University Press, 1984.

Brokaw, Tom. *The Greatest Generation*. London: Pimlico, 2002.

Broszat, Martin. *The Hitler State: The Foundation and Development of the Internal Structure of the Third Reich*. New York and London: Longman, 1981.

Bruns, Ingeborg. *Als Vater aus dem Krieg heimkehrte: Töchter erinnern sich*. Frankfurt: Fischer Taschenbuch Verlag, 1991.

Buck, Pearl S. *How It Happens: Talk about the German People, 1914–1933, with Erna von Pustau*. Reprinted in *The German Inflation of 1923*, edited by Fritz K. Ringer, 119–46. New York: Oxford University Press, 1969.

Bude, Heinz. *Bilanz der Nachfolge: Die Bundesrepublik und der Nationalsozialismus*. Frankfurt: Suhrkamp Verlag, 1992.

———. "The German *Kriegskinder*: Origins and Impact of the Generation of 1968." In Roseman, *Generations in Conflict*, 290–305.

Busse-Wilson, Elisabeth. "Liebe und Kameradschaft" (1925). In Schade, *Ein Weibliches Utopia*, 246–53.

Confino, Alon. *Germany as a Culture of Remembrance: Promises and Limits of Writing History*. Chapel Hill: University of North Carolina Press, 2006.

———. "Prologue: The Historian's Representations." In Confino, *Germany as a Culture of Remembrance*, 1–22.

———. "Traveling as a Culture of Remembrance: Traces of National Socialism in West Germany, 1945–1960." In Confino, *Germany as a Culture of Remembrance*, 235–54.

Crew, David F., ed. *Nazism and German Society, 1933–1945*. London and New York: Routledge, 1994.

Cubitt, Geoffrey. *History and Memory*. Manchester: Manchester University Press, 2007.

Dahrendorf, Ralf. *Society and Democracy in Germany*. Garden City, NY: Doubleday, 1969.

Daniel, Ute. *Kompendium Kulturgeschichte: Theorien, Praxis, Schlüsselwörter*. Frankfurt: Suhrkamp Verlag, 2001.

Dean, Carolyn J. "Indifference and the Language of Victimization." In *The Fragility of Empathy After the Holocaust*, 76–105. Ithaca: Cornell University Press, 2004.

Dörner, Bernward. *Die Deutschen und der Holocaust: Was niemand wissen wollte, aber jeder wissen konnte*. Berlin: Ullstein Verlag, 2007.

Dörr, Margarethe. "*Wer die Zeit nicht miterlebt hat . . .*": Frauenerfahrungen im Zweiten Weltkrieg und in den Jahren danach, 4 vols. Frankfurt: Campus Verlag, 1998.

Einfeldt, Anne-Katrin. "Auskommen—Durchkommen—Weiterkommen: Weibliche Arbeitserfahrungen in der Bergarbeiterkolonie." In Niethammer, "*Die Jahre weiß man nicht*," 267–96.

———. "Zwischen alten Werten und neuen Chancen: Häusliche Arbeit von Bergarbeiterfrauen in den fünfziger Jahren." In Niethammer, "*Hinterher merkt man*," 149–90.

Eley, Geoff. Foreword to Lüdtke, *The History of Everyday Life*, vii–xiii.

———. "Labor History, Social History, Alltagsgeschichte: Experience, Culture, and the Politics of Everyday Life—A New Direction for German Social History?" *Journal of Modern History* 61 (1989): 297–343.

Engelmann, Bernt. *Im Gleichschritt marsch: Wie wir die Nazizeit erlebten, 1933–1939*. Cologne: Kiepenhauer und Witsch, 1982.

Erdheim, Mario. "Die tryrannische Instanz im Innern: Wie totalitäre Herrschaft die Psyche beschädigt." *Journal für Geschichte* 2 (1982): 16–20.

Evans, Richard J. "Coercion and Consent in Nazi Germany." *Proceedings of the British Academy* 151 (2007): 53–81.

Feldman, Gerald. *The Great Disorder: Politics, Economics, and Society in the German Inflation, 1914–1924*. New York: Oxford University Press, 1993.

Fogt, Helmut. *Politische Generationen: Empirische Bedeutung und theoretisches Modell*. Opladen: Westdeutscher Verlag, 1982.

Förster, Alice, and Birgit Beck. "Post-traumatic Stress Disorder and World War II: Can a Psychiatric Concept Help Us Understand Postwar Society?" In Bessel and Schumann, *Life After Death*, 15–35.

Frei, Norbert. "Auschwitz und die Deutschen: Geschichte, Geheimnis, Gedächtnis." In Frei, *1945 und Wir*, 156–220.

———. "Epochenjahr 1933: Der 30. Januar entschwindet dem historischen Bewußtsein." In Frei, *1945 und Wir*, 83–96.

———. "Erinnerungskampf: Der 20. Juli 1944 in den Bonner Anfangsjahren." In Frei, *1945 und Wir*, 129–44.

———. *National Socialist Rule in Germany: The Führer State, 1933–1945*. Oxford: Blackwell, 1993.

———. "'Volksgemeinschaft': Erfahrungsgeschichte und Lebenswirklichkeit der Hitler-Zeit." In Frei, *1945 und Wir*, 107–28.

———. "Wie modern war der Nationalsozialismus?" *Geschichte und Gesellschaft* 19 (1993): 367–87.

———. *1945 und Wir: Das Dritte Reich im Bewußtsein der Deutschen*. Munich: C. H. Beck Verlag, 2005.

Frevert, Ute. *Women in German History: From Bourgeois Emancipation to Sexual Liberation*. New York: Berg, 1993.

Friedländer, Saul. *Nazi Germany and the Jews: The Years of Persecution, 1933–1939*. New York: Harper Collins, 1997.

———. "The Wehrmacht, German Society, and the Knowledge of the Mass Extermination of the Jews." In Bartov, Grossmann, and Nolan, *Crimes of War*, 17–30.

———. *The Years of Extermination: Nazi Germany and the Jews, 1939–1945*. New York: Harper Collins, 2007.

Fritzsche, Peter. *Germans into Nazis*. Cambridge, MA: Harvard University Press, 1998.

———. *Life and Death in the Third Reich*. Cambridge, MA: Harvard University Press, Belknap Press, 2008.

———. *Rehearsals for Fascism: Populism and Political Mobilization in Weimar Germany*. New York: Oxford University Press, 1990.

Galinski, Dieter, Ulrich Herbert, and Ulla Lachauer, eds. *Nazis und Nachbarn: Schüler erforschen den Alltag im Nationalsozialismus*. Reinbek: Rowohlt Verlag, 1981.

Gellately, Robert. *Backing Hitler: Consent and Coercion in Nazi Germany*. Oxford: Oxford University Press, 2001.

———. *The Gestapo and German Society: Enforcing Racial Policy, 1933–1945*. Oxford: Clarendon, 1990.

Gerstenberger, Heide. "Alltagsforschung und Faschismustheorie." In *Normalität oder Normalisierung? Geschichtswerkstätten und Faschismusanalyse*, edited by Heide Gerstenberger and Dorothea Schmidt, 35–49. Münster: Westfälisches Dampfboot, 1987.

Glaser, Ernst. *The Class of 1902*. New York: Viking, 1929.

Gordon, Sarah. *Hitler, Germans, and the "Jewish Question."* Princeton, NJ: Princeton University Press, 1984.

Grele, Ronald J. "Ziellose Bewegung: Methodische und theoretische Probleme der Oral History." In Niethammer, *Lebenserfahrung*, 195–220.

Grossmann, Atina. "A Question of Silence: The Rape of German Women by Occupation Soldiers." In *West Germany under Construction: Politics, Society, and Culture in the Adenauer Era*, edited by Robert G. Moeller, 33–52. Ann Arbor: University of Michigan Press, 1997.

———. "Trauma, Memory, and Motherhood: Germans and Jewish Displaced Persons in Post-Nazi Germany, 1945–1949." In Bessel and Schumann, *Life After Death*, 93–127.

Gründel, E. Günther. *Die Sendung der Jungen Generation*. Munich: C. H. Beck'sche Verlagsbuchhandlung, 1932.

Haffner, Sebastian. *Geschichte eines Deutschen: Die Erinnerungen, 1914–1933*. Stuttgart and Munich: Deutsche Verlagsanstalt, 2000.

———. *The Meaning of Hitler*. Cambridge, MA: Harvard University Press, 1979.

Hagemann, Karen, and Stefanie Schüler-Springorum, eds. *Home/Front: The Military, War and Gender in Twentieth-Century Germany*. Oxford: Berg, 2002.

Halbwachs, Maurice. *The Collective Memory*. New York: Harper Colophon, 1980.

Hartmann, Gertrud. "Spuren des Nationalsozialismus bei nicht-jüdischen Kindern, Jugendlichen und ihren Familien." In *Erinnerung einer Profession: Erziehungsberatung, Jugendhilfe und Nationalsozialismus*, edited by Renate Cogoy, 231–40. Münster: VOTUM Verlag, 1989.

Heim, Susanne. "The German-Jewish Relationship in the Diaries of Victor Klemperer." In Bankier, *Probing the Depth*, 312–25.

Heineman, Elizabeth D. "The Hour of the Woman: Memories of Germany's 'Crisis Years' and West German National Identity." In Schissler, *The Miracle Years*, 21–56.

———. *What Difference Does a Husband Make? Women and Marital Status in Nazi and Postwar Germany*. Berkeley: University of California Press, 1999.

Hellfeld, Matthias von. *Bündische Jugend und Hitlerjugend: Zur Geschichte von Anpassung und Widerstand, 1930–1939*. Cologne: Verlag Wissenschaft und Politik, 1987.

Herbert, Ulrich. "Apartheid nebenan: Erinnerungen an die Fremdarbeiter im Ruhrgebiet." In Niethammer, *"Die Jahre weiß man nicht,"* 233–66.

———. "Drei politische Generationen im 20. Jahrhundert." In Reulecke, *Generationalität*, 95–114.

———. "'Generation der Sachlichkeit': Die völkische Studentenbewegung." In Bajohr, Johe, and Lohalm, *Zivilisation und Barbarei*, 115–44.

———. "Good Times, Bad Times: Memories of the Third Reich." In Bessel, *Life in the Third Reich*, 97–110.

———. "Zur Entwicklung der Ruhrarbeiterschaft 1930 bis 1960 aus erfahrungsgeschichtlicher Perspektive." In Niethammer and Plato, *"Wir kriegen jetzt andere Zeiten,"* 19–52.

Herzog, Dagmar. "Hubris and Hypocrisy, Incitement and Dismissal: Sexuality and German Fascism." In *Sexuality and German Fascism*, edited by Dagmar Herzog, 1–21. New York: Berghahn Books, 2005.

———. *Sex After Fascism: Memory and Morality in Twentieth-Century Germany.* Princeton, NJ: Princeton University Press, 2005.

Hoerning, Erika M. "Frauen als Kriegsbeute: Der Zwei-Fronten-Krieg, Beispiele aus Berlin." In Niethammer and Plato, *"Wir kriegen jetzt andere Zeiten,"* 327–44.

Hopster, Norbert, and Ulrich Nassen. "Vom 'Bekenntnis' zum 'Kampf': Jugend und Jugendliteratur auf dem Weg ins 'jugendliche Reich.'" In Koebner, Janz, and Trommler, *"Mit uns zieht die neue Zeit,"* 546–62.

Hüppauf, Bernd. "Langemarck, Verdun, and the Myth of a New Man in Germany After the First World War." *War and Society* 6 (1988): 70–103.

Jaeger, Hans. "Generationen in der Geschichte: Überlegungen zu einer umstrittenen Konzeption." *Geschichte und Gesellschaft* 3 (1977): 429–52.

Janz, Rolf-Peter. "Die Faszination der Jugend durch Rituale und sakrale Symbole: Mit Anerkennung zu Fidu, Hesse, Hofmannsthal und George." In Koebner, Janz, and Trommler, *"Mit uns zieht die neue Zeit,"* 310–37.

Johnson, Eric A. *Nazi Terror: The Gestapo, Jews, and Ordinary Germans.* New York: Basic Books, 1999.

Johnson, Eric A., and Karl-Heinz Reuband. *What We Knew: Terror, Mass Murder and Everyday Life in Nazi Germany.* Cambridge: Basic Books, 2005.

Karutz, Annemarie. *Von der Idealisierung des Nationalsozialismus zur Idealisierung des Kommunismus: Eine biografietheoretische Verlaufsstudie frühere SED-Genossen von 1990 bis 1999.* Giessen: Psychosozial-Verlag, 2003.

Kater, Michael H. "Bürgerliche Jugendbewegung und Hitlerjugend in Deutschland von 1926 bis 1939." *Archiv für Sozialgeschichte* 17 (1977): 127–74.

———. "Generationskonflikt als Entwicklungsfaktor in der NS-Bewegung vor 1933." *Geschichte und Gesellschaft* 11 (1985): 217–43.

———. *Hitler Youth.* Cambridge, MA: Harvard University Press, 2004.

Kempowski, Walter. *"Haben Sie davon gewußt?" Deutche Antworten.* Hamburg: Albrecht Knaus Verlag, 1979.

Kershaw, Ian. "Alltägliches und Außeralltägliches: Ihre Bedeutung für die Volksmeinung, 1933–1939." In *Die Reihen fast geschlossen: Beiträge zur Geschichte des Alltags unterm Nationalsozialismus*, edited by Detlev Peukert and Jürgen Reulecke, 273–92. Wuppertal: Peter Hammer Verlag, 1981.

———. "German Popular Opinion and the 'Jewish Question,' 1939–1943: Some Further Reflections." In *Die Juden im nationalsozialistischen Deutschland, 1933–1943*, edited by Arnold Paucker et al., 365–86. Tübingen: J. C. B. Mohr, 1986.

———. *The Hitler Myth: Image and Reality in the Third Reich.* New York: Oxford University Press, 1987.

———. *The Nazi Dictatorship: Problems and Perspectives of Interpretation*. New York: Oxford University Press, 2000.

———. *Popular Opinion and Political Dissent in the Third Reich, 1933–1945*. Oxford: Clarendon, 1983.

Kienitz, Sabine. "Body Damage: War Disability and Constructions of Masculinity in Weimar Germany." In Hagemann and Schüler-Springorum, *Home/Front*, 181–204.

Koebner, Thomas, Rolf-Peter Janz, and Frank Trommler, eds. *"Mit uns zieht die neue Zeit": Der Mythos Jugend*. Frankfurt: Suhrkamp Verlag, 1985.

Kohler, Mathilde Anna. "'Irgendwie windelt man sich durch, mit großen Unbehagen': Dienste und Einsätze der Studentinnen an der Universität Wien, 1938–1945." In *Töchter-Fragen N-S Frauen Geschichte*, edited by Lerke Gravenhorst and Carmen Tatschmurat, 237–51. Freiburg: Kore Verlag, 1990.

Kohut, Heinz. "From a Letter to a Colleague of September 1978." In *The Search for the Self*, 4:577–91.

———. "On Leadership." In *The Search for the Self*, 3:103–28.

———. *The Search for the Self: Selected Writings of Heinz Kohut*, edited by Paul H. Ornstein. 4 vols. Madison, CT: International Universities Press, 1978–91.

Kohut, Thomas A. "Kaiser Wilhelm II and His Parents: An Inquiry into the Psychological Roots of German Policy towards England Before the First World War." In *Kaiser Wilhelm II: New Interpretations*, edited by John C. G. Röhl and Nicolaus Sombart, 63–89. Cambridge: Cambridge University Press, 1982.

Koonz, Claudia. *Mothers in the Fatherland: Women, the Family, and Nazi Politics*. New York: St. Martins, 1987.

———. *The Nazi Conscience*. Cambridge, MA: Harvard University Press, 2003.

Krockow, Christian Graf von. *Hour of the Women*. New York: Harper Collins, 1991.

Kruedener, Jürgen Freiherr von. "Die Entstehung des Inflationstraumas: Zur Sozialpsychologie der deutschen Hyperinflation 1922/23." In *Konsequenzen der Inflation*, edited by Gerald D. Feldman et al., 213–86. Berlin: Colloquium Verlag, 1989.

Kulka, Otto Dov. "The German Population and the Jews: State of Research and New Perspectives." In Bankier, *Probing the Depth*, 271–81.

Kulka, Otto Dov, and Aron Rodrigue. "The German Population and the Jews in the Third Reich: Recent Publications and Trends in Research on German Society and the 'Jewish Question.'" *Yad Vashem Studies* 16 (1984): 421–35.

Laqueur, Walter Z. *Young Germany: A History of the German Youth Movement*. London: Routledge and Kegan Paul, 1962.

Lessing, Theodor. *Geschichte als Sinngebung des Sinnlosen*. Munich: C. H. Beck'sche Verlagsbuchhandlung, 1921.

Linse, Ulrich. "'Geschlechtsnot der Jugend': Über Jugendbewegung und Sexualität." In Koebner, Janz, and Trommler, *"Mit uns zieht die neue Zeit,"* 245–309.

Loewenberg, Peter. "The Psychohistorical Origins of the Nazi Youth Cohort." *American Historical Review* 76 (1971): 1457–1502.

Longerich, Peter. *"Davon haben wir nichts gewusst!" Die Deutschen und die Judenverfolgung, 1933–1945*. Munich: Siedler Verlag, 2006.

Lübbe, Hermann. "Der Nationalsozialismus im deutschen Nachkriegsbewußtsein." *Historische Zeitschrift* 3 (1983): 579–99.

Lüdtke, Alf. "The Appeal of Exterminating 'Others': German Workers and the Limits of Resistance." In *The Third Reich: The Essential Readings*, edited by Christian Leitz, 155–77. Oxford: Blackwell, 1999.

———. "'Coming to Terms with the Past': Illusions of Remembering, Ways of Forgetting Nazism in West Germany." *Journal of Modern History* 65 (1993): 542–72.

———, ed. *The History of Everyday Life: Reconstructing Historical Experiences and Ways of Life*. Princeton, NJ: Princeton University Press, 1995.

———. "Introduction: What Is the History of Everyday Life and Who Are Its Practitioners?" In Lüdtke, *The History of Everyday Life*, 3–40.

Mallmann, Klaus-Michael, and Gerhard Paul. "Omniscient, Omnipresent, Omnipotent? Gestapo, Society and Resistance." In Crew, *Nazism and German Society*, 166–96.

———. "Sozialisation, Milieu und Gewalt: Fortschritte und Probleme der neueren Täterforschung." In *Karrieren der Gewalt: Nationalsozialistische Täterbiographien*, edited by Klaus-Michael Mallmann and Gerhard Paul, 1–32. Darmstadt: Wissenschaftliche Buchgesellschaft, 2004.

Mann, Golo. *Erinnerungen und Gedanken: Eine Jugend in Deutschland*. Frankfurt: Fischer Verlag, 1986.

Mann, Klaus. *Kind dieser Zeit*. Berlin: Transmare Verlag, 1932.

Mannheim, Karl. "The Problem of Generations." In Karl Mannheim, *Essays on the Sociology of Knowledge*, edited by Paul Kecskemiti, 276–322. New York: Oxford University Press, 1952.

Mansel, Jürgen, Gabriele Rosenthal, and Angelika Tölke, eds. *Generationen-Beziehungen, Austausch und Tradierung*. Opladen: Westdeutscher-Verlag, 1997.

Maschmann, Melita. *Fazit: Mein Weg in der Hitler-Jugend*. Munich: Deutschertaschenbuch Verlag, 1983.

Massing, Almuth, and Ulrich Beushausen. "'Bis ins dritte und vierte Glied': Auswirkungen des Nationalsozialismus in den Familien." *Psychosozial* 9 (1986): 27–42.

Matzke, Frank. *Jugend bekennt: So sind wir!* Leipzig: Philipp Reclam, 1930.

Meyer, Sibylle, and Eva Schulze. "'Als wir wieder zusammen waren, ging der Krieg im Kleinen weiter': Frauen, Männer und Familien im Berlin der vierziger Jahre." In Niethammer and Plato, *"Wir kriegen jetzt andere Zeiten,"* 305–26.

———. *Von Liebe sprach damals keiner: Familienalltag in der Nachkriegszeit*. Munich: C. H. Beck Verlag, 1985.

Mitscherlich, Alexander, and Margarethe Mitscherlich. "Die Unfähigkeit zu trauern—Womit zusammenhängt: Eine deutsche Art zu lieben." In *Die Unfähigkeit zu trauern: Grundlagen kollektiven Verhaltens*, 13–85. Munich: R. Piper Verlag, 1967.

Möding, Nori. "'Ich muß irgendwo engagiert sein—fragen Sie mich bloß nicht, warum': Überlegungen zu Sozialisationserfahrungen von Mädchen in NS-Organisationen." In Niethammer and Plato, *"Wir kriegen jetzt andere Zeiten,"* 256–304.

Moeller, Robert G. "'The Last Soldiers of the Great War' and Tales of Family Reunions in the Federal Republic of Germany." *Signs: Journal of Women in Culture and Society* 24 (1998): 129–45.

———. *Protecting Motherhood: Women and the Family in the Politics of Postwar West Germany.* Berkeley: University of California Press, 1993.

———. "Remembering the War in a Nation of Victims: West German Pasts in the 1950s." In Schissler, *The Miracle Years*, 83–109.

———. *War Stories: The Search for a Usable Past in the Federal Republic of Germany.* Berkeley: University of California Press, 2003.

Mommsen, Hans. "Generationenkonflikt und politische Entwicklung in der Weimarer Republik." In Reulecke, *Generationalität*, 115–26.

———. "Nationalsozialismus als vorgetäuschte Modernisierung." In Pehle, *Der historische Ort*, 31–46.

———. *Der Nationalsozialismus und die deutsche Gesellschaft.* Reinbek: Rowohlt Taschenbuch Verlag, 1991.

Mommsen, Hans, and Dieter Obst. "Die Reaktion der deutschen Bevölkerung auf die Verfolgung der Juden, 1933–1943." In *Herschaftsalltag im Dritten Reich: Studien und Texte*, edited by Hans Mommsen and Susanne Willems, 374–421. Düsseldorf: Schwann, 1988.

Moser, Tilmann. "Die Unfähigkeit zu trauern: Hält die These einer Überprüfung stand? Zur psychischen Verarbeitung des Holocaust." In *Vorsicht Berührung: Über Sexualisierung, Spaltung, NS-Erbe und Stasi Angst*, 203–20. Frankfurt: Suhrkamp Verlag, 1992.

Mosse, George. "Shell-Shock as a Social Disease." *Journal of Contemporary History* 35 (2000): 101–8.

Müller-Hohagen, Jürgen. *Verleugnet, verdrängt, verschwiegen: Die seelischen Auswirkungen der Nazizeit.* Munich: Kösel-Verlag, 1988.

Münkel, Daniela. "'Volksgenossen' und 'Volksgemeinschaft': Anspruch und Wirklichkeit." In *Die Deutschen im 20. Jahrhundert*, edited by Edgar Wolfrum, 159–68. Darmstadt: Primus Verlag, 2004.

Niethammer, Lutz. "Einführung." In Niethammer, *Lebenserfahrung*, 7–33.

———. "Einleitung des Herausgebers." In Niethammer, *"Die Jahre weiß man nicht,"* 7–29.

———. "Fragen—Antworten—Fragen: Methodische Erfahrungen und Erwägungen zur Oral History." In Niethammer and Plato, *"Wir kriegen jetzt andere Zeiten,"* 392–445.

———. "Heimat und Front: Versuch zehn Kriegserinnerungen aus der Arbeiterklasse des Ruhrgebietes zu verstehen." In Niethammer, *"Die Jahre weiß man nicht,"* 163–232.

———, ed. *"Hinterher merkt man, daß es richtig war, daß es schiefgegangen ist." Nachkriegserfahrungen im Ruhrgebiet, 1930–1960.* Bonn: Verlag J. H. W. Dietz Nachfolger, 1983.

———, ed. *"Die Jahre weiß man nicht, wo man die heute hinsetzen soll." Faschismus Erfahrungen im Ruhrgebiet: Lebensgeschichte und Sozialkultur im Ruhrgebiet, 1930–1960.* Bonn: Verlag J. H. W. Dietz Nachfolger, 1986.

———. "Juden und Russen im Gedächtnis der Deutschen." In Pehle, *Der historische Ort*, 114–34.

———, ed. *Lebenserfahrung und kollektives Gedächnis: Die Praxis der 'Oral History.'* Frankfurt: Suhrkamp Verlag, 1985.

———. "'Normalization' in the West: Traces of Memory Leading Back into the 1950s." In Schissler, *The Miracle Years*, 237–65.

———. "Privat-Wirtschaft: Erinnerungsfragmente einer anderen Umerziehung." In Niethammer, *"Hinterher merkt man,"* 17–105.

Niethammer, Lutz, and Alexander von Plato, eds. *"Wir kriegen jetzt andere Zeiten." Auf der Suche nach der Erfahrung des Volkes in nachfaschistischen Länder: Lebensgeschichte und Sozialkultur im Ruhrgebiet, 1930 bis 1960.* Bonn: J. H. W. Dietz Nachfolger, 1985.

Nolzen, Armin. "Inklusion und Exklusion im 'Dritten Reich': Das Beispiel der NS-DAP." In Bajohr and Wildt, *Volksgemeinschaft*, 60–77.

Olick, Jeffrey K. *In the House of the Hangman: The Agonies of German Defeat, 1943–1949.* Chicago: University of Chicago Press, 2005.

Owings, Alison. *Frauen: German Women Recall the Third Reich.* New Brunswick, NJ: Rutgers University Press, 2005.

Patel, Kiran Klaus. *Soldiers of Labor: Labor Service in Nazi Germany and New Deal America, 1933–1945.* Cambridge: Cambridge University Press, 2005.

Paul, Gerhard, and Klaus-Michael Mallmann. "Die Gestapo: Weltanschauungsexekutive mit gesellschaftlichem Rückhalt." In *Die Gestapo im Zweiten Weltkrieg: "Heimatfront" und besetztes Europa*, edited by Gerhard Paul and Klaus-Michael Mallmann, 599–650. Darmstadt: Wissenschaftliche Buchgesellschaft, 2000.

———. *Milieus und Widerstand: Eine Verhaltensgeschichte der Gesellschaft im Nationalsozialismus.* Bonn: Verlag J. H. W. Dietz Nachfolger, 1995.

Pehle, Walter, ed. *Der historische Ort des Nationalsozialismus: Annäherungen.* Frankfurt: Fischer Verlag, 1990.

Petö, Andrea. "Memory and the Narrative of Rape in Budapest and Vienna in 1945." In Bessel and Schumann, *Life After Death*, 129–48.

Peukert, Detlev. "Alltag und Barbarei: Zur Normalität des Dritten Reiches." In *Ist der Nationalsozialismus Geschichte? Zu Historisierung und Historikerstreit*, edited by Dan Diner, 142–53. Frankfurt: Fischer Verlag, 1987.

———. *Inside Nazi Germany: Conformity, Opposition, and Racism in Everyday Life.* New Haven: Yale University Press, 1987.

Pinder, Wilhelm. *Das Problem der Generation in der Kunstgeschichte Europas.* Berlin: Frankfurter Verlags-Anstalt, 1926.

Pine, Lisa. *Nazi Family Policy, 1933–1945.* Oxford: Berg, 1997.

Plato, Alexander von. "The Hitler Youth Generation and Its Role in the Two Post-war German States." In Roseman, *Generations in Conflict*, 210–26.

———. "Nachkriegssieger: Sozialdemokratischer Betriebsräte im Ruhrgebiet—Eine lebensgeschichtliche Untersuchung." In Niethammer, *"Hinterher merkt man,"* 311–58.

———. "Oral History als Erfahrungswissenschaft: Zum Stand der 'mündlichen Geschichte' in Deutschland." *BIOS: Zeitschrift für Biographieforschung und Oral History* 1 (1991): 97–119.

Pohl, Dieter. "Das NS-Regime und das internationale Bekanntwerden seiner Verbrechen." In Bajohr and Pohl, *Der Holocaust als offene Geheimnis*, 81–129.

Prinz, Michael. "Die soziale Funktion moderner Elemente in der Gesellschaftspolitik des Nationalsozialismus." In Prinz and Zitelmann, *Nationalsozialismus und Modernisierung*, 297–327.

Prinz, Michael, and Rainer Zitelmann, eds. *Nationalsozialismus und Modernisierung.* Darmstadt: Wissenschaftliche Buchgesellschaft, 1991.

———. "Vorwort." In Prinz and Zitelmann, *Nationalsozialismus und Modernisierung,* vii–xi.

Prümm, Karl. "Jugend ohne Vater: Zu den autobiographischen Jugendromanen der späten zwanziger Jahre." In Koebner, Janz, and Trommler, *"Mit uns zieht die neue Zeit,"* 563–89.

Raabe, Felix. *Die Bündische Jugend: Ein Beitrag zur Geschichte der Weimarer Republik.* Stuttgart: Brentano Verlag, 1961.

Rabinbach, Anson. "Response to Karen Brecht." In "In the Aftermath of Nazi Germany: Alexander Mitscherlich and Psychoanalysis—Legend and Legacy." *American Imago* 52 (1995): 313–28.

Reese, Dagmar. "The BDM Generation: A Female Generation in Transition from Dictatorship to Democracy." In Roseman, *Generations in Conflict,* 227–46.

———. *Growing Up Female in Nazi Germany.* Ann Arbor: University of Michigan Press, 2006.

Reese-Nübel, Dagmar. "Kontinuitäten und Brüche in den Weiblichkeitskonstruktionen im Übergang von der Weimarer Republik zum Nationalsozialismus." In *Soziale Arbeit und Faschismus: Volkspflege und Pädagogik im Nationalsozialismus,* edited by Hans-Uwe Otto and Heinz Sünker, 223–41. Bielefeld: Karin Böllert-KT Verlag, 1989.

Reinecker, Herbert. *Die Illusionen der Vergangenheit: Ein persönlicher Zeitbericht.* Frankfurt: Ullstein Verlag, 1992.

Rempel, Gerhard. *Hitler's Children: The Hitler Youth and the S.S.* Chapel Hill: University of North Carolina Press, 1989.

Reulecke, Jürgen. "Einführung: Lebensgeschichten des 20. Jahrhunderts—im 'Generationencontainer'?" In Reulecke, *Generationalität,* vii–xv.

———, ed. *Generationalität und Lebensgeschichte im 20. Jahundert,* Schriften des Historischen Kollegs 58. Munich: Oldenbourg Verlag, 2003.

———. "Generationen und Biografien im 20. Jahrhundert." In *Psychotherapie in Zeiten der Veränderung,* edited by Bernhard Strauss and Michael Geyer, 26–40. Wiesbaden: Westdeutscher Verlag, 2000.

———. "Hat die Jugendbewegung den Nationalsozialismus vorbereitet? Zum Umgang mit einer falschen Frage." In Reulecke, *"Ich möchte einer werden,"* 151–76.

———. *"Ich möchte einer werden so wie die . . .": Männerbünde im 20. Jahrhundert.* Frankfurt: Campus Verlag, 2001.

———. "'In Unruhe Leben': Jugendbewegte Väter und studentenbewegte Söhne in den späten 1960er Jahren." *Historische Jugendforschung, Jahrbuch des Archivs der deutschen Jugendbewegung* 4 (2007): 51–66.

———. "Männerbund versus Familie: Bürgerliche Jugendbewegung und Familie in Deutschland im ersten Drittel des 20. Jahrhunderts." In Koebner, Janz, and Trommler, *"Mit uns zieht die neue Zeit,"* 199–223.

———. "Neuer Mensch und neue Männlichkeit: Die 'junge Generation' im ersten Drittel des 20. Jahrhunderts." In *Jahrbuch des Historischen Kollegs* 6 (2001), edited by Lothar Gall, 109–38. Munich: Oldenbourg Verlag, 2002.

———. "'. . . und sie werden nicht mehr frei ihr ganzes Leben!': Jungmannschaft der Weimarer Republik auf dem Weg in die Staatsjugend des 'Dritten Reiches.'" In Reulecke, *Ich möchte einer werden,* 129–50.

———. "'Wir reiten die Sehnsucht tot' oder: Melancholie als Droge. Anmerkungen zum bündischen Liedgut." In Reulecke, *Ich möchte einer werden,* 103–28.

Riegger, Luise. "Die Frau in der Jugendbewegung." In *Die Kultur der Frau: Eine Lebenssymphonie der Frau des XX. Jahrhunderts,* edited by Ada Schmidt-Beil, 237–45. Berlin-Frohnau: Verlag für Kultur und Wissenschaft, 1931.

Roseman, Mark, ed. *Generations in Conflict: Youth Revolt and Generation Formation in Germany, 1770–1968.* Cambridge: Cambridge University Press, 1995.

———. "National Socialism and Modernisation." In *Fascist Italy and Nazi Germany: Comparisons and Contrasts,* edited by Richard Bessel, 197–229. Cambridge: Cambridge University Press, 1996.

———. *The Past in Hiding.* London: Penguin, 2000.

Rosenthal, Gabriele. *"Als der Krieg kam, hatte ich mit Hitler nichts mehr zu tun":* *Zur Gegenwärtigkeit des "Dritten Reiches" in Biographien.* Opladen: Leske und Budrich, 1990.

———. "Antisemitismus im lebensgeschichtlichen Kontext: Soziale Prozesse der Dehumanisierung und Schuldzuweisung." *Österreichische Zeitschrift für Geschichtswissenschaften* 3 (1992): 449–79.

———. "Erzählbarkeit, biographische Notwendigkeit und soziale Funktion von Kriegserzählungen. Zur Frage: Was wird gerne und leicht erzählt." *BIOS: Zeitschrift für Biographieforschung und Oral History* 6 (1993): 5–24.

———. "Kollektives Schweigen zu den Nazi-Verbrechen: Bedingungen der Institutionalisierung einer Abwehrhaltung." *Psychosozial* 15 (1992): 22–33.

———. *" . . . wenn alles in Scherben fällt . . ." Von Leben und Sinnwelt der Kriegsgeneration: Typen biographischer Wandlungen.* Opladen: Leske und Buderich, 1987.

———. "Zur interaktionellen Konstitution von Generationen: Generationenabfolgen in Familien von 1890 bis 1970 in Deutschland." In Mansel, Rosenthal, and Tölke, *Generationen-Beziehungen, Austausch und Tradierung,* 57–73.

Rupp, Susanne. "Zur Herausbildung von Generationseinheiten und Generationsbeziehungen bei Angehörigen der Weimarer Jugend- und Hitlerjugendgenerationen." In Mansel, Rosenthal, and Tölke, *Generationen-Beziehungen, Austausch und Tradierung,* 205–17.

Rusinek, Bernd A. "Krieg als Sehnsucht: Militärischer Stil und 'junge Generation' in der Weimarer Republik." In Reulecke, *Generationalität,* 127–44.

Schade, Rosemarie. *Ein Weibliches Utopia: Organisationen und Ideologien der Mädchen und Frauen in der bürgerlichen Jugendbewegung, 1905–1933.* Burg Ludwigstein: Archiv der deutschen Jugendbewegung, 1996.

Schäfer, Hans Dieter. "Das gespaltene Bewußtsein: Über Lebenswirklichkeit in Deutschland, 1933–1945." In *Das gespaltene Bewußtsein: Über deutsche Kultur und Lebenswirklichkeit, 1933–1945,* 114–62. Munich: Carl Hanser Verlag, 1983.

Schelsky, Helmut. *Die skeptische Generation: Eine Soziologie der deutschen Jugend.* Düsseldorf: Eugen Diederichs, 1957.

Schissler, Hanna, ed. *The Miracle Years: A Cultural History of West Germany, 1949–1968.* Princeton, NJ: Princeton University Press, 2001.

———. "'Normalization' as Project: Some Thoughts on Gender Relations in West Germany during the 1950s." In Schissler, *The Miracle Years,* 359–75.

Schmidt, Margot. "Krieg der Männer—Chance der Frauen?" In Niethammer, *"Die Jahre weiß man nicht,"* 133–62.

Schmidt-Harzbach, Ingrid. "Eine Woche im April. Berlin 1945. Vergewaltigung als Massenschicksal." *Feministische Studien* 3 (1984): 51–65.

Schmitt-Sasse, Joachim. "'Der Führer ist immer der Jüngste': Nazi Reden an die deutsche Jugend." In Koebner, Janz, and Trommler, *"Mit uns zieht die neue Zeit,"* 128–49.

Schoenbaum, David. *Hitler's Social Revolution: Class and Status in Nazi Germany, 1933–1939.* Garden City, NY: Doubleday, 1966.

Schröder, Hans Joachim. *Die gestohlenen Jahre. Erzählgeschichten und Geschichtserzählungen im Interview: Der Zweite Weltkrieg aus der Sicht ehemaliger Mannschaftssoldaten.* Tübingen: Max Niemeyer Verlag, 1992.

Schulz, Hermann, Hartmut Radebold, and Jürgen Reulecke. *Söhne ohne Väter: Erfahrungen der Kriegsgeneration.* Berlin: Christoph Links Verlag, 2004.

Schwarz, Gudrun. "'During Total War, We Girls Want to Be Where We Can Really Accomplish Something': What Women Do in Wartime." In Bartov, Grossmann, and Nolan, *Crimes of War,* 121–37.

Seidel, Heinrich Ulrich. *Aufbruch und Erinnerung: Der Freideutsche Kreis als Generationseinheit im 20. Jahrhundert.* Witzenhausen: Archiv der deutschen Jugendbewegung, 1996.

———. "'Wir waren so himmelblaue Idealisten': Die Eltern der 68er am Beispiel der Mitglieder des Freideutschen Kreises." *Westfälische Forschungen* 48 (1998): 55–68.

Smith, Arthur L. *Heimkehr aus dem Zweiten Weltkrieg: Die Entlassung der deutschen Kriegsgefangenen.* Stuttgart: Deutsche-Verlags-Anstalt, 1985.

Stachura, Peter D. *The German Youth Movement, 1900–1945: An Interpretive and Documentary History.* New York: St. Martin's, 1981.

Stargardt, Nicholas. *Witnesses of War: Children's Lives under the Nazis.* London: Pimlico, 2006.

Steinbacher, Sybille. "Differenz der Geschlechter? Chancen und Schranken für die 'Volksgemeinschaft.'" In Bajohr and Wildt, *Volksgemeinschaft,* 94–104.

Stephenson, Jill. *Women in Nazi Germany.* Harlow: Pearson Education, 2001.

Stierlin, Helm. "Der Dialog zwischen den Generationen über die Nazizeit." *Familiendynamik* 7 (1982): 31–48.

Stokes, Lawrence D. "The German People and the Destruction of the European Jews." *Central European History* 6 (1973): 167–91.

Strecker, Gabriele. *Überleben ist nicht genug: Frauen 1945–1950.* Freiburg: Herder Verlag, 1981.

Suhrkamp, Peter. "Söhne ohne Väter und Lehrer: Die Situation der bürgerlichen Jugend." *Die Neue Rundschau* 43 (May 1932): 681–96.

Szepansky, Gerda. *"Blitzmädel," "Heldenmutter," "Kriegerwitwe."* Frankfurt: Fischer Taschenbuch Verlag, 1986.

Tönnies, Ferdinand. *Gemeinschaft und Gesellschaft: Grundbegriffe der reinen Soziologie*. Darmstadt: Wissenschaftlich Buchgesellschaft, 2005.

Tröger, Annemarie. "German Women's Memories of World War II." In *Behind the Lines: Gender and the Two World Wars*, edited by Margaret Higonnet, Jane Jensen, Sonya Michel, and Margaret Weitz, 285–99. New Haven: Yale University Press, 1987.

Ullrich, Volker. "'Wir haben nichts gewußt'—Ein deutsches Trauma." *1999: Zeitschrift für die Sozialgeschichte des 20. und 21. Jahrhunderts* 4 (1991): 11–46.

Unruh, Trude. *Trümmerfrauen: Biografien einer betrogenen Generation*. Fulda: Klartext Verlag, 1987.

Verhey, Jeffrey. *The Spirit of 1914: Militarism, Myth and Mobilization in Germany*. Cambridge: Cambridge University Press, 2000.

Wangh, Martin. "National Socialism and the Genocide of the Jews." *International Journal for Psychoanalysis* 45 (1964): 386–94.

Welzer, Harald. "Das gemeinsame Verfertigen von Vergangenheit im Gespräch." In Welzer, *Das soziale Gedächtnis*, 160–78.

———. "Das soziale Gedächtnis." In Welzer, *Das soziale Gedächtnis*, 9–16.

———, ed. *Das soziale Gedächtnis: Geschichte, Erinnerung, Tradierung*. Hamburg: Hamburger Edition, 2001.

Wierling, Dorothee. *Geboren im Jahr Eins: Der Jahrgang 1949 in der DDR. Versuch einer Kollektivbiographie*. Berlin: Christoph Links Verlag, 2002.

———. "The Hitler Youth Generation in the GDR: Insecurities, Ambitions, and Dilemmas." In *Dictatorship as Experience: Towards a Socio-Cultural History of the GDR*, edited by Konrad Jarausch, 301–24. New York: Berghahn Books, 1999.

———. "Mission to Happiness: The Cohort of 1949 and the Making of East and West Germans." In Schissler, *The Miracle Years*, 110–25.

Wildt, Michael. "Continuities and Discontinuities of Consumer Mentality in West Germany in the 1950s." In Bessel and Schumann, *Life After Death*, 211–29.

———. *Generation des Unbedingten: Das Führerkorps des Reichssicherheitshauptamtes*. Hamburg: Hamburger Edition, 2003.

———. "Die Ungleichheit des Volkes: 'Volksgemeinschaft' in der politischen Kommunikation der Weimarer Republik." In Bajohr and Wildt, *Volksgemeinschaft*, 24–40.

———. "Violence against Jews in Germany, 1933–1939." In Bankier, *Probing the Depth*, 181–209.

———. *Volksgemeinschaft als Selbstermächtigung: Gewalt gegen Juden in der deutschen Provinz, 1919 bis 1939*. Hamburg: Hamburger Edition HIS Verlaggesellschaft, 2007.

Wilke, Gerhard. "Village Life in Nazi Germany." In Bessel, *Life in the Third Reich*, 17–24.

A Woman in Berlin: Eight Weeks in the Conquered City, a Diary. New York: Metropolitan, 2005.

Zinnecker, Jürgen. "'Das Problem der Generationen': Überlegungen zu Karl Mannheims kanonischen Text." In Reulecke, *Generationalität*, 33–58.

Zweig, Stefan. *Die Welt von Gestern: Erinnerungen eines Europäers*. London: Hamish Hamilton, 1941.

INDEX

Ahlborn, Knut, 52n, 53, 191n
Ahnenforschung ("ancestral research"), 131–32
air raids, 114–15, 118, 145–46, 169
Altenberg monastery, 2
anti-Semitism. *See also* genocide; Jewish people
    among interviewees, 11, 34, 55, 131–38, 140–41
    1968 generation and, 235–36
    rejection of Nazi stereotypes and, 133–35
    during the Third Reich, 167–72
    Volksgemeinschaft and, 159–60
    youth movement and, 34, 69
Arctic Ocean, in World War II, 96–97
Arnim, Gabriele von, 235
Aryan racial stereotype, 131–32
asceticism
    postwar ideals and, 213–14
    as youth movement value, 29–31, 53, 66–67
Auschwitz, 163, 166
Austria, annexation of, 88
authority of historical experience
    over human beings, 238–41
    over memories, 241–42

Autobahns, 98n, 106
Autsch, Sabiene, 3, 303n32

Bajohr, Frank, 167, 168, 170
Balkans, in World War II, 92–93, 98
Bankier, David, 165–66
Bar-On, Dan, 234
barter economy, 183, 184, 195
Baumann, Hans, 103
Bäumer, Gertrud, 44, 224
Baumgarten, Otto, 75
BBC, 163–64
Beck, Birgit, 306n49
"Beck, Magdalene" (composite interviewee), 100–123, 280n96
Berlin
    evacuation from, 114–15
    in Third Reich, 39–40, 57–58, 106–7, 111, 114–15, 117
    after World War I, 24–26, 44, 49
Bessel, Richard, 73, 74, 233
Biess, Frank, 226, 236
Borchert, Wolfgang, 227
bourgeois tradition. *See* elitism
Breuer, Hans, 77
Brokaw, Tom, 237–41
Broszat, Martin, 154, 159